Chick Lit

Chick Lit

The New Woman's Fiction

Edited by Suzanne Ferriss
and Mallory Young

Routledge
Taylor & Francis Group

New York   London

Published in 2006 by
Routledge
Taylor & Francis Group
270 Madison Avenue
New York, NY 10016

Published in Great Britain by
Routledge
Taylor & Francis Group
2 Park Square
Milton Park, Abingdon
Oxon OX14 4RN

Printed in the United States of America on acid-free paper
10 9 8 7 6 5 4 3 2 1

International Standard Book Number-10: 0-415-97502-6 (Hardcover) 0-415-97503-4 (Softcover)
International Standard Book Number-13: 978-0-415-97502-5 (Hardcover) 978-0-415-97503-2 (Softcover)
Library of Congress Card Number 2005013904

Library of Congress Cataloging-in-Publication Data

Chick lit : the new woman's fiction / edited by Suzanne Ferriss and Mallory Young.
    p. cm.
  Includes bibliographical references and index.
  ISBN 0-415-97502-6 (alk. paper) -- ISBN 0-415-97503-4 (pbk. : alk. paper)
   1. American fiction--Women authors--History and criticism. 2. English fiction--Women authors--History and criticism. 3. Women--Books and reading--English-speaking countries. 4. Women and literature--English-speaking countries. 5. Single women in literature. 6. Young women in literature. 7. Women in literature. I. Ferriss, Suzanne, 1962- II. Young, Mallory, 1952- III. Title.

PS374.W6C48 2005
813'.54093522--dc22

2005013904

Taylor & Francis Group
is the Academic Division of Informa plc.

Visit the Taylor & Francis Web site at
http://www.taylorandfrancis.com

and the Routledge Web site at
http://www.routledge-ny.com

For Ann and Mary Ellen, Ada and Rowena

Contents

Acknowledgments   ix

Introduction

SUZANNE FERRISS AND MALLORY YOUNG   1

Part I   The Hatching of a Genre: Origins and Influences

1   Who's Laughing Now? A Short History of Chick Lit
and the Perversion of a Genre

CRIS MAZZA   17

2   Tradition and Displacement in the New Novel of Manners

STEPHANIE HARZEWSKI   29

3   Mothers of Chick Lit? Women Writers, Readers, and
Literary History

JULIETTE WELLS   47

4   Narrative and Cinematic Doubleness: *Pride and Prejudice*
and *Bridget Jones's Diary*

SUZANNE FERRISS   71

Part II   Free Range: Varieties and Variations

5   "Sistahs Are Doin' It for Themselves": Chick Lit in
Black and White

LISA A. GUERRERO   87

6   Long-Suffering Professional Females: The Case of
    Nanny Lit
    ELIZABETH HALE   103

7   You Are Not Alone: The Personal, the Political, and
    the "New" Mommy Lit
    HEATHER HEWETT   119

8   Chick Lit Jr.: More Than Glitz and Glamour for Teens
    and Tweens
    JOANNA WEBB JOHNSON   141

9   Ya Yas, Grits, and Sweet Potato Queens: Contemporary
    Southern Belles and the Prescriptions That Guide Them
    ELIZABETH B. BOYD   159

10 Bridget Jones and Hungarian Chick Lit
    NÓRA SÉLLEI   173

**Part III   Sex and the Single Chick: Feminism and Postfeminism,
            Sexuality and Self-Fashioning**

11 About a Girl: Female Subjectivity and Sexuality in
    Contemporary 'Chick' Culture
    A. ROCHELLE MABRY   191

12 No Satisfaction: *Sex and the City, Run Catch Kiss*, and the
    Conflict of Desires in Chick Lit's New Heroines
    ANNA KIERNAN   207

13 Fashionably Indebted: Conspicuous Consumption,
    Fashion, and Romance in Sophie Kinsella's
    Shopaholic Trilogy
    JESSICA LYN VAN SLOOTEN   219

14 Supersizing Bridget Jones: What's Really Eating the
    Women in Chick Lit
    ALISON UMMINGER   239

    Afterword: The New Woman's Fiction
    SHARI BENSTOCK   253

    Selected Bibliography   257

    Contributors   261

    Index   265

Acknowledgments

We want to thank our editor at Routledge, Matthew Byrnie, for seeing the promise in our first fledgling proposal and coming along with us as it took wing. Suzanne benefited from the support of the Farquhar College of Arts and Sciences at Nova Southeastern University and the Department of English at the University of Trier. Mallory is grateful to the Department of English and Languages at Tarleton State University and to Mark Shipman and Donald L. Zelman, who provided release time for completion of the manuscript.

At home, our thanks go to Steven and Craig for wise guidance, editorial expertise, and all-around support—and for never letting us take ourselves too seriously. Their competing title and cover mock-up featuring us as biker chicks will always make us laugh—and will never be revealed publicly.

Finally, we acknowledge the fabulous women who have inspired us: friends and colleagues, teachers and students, writers and artists—and especially our mothers and sisters, to whom this book is dedicated.

Introduction

SUZANNE FERRISS AND MALLORY YOUNG

It's hip. It's smart. It's fun. It's about you!

—Chicklitbooks.com

In the fall of 2003, the *Baltimore City Paper* published an introduction to chick lit called "Chick Lit 101." Author Lizzie Skurnick offered as a sidebar a tongue-in-cheek quiz—"Did I Just Buy Chick Lit?"—with ten multiple-choice questions about the book's cover, author, main character, and themes. The point, naturally, was to establish the genre's formulas. Take question 7: "Does she work at: a) a women's magazine, b) a newspaper, c) a TV station, d) any other organization that can be linked, however tenuously, to 'the media'?" Naturally, choice a, b, c, or d fits the formula.

Together, our epigram from a chick-lit fans' Web site and the paper's sarcastic chick-lit quiz clearly indicate the opposing responses chick lit has inspired. These responses have indeed tended toward extremes. On one hand chick lit attracts the unquestioning adoration of fans; on the other it attracts the unmitigated disdain of critics.

Such criticisms have become almost as common as the genre's ubiquitous pink, fashion-conscious covers. Highbrow critics, perhaps inevitably, have dismissed chick lit as trashy fiction. In Britain venerated novelists such as Beryl Bainbridge and Doris Lessing have weighed in against the "chickerati." Bainbridge described chick lit as "a froth sort of thing" that "just wastes time." Lessing added, "It would be better, perhaps, if [female

Nastiness against the image [handwritten annotation]

novelists] wrote books about their lives as they really saw them, and not these helpless girls, drunken, worrying about their weight" ("Bainbridge").

But chick lit does have its defenders as well, such as novelist Jenny Colgan. Of Fielding's *Bridget Jones's Diary*, she said, "It's a terrific book and it has sold more than two million copies. They have not all been bought by lovelorn single women in London" (qtd. in Gibbons). Jeanette Winterson, who identifies her work as "unashamedly high art," admitted she has "no problem" with chick lit ("Bainbridge").

Critics and defenders alike are responding to the genre's amazing commercial success. Chick lit has been called a "commercial tsunami" (Zernike 1). In 2002, for instance, chick-lit books earned publishers more than $71 million (Cabot), prompting publishers such as Harlequin, Broadway, and Pocket Books to create separate imprints dedicated to the genre. In the same year seven chick-lit books occupied *Publishers Weekly* best-seller lists for ninety weeks (Gelsomino 28). Popular publications such as *Entertainment Weekly* regularly highlight chick-lit titles. Three were reviewed recently under the clever heading "Feeding Your Heroine Addiction" (Armstrong and Cruz). A panel was held at the Women's National Book Association in New York, January 2004, called "Is Chick Lit Chic?" (Zernike 2). Fans of the genre even have their own Web sites, in both Britain (www.chicklit.co.uk) and the United States (www.chicklit.us and www.chicklitbooks.com).

Chick lit's popularity—and lucrative possibilities—do not stop with print. Not only writers and journalists but also film producers have been riding the wave. The film versions of the two Bridget Jones novels have proved the genre's crossover potential. The first novel published by Harlequin's chick-lit imprint Red Dress Ink, *See Jane Date* by Melissa Senate, was made into a TV movie starring *Buffy the Vampire Slayer*'s Charisma Carter (Ward). Hilary Swank recently purchased the rights to *Family Trust*, the new novel by *Legally Blonde* author Amanda Brown, and Gigi Levangie Grazer's *Maneater* was optioned for more than $1 million even before the book appeared in stores (Skurnick). Chick lit is big business.

It is hardly surprising, then, that chick lit raises eyebrows and concerns. Yet for all the popular attention it has drawn, it has received little serious or intelligent discussion. The discourse surrounding the genre has been polarized between its outright dismissal as trivial fiction and unexamined embrace by fans who claim that it reflects the realities of life for contemporary single women. Chick lit's astounding popularity as a cultural phenomenon calls for a more considered response. In addition, as this volume reveals, a serious consideration of chick lit brings into focus many of the issues facing contemporary women and contemporary culture—issues of identity, of race and class, of femininity and feminism, of consumerism and self-image. Rather than simply accepting that we "know it when we see it," we examine in this collection the contemporary phenomenon that is chick lit from a variety of angles, from its place in literary history to its engagement with contemporary culture.

The Hatching of a Genre: Origins and Influences

The genesis of chick lit is punctuated with irony. Novelist Cris Mazza, coeditor of *Chick-Lit: Postfeminist Fiction* (FC2, 1995) and *Chick-Lit: No Chick Vics* (FC2, 1996), argues convincingly that she was the first to use the term "chick lit" in print—but for ironic purposes. In "Who's Laughing Now?: A Short History of Chick-Lit and the Perversion of a Genre," she traces how the term worked its way into print after her anthologies were published and reviewed, focusing on the difference between her mocking use of "chick lit" and its subsequent emergence as a type of brand name in the publishing industry.

In the ten years since Mazza and her coeditor Jeffrey DeShell first used the term, chick lit has acquired a fixed definition, mocked not only in the "Chick Lit 101" article but also in various recipes and formulas published in the popular press. From the perspective of literary criticism, we can define it as a form of women's fiction on the basis of subject matter, character, audience, and narrative style. Simply put, chick lit features single women in their twenties and thirties "navigating their generation's challenges of balancing demanding careers with personal relationships" (Cabot).

As popular women's fiction, chick lit has been likened to the contemporary romance popularized by Harlequin in the United States and Mills and Boon in Britain.[1] But here, too, the connection might be an ironic one. Janice Radway's influential work on the romance identifies that genre's single unassailable tenet: the primacy of the male–female couple. The heroine must be connected with one, and only one, man. Yet, as Stephanie Harzewski explains in her essay "Tradition and Displacement in the New Novel of Manners," that requirement, along with others, has been subtly subverted by chick-lit novels. Supporters claim that, unlike traditional, convention-bound romance, chick lit jettisons the heterosexual hero to offer a more realistic portrait of single life, dating, and the dissolution of romantic ideals.

Both fans and authors of chick lit contend the difference lies in the genre's realism. Chicklit.us explains that it reflects "the lives of everyday working young women and men" and appeals to readers who "want to see their own lives in all the messy detail, reflected in fiction today." The typical chick-lit protagonist is, as a result, not perfect but flawed, eliciting readers' compassion and identification simultaneously. Heroines deploy self-deprecating humor that not only entertains but also leads readers to believe they are fallible—like them. "The heroine of these books can be rude, shallow, overly compulsive, neurotic, insecure, bold, ambitious, witty or surprisingly all of the above—but we love them anyway!" (chick-lit.us). Invoking the "physical stuff of everyday life" (Jernigan 70), chick lit's often criticized investment in fashion and cocktails, from this perspective, is not simply superficial but a reflection of consumer culture.

Author Jennifer Weiner claims chick lit has "an authenticity frequently missing from women's fiction of the past." She says, "I think that for a long time, what women were getting were sort of the Jackie Collins, Judith Krantz kind of books—sex and shopping, glitz and glamour, heroines that were fun to read about, but just felt nothing like where you were in your life" (qtd. in Cabot). Her novel *Good in Bed,* by contrast, was inspired by a rough breakup she experienced. Others, such as Plum Sykes, Lauren Weisberger, and the authors of *The Nanny Diaries,* have mined their professional and personal experiences as inspiration for their novels' plots. The result of such realistic elements is the perception that chick lit is not fiction at all. So intent are Bridget Jones's fans, for example, on identifying the author with her protagonist that Helen Fielding has had to distance herself from her character: "At one point I was going to put a sign around my neck that said, 'No, I am *not* Bridget Jones' " (qtd. in de Vries 6).

Such identification is augmented by chick lit's narrative style. Fielding's novel suggested spontaneity and candor with its use of the diary form. Others exploit the confessional style of letters and e-mails, or simply employ first-person narration to craft the impression that the protagonist is speaking directly to readers. These narrative techniques not only appeal to readers but also link chick lit significantly with a large body of women's fiction from earlier generations.

When we consider the origins of chick lit, a single urtext clearly presents itself: Helen Fielding's *Bridget Jones's Diary* (1996). The entire chick-lit phenomenon is invariably traced back to this single novel. But as in other cases in which a many-branched genre appears to grow from a single stalk, the genesis of chick lit may not be so simple. After all, *Bridget Jones*—much like the Homeric epics or the first eighteenth-century British novels—could hardly have sprung fully formed from Fielding's brain.

The most obvious of Fielding's sources is well-known to be Jane Austen's *Pride and Prejudice,* from which Fielding admittedly borrowed much of her plot and many of her characters. Juliette Wells points out, however, that although Austen's work, together with a long tradition of women's writing, precedes Fielding's novel, chick lit cannot justifiably make a claim to comparable literary status. Still, chick lit's popularity leads to significant issues surrounding the reception of women's literature. As Wells argues, "To judge whether an individual work of chick lit, or the genre as a whole, has literary merit is to participate in a long tradition of discounting both women writers and their readers." Wells concludes, "Chick lit is certainly one of the next generations of women's *writing* but, in spite of its capacity to invoke the questions that long swirled around women's literary writing, it is not the next generation of women's *literature.*"

However we choose to judge its literary merit, the phenomenon now referred to as chick lit clearly does flow—albeit in numerous directions—from the original source of Bridget Jones. And Bridget Jones is a direct literary descendant of Austen's Elizabeth Bennet. Considering the relationship between the two characters and the two texts allows us to focus simultaneously on chick lit's literary ancestry and its contemporary nature. As Suzanne Ferriss points out, Austen's work is transformed both in Fielding's popular book and in the film version: "In each instance, the transformation exploits the distinctive and incommensurate qualities of literature and cinema to represent the psychological development of a female character searching for self-esteem and security." *Bridget Jones*—and the genre of chick lit it spawned—proves to be indebted to women's literature of the past—and, at the same time, completely independent of it.

Free Range: Varieties and Variations

As Kathryn Robinson explains, "Anyone familiar with Jane Austen's oeuvre will immediately recognize in chick lit a kindred wit, the same obsession with choosing a mate, and a shared attention to the dailiness of women's lives." Those same defining characteristics have continued to appear in each new form of chick lit. In the decade since *Bridget Jones,* it has crossed the divides of generation, ethnicity, nationality, and even gender. Leaping the generation gap, it has given rise on one side to "hen lit" (or "matron lit" or "lady lit")—chick lit focused on women over forty—and on the other to adolescent chick lit or what Joanna Johnson calls "chick lit jr." Johnson identifies a parallel chick-lit world targeting adolescents. She argues that, like their adult counterparts, junior chick-lit novels affirm flawed women, acknowledging their insecurities and offering lessons in negotiating relationships. Between these two extremes "mommy lit" finds its place, adding new complexity to the old question, "Can women have it all?" Heather Hewett points out in "You Are Not Alone: The Personal, the Political, and the 'New' Mommy Lit" that novels focused on motherhood, such as Allison Pearson's *I Don't Know How She Does It,* both stage and complicate issues of middle-class maternity, an area rife with political implications.

Crossing the racial divide, we find Ethnick lit, including such subgenres as "Sistah lit" and "Chica lit." Lisa Guerrero shows that such novels as Terry McMillan's *Waiting to Exhale*—which, not incidentally, predates *Bridget Jones* by four years—change the focus from the naive single white woman seeking a fairy-tale romance to a more experienced black woman opting for the reality of friendship. Other recent chick-lit novels present the lives, loves, and friendships of Latina heroines, whereas chick-lit works focusing on second-generation Chinese American and Indian American protagonists have also made their debut.

Although chick lit began as a British and American phenomenon (with Candace Bushnell's *Sex and the City* often considered a second major source along with *Bridget Jones*), international versions have developed, including the Indonesian "sastra wangi" (or "fragrant literature") and Hungarian chick lit. In this instance, the genre's exportation has generated not only new texts but also a new discourse. In her essay "Bridget Jones and Hungarian Chick Lit," Nóra Séllei contends that Zsuzsa Rácz's chick-lit novel *Stop Mammatheresa!* has brought to the surface symptoms of a changing postcommunist society, with anxieties about shifting gender roles revealed not only in the fictional text but also in the critical responses to it.

Perhaps even more surprising than these transformations has been the development of Christian chick lit, or "church lit." Whereas Jewish authors and heroines have appeared from the onset of chick lit, the protagonists' religion is not a focus of the novels. In the case of church lit, however, it is. The immediate question here might be, "Can church lit girls be as devoted to their Prada as they are to their prayer beads?" (Gelsomino 31). Does the genre's emphasis on consumerism and sexual escapades necessarily clash with Christian values? Apparently, writers and readers are not troubled by the apparent conflict. Interestingly, church lit seems to be picking up on many other chick-lit subgenres, with faith-based versions of adolescent chick lit, mommy lit, southern lit, and African-American lit all currently appearing. Harlequin's new Steeple Hill Cafe line is devoted entirely to Christian chick lit. According to the editorial director Joan Marlow Golan, "The Cafe heroine's challenge is to face her dilemmas with faith and humor, turning to Jesus as the Ultimate Best Friend who will help her with—in the words of our tagline—'life, faith, and getting it right'" (qtd. in Gelsomino 31–32).

Each of these manifestations has molded the original form in new ways, proving chick lit's resiliency and adaptability. Finally, even the presumed absolute boundary of gender has been traversed with the advent of "lad lit" (or "dick lit"), including novels by Nick Hornby, Scott Mebus, and Kyle Smith. Black novelists E. Lynn Harris and Eric Jerome Dickey have established themselves among "the few kings of popular African-American fiction for women" (Lee B1). Although not nearly as successful as its sister genre, lad lit represents the extent of chick lit's remarkable ability to transform itself into new varieties.

Even within the mainstream literature focused on white, middle-class, twenty- and thirtysomething professional women, the genre has proliferated, giving rise to "bride lit" or "wedding fic"—or, in less flattering terms, "Bridezilla" novels—as well as regional variations including what might be termed "southern fried chick lit." Elizabeth Boyd points out in "Ya Yas, Grits, and Sweet Potato Queens: Contemporary Southern Belles and the Prescriptions that Guide Them" that southern chick lit alternately upholds and subverts the anachronous but entrenched prescriptions guiding views of southern womanhood. She notes a resurgence in "how to be a belle books" following the 1996 publication of Rebecca Wells's *Divine Secrets of the Ya Ya Sisterhood*. The popularity of these works throughout the United States indicates that such gender prescriptions still affect twenty-first-century women across regional boundaries. It becomes clear that the women who read contemporary belle manuals—or the antibelle works that skewer them—feel caught between their postmodern, feminist lives and the prescriptions that still expect them to maintain a traditional feminine image.

Novels focusing more specifically on the work world, such as Lauren Weisberger's *The Devil Wears Prada* and Emma McLaughlin and Nicola Kraus's *The Nanny Diaries*, have also formed a subgroup of their own. Although most chick fiction tends to present work as a background and means to the more important concern of shopping—whether for shoes or mates—these novels treat the professional world as the ultimate chick challenge. Elizabeth Hale notes that surprisingly, however, many of these books drop the cover of escapist fantasy and portray women's working conditions as demeaning and ultimately destructive.

Sex and the Single Chick: Feminism and Postfeminism, Sexuality, and Self-Fashioning

In spite of these various metamorphoses, however, critics have made the argument that chick lit has failed to offer true diversity. Jessica Jernigan, writing for *Bitch* magazine, decries the fact that ultimately "there's so much cloying sameness to chick lit" (71). "Most chick lit," she continues, "is grounded in a jumbled, half-fantasy version of reality, a reality in which a better wardrobe, a better body, and a better man are not yet out of reach" (74).

It is indeed impossible to deny that the overwhelming majority of chick lit continues to focus on a specific age, race, and class: young, white, and middle. But it is equally impossible to deny that the demand for and popularity of fiction focusing on protagonists beyond those categories is growing exponentially. Black chick lit, in particular, has experienced a burst of popularity since 2004. Although Terry McMillan remains the original progenitor of popular black women's fiction, most of the recent crop of black chick-lit titles owe more to *Sex and the City* than *Waiting to Exhale*. As Lyah Beth LeFlore, coauthor of the successful *Cosmopolitan Girls,* said, "I loved that show, but when you watched, it was as if the only people in New York living fabulous lives were 30-something-year-old white women, and that's a complete fallacy" (Ogunnaike). LeFlore and numerous other African-American authors responded with books focused on educated, professional, "decidedly middle to upper class" black women negotiating exciting urban careers and rocky love lives (Ogunnaike). Major chain bookstore buyers, consumer researchers, and publishing company executives agree that the market for such books is a lucrative one—and that the audience will likely be made up of black and white fans alike. Indeed the novels studiously avoid references to racial inequality or specifically black problems and concerns. As Tia Williams, an African-American chick-lit author, claims, "Recent black fiction has been full of whiny, suffering-from-hair-politics, my-man-done-me-wrong women. Sounds pat, but many people still think you need to be downtrodden to be truly black" (qtd. in Ogunnaike). It is this crucial thematic difference that most clearly distinguishes these authors from Terry McMillan and African-American authors of literary fiction. And it is here too that critics—particularly feminist critics—will find chick lit avoiding serious treatment of cultural, political, and social concerns.

Latina protagonists also figure in numerous chick-lit works, including those of Mary Castillo, Sofia Quintero, Berta Platas, and Caridad Scordato, all featured in a 2005 anthology *Friday Night Chicas* (Gelsomino). Alisa Valdes-Rodriguez has achieved particular success with her chick-lit offerings *The Dirty Girls Social Club* (2003) and *Playing with Boys* (2004). Valdes-Rodriguez's books do, according to Suzanne Leonard, complicate stereotypes of Hispanics: "Her characters are all aware that the Latina stereotype has itself become another marketing ploy." Still, as Leonard suggests, the same accusations made against writers of mainstream chick lit can be applied to these works. "Rodriguez's idea of 'making it' is grounded in wish-fulfillment. ... Rodriguez, like too many chick-lit authors," Leonard concludes, "sees women's lives in very narrow terms—ambiguity has very little place in the realm of chick lit" (D6).

But ambiguity lies at the genre's core. Cris Mazza and Jeffrey DeShell originally employed the term "chick lit" ironically to refer to postfeminist attitudes; in her words, "not to embrace an old frivolous or coquettish image of women, but to take responsibility for our part in the damaging, lingering stereotype." In perhaps another ironic twist, when the term was taken up with no evident irony to refer to the popular genre of women's fiction, it only heightened the controversy regarding the distinction between feminism and postfeminism. Reactions to chick lit are divided between those who expect literature by and about women to advance the political activism of feminism, to represent women's struggles in patriarchal culture and offer inspiring images of strong, powerful women, and those who argue instead that it should portray the reality of young women grappling with modern life. The generations of women coming of age after the women's movement of the 1960s find themselves in an ambiguous position: they have indubitably benefited from feminism's push for education and access to the professions, but they still experience pressures from without and desires from within for romance and family. In short, they are caught between competing demands to be strong and independent while retaining their femininity. Is chick lit advancing the cause of feminism by appealing to female audiences and featuring empowered, professional women? Or does it rehearse the same patriarchal narrative of romance and performance of femininity that feminists once rejected?

In addition to Lessing and Bainbridge, those influenced by second-wave feminism, emphasizing contemporary women's fight for equality and access to professions, have disparaged chick lit as "unserious" and antifeminist. Anna Weinberg's criticisms are exemplary: "Inside their dust jackets covered with shopping bags, martini glasses, shoes or purses, many of these titles really are trash: trash that imitates other, better books that could have ushered in a new wave of smart, postfeminist writing" (qtd. in Skurnick). Helen Fielding answered such charges with characteristic aplomb: "Sometimes I have had people getting their knickers in a twist about Bridget Jones being a disgrace to feminism. But it is good to be able to represent women as they actually are in the age in which you are living" (qtd. in Ezard). She adds, "If we can't laugh at ourselves without having a panic attack over what it says about women, we haven't got very far with our equality" (qtd. in Razdan). Chick-lit reader and author Alesia Holliday warns, "What frightens me about the slew of articles trashing the new chick lit genre ... is the subtle sexist bias in all of them" (qtd. in Gelsomino 28). Partly at issue may indeed be differences in tone. In the minds of many chick-lit detractors, feminist means serious, and chick lit's humor marks it as unserious.

Taking chick lit seriously, however, leads to more complicated responses. As Rochelle Mabry notes, Bridget Jones takes her boss's e-mail about her short skirt not as sexual harassment but as an opportunity for flirtation, which she eagerly embraces. Rather than presenting their protagonists as subordinate to male advances, chick-lit authors present women as sexual agents. They give their female protagonists a number of sexual partners and experiences. To Mabry, the women of Candace Bushnell's *Sex and the City*, with their frank discussions of sex, represent "the desires and attempts of many real-life contemporary women to investigate the mysteries of modern sexual relationships and gender roles on their own terms." She, along with Harzweski and others, argues that contemporary literature and films deemphasize a central romance and highlight the female protagonist's nonromantic relationship with her close community of mostly female friends, thus suggesting that contemporary women can express their desires outside the frame of patriarchally defined heterosexual monogamy.

By contrast, Anna Kiernan questions whether the genre offers alternative images of female sexuality at all in her essay "No Satisfaction: *Sex and the City, Run Catch Kiss*, and the Conflict of Desires in Chick Lit's New Heroines." She argues that by treating sex in businesslike fashion as a form of exchange, the women in *Sex and the City* merely invert the traditionally gendered sexual roles, placing women in a position of power over men. "Doesn't it simply reinstate the limitations of the value system that feminism purports to reject, namely the objectification of women?" she asks. She does find, however, that one chick-lit novel, Amy Sohn's *Run Catch Kiss*, features a character fraught with anxieties about conforming to sexual expectations for women who plays out feminist debates about pornography and pleasure.

On a related front, the genre has also been criticized for presenting love as "just another commodity, more or less indistinguishable from a Lulu Guinness handbag. The tendency of chick-lit authors to assign the same narrative weight to such disparate and disproportionate phenomena as peep-toe pumps and marriage makes reading their stories as confounding as flipping through women's magazines, with their unsettling mix of relationship advice, fashion photography and beauty advertorials" (Jernigan 71). The visibility fashion and consumerism have achieved within—and on—the covers of chick lit has also marked it for feminist disapprobation. Fashion has been dismissed by feminists as frivolous, as inculcating women with a debilitating femininity and making them the unwitting dupes of capitalism. But feminist condemnations have coexisted with claims that fashion provides women with a means of expressing identity. As cultural critic Elizabeth Wilson argued, "While feminists with one voice condemn the consumeristic poison of fashion, with another they praise the individualism made possible by dress" (237). The same central ambiguity applies to chick lit.

Is chick lit "buying in" to a degrading and obsessive consumer culture, or is it ultimately exposing the limitations of a consumerist worldview? Numerous chick-lit novels focus on the simultaneous pleasures and dangers of consumerism. Sophie Kinsella's *Shopaholic Trilogy*, for example, fuses consumerism, fashion, and identity, as its fashionista protagonist Becky Bloomwood engages in retail therapy and consumption binges to assuage her insecurities about love and personal fulfillment. In considering Kinsella's works, Jessica Van Slooten explores the role that fashion plays in shaping the chick-lit heroine's relationship to money, herself, and her love interests. She also considers the commodification of chick lit, questioning the novels' status as fashionable objects to be consumed by bookstore shoppers. Perhaps the ideal conflation of these themes appeared in the marketing scheme promoting the publication of Kinsella's fourth Shopaholic novel, *Shopaholic and Sister* (2005). Each new hardcover book was adorned with a bright lime green and hot pink sleeve announcing the opportunity to "Celebrate this new Shopaholic novel—Win a London Shopping Spree-for-Two!" The grand prize, described inside the sleeve, was, quite appropriately, "a 6-day/5-night London getaway with your best 'shopping sister,' and a $5000.00 cash prize plus lunch with Sophie Kinsella."

Chick lit's concern with shopping, fashion, and consumerism leads to an arguably obsessive focus on skin-deep beauty. From the moment of Bridget Jones's opening diary entry—"29 lbs. (but post-Christmas)"—chick lit has emphasized women's appearance and, more specifically, weight. The intimate connection between a woman's appearance and the chances of her (real or perceived) success in bedrooms and boardrooms is an issue that has long been central to discussions of feminism. Naomi Wolf's controversial landmark study *The Beauty Myth* (1991) is a case in point. Once again detractors find chick lit's obsession with appearance a cause for disdain, but chick lit's focus on weight does not necessarily mean that it endorses cultural expectations of women's beauty. According to Alison Umminger's "Supersizing Bridget Jones: What's Really Eating the Women in Chick Lit," such a focus reveals that the "quest for a partner is entirely secondary to the ongoing battle chick lit's heroines are engaging with themselves." She observes, "While the Bridget Jones's and Jemima J's of the new millennium are free agents relative to their sister characters of past centuries, their freedom is mitigated by the self-imposed and culturally sanctioned tyranny of hating their own bodies." Umminger notes that numerous chick-lit novels, such as Jennifer Weiner's *Good in Bed*, have presented truly overweight heroines who struggle with body image—and therefore self-image—on a daily basis. Nonetheless, such novels may unconsciously reinforce some of the more destructive appearance-related biases in contemporary society.

The New Woman's Fiction

The subtitle of this collection is intentionally ambiguous. Chick lit is simultaneously fiction about and for the "new woman," the contemporary reader of our postfeminist culture, and a new "woman's fiction," a form of popular literature (largely) written by women for a female audience. In the afterword, Shari Benstock accounts for chick lit in this dual sense, identifying the significant ways it engages with contemporary culture and situating it in relation to the new woman's fiction of the twentieth century. She also suggests possibilities for further investigations of chick lit and women's fiction.

Like her, we believe that, contrary to announcements of chick lit's imminent demise, the genre is rife with possibilities and potential. Tara Gelsomino notes that the genre offers opportunities to young women writers: "Because of its newness, chick lit is one of the few genres that is completely open to debut novelists and has offered incredible opportunities for young women to make an impact in the male-dominated publishing industry. (If that's not feminist, what is?) Indeed, its boundless potential for opportunity is the very quality that seems to ensure chick lit's future survival in the publishing arena" (104). We would add that this volume proves the same is true for young voices in scholarship. Even if chick lit's popularity were to diminish, the body of work amassed over the past decade alone raises issues and questions about subjectivity, sexuality, race, and class in women's texts for another generation of women to ponder.

Note

1. Harlequin's creation of a separate chick-lit imprint, Red Dress Ink, appears to underscore the distinction while retaining the link between genres. Members of the Romance Writers of America have recently established a separate chick-lit chapter, Chick Lit Writers of the World (www.chicklitwriters.com), suggesting the genres share a heritage at the very least.

Works Cited

Armstrong, Jennifer, and Clarissa Cruz. "Chick Lit 101: Feeding Your Heroine Addiction." *Entertainment Weekly* 16, Jan. 2004: 74.
"Bainbridge Denounces Chick-Lit as 'Froth.'" *Guardian Unlimited* 23, Aug. 2001. <http://books.guardian.co.uk/bookerprize2001/story/0,1090,541335,00.html>.
Cabot, Heather. "Chick Lit: Genre Aimed at Young Women Is Fueling Publishing Industry." abcnews.com 30, Aug. 2003. <http://abcnews.go.com/sections/wnt/Entertainment/chicklit030830.html>.
De Vries, Hilary. "Bridget Jones? No, It's Jane Bond." *New York Times* 6, June 2004: 6.

Ezard, John. "Bainbridge Tilts at 'Chick Lit' Cult: Novelist Says Bridget Jones Genre Is Just a Lot of Froth." *The Guardian* 24, Aug. 2001. <http://books.guardian.co.uk/departments/generalfiction/story/0,6000,541954,00.html>.

Gelsomino, Tara. "Growing Pains." www.RomanticTimes.com. Aug. 2004: 28–29, 31–32, 104.

Gibbons, Fiachra. "Stop Rubbishing Chick Lit, Demands Novelist." *Guardian Unlimited* 21, Aug. 2003.

Jernigan, Jessica. "Slingbacks and Arrows: Chick Lit Comes of Age." *Bitch* Summer 2004: 68–75.

Lee, Felicia R. "Chick-Lit King Imagines His Way into Women's Heads." *New York Times* 29, July 2004: B1, B5.

Leonard, Suzanne. "All Too Familiar." Rev. of *Playing with Boys,* by Alisa Valdes-Rodriguez. *Fort Worth Star-Telegram* 19, Sept. 2004: D6.

Ogunnaike, Lola. "Black Writers Seize Glamorous Ground around 'Chick-Lit.'" *New York Times* 31, May 2004. <http:www.nytimes.com/2004/05/31/books/31CHIC.html>.

Radway, Janice A. *Reading the Romance: Women, Patriarchy, and Popular Literature.* Chapel Hill: University of North Carolina Press, 1984.

Razdan, Anjula. "The Chick Lit Challenge: Do Trendy Novels for Young Women Smother Female Expression—Or Just Put a Little Fun in Feminism?" *Utne* Mar.–Apr. 2004, 20–2.

Robinson, Kathryn. "Why I Heart Chick Lit." *Seattle Weekly* 22–28, Oct. 2003. <http://www.seattleweekly.com/features/o343/031022_arts_books_chicklit.php>.

Skurnick, Lizzie. "Chick Lit 101: A Sex-Soaked, Candy-Colored, Indiscreet Romp through the Hottest Gal Tales of the Season." *Baltimore City Paper* 10, Sept. 2003. <http://www.citypaper.com/2003-09-10/bigbooks.html>.

Ward, Alyson. "Black Authors Getting in on the 'Chick Lit' Circuit." *Fort Worth Star-Telegram* 2, Sept. 2003.

Wilson, Elizabeth. *Adorned in Dreams: Fashion and Modernity.* London: Virago, 1985.

Wolf, Naomi. *The Beauty Myth: How Images of Beauty Are Used against Women.* New York: William and Morrow, 1991.

Zernike, Kate. "Oh, to Write a 'Bridget Jones' for Men: A Guy Can Dream." *New York Times* 22, Feb. 2004: 9.1–2.

PART I

The Hatching of a Genre: Origins and Influences

1

Who's Laughing Now? A Short History of Chick Lit and the Perversion of a Genre

CRIS MAZZA

Ten years ago, in the winter of 1995, Jeffrey DeShell and I sat on the floor of his living room, brainstorming what title we would give to the anthology we had just finished. To name the book effectively, we had to boil down into a single concept what we had asserted in choosing, from more than four hundred submissions, the final twenty-two stories. Our original goal had been to determine how, in a post-Barth-and-Barthelme era, women's experiments with form and language might be distinct from men's. But that line of inquiry was overshadowed by the emergence of something larger, more exciting than a mere study of form. We had uncovered an atmosphere, an aura, exemplified by this example from "In the Guise of an Explanation of My Aunt's Life" by Kat Meads:

> For the sake of believability, suppose … that this family assumed all families cheated on taxes, disliked their children, killed squawking chickens bare-handed, ate calf brains with pleasure … that they accepted with humor and grace the sad but universal banality of all deviance, rendering the concept of secrecy bogus, understanding this page reveals nothing a hundred pages written by a hundred others have not already revealed, reducing the idea of family secret to the level of a bad knock-knock joke. … Sixty-two and three-quarters

17

she was when the lid blew off, more than sixteen thousand days of cooking-cleaning-toenail clipping-monthly bleeding behind her. (53–54)

The fictions we had compiled were simultaneously courageous and playful; frank and wry; honest, intelligent, sophisticated, libidinous, unapologetic, and overwhelmingly emancipated. Liberated from *what*? The grim anger that feminists had told us ought to be our pragmatic stance in life. The screaming about the vestiges of the patriarchal society that oppressed us. Liberated to *do* what? To admit we're part of the problem. How empowering could it be to be *part* of the problem instead of just a victim of it? I can't remember the titles we rejected, but the one we ultimately chose encompassed all of the above: *Chick-Lit: Postfeminist Fiction* (FC2, 1995).

Immediately we feared it would be too inflammatory, would discredit our project, would brand us literary heretics. We almost changed it. But then, how could it backfire if it was so obviously sardonic? Or, as Kelly Vie in *two girls review* perfectly put it in her review of *Chick-Lit*: "One generation of women writers wrote 'shit happens.' The next writes, 'yeah, it still does, but I've stuck my fingers in it.'" This was the ironic intention of our title: not to embrace an old frivolous or coquettish image of women but to take responsibility for our part in the damaging, lingering stereotype.

What we couldn't anticipate was that less than ten years later our tag would be greasing the commercial book industry machine. I've conducted no extensive research into culture and society to explain why chick lit was "originated" all over again, about three years after *Chick-Lit: Postfeminist Fiction* was published. But a stroll through any bookstore confirms that chick lit's second incarnation looks not at all like its first (see figure 1.1). Somehow chick lit had morphed into books flaunting pink, aqua, and lime covers featuring cartoon figures of long-legged women wearing stiletto heels. What follows is a simple synopsis from a perplexed author wondering how this all got away from us.

In fall of 1995, *Chick-Lit: Postfeminist Fiction* was released. Reviewers would not have been interested in yet another anthology of fiction by women, but they were openly intrigued by this idea of postfeminism. "One narrator's aunt goes berserk in her kitchen, another's mother is transformed into a ravenous infant … and a couple decides whether to have children by playing board games," wrote *Columbus Dispatch* book critic Margaret Quamme, who also made a chart to accompany her review:

Prefeminism	Feminism	Postfeminism
kitchen	protest march	psychiatrist's office
shirtwaists	power suits	lots of leather
white rice	brown rice	sushi
Donna Reed	Gloria Steinem	Madonna
Rhett Butler	Alan Alda	anonymous sweaty cowboys
romantic	heroic	ironic

In fictions that "break the boundaries of politeness," Quamme concluded, "if feminism proposes to improve life by making social and political changes, postfeminism answers that large portions of life can't be dealt with so rationally."

We knew we'd found some kind of itch that had been waiting to be scratched, even if it was not always expressed the way we would have articulated it: "What does this weird title mean?" asked a reviewer in the San Francisco Bay area's *Express Books* (Hagar). But despite that reviewer's parenthetical aside, "(ooo, I just luv that word!)," a spelling I'd last seen used by cheerleaders in each other's yearbooks, most of the first responses were not saucy or giddy but ranged from astonishment to gratitude.

"I was and remain repelled by very right-minded women who were, in the '80s and '90s, writing and reading like Stalinists," says former FC2 publisher Curtis White, in describing how he hoped 1995's *Chick-Lit: Postfeminist Fiction* would affect American literature. "They had forgotten that literature is an art, that art functions through irony, and that all the sincerity in the world doesn't make bad art good."

Professors of literature likewise saw artistic, as well as cultural, value in *Chick-Lit: Postfeminist Fiction*. Cam Tatham, associate professor of English at the University of Wisconsin, Milwaukee, says he put *Chick-Lit: Postfeminist Fiction* on his syllabus because, "I wanted to give students a sense of what had happened to conventional feminism, expressed through cutting-edge texts." Tatham thought that chick lit helped readers "move beyond the too-familiar issues/questions of conventional feminism, deterritorializing views of victimizer/victimized."

Pamela Caughie, professor of English and Women's Studies at Loyola University in Chicago, also teaches postfeminist fiction. She sums up the genre that we were trying to capture in Chick Lit this way: "Postfeminist fiction does not conform to a set of beliefs about the way women are or should be. Indeed, the very writing that goes by this name resists the kind of certainty, conclusiveness and clear-cut meaning that definition demands." Caughie further describes the genre by pointing out that the

Figure 1.1 Cover of *Chick-Lit: Postfeminist Fiction,* Fiction Collective 2, 1995 (artwork by Andi Olsen).

characters in postfeminist fiction might be "seen as confident, independent, even outrageous women taking responsibility for who they are, or as women who have unconsciously internalized and are acting out the encoded gender norms of our society."

Hearing these diagnostic comments after the fact helped me fully appreciate that one doesn't have to be a student of a movement to be a product of it. Certainly while writing my own work I did not have these theoretical summaries in my head, but one could argue that, as an editor, I should have. Simply, I was pleased to see that what I'd done on more of a gut level—shoving fiction by women into a different direction—was validated by literary and feminist scholars.

Responses such as these from critics and reviewers further elucidated our message and helped us focus the theme of the anthology's successor, *Chick-Lit 2 (No Chick Vics)*, published in 1996 (with a third editor, Elisabeth Sheffield).

After the release of *Chick-Lit 2*, something happened that could have set the course for chick lit to carry on as fiction that transgressed the mainstream or challenged the status quo, instead of becoming what it is now: career girls looking for love. When *Chick-Lit 2* was reviewed in the *Washington Post* by Carolyn See, besides admitting that she sounded "like a grizzled old veteran down at the American Legion Hall with my medals clanking" when she demanded more plot, See observed, "You never saw so many wigs and crew cuts bleached white, or so many female genitalia. ... Not many straight women here either. ... The National Endowment for the Arts [NEA] funded part of this enterprise, and it is couched in words and concepts that are sure to give Jesse Helms a conniption fit."

We believe it was Focus on the Family, a conservative watchdog organization, that spotted See's comment and forwarded the review to Congressman Peter Hoekstra (R, MI), chair of the House Subcommittee on Oversight and Investigations, who pronounced the book "an offense to the senses." An investigation ensued. Four of the books FC2 published that year were included (those supported by the NEA), and at one point Helms was seen holding one of the volumes aloft as he addressed his colleagues about the NEA.

But we weren't Mapplethorped. Sales stayed at about what they would have been—decent to good for an independent-press book, fueled by university course adoptions. The NEA was spanked (ambiguously charged with making an effort not to fund offensive material), and despite See's prediction, "and then the writers here can get all prissy and righteous—which isn't as hard as it might seem, even if you're all dolled up in minis and teddies and nose rings and black lipstick," we didn't meet on the

Capitol steps. The little flurry failed to forever stamp the term *chick lit* as transgressive, visionary, or even smart.

Looking back now, I suspect if we *had* met on the Capitol steps in a news-conference protest (sans teddies), chick lit couldn't, or maybe wouldn't, have been co-opted. At least not without taking us along.

In May 1996 the *New Yorker* published an essay by James Wolcott titled, "Hear Me Purr: Maureen Dowd and the rise of postfeminist chick-lit." There was our title! Although backward and not capitalized. Had Wolcott independently come up with and paired those two words? No, it could hardly be argued that he had, considering that he referenced our anthology later in the article:

> One can spot this Noxzema gleam in the first-person exploits of Lynn Snowden, in the sex chat of Cynthia Heimel, *Details'* Anka Radakovich, and ... in pop-fiction anthologies like "Chick-Lit," where the concerns of female characters seem fairly divided between getting laid and not getting laid.

We had to assume it was our anthology he referred to, because nothing else titled *Chick-Lit* was in print at the time. But Wolcott's characterization of the anthology as "pop-fiction" would hardly apply to *Chick-Lit: Postfeminist Fiction*. Neither did his summary of the stories *Chick-Lit* contained. Still, it's hard to deny that Wolcott's reference to our book was proof that he had at least seen it, if not read it. So the use of "postfeminist chick-lit" in Wolcott's subtitle could be no accident.

And Wolcott seemed to conclude that our anthology was part of some kind of movement. Although he never directly (except in the title) called the movement "chick lit," he did refer to the writers of whom he spoke as *chicks*. "Today," he wrote, "a chick is a postfeminist in a party dress, a bachelorette too smart to be a bimbo, too refined to be a babe, too boojy to be a bohemian." And in his summary, "The butch sensibility that imbued so much female writing in the seventies didn't moderate or modulate into maturity. Instead, too much feminist and postfeminist writing has reverted in the nineties to a popularity-contest coquetry."

In this last paragraph of his essay, Wolcott seemed to be describing not *Chick-Lit: Postfeminist Fiction* but the chick lit yet to come.

Meanwhile, reviews of the two *Chick-Lit* anthologies had continued to appear, even in international publications. Nicholas Royle, novelist and book critic for *Time Out: London,* wrote, "The 'postfeminist' thing means we aren't just getting our ears boxed by rant after rant." After flagging several of the stories for special mention (none about dating or careers), he concluded by saying, "[This book] deserves to break out of the US and hit the UK. ... In the meantime, UK publishers, isn't it time for 'Brit Chick-Lit'?"

At least that's what he wrote in the version of the review he sent to me in 1996. "But for some reason," Royle said to me recently, "(space? stupidity? bizarre prophecy?) the last line, the very last sentence, didn't make it into the printed version."

I choose bizarre prophecy—because it was the British book industry, two years later, that took *chick lit* and ran with it. Perhaps this development was aided by the rise of the Internet, homogenizer of the world. Three of our *Chick-Lit* authors had started a Web site called the Postfeminist Playground. "The point of liberation," the Web site said, "is that at some point, even if you're not totally liberated, you start trotting around flaunting your freedom." For a while the site paid homage to its inspiration, the *Chick-Lit* anthologies, even quoting from the introductions. But eventually, in the bustle of their movie, book, and music reviews, some original fiction—by both men and women—and especially the advice columns, fashion critiques, and bulletin board arguments with angry feminists, the site dropped all mention of *Chick-Lit: Postfeminist Fiction* and *Chick-Lit 2: No Chick Vics*. Whatever we'd attempted or accomplished in the anthologies was already slipping away. Or as Curtis White put it,

> Chick lit has experienced that age old commodification shuffle. It was once strong and a force for something liberating. Now it's been co-opted by people selling things. That's okay. Let's move on. Chick lit is dead. Long live chick lit.

The Postfeminist Playground went off the Net in late 1998. The end of the story for the Postfeminist Playground, however, is a stark allegory for the larger picture of what happened to *Chick-Lit: Postfeminist Fiction*. The owners neglected to retain rights to the domain name, so when their site went off the Net, a pornography site snatched the title.

As the Postfeminist Playground was shutting down, the British book industry took center stage with the publication of Helen Fielding's *Bridget Jones's Diary*. I didn't take note at the time whether the chick-lit label was put to use in *Diary*'s initial publicity. On the current Amazon page for Fielding's book, *chick lit* is not used in initial reviews for the American hardback edition from *Publishers Weekly, Kirkus, New York Times Book Review,* and the others.

Bridget Jones's Diary, however, is heralded in almost every book-industry news item that discusses this new chick lit. In fact, when Anna Weinberg, writing for *Book Magazine* in summer 2003, was beginning what the magazine called an exposé on chick lit, she said she had "just embarked on a chick lit crash course," and then credited *Bridget Jones's Diary* as "the eve of the genre." In her crash course, she didn't even go back as far as 1995 and never mentioned the anthology (the only *book*) that ever took *Chick-Lit* as its title.

By May 2004, Newsday.com reported, "Jump-started with Helen Fielding's *Bridget Jones's Diary* ... bolstered by TV's *Sex and the City*, [chick-lit books have] swelled to at least 240 new novels a year, according to ... *Publishers Weekly*" (Jacobson). But if the new chick lit is not what we identified in *Chick-Lit: Postfeminist Fiction,* then what is it? In 2003, chick-litbooks.com (privately written and maintained by Rian Montgomery), declared,

> Let me start out by telling you what Chick Lit *is NOT*:
>
> • Lame and ridiculous
> • Cheesy romance novels
> • Bad influence on women
> • Brain-numbing fluff
>
> [Chick-lit] books are entertaining, interesting, and many women can identify with them. The plots usually involve a woman in her 20s or 30s, going through everyday problems and challenges with her boyfriend, job, living situation, marriage, dating life, etc.

The titles featured on this site's new books page that year included *Life à la Mode,* "Will she take the first step with a shy co-worker she likes? Will she stand up to her annoying boss at work? Will she take a chance at life, love and happiness?" and *The Dewey Decimal System of Love,* "She works in a library, looks about half of her age, and is in love for the first time that she could remember. Ally realizes that she needs to pry her nose out of the books and take a chance at life."

Then there is www.chicklit.co.uk (a more commercial site that provides a way to buy British books through Amazon.com.uk). "You'll flip over our lineup of the very best of British Chick Lit!" In 2004, a "What Is Chick Lit?" page on the site read,

> Chick Lit refers to modern literature for women—that is written about late twenty and thirtysomething singles (aka singletons) as they search for the perfect partner. ... Chick Lit is very different from the standard romance novels. ... These books [usually] reflect the lives of everyday working young men and women ... and give

fresh insight into relationships. ... You won't find the usual corny love scenes here.

The site's suggestion for a "great girlfriend/shower gift" is *The Handbag Book of Girly Emergencies.*

These days, Nicholas Royle, who narrowly escaped the credit for calling on British publishers to do a version of *Chick-Lit,* looks at the British chick-lit industry and says, "[FC2's] bold, ground-breaking anthology has seen its title hijacked by the media on behalf of a sub-genre of popular fiction that is sociologically banal, intellectually inert and about as much use as yesterday's TV listings."

Despite some British writers' chagrin that the plethora of new-generation romance novels whose titles too often begin with "diary of a" might have originated in Britain, there are others who believe commercial chick lit had an American "founding mother." Laura Miller, columnist for the *New York Times Book Review,* says,

> *Fear of Flying* was one of the first and most successful popular confessional novels about a flawed but endearing young woman trying to sort out her life in a world that suddenly allowed women a lot more leeway. In that, and in the book's humor and frankness, it now seems like a predecessor to what we now call Chick-Lit. Isadora is a product of the '70s, though, and as a result she's a lot less conventional in her aspirations and the conclusion of the novel is less romantic. The impression is less that her quandary will be resolved by settling on the right man and more that she needs to get over her romantic belief that the right man is the answer. Contemporary chick-lit heroines sometimes try to tell themselves that they need to avoid hinging their lives on a man, but the genre makes them do it anyway.

Miller adds, "I *still* say in defense of chick lit that nobody else is writing as much about (middle-class) young women's work lives."

Other critics have chimed in with mixed support, as many articles on the genre cite professors designing literature courses that feature popular chick lit, and doctoral students of literature are beginning to do dissertations on the subject. "Helen Fielding's re-visioning of Austen's *Pride and Prejudice* and *Persuasion* ... anchors the genre in respectable literary origins," says Stephanie Harzewski, a doctoral student in literature at the University of Pennsylvania.

Yet, these new novels of manners typically opt for transparency and humor over nuance and irony. As with most of popular fiction, high readability is part of the formula and an impediment when evaluating chick lit as literary. ... While offering a remedy to relatively humorless feminist polemics, the genre is nearly oblivious to social concerns beyond the protagonist's rather narrow world.

According to *Publishers Weekly* in 2004, five mainstream publishers had chick-lit imprints (accounting for those 240 new novels each year). The "genre aimed at young women is fueling [the] publishing industry," said abcnews.com in a 2003 article by Heather Cabot. In fact, Cabot reports, the trend has even spawned a new way to create novels:

A group of six Brooklyn-based friends have met once a month over Sunday brunch to discuss their story development and characters. They strive to imbue their books with a tone that's similar to their chats among girlfriends. "It has every single element: Oh, I'm so fat, Oh, I want a date, Oh, I don't make enough money," explained 32-year-old Elise Miller.

It does seem most revealing when the authors themselves discuss their genre. In 2003, the *Guardian Unlimited,* online issue of the Guardian Newspapers Ltd., reported about an angry author who "tore into 'hairy-legged' female book critics who looked down their noses at chick-lit" at the Edinburgh book festival. Fiachra Gibbons, reporter for the *Guardian,* got it all in two sentences:

The author of *Amanda's Wedding* said a whole generation of writing about young women's lives was being trashed by commentators who took one look at a "fluffy pink cover" and got out their knives. ... The 32-year-old writer blamed what she called the "hairy-leggers" in the critical establishment for perpetuating the myth that anything in a pastel cover had to be pap.

But then this author of *Amanda's Wedding* is quoted one time too many: "It's time we reclaimed the name."

In "Books and the Single Girl," one author was quoted as saying, "I think the term is meant to be pejorative, to put women down: Oh, you silly little women with your silly little concerns." Another author, Plum Sykes, said, "I think a man might have invented it. I don't think girls would label themselves that way" (Jacobson).

As one who believes she helped coin the term, I'd like to raise my hand and offer, Would you like proof?

A quick look at the word origin Web site called the Word Spy—which is also a book, *The Word Spy: The Word Lovers Guide to Modern Culture* by Paul McFedries—indirectly confirms that FC2's anthology was the first to use the term *chick lit* in print, even though Word Spy provides an incorrect first citation:

Earliest Citation:

Anyway, I still adore his writing, and he's still my hero, but I'm really very sad to see Wolcott decrying postfem chick lit as mere "popularity-contest coquetry." (I think he's jealous.) He doesn't even like Cynthia Heimel or Julie Burchill, from what I can tell. Vicki Hengen, "Pictures perfect; rock gems; chick lit," *The Boston Globe*, May 22, 1996.

Couldn't the Word Spy see that *this* May '96 citation in the *Boston Globe* is indirectly quoting James Wolcott from his 1996 *New Yorker* article? Why didn't the Word Spy cite Wolcott's piece as the earliest citation? The Word Spy should have done his fact-checking, gone to Wolcott's article to see if, in fact, there was an earlier published reference to *chick lit* there. And he would've found it. And if he'd looked even harder, he would've seen that *in* that 1996 *New Yorker* essay, Wolcott was referencing an even *earlier* use of chick lit, a 1995 book called *Chick-Lit: Postfeminist Fiction.*

When we titled our anthology *Chick-Lit,* it was not to reduce the contributing authors into shopping-and-dieting airheads. It was a way of saying, "Careful, if you think you know us." Flash back to the '70s, high school English. Eleventh-grade American Literature introduced me to exactly two female characters, both dealing with accusations and convictions having to do with their sex: Hester Prynne (convicted adulteress in *The Scarlet Letter,* written by a man) and Abigail Williams (adulteress in *The Crucible,* written by a man). The other authors on our list included Twain, Crane, Hemingway, Fitzgerald, Salinger, and Willard Motley, who we weren't told was African American. In twelfth-grade Creative Writing, my first story featured a concentrated emotional crisis belonging to a teen-aged boy. When the teacher asked me why I'd chosen to write about a boy, I actually answered, "Because it's more important that this happened to a boy."

But that literary landscape was already quickly changing into the one we've known for at least twenty-five years. For at least that long, writers with double-X chromosomes have been set apart, frequently called "women writers" while the others remain, simply, wholly, "writers." What these women writers produce has been "women's fiction," and the rest, unconditionally, is "fiction" (or even "literature"). The translation to me always has been that men write about what's important; women write about what's important *to women.* So our title of *Chick-Lit* was meant to point out this delusion, this second-class differentiation; not pretend it isn't there. Our titling gesture was similar to comedian Dick Gregory's title for his autobiography, *Nigger.* Here's who we are, plus what you (still) think of us thrown back in your face.

But now, how is anyone to make a distinction? The chicks in commercial chick lit, along with Hooters restaurants and celebrity boxing, have stripped themselves of irony.

Works Cited

Cabot, Heather. "Chick Lit: Genre Aimed at Young Women Is Fueling Publishing Industry." abcnews.com. 30, Aug. 2003. <http://abcnews.go.com/sections/wnt/Entertainment/chicklit030830.html>.

Caughie, Patricia. E-mail interview. Sept. 2004.

Chick Lit (formerly Chick Lit USA). www.chicklit.us.com.

Chick Lit Books. www.chicklitbooks.com.

Gibbons, Fiachra. "Stop Rubbishing Chick-lit, Demands Novelist." *Guardian Unlimited* 21, Aug. 2003. <www.guardian.co.uk>.

Hagar, Laura. "All the News That Fits about Print: Postfeminist Chick Lit." *Express Books* Nov. 1997.

Harzewski, Stephanie. E-mail interview. Sept. 2004.

Hengen, Vicki. "Pictures Perfect; Rock Gems; Chick Lit." *The Boston Globe* 22, May 1996.

Jacobson, Aileen. "Books and the Single Girl." Newsday.com, 11, May 2004.

McFedries, Paul. "Chick Lit." The Word Spy. www.wordspy.com.

Meads, Kat. "In the Guise of an Explanation of My Aunt's Life." *Chick-Lit: Postfeminist Fiction.* Tallahassee, FL: FC2, 1995. 52–57.

Miller, Laura. E-mail interview. Aug. 2004.

The Postfeminist Playground. www.pfplayground.com.

Quamme, Margaret. "'Chick-Lit' Makes Engrossing, Provocative Reply to Feminism." *The Columbus Dispatch* 28, Jan. 1996: 6G.

Royle, Nicholas. "Yarn in the USA." *Time Out: London* 3, July 1996.

See, Carolyn. "Chick-Lit Lays an Egg." *Washington Post* 20, Dec. 1996.

Tatham, Cam. E-mail interview. Sept. 2004.

Vie, Kelly. *two girls review.*

Weinberg, Anna. "She's Come Undone." *Book Magazine* July–Aug. 2003: 47–49.

Wolcott, James. "Hear Me Purr: Maureen Dowd and the Rise of Postfeminist Chick Lit." *The New Yorker* 20, May 1996: 54–59.

2

Tradition and Displacement in the New Novel of Manners

STEPHANIE HARZEWSKI

> There seems little doubt that most modern romance formulas are affirmations of the ideal of monogamous marriage and feminine domesticity. No doubt the coming of age of women's liberation will invent significantly new formulas for romance, if it does not lead to the total rejection of the moral fantasy of love triumphant.
>
> —John Cawelti (1976)

In "Silly Novels by Lady Novelists," George Eliot surveys mid-Victorian romance fiction to assess this popular reading as a "genus with many species" pervaded by a "silliness," whether "frothy," "prosy," "pious," or "pedantic" in quality (140). It is not women writing novels that elicits anxiety for Eliot but that men—and women—interpret sentimental or romance fiction as definitive statements on women's prose craftsmanship. In addition, characteristics that contribute to such novels' infectious quality and commercial appeal can be appropriated to support gender stereotypes, specifically that all women are dreamy, artificial, or silly. Eliot's apprehension is not unfounded when we consider the history of the novel. From its rise in the eighteenth century, the genre provoked unfavorable response related to its position at the intersection of gender, sexuality, and commerce. As a new class of women writers seized on improved printing technologies and an expanding middle-class reading public, many achieved popular recognition and sizeable capital, inciting the wrath of their male counterparts. The novel, a displacement of the prose romance, as Northrop Frye demonstrated, finds its origins in anxiety over the nexus of female sexuality, authorship, and audience (38). This anxiety was manifested in frequent attacks on romantic fiction and, in later decades, popular romance. For instance, in his 1728–29 *The Dunciad*, Alexander Pope cast Eliza Haywood, the most prolific woman author of eighteenth-century England, as a publishers' pissing contest trophy, attempting to put the Danielle Steele of her day in her proper critical place. William Dean Howells classified women's nineteenth-century popular domestic novels under "dubiosities," while Nathaniel Hawthorne, in an 1895 letter to his publisher William Tickner, cursed the "d__d mob of scribbling women," an invective surely motivated in part by their staggering sales (Howells 383; Marks 14).

Though the last two decades of second-wave feminist scholarship have accomplished a recovery and more nuanced consideration of so-called silly lady novelists, recent years have seen a resurgence of antinovel sentiment directed at a new segment of women authors. They have been classified by the neologism *chickerati*, scribblers of chick lit, popular fiction characterized by its antagonists as consisting of "connect-the-dot plots" recognized by "identikit covers" (Thomas). Dame Beryl Bainbridge, five-time Booker nominee, denounces this latest development in prose romance as "froth," whereas Doris Lessing deems it "instantly forgettable" (Ezard). They, as well as a growing number of women journalists, are defensive that this genre not only will be taken as representative "women's writing" but also will disqualify aspiring and younger women writers from critical recognition. As increasing numbers of titles are pigeonholed into this classification, showcased in bookstore displays titled "It's a Girl Thing,"[1] this transatlantic media phenomenon has been the recipient of increased ire by women critics fearful, like Eliot, of frothiness becoming the only suitable literary expression.[2]

Those wishing to validate this fiction are confronted with a critical double bind, as they must not only recognize a new mode currently outside of the canon but also risk confirming stereotypes suggested by its label. Many of the books' titles operate as a further roadblock with, for example, *See Jane Date*, implying a grade-school mentality; *Me Times Three*, an irritating narcissism; and *Run Catch Kiss*, a primitive take on love and sexuality. The genre's kitschy, typically paperback covers conjure a quick-fix consumable status, fueling the derisory classification of chick lit as "snack-food literature" (Barrientos). Generic epithets such as "year-long beach reading" and "the treadmill book club" evoke escapism and mindless ephemerality (Amazon.com list; Napalkova). Most important, in attempting to classify chick lit, we face the daunting prospect of determining what recent fiction by women featuring a female protagonist or a cast of women characters is *not* chick lit.[3] In the past two years, the movement has assumed, deservedly or not, gargantuan proportions, most recently filtering into the mystery and young adult genres as well as newly named subsets such as *mommy lit* and *hen lit* (the latter for the over-fifty reader).[4]

Although chick lit may be a trend, it causes us to reexamine major debates surrounding the novel and literary value. In displacing the popular romance, the genre has clearly revived anxieties over the novel's commercial origins as well as the role of the female writer and reader. Chick lit has adapted several major literary traditions, including traditional prose romance, popular romance, and the novel of manners. Considering its connections to each of these traditions will help clarify both its place in literary history and the reactions it provokes.

Chick Lit and Prose Romance

Although we now equate the term *romance* with its popular incarnation, often referred to as the Harlequin romance after its chief publisher, chick lit's ties are stronger to the original prose romance, particularly in terms of accusations regarding its literary merit. *Romance* is a term that has been used at different times to refer to a variety of fictional works involving some combination of the following: high adventure, thwarted love, mysterious circumstances, arduous quests, and improbable triumphs. The term *romance* derives from the French and was first used exclusively to refer to medieval romances (sometimes called "chivalric romances") written in French and composed in verse. These narratives were concerned with knightly adventure, courtly love, and chivalric ideals, often set at the court of King Arthur. Later the term was used to refer to any medieval romance, whether in verse or prose, and regardless of country of origin.

Prose romance has always spurred debate among its contemporaries over the woman writer's moral and financial status as well as the genre's educational and entertainment benefits, especially in regard to women readers.[5] Romances were deemed "dangerous fictions" and "instruments of debauchery" by Oliver Goldsmith in 1761 (232). Though works commonly closed with a marriage, consent of parents, and a ceremony prescribed by law, the plot is rife with passages that in their "overthrow of laudable customs" expose virtue to the most dangerous attacks (232). Dramatist Richard Cumberland in 1785 cautioned against reading the romance for the stories' capacity to lead female readers into affectation and false character (333). Similarly, John Trumbull in *The Progress of Dullness* (1773) mock-grieved romance's bluster as it fills ladies' heads "brimfull of purling rills" and "swells the mind with haughty fancies," "am'rous follies," and "whims" (19). Sometimes titled *The Progress of Coquetry,* his text associates romance reading with flights of fancy in women.

Such accusations, however, do not go unchallenged. Clara Reeve's *Progress of Romance,* originally published in 1785, directly refuted Trumbull's charges. The text consists of a series of dialogues among the romantically named Euphrasia, Sophronia, and Hortensius. Euphrasia, Reeve's mouthpiece, portrays the romance as a respectable genre, one that inspires its readers to emulate the ideal virtue of its characters. In its first volume, Euphrasia argues that romance and epic derive from the same source, pointing out that both describe idealized characters and fabulous adventures. Reeve charges "modern romances" of the seventeenth century with confounding truth and fiction, yet asserts that the aims of romance and "true history" are contiguous; that is, they provide examples of heroic virtue for readers to imitate. *The Progress of Romance* endeavors to break down the distinctions between romance, epic, and history, with the ultimate goal of rescuing the romance's respectability in terms of moral and literary merit.

The history of the novel in English is a history of secession and appropriation from the romance. Critics cast the early novel reader as they did the romance reader—that is, as a vulnerable female. This gendering persisted throughout the eighteenth century and carried well into the next. In the first half of the eighteenth century, those who condemned novels condemned them as a whole. The distinction between good and bad, moral and corrupt novels did not occur until midcentury (Warner 8). After the success of *Pamela* (1740), *Joseph Andrews* (1742), *Clarissa* (1747–48), and *Tom Jones* (1749), critics shifted the terms of the debate, not denouncing novels as a class but discerning what kinds of novels should be read and what kinds should be written (Warner 8). In the works of Richardson and Fielding, critics found merit, morality, and a male authorial model. Claiming Richardson and Fielding enabled critics to begin to define the "English" novel and separate the novel from the prose romance's French affiliations. The latter form was coded as feminine; the former as masculine.[6] This marked the triumph of realism over novels of amorous intrigue, deemed unrealistic because they were inappropriately factual as in the case of Delarivière Manley's "scandal fiction" or simply fantasy like Haywood's best-selling *Love in Excess* (Warner 88).

Chick lit continues this gendered debate about the novel's value. Like the first novels, chick lit emerged as a subset of commercial print entertainments: its foundational texts, Candace Bushnell's *Sex and the City* and Helen Fielding's *Bridget Jones's Diary*, were both originally newspaper columns published in book form in 1996. Numerous chick-lit authors are former or current media professionals, the sector in which heroines are typically employed. For instance, the author of *A Connecticut Fashionista in King Arthur's Court* is Marianne Mancusi, an Emmy-award-winning TV news producer; *Carrie Pilby* author Caren Lissner edits a chain of weekly newsletters; and best-selling authors Jennifer Weiner and Karen E. Quinones Miller both worked as *Philadelphia Inquirer* journalists.[7] Plots are also closely connected to the world of popular culture. Jennifer O'Connell's *Bachelorette #1* (2003) and Alesia Holliday's *American Idle* [*sic*] (2004) directly reference and draw their plots from the concurrent media phenomenon reality TV. Chick lit presents itself as a literary form yet does not avoid alliances with popular entertainment. As a result, it calls attention to the tensions between high and popular culture.

Although the literary merit of these novels is questionable, the genre's status as a media icon is not. Anna Weinberg's "Make Your Own Chick-Lit Novel!" is a satirical recipe designed to suggest its middling merit and mock its distinct visual identity (see figure 2.1). NPR's *Fresh Air* critic Maureen Corrigan has assessed the genre as a "veritable Pepto-Bismol tidal wave." The novels have brought a new visual contribution to the marketplace. This contribution reveals, for some, embarrassingly, a strong interplay with advertising and commodity culture. Victoria's Secret, for example, which for several years has featured pink and white pinstripe cosmetic and accessory cases as part of its permanent inventory, brought this signature motif to a new level in 2003: the company introduced a formfitting "pyjama" short line, bearing strong resemblance to RDI covers such as Ariella Papa's *Up and Out* (2003). This valorization of pink has failed to cross over to the genre's reception: critics such as Corrigan have labeled its protagonists "powderpuff girls," perhaps unaware of the genre's interchange with the beauty industry. For instance, "Lucky Chick" body care products, featuring an icon of a woman in a pink turban with her arms outstretched like a diva, aim to cultivate "a positive attitude focused on fun and pampering," dovetailing with that of the genre's protagonists. Former *Lucky* magazine beauty department alum Tia Williams has inspired a lip gloss shade named after the heroine of her novel *The Accidental Diva* ("Hot Gloss").[8] The genre has permeated the realm of writing materials, as both the R. Nichols and Caspari stationery lines feature chick-lit-inspired designs. Chick lit's association with pink is not only a textbook case of the novel's feminization, compounded with covers

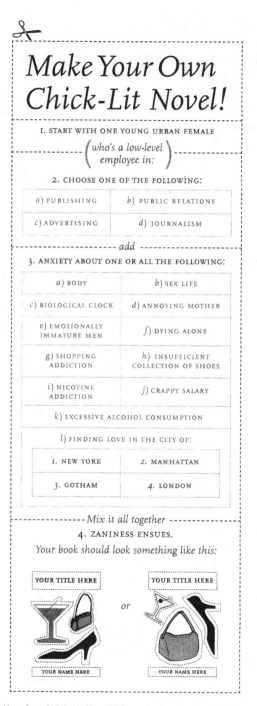

Figure 2.1 "Make Your Own Chick-Lit Novel!" from *Book* magazine, July–August 2003.

frequently featuring an exposed female knee, but also a marketing move to attract and bring back readers through a recognizable visual appeal. It participates in a feedback loop with fashion trends, as pink for several seasons has been the new black.[9]

On this point of fashion, the genre's reception history exhibits notable parallels with censure surrounding early English novels. Francis Coventry, author of the satirical novel *The History of Pompey the Little* (1751), credited novelist Henry Fielding for persuading female readers of amatory trifles to "leave this extravagance to their Abigails with their cast cloths" (qtd. in Warner 8). Romance reading is not only pathological but also here associated with women's rabid appetite for new fashions. The novels should, like their old dresses, be passed on to the maid, exchanged for a more sensible text. However farcical these arguments may be three centuries later, the connection between frivolous novels and fashion has resurfaced with chick lit, as critics, judging a book by its cover, have conflated its fashion-conscious exterior with inferior literature. Admittedly, a fixation with clothes permeates the genre in content and form. For instance, covers more often than not feature stylish female clothing or high heels. Simon and Schuster/Pocket Books' Downtown Press imprint logo is a shopping bag, while the imprint titles Strapless and Red Dress Ink reflect their protagonists' typically strong penchant for apparel. Avon Trade, an imprint of HarperCollins, features a tote purse as its logo, the imprint slogan—"because every great bag deserves a great book!"—exclaims a marriage between accessories and reading. Its order privileges the bag, making the "book" ultimately a complementary accessory. Chick-lit-inspired self-help, such as Jacqueline Williams's *The Handbag Book of Girlie Emergencies* (2001/2002), blurs the categories of book and accessory. And finally, not surprisingly, a substratum of texts presents a satirical treatment of the Manhattan fashion sector. Chick lit's fashion and shopping fetish further genders this by-women, for-women genre and compounds its affiliations with mass culture, however upscale (Radway 193).

The genre offers a case study of the novel's difficulty in breaking free of its commercial origins. Chick lit's denigration stems in part from its gendered reclamation of the novel's commodity roots. The connection goes beyond an interest in fashion to a full-fledged embracing of commercialism in all its manifestations. For instance, many chick-lit authors maintain Web sites with links to book vendors along with managing promotional listservs. Ford Motor Company made a deal with best-selling chick-lit author Carole Matthews to feature one of its cars in her novel *The Sweetest Taboo* (2004). The product placement has the heroine driving a Ford Fiesta. "She's red, raunchy and drives like a dream," reads a snippet from the book ("Literature, Sponsored by ..."). Novels about women who work in the media industry who like to shop are written by former, sometimes current, media professionals who like to shop. Some, I suspect, write to shop. Back cover author bios, such as Michelle Cunnah's, unabashedly reveal the novelist's affinity for consumption. Shanna Swendson, a member of Yahoo!'s ChickLit discussion board, encourages her virtual sisters to persevere in writing "these books that others may dismiss as fluff." The novelist concludes her post with a defense of shopping: "Now's I'm off to Barnes and Noble with my Master Card to spend more money than I should. It's market research right?" Author of the best-selling Shopaholic series, Sophie Kinsella in 2003 participated as one of the "bridal industry superstars" in the annual "Wedding March on Madison" bridal weekend sponsored by *Brides* and *Modern Bride*. Melissa Senate, author of *See Jane Date* (2001), Red Dress Ink's debut title, participated in a reading with RDI authors Lynda Curnyn and Wendy Markham on October 1, 2003, as a cross-promotion with Bloomingdale's Manhattan flagship store. Attendees who purchased $100 worth of Y.E.S. clothing received an autographed book of their choice and an introduction to the author who sat in the center of one of the clothing aisles.

Chick Lit and Popular Romances

This critique of chick lit's commodity roots also links it to the popular romance, or Harlequin. Germaine Greer, in the best-selling feminist classic *The Female Eunuch* (1970), offers one of the first critiques of formula romances. For Greer, these novels merit one-word classifications, specifically, "trash" and "mush" (185). By presenting an "utterly ineffectual heroine" the novels thwart female liberation aimed at counteracting the fiction's capacity to breed "sterile self-deception" (185). The female reader is masochistic, "cherishing [her] chains of bondage," a slave to the romantic myth (176). Susan Ager of the *Detroit Free Press* denounced the romance novel as not merely "bad" for women but emphatically "Evil," judging it "more crippling than high heels" and "worse than whipped cream," the latter, of course, edible froth (qtd. in Grescoe 217). Even more judgment-neutral studies of the Harlequin empire cannot entirely escape casting the romance as fundamentally commercial, and therefore inferior as literature. For instance, *Merchants of Venus*, Paul Grescoe's book-length examination of the world's largest paperback publisher, implies in its title that Harlequin does not so much create novels as sell them. Furthermore, these novels are not inherently literary as much as products of and about a female grotesque. His title's allusion to Shakespeare, however playful, instead demarcates the modern romance from "authentic" literature by connoting a keen hunger for commerce.

The Harlequin romance boomed in the early 1970s and coexisted, though antagonistically, with the concurrent proliferation of second-wave manifestos.[10] Chick lit established itself as a commercial genre by the late 1990s and worked in tandem with postfeminism. The genre has its origin, as did the Harlequin romance, in North America and the United Kingdom (Paizis 10). Although some chick-lit authors, such as Melissa Senate, are former romance novel editors, and numerous others, such as Lisa Cach and Swendson, also write romance fiction, not all of chick lit ends with what Grescoe identified as the modern romance's one defining constant, the inevitable happy ending (2). Scholars such as Ann Barr Snitow have attributed the Harlequin boom of the 1970s to the books' ability to offer an archetypal, fixed image of the exchange between men and women at the very moment of "confusing, shifting, frightening" social actualities (150). Chick lit, by contrast, responds to upheavals in the dating and mating order through a mixed strategy of dramatization, farce, and satire. Daughters of educated baby boomers, chick-lit heroines, in their degree of sexual autonomy and professional choices, stand as direct beneficiaries of the women's liberation movement. Yet they shift earlier feminist agendas, such as equal pay for equal work, to lifestyle concerns. Unlike earlier generations, chick protagonists and their readers have the right to choose; now the problem is too many choices, a dilemma *Sex and the City*'s Carrie Bradshaw contemplates on her Mac laptop.

According to the Romance Writers of America's official definition, the love story is the central focus of the romance novel, and the end of the book is emotionally satisfying as its climax resolves the love story ("RWA Defines"). Its main plot must involve a man and woman falling in love and its conflict center on the pair struggling to make the relationship work. This core attribute draws from the standard romance plot, where two people fall in love and must complete a quest or overcome some sort of obstacle before they finally marry. The traditional romance presents a narrative that emphasizes action or plot over character development, and often lacks clear causal impetus, instead depending on deus ex machina resolutions.

Chick lit replicates romance conventions in the heroine's union with Mr. Right, though this is not requisite. Frequently Mr. Right turns out to be Mr. Wrong or Mr. Maybe. The quest for self-definition and the balancing of work with social interaction is given equal or more attention than the relationship conflict. The desire to be beautiful, rich, and adored receives ultimate validation when the heroine enters the realm of narrative, circulated in the gossip papers or photographed by paparazzi as an exciting artist, editor, or new millennium style icon. Chick lit's depiction of serial dating strays from what Harlequin readers have articulated as the "one woman—one man" cardinal tenet: the stipulation that a romance focuses only on one male complement for the heroine (Radway 171). Although the Harlequin romance may contain scenes of playful banter, chick lit deliberately aims for a humorous effect: Bridget Jones's popularity stems in part from her ability to laugh at her self-improvement quests.[11] The protagonists' self-deprecating humor, readers claim, lends the novels an identifiable, friendly voice and approachable comfort level.

An offshoot of romantic comedy, chick lit virtually jettisons the figure of the heterosexual hero, with Manolo Blahniks upstaging men.[12] The genre relegates the hero to a cipher as the protagonist's suitor or fiancé becomes like the men in bridal magazines, that is, a shadow presence or pleasingly pat background figure. Instead, a gay male best friend operates prominently.[13] More often than not we know more about the Plaza Hotel, the wedding reception venue par excellence, than of the heroine's groom. Sometimes the hero is even upstaged by someone from outside his species: in Elizabeth Young's *A Girl's Best Friend* (2003), Henry, the protagonist's wolfhound mix, occupies the alpha male slot. Kathleen Tessaro's international best-seller *Elegance* (2003) presents a closeted gay male as the heroine's husband. She evaluates her desire for her thoughtful but libido-challenged spouse: "The truth is I don't want him to notice me, to cuddle me, to touch me, or to say how pretty I am. I just want him to leave me alone. After all that, I don't want to fuck him either" (90). The cardboard groom in some texts enters the realm of the corpse, as Bushnell's Mary Winters of *Four Blondes* (2000) confesses this death wish: "I wanted to be a painter. But I had the big white fantasy—that dream you have about your wedding day. And then it comes true. And then, almost immediately afterward, you have the black fantasy. … You have this vision of yourself, all in black. Still young, wearing a big black hat, and a chic black dress. And you're walking behind your husband's casket. … You still have your children and you're still young, but you're … free" (243–44). Significantly, though popular romance covers feature a riveting hero of phallic intensity, no such figure makes chick lit's cover iconography.

The genre's typical first-person female narrator and confessional mode render direct male speech at least once removed. Underdeveloped male characters may stem in part from authorial inexperience as numerous novels are debut works. But it is also an effect of the formula itself: though standard features of mainstream fiction—plot, setting, general linearity—appear in these popular works, many novels approach the monologue form.[14] The frequency of the *I* pronoun facilitates the heroine's development, or, as critics have claimed, produces a juvenile solipsism.

That many of chick lit's heroines are orphans, itself a romance trope, indicates the legacies of the Cinderella story and classic heroine-centered novels such as Brontë's *Jane Eyre*. Significantly, Jane, a textbook match with readers' identification with an Everywoman, is a recurring name in the genre.[15] The orphan trope, common also to the romance genre, reflects the continuing concerns over single status for women. A growing body of feminist social science has sought to replace negative images of female singleness—waste, desiccation, and barrenness—with affirmative models. For example, *singularity* is transformed from incompleteness to a state of readiness, of openness and self-sufficiency. Yet, women are still feeling apprehensive, lonely, or frustrated, as sociologist Marcelle Clements frankly appraises: "It's not that there are no men, it's that there are no men she wants to want, or who would want her the way she wants to be wanted" (25). By offering literary representations of social observations such as Clements's, chick lit has worked to lend the popular romance a greater, and, more important, contemporary, psychological realism. Although many protagonists share the optimism of Jane Austen's heroines, a sobering, darker element, what Katherine Marsh named "the failure of sex to answer post-feminist women's longing for real human connection" underlies the genre (41, 44). As the novels do not necessarily culminate in marriage, the books present a more realistic portrait of single life and dating, exploring, in varying degrees, the dissolution of romantic ideals or exposing those ideals as unmet, sometimes unrealistic, expectations.

Chick lit transports elements of the romance into an urban setting, as opposed to Harlequins, which, critics such as Snitow have noted, avoid references to local detail beyond the merely scenic (148). In this sense, the genre offers what critic Michael McKeon termed *emplacement* (14). On romance covers there is an absence of work and the city, the latter frequently foregrounded in chick lit (Paizis 57–58). The degree of verisimilitude devoted to the protagonist's day-to-day working life, characteristically in the media sector, reflects the genre's Harlequin "career romance" legacy. While in the mid-seventies the typical Harlequin heroine either was just emerging from home or was a secretary or nurse who quit her job at marriage, by the late seventies many Harlequin heroines had unusual and interesting, if not bizarre, careers (Rabine 167). In the frequency of its heroines having crushes on or full-fledged affairs with their bosses or senior colleagues, chick lit is an extension of series such as Harlequin's Temptations, where the boss figure remains the prototype for the career romance hero (Rabine 168, 170). Yet analysts of the career romance have noted that when the romantic plot begins to thicken, the heroine's job that initially imbued her with glamour then becomes temporary. Ann Rosalind Jones asserts that women's work operates merely "cosmetically," as the negotiation between absorbing job responsibilities and total commitment to a man inevitably undermines the romance's attempt at verisimilitude (207). In its greater integration of the world of urban work into the romance plot, chick lit offers arguably less romance than its predecessor but more realism.

The final difference between the romance and chick lit appears in the status of money in the marriage contract. The romance has traditionally opposed love and monetary gain, as the gold digger or social climber functions as a foil to the less worldly heroine. Chick lit offers the revenge of the husband hunter, typically united with a man she does love but who is conveniently well appointed. Whereas popular romance novels must be careful, as Tania Modleski notes, to show that the heroine never machinates for a man and his estate (48), many American chick-lit novels, such as Gigi Levangie Grazer's *Maneater* (2003), invert, or certainly complicate, this trope, often diffusing it through humor or presenting semifarcical husband hunting tales of cunning and endeavor. For instance, in the initial sentence of Bushnell's "Nice N'Easy" (one of the novellas included in *Four Blondes*), the third-person limited narrator objectively informs us that thirty-two-year-old Manhattanite Janey Wilcox spent the past ten summers in the Hamptons without renting a house or paying for anything except an occasional Jitney ticket. In the early nineties Janey's modeling success earned her a part in an action flick. Janey never acted again, but with her semi-celebrity status as a "thinking man's sex symbol" established, she figured out that, as long as she maintained her high-finish exterior, she could "get … things and keep on getting them" (3). That Janey had no money was irrelevant, as long as she had rich friends and could get rich men. The secret for getting men was simply to abandon any illusions about marrying them: "There was no rich man in New York who would turn down a regular blow job and entertaining company with no strings attached. Not that you'd want to marry any of these guys anyway" (3). Janey forgoes the long-term investment of a committed relationship for the quick return of a prime area Hamptons rental, and, usually, as a fringe benefit, the man's car. She sells herself seasonally as what economists Samuel Cameron and Alan Collins termed a "recreational consumption good" and, realtor-like, appraises men based on their ability to offer "location, location" (126).

When a friend asks her whether she worries if men will figure out they're being used for their houses, she replies, "I'm a feminist. … It's about the redistribution of wealth" (10). In the end, Janey secures an eight-million-dollar windfall contract with Victoria's Secret and pulls her Porsche Boxster convertible, a bonus from Victoria's Secret, into the driveway of the five-bedroom house with sauna, Jacuzzi, and pool she has rented. We can only wonder if Bushnell is offering a case study or self-help template for what we might call "yuppie feminism," in which the self-conscious use of the female form as a type of currency is offered as a materialist ethos.

Chick Lit and the Novel of Manners

With Edith Wharton and Jane Austen as acknowledged precedents, much of the chick-lit genre revisits the "class without money" conflict that pervades the novel of manners tradition. Heroines on an entry- to mid-level publishing salary typically wrestle with a barrage of material temptations, often succumbing to hefty credit card debt. Chick lit reinterprets the legacies of the novel of manners and domestic fiction's marriage plot, chronicling the heroines' fortunes on the marriage market and assessing contemporary courtship behavior, dress, and social motives.[16] But chick lit's indebtedness to the novel of manners goes beyond such general thematic similarities. It is a critical commonplace that Helen Fielding's *Bridget Jones's Diary* co-opts Austen's *Pride and Prejudice,* while Chris Dyer's lesser-known *Wanderlust* (2003) advertises itself as an Austen-inspired novel of "Sex and Sensibility." In interviews, Tama Janowitz has stated she intended *A Certain Age* (1999) as a modern version of *The House of Mirth* (Buchwald); Candace Bushnell's *Trading Up* (2003) contains direct allusions to Wharton's novel as well as strong thematic parallels with *The Custom of the Country,* as Bushnell has acknowledged Wharton as a principal literary influence.[17] Appropriations from classic novels of manners may merely operate on a literal level, as Michelle Cunnah's *32AA* (2003) features a half-British protagonist often called Emma. The naming device signals continuity with Austenesque subjects, namely, courtship, coming of age, and erroneous judgments about male suitors rectified in an actual or imminent union.

Chick lit presents a new novel of manners not as an exaggerated version of its codes but as a synthesis of diverse popular and literary forms. For example, Kathleen Tessaro's *Elegance* doubles as a self-help book on the subject of its title. London box-office sales clerk Louise Canova stumbles upon a forty-year-old encyclopedia of style by French fashion expert Genevieve Antoine Dariaux, and the novel structures its chapters around sections reprinted from Dariaux's 1964 tome. Advice on apparel suitable for a yachting excursion complements the protagonist's attempt to attend the male love interest's boat christening party. The lighthearted *How to Meet Cute Boys* (2003) by Deanna Kizis includes dating and relationship statistics as well as quizzes and magazine articles from the *Cosmopolitan*-like magazine its L.A. protagonist edits. Laura Wolf's debut novel, *Diary of a Mad Bride* (2002), chronicles a year in the life of twenty-nine-year-old associate features editor Amy Thomas, who unexpectedly becomes engaged and finds herself mutating into a mad bride. From this point her diary is transformed into a wedding planner. Amy begins by making a twenty-item wedding "To Do" list, which, after she consults some bridal magazines, grows to seventy items. The list, which appears in full in the text, is reprinted several times with lines through its completed or jettisoned tasks. The diary finally doubles as a keepsake book as it features a reprint of the invitation, wedding gift thank-you notes, and a series of "while you were out" messages, the last by Amy's assistant, who, exasperated by a delegated wedding-related work overload, conveys her resignation.

Elise Juska's debut novel *Getting over Jack Wagner* (2003) offers another case study of chick lit's embrace of popular forms. Twenty-six-year-old Philadelphian copywriter Eliza Simon has a predilection for dating rock stars. Yet none have made it past their basement, garage, or local gig. And none have approached the object of her initial crush, singer and soap opera star Jack Wagner, "Frisco" of *General Hospital*. The funky moral is as follows: only by looking level-headedly at her past and material objects, namely, her 1980s music collection, can she hear a different kind of song and begin to lead a more grounded life.[18]

The first-person account culminates with neither an engagement nor a marriage, as the protagonist moves from seeking experience vicariously through intense but amateur musicians to looking within herself as a source of real possibilities. At the same time, the novel comments self-consciously on the act of writing the novel itself. We learn that Eliza's previous project was called "Movies That Smell," based on the concept that moviegoers can inhale the scenes as viewed:

Examples:

a. *Mystic Pizza* = Italian sausage and pepperoni.
b. *Beaches* = sunscreen and ocean breeze. (24)

She hits a dead end, though, when a friend questions how to render a war movie into olfactory form. That many movies are set in major, air-polluted cities poses another conundrum. Her new project is intended to serve as a guide to dating rock stars. Eliza directly presents its crossover quality and her authorial intent:

> It will be a guide to dating rock stars. It will be part fiction, part nonfiction. It will be part humor, part personal health. It will qualify as sociology, how-to, reference, and the performing arts. Each chapter will focus on a different kind of musician—an ambassador from the instrumental genre, if you will—and what to expect (and not to expect) if you date them. I consider it a public service, a way of using any collective experience to better the world. Maybe, as a bonus, I'll figure out where my own rock star is hiding. (23)

The novel formally mimics the principles of the never-written manual. Each chapter begins with songs from a mix tape readers can play as they read along, capturing the tone and lyric of life in a certain moment. Most chapters are titled after a different musician and open with a list of songs drawn and mixed from Eliza's own collection. The penultimate chapter concludes with a list of concerns about Eliza's book, which by this time is no longer a rock star dating guide but the novel itself.

The merging of the original, unwritten book with that of the actual narrative parallels Eliza's development of a more integrated and authentic self. She concedes, "Though the rock stars might be the ones up on the makeshift stage, it's always been me performing" (247). The final chapter jettisons the subject of dating angst for domestic fiction as it features an informal mother–daughter reunion and sharing of long-suppressed confidences. The book's (unnumbered) last page serves as the cover jacket of the unfinished book, with both sides of the tape mix titles in place, the tape's title matching that of Juska's novel.

It appears, approximately three centuries later, that the novel has come full circle, or, in its partial parody and reformulation of prose romance conventions, has renewed this cycle. This new novel offers a backward glance at earlier debates around the long-standing tensions among gender, commerce, and literary culture. In its triumvirate embrace of shopping, femininity, and mass culture, the genre of chick lit greets the novel's closet skeletons in a new marketplace.

Notes

1. Title of Barnes & Noble book display, Philadelphia, Pennsylvania, summer 2003.
2. See, for example, journalist Hanne Blank's *Baltimore City Paper* big books feature "Don't Hate Me Because I'm Cute," which references Eliot's essay to argue for the vapidity of the chick-lit genre. Blank bemoans that silly novels by lady novelists are back in vogue, appearing on top-seller lists "like candy-colored mushrooms in the front lawn of literature" yet also acknowledges that pejoratives targeted at women writing to the female reader are a sexist commonplace in literary history.
3. This gender classification will become further complicated as male writers, such as "B.D. Garnder" and "E. Lynn Harris," have jumped on the chick-lit bandwagon.
4. Young adult *Sex and the City*–inspired imprints such as Little, Brown's *Gossip Girl* and *The A-List* have produced best-sellers such as Cecily von Ziegesar's *All I Want Is Everything* (2002).
5. Annette Townend locates judgment of the romance as "unserious" literature as early as the end of the sixteenth century, which she posits as the consequence of the shift from a male to female protagonist and the transition to a single-sex readership (19). For Gillian Beer, the "feminine" temper of the genre can be traced to the increased role of women as the chief distinction between Arthurian romance and earlier related Carolingian literature (25).
6. In his *History of the English Novel*, Ernest Baker judged scandal chroniclers such as Haywood and Delarivière Manley as "very enterprising" yet, compared to their predecessor Aphra Behn, too under the sway of "foreign fashions" (Warner 107). The former he deems as insufficiently English, an appraisal with gender implications given the coding of France as feminine.

7. Chick-lit authors as current or former media professionals invite parallels with the occupational history of early-eighteenth-century English novelists: many, as Lennard Davis has shown, were directly associated with journalism (101). We know that Eliza Haywood, the most important producer of popular fiction before Samuel Richardson, was a journalist and distributor of political pamphlets; Henry Fielding and William Defoe wrote and edited newspapers; playwright and novelist Aphra Behn penned political pieces, as did her contemporary Mary Manley; and satirist Jonathan Swift authored journalistic pieces and political pamphlets (175). Critics, such as Davis, have classified these early novelists as inheritors of news discourse, who, fittingly, viewed themselves writing about the events of the world as a reporter might perceive them; their attempts at verisimilitude and realism enable us to view the novel as what Davis has thoughtfully called a "factual fiction." Numerous chick-lit protagonists report within the fiction world of their novel on topics such as mating patterns, society gossip, local news, and the media industry.
8. *Lucky* magazine is a periodical devoted to women's shopping culture. Lucky Chick's marketing slogan, "products for a lucky lifestyle," may allude to the publication.
9. We can hypothetically consider this a response from the fashion industry to a dark political and economic climate. These flashes of optimism and gaiety may appear irresponsible or immature for such a backdrop. Such accusations can be leveled at its New York heroines oblivious to September 11th and its aftermath.
10. With the introduction of the new Sensual Historical in 1972 (*The Flame and the Flower* by Kathleen Woodwiss) and the Sweet/Savage Historical in 1974 (*Sweet Savage Love* by Rosemary Rogers), the romance market exploded and historicals became popular after a twenty-plus-year relative absence (Ramsdell 8).
11. See Franken (731–32) for a discussion of how Fielding's novel parodies the novel of education and its female protagonist's unilinear character development.
12. See Harzewski for an analysis of this phenomenon in the HBO series *Sex and the City.*
13. Sometimes chick lit overlaps its dating adventures with the AIDS story, as the illness and untimely demise of the best friend is intended to balance what can be construed as the self-absorption of the heroine. Although it can be argued that the sacrifice of the gay best friend, always depicted as more handsome and stylish than his straight counterpart, allows for the heterosexual union of the couple, I suspect this trope attempts to counter critical accusations of solipsism. In addition, it could be interpreted as an inversion of love-struck female fatality especially rife in Victorian literature; for example, Eliot's *Adam Bede,* Wilde's *The Picture of Dorian Gray,* and Tennyson's "The Lady of Shalott."
14. Not all of the genre confines itself to the first person. The works of Bushnell, for example, employ third-person narration, as does Marian Keyes's *Sushi for Beginners* (2001).
15. See also Whitehead 49.
16. Criticisms of the chick-lit heroine's man-catching preoccupation echo those made of Jane Austen's oeuvre. For example, William Forsyth in 1871 bewailed the novels' "constant husband-hunting," a feature that left readers feeling that the sole rationale of a young lady's existence (337, 334–35).
17. An advertisement for *Trading Up*'s paperback edition proclaims "Sex … without sensibility" in a partial parody of Austen's novel.
18. This "music of our lives" trope figured prominently in Downtown Press's 2003 releases. For example, in Emily Franklin's *Liner Notes,* mother–daughter reminiscences are sparked by 1980s tapes the two listen to on a cross-country trip, with the tunes operating as figurative road signs.

The author gratefully acknowledges the American Association of University Women and the Woodrow Wilson Foundation, whose awards of a dissertation fellowship and dissertation grant in women's studies, respectively, supported the writing of this essay. Rita Barnard's translation of Christien Franken's article "Me and Ms. Jones: Love, Romance, and Motherhood in English-Language 'Single Women' Novels," from Dutch to English, is especially appreciated.

Works Cited

Barrientos, Tanya. "Sassy, Kicky 'Chick Lit' Is the Hottest Trend in Publishing." *Philadelphia Inquirer.* 28, May 2003. 19, Aug. 2003. <http://www.ledgerenquirer.com/mld/ledgeren-quirer/entertainment/5960564.html>.

Beer, Gillian. *The Romance.* London: Methuen, 1970.

Blank, Hanne. "Don't Hate Me Because I'm Cute." *Baltimore City Paper Online.* 10–16, Sept. 2003. 23, Sept. 2003. <http://www.citypaper.com/2003-09-10/bigbooks2.html>.

Buchwald, Laura L. "My Lunch with Tama." Bold Type. <http://www.randomhouse.com/boldtype/0899/janowitz/interview.html>.

Bushnell, Candace. *Four Blondes.* New York: Atlantic Monthly Press, 2000.

———. *Sex and the City.* New York: Atlantic Monthly Press, 1996.

———. *Trading Up.* New York: Hyperion, 2003.

Cameron, Samuel, and Alan Collins. *Playing the Love Market: Dating, Romance and the Real World.* London: Free Association, 2000.

Cawelti, John G. *Adventure, Mystery, and Romance: Formula Stories as Art and Popular Culture.* Chicago: University of Chicago Press, 1976.

Clements, Marcelle. *The Improvised Woman: Single Women Reinventing Single Life.* New York: Norton, 1998.

Corrigan, Maureen. " 'Pink' Books." Rev. of the chick-lit genre. Fresh Air. WHYY-FM, Philadelphia. 7, July 2003.

Cumberland, Richard. Letter. *The Observer* 27 (1785). Reprinted in *Novel and Romance, 1700–1800: A Documentary Record.* Ed. Ioan Williams. New York: Barnes and Noble, 1970. 332–35.

Cunnah, Michelle. *32AA.* New York: Avon Trade, 2003.

Dariaux, Genevieve Antoine. *Elegance: A Complete Guide for Every Woman Who Wants to Be Well and Properly Dressed on All Occasions.* New York: Doubleday, 1964.

Davis, Lennard J. *Factual Fictions: The Origins of the English Novel.* Philadelphia: University of Pennsylvania Press, 1996.

Dyer, Chris. *Wanderlust: A Novel of Sex and Sensibility.* New York: Plume, 2003.

Eliot, George. "Silly Novels by Lady Novelists." *Westminster Review* (October 1856). Reprinted in *Selected Essays, Poems and Other Writings.* Ed. A.S. Byatt and Nicholas Warren. London: Penguin, 1990, 140–63.

Ezard, John. "Bainbridge Tilts at 'Chick Lit' Cult." *The Guardian* 24, Aug. 2001. 1, June 2003. <http://books.guardian.co.uk/departments/generalfiction/story/0,6000,541954,00.html>.

Fielding, Helen. *Bridget Jones's Diary,* London: Picador, 1996.

Forsyth, William. *The Novels and the Novelists of the Eighteenth Century, in Illustration of the Manners and Morals of the Age.* 1871. London: Kennikat, 1970.

Franken, Christien. "Me and Ms. Jones: liefde, romantiek en moedderschap in Engelstalige 'singlewomen'-romans." *De Gids* 63.9 (2000): 29–36.

Frye, Northrup. *The Secular Scripture: A Study of the Structure of Romance.* Cambridge: Harvard University Press, 1976.

Goldsmith, Oliver. "From a Letter Written in the Character of Lien Chi Altangi, 1761." *Novel and Romance, 1700–1800: A Documentary Record.* Ed. Ioan Williams. New York: Barnes and Noble, 1970. 232–33.

Grazer, Gigi Levangie. *Maneater.* New York: Downtown Press, 2003.

Greer, Germaine. *The Female Eunuch.* New York: McGraw-Hill, 1971.

Grescoe, Paul. *Merchants of Venus: Inside Harlequin and the Empire of Romance.* Vancouver: Raincoast Books, 1996.

Harzewski, Stephanie. "The Limits of Defamiliarization: *Sex and the City* as Late Heterosexuality." *The Feminist and the Scholar Online: A Webjournal Published by the Barnard Center for Research on Women* 3.1 (Fall 2004). <http://www.barnard.edu/sfonline/hbo/harzewski_01.htm>.

Holliday, Alesia. *American Idle.* New York: Dorchester, 2004.

"Hot Gloss." *Lucky* July 2004: 100.

Howells, William Dean. Rev. of *A Terrible Temptation,* by Charles Reade. *Atlantic Monthly* 28 September 1871: 383–84.

Jones, Ann Rosalind. "Mills and Boon Meets Feminism." *The Progress of Romance: The Politics of Popular Fiction.* Ed. Joan Radford. London: Routledge, 1986. 195–218.

Juska, Elisa. *Getting over Jack Wagner.* New York: Downtown Press, 2003.

Keyes, Marian. *Sushi for Beginners*. Dublin: Poolbeg, 2001.

Kizis, Deanna. *How to Meet Cute Boys*. New York: Warner, 2003.

"Literature, Sponsored by…" *The Writer* July 2004: 8.

Marks, Pamela. "The Good Provider in Romance Novels." *Romantic Conventions*. Ed. Anne Kaler and Rosemary E. Johnson-Kurek. Bowling Green, OH: Bowling Green State University Popular Press, 1991. 10–22.

Marsh, Katherine. "Fabio Gets His Walking Papers: Can Harlequin Rekindle Romance in a Post-Feminist World?" *Washington Monthly* Jan.–Feb. 2002: 39–44.

Matthews, Carole. *The Sweetest Taboo*. New York: Avon Trade, 2004.

McKeon, Michael. *The Origins of the English Novel, 1600–1740*. Baltimore: Johns Hopkins University Press, 1987.

Modleski, Tania. *Loving with a Vengeance: Mass-Produced Fantasies for Women*. Hamden CT: Archon, 1982.

Napalkova, Ekaterina. "The Treadmill Book Club: Finding the Literary Value of 'Chick Lit' in Candace Bushnell's 'Nice N'Easy." Unpublished student essay. June 2003.

O'Connell, Jennifer L. *Bachelorette #1*. New York: New American Library, 2003.

Paizis, George. *Love and the Novel: The Poetics and Politics of Romantic Fiction*. Houndsmills, Basingstoke: Macmillan; New York: St. Martin's, 1998.

Papa, Ariella. *Up and Out*. Ontario: Red Dress Ink, 2003.

Pope, Alexander. *The Dunciad, Variorum. With the Prolegomena of Scriblerus*. London: A. Dod, 1729.

Rabine, Leslie W. *Reading the Romantic Heroine: Text, History, Ideology*. Ann Arbor: University of Michigan Press, 1985.

Radway, Janice. *Reading the Romance: Women, Patriarchy, and Popular Literature*. Chapel Hill: University of North Carolina Press, 1984.

Ramsdell, Kristin. *Happily Every After: A Guide to Reading Interests in Romance Fiction*. Littleton, CO: Libraries Unlimited, 1999.

Reeve, Clara. *The Progress of Romance through Times, Countries, and Manners*. Vol. 1. 1785. New York: Garland, 1970.

"RWA Defines the Romance Novel." c. 1999. 22, Sept. 2004. <http://www.rwanational.org/PressReleaseRWADefinesRomance.cfm>.

Senate, Melissa. *See Jane Date*. Ontario: Red Dress Ink, 2001.

Snitow, Ann Barr. "Mass Market Romance: Pornography for Women Is Different." *Radical History Review* (Spring/Summer 1979): 141–61.

Sohn, Amy. *Run Catch Kiss: A Gratifying Novel*. New York: Simon and Schuster, 1999.

Swendson, Shanna. "The Relevance of Chick Lit." Online posting. 1, Dec. 2003. Yahoo!'s ChickLit Discussion Group. <http://groups.yahoo.com/group/ChickLit/ message/14391>.

Tessaro, Kathleen. *Elegance*. New York: Avon Trade, 2003.

Thomas, Scarlett. "The Great Chick Lit Conspiracy." *The Independent* 4, Aug. 2002. 1, June 2003. <http://enjoyment.independent.co.uk/books/features/story.jsp?story=321729>.

Townend, Annette. "Historical Overview." *Words of Love: A Complete Guide to Romance Fiction*. Ed. Eileen Fallon. New York: Garland, 1984. 3–29.

Trumbull, John. *The Progress of Dullness. Part Third, and Last: Sometimes Called, the Progress of Coquetry*. New Haven: Printed by Thomas and Samuel Green, 1773.

Warner, William B. *Licensing Entertainment: The Elevation of Novel Reading in Britain, 1684–1750*. Berkeley: University of California Press, 1998.

Whitehead, Barbara Dafoe. *Why There Are No Good Men Left: The Romantic Plight of the New Single Woman*. New York: Broadway Books, 2003.

Williams, Jacqueline. *The Handbag Book of Girlie Emergencies*. 2001. San Diego, CA: Laurel Glen, 2002.

Williams, Tia. *The Accidental Diva*. New York: Penguin, 2004.

Wolf, Laura. *Diary of a Mad Bride*. New York: Delta, 2002.

Young, Elizabeth. *A Girl's Best Friend*. New York: Avon Trade, 2003.

3

Mothers of Chick Lit? Women Writers, Readers, and Literary History

JULIETTE WELLS

A recent *New Yorker* cartoon showed a woman in a window seat, apparently engrossed in her book. Across the room, which has built-in bookcases to the ceiling, a man is interrupted in his own reading by a persistent little boy. "Go bother your mother," says the man. "She's only reading chick lit."

By now, the assumptions embedded in this gag line about the insignificance of chick lit and its exclusive appeal to women readers—related phenomena, perhaps?—are familiar to us all. (Cynical *New Yorker* readers, noticing that the cartoonist is a man, may conclude that he is not only satirizing the currently fashionable denigration of chick lit but also participating in it.) For readers acquainted with women's literary history, however, the cartoon evokes additional associations. Charlotte Brontë's highly successful novel *Jane Eyre* (1847), for instance, opens with a scene of a young woman in a window seat with a favorite book; when a boorish male relation interrupts her reading, she throws her book at him, although she knows that she will be punished for her audacity.

What women choose to read, and to write, have been hot topics in discussions of fiction, and in fiction itself, since the English novel came into being approximately three hundred years ago. As a recent interview with Plum Sykes suggests, the present-day success of chick lit invites many of the same questions that have been posed for centuries regarding women readers and writers. Asked by Deborah Solomon if "the label chick-lit is a fair description" of her 2004 novel *Bergdorf Blondes*, Sykes, a well-known New York socialite, responded,

> Honestly, if Edith Wharton published *The Custom of the Country* now, it would be considered chick-lit. It's a way to kind of suppress these books, which are doing very well.
>
> [Solomon:] In other words, you don't like being called a chick-lit writer.
>
> [Sykes:] Well, it is nice to be considered literature of any kind. (Solomon 13)

What makes literature "literature," and does women's writing count? What does a woman author's financial success or social position indicate about the quality of her writing? Do novels have literary merit, especially if they focus on women's experiences, high society, or money and fashion? Does great popularity, especially among women readers, disqualify a novel from being considered literary?

When reviews of chick-lit novels and articles about the genre's commercial success do pose questions such as these, they generally do so without any acknowledgment that such questions, and women's writing in general, have a history. Because chick lit's writers are exclusively women and its readers overwhelmingly so, perceptions of the genre are affected by entrenched views that women's writing is inferior to men's and that women readers prefer lightweight novels to literary ones. To judge whether an individual work of chick lit, or the genre as a whole, has literary merit is to participate in a long tradition of discounting women writers and their readers. Acknowledging this does not make it impossible to consider the question of chick lit's literary merit and its debts to the tradition of women's writing; it means, instead, that such an endeavor must be undertaken with full awareness of how women writers historically have fared in the literary marketplace.

Reviews of chick lit rarely invoke women writers of previous generations, with the exception of Jane Austen, thanks to her enduring prominence in our popular culture. Writers of chick lit, by contrast, frequently invite us to view their works as descendants of women's literary classics: Plum Sykes by invoking Edith Wharton, Helen Fielding by modeling *Bridget Jones's Diary* on Austen's *Pride and Prejudice,* and Emma McLaughlin and Nicola Kraus by choosing a passage about governesses from *Jane Eyre* as the epigraph to their 2002 novel *The Nanny Diaries*. Although such allusions may be marketing tactics, they also encourage readers to see chick-lit novels not as a brief publishing phenomenon but as the next generation of women's literature, a perspective that ennobles both its writers and its readers. Is it true?

Chick lit is certainly one of the next generations of women's *writing* but, in spite of its capacity to invoke the questions that long swirled around women's literary writing, it is not the next generation of women's *literature*. The reactions chick lit provokes and the claims made for it by its authors do have identifiable roots in the history of women's writing, as do many of the genre's characteristic elements: the heroine's search for an ideal romantic partner; her maturation and growth in self-knowledge, often aided by friends and mentors; and her relationship to conventions of beauty. Chick lit departs from its predecessors, however, in several ways: its emphasis on the role of sexual adventures in the romantic quest; the nature of the conclusion to the romantic plot; the importance of the heroine's experiences in the world of work and her evolution as a professional woman; the delight and consolation the heroine finds in indulging herself, particularly in consumer goods; and the privileging of entertainment value, particularly humor, over any challenging or experimental content or style. Except for the last, these distinctions reflect the profound changes in social mores that have affected what women authors can write about and what readers wish to read. The final distinction indicates that chick lit positions itself firmly as entertaining rather than thought provoking, as fiction rather than literature.

The Love Plot

Every chick-lit novel centers on a love plot, although the nature of that plot varies according to its heroine's age and marital status. If single and unattached, like Helen Fielding's Bridget Jones and countless others, she will attempt relationships, only one of which will ultimately prove worthwhile—often with the man who seemed least likely or attractive at first, a twist borrowed from Austen's *Pride and Prejudice*. If the heroine begins the novel with an admirable boyfriend, as does Andrea Sachs of Lauren Weisberger's *The Devil Wears Prada,* she will place the relationship in jeopardy by trying his patience and toying with a more glamorous man. If happily married, she will discover that her husband has been having an affair and will either patch things up with him after an interval of freedom, as does Maggie in Marian Keyes's *Angels,* or endure his departure and begin a new (or renew an old) relationship, as does Rose Lloyd in Elizabeth Buchan's *Revenge of the Middle-Aged Woman.*[1] These plots are exclusively heterosexual, although a very distant whiff of lesbianism occasionally provides titillation: one of Emma Corrigan's embarrassing secrets in Sophie Kinsella's *Can You Keep a Secret?*, for instance, is having once had "this weird lesbian dream about [her] flatmate Lissy" (2).

Few, if any, chick-lit novels end with the heroine's wedding; much more common are mutual declarations of love after a long and tumultuous period of misunderstandings, with future marriage likely but not guaranteed. Typical is Janice Kaplan and Lynn Schnurnberger's *Botox Diaries,* which ends with the heroine, Jess, and her newly acknowledged boyfriend watching a child sing "I'm getting married in the morning!," part of a song from *My Fair Lady:* "Maybe not in the morning," Jess thinks, "gazing into [her boyfriend's] glimmering blue eyes. But anything's possible" (296). Sometimes, in true Hollywood tradition, the novel ends with a kiss, as does the final story of Melissa Bank's *The Girls' Guide to Hunting and Fishing.* Although a chick-lit heroine rarely aims to be wedded by the final page, one of her female relatives or friends is likely to think of little else, a preoccupation that the novelist generally satirizes. Sophie Kinsella's character Jemima, for instance, has been schooled by her mother in how to get, as she calls it, "a rock on her finger" (151), and strives to impart this knowledge to her roommate, the heroine.

A chick-lit novel without a few satisfying—or, alternatively, ridiculous—sex scenes is hard to find. With the exception of the subgenre of Christian chick lit, whose writers make a point of preserving their heroines' and their readers' purity, most chick-lit novelists, like contemporary writers in every genre, view sex as a necessary part of romantic exploration. Chick lit's characters certainly talk and joke about sex and genitals: Plum Sykes's narrator, for instance, seems constantly to be mentioning Brazil or South America, her code words for intercourse (derived from the Brazilian bikini wax, to which she is devoted). Yet chick-lit sex scenes are rarely either extensive or graphic, and they are narrated matter-of-factly rather than in purple prose, factors that distinguish the genre from pornography, erotica, and romance novels. Kaplan and Schnurnberger's handling of Jess's sex scenes with her French ex-husband Jacques is representative: "Jacques doesn't seem to notice that I'm not totally on his wavelength, and within minutes, he explodes with pleasure inside me. I don't exactly fake it, but I make a few murmurings of satisfaction, truly enjoying his excitement" (171).

Of these three characteristics—a central love plot, a conclusion with the heroine happily paired off but not married, and frank sex scenes—chick lit shares only the first with its predecessors in women's literary history. The suspense inherent in romantic quests, visible in literary genres throughout history, has been essential to novels by and about women since the earliest days of prose fiction in English. The story of a heroine finding her proper mate in the face of obstacles and misunderstandings can be found in Samuel Richardson's *Pamela* (1741), Frances Burney's *Evelina* (1778), and all of the novels of Jane Austen (published 1811–18), among many others. Unlike chick lit, some of whose heroines are aged forty or fifty, novels of the eighteenth and early nineteenth centuries focused exclusively on the courtship of young, single women. The heroines of Jane Austen's novels, which are often considered the apex of English romantic comedy, are all in their teens and twenties; any stories of older women's finding love, as does the former governess Miss Taylor in *Emma* (1816), are peripheral. Later, Victorians, particularly George Eliot, took an interest in young widows' search for love as well: both Dorothea Brooke of *Middlemarch* (1871–72) and Gwendolen Harleth of *Daniel Deronda* (1876) survive disastrous first marriages and seek more suitable partners.

A much more significant difference between the love plots of chick lit and of earlier women's novels than the age of the heroine is her level of sexual experience and attitude toward sex—what would have been called her "virtue" in the eighteenth and nineteenth centuries. Respectable young women of those eras showed no interest in sex outside of marriage and admitted only very obliquely to pleasure within marriage: a far cry indeed from our own day, in which chick-lit heroines happily discuss their orgasms and G-spots. Since reading fiction, then as now, involved sympathizing with characters and imagining oneself in their place, novels that featured morally questionable characters or that did not appropriately punish behavioral lapses were harshly criticized for their potentially harmful effect on readers.[2] Charlotte Brontë's very popular *Jane Eyre,* for instance, was highly controversial in part because its heroine responded sensually to her lover (albeit in ways that may seem very tame to present-day readers). Listening to Mr. Rochester sing, for instance, Jane feels that his voice "find[s] a way through the ear to the heart and there wake[s] sensation strangely" (225). Although the primary sensation that Rochester's singing awakes in Jane's heart is clearly emotional, Brontë's repeated references to the potency of his voice—it "severs" the air, conveys his "force," is "deep and full" (225)—indicate that Jane is affected physically by its evident virility.

In addition to not wanting or thinking about sex, a "virtuous" woman of the eighteenth or nineteenth century would have neither confessed to being in love with a man until she had received a proposal of marriage from him nor admitted to having been in love with more than one man. Thanks to great changes in social mores and ideals of femininity, these requirements seem rather absurd to us today, but they were deeply important to earlier generations of writers and readers. A heroine—or, indeed, a real woman—who acknowledged her love before she had been proposed to was held to be imperiling her virtue, and falling in love more than once hinted at moral unreliability. Charlotte Brontë got in trouble with her reviewers here, too. She made it plain to the readers that both Jane Eyre and the heroine of *Villette* (1853), Lucy Snowe, are in love long before they receive proposals, and Lucy falls in love twice: first with a handsome Englishman who doesn't return her affections, and then with an eccentric Belgian who does.

Given the cultural preoccupation with women's virtue, it is hardly surprising that marriage, traditionally the end of theatrical comedies, long served as the conclusion of novels as well. Frances Burney ended her novel with Evelina assuring her correspondent that "she [has] united herself for ever with the object of her dearest, her eternal affection!" (436), while Austen declared of the hero and heroine's wedding that concludes *Emma* that "the wishes, the hopes, the confidence, the predictions of the small band of true friends who witnessed the ceremony, were fully answered in the perfect happiness of the union" (440). For authors like Burney and Austen, to stop at all short of a wedding scene—as do so many chick-lit writers—would be to leave the heroine's fate unsecured and her virtue still in question.

The Heroine's Maturation

Chick-lit heroines are invariably more likeable than the characters around them, usually because of their endearing faults rather than because they are paragons. What makes Fielding's Bridget Jones appealing, for example, is her all-too-human ineptitude, which contrasts with the irritating competence of her coworker Perpetua, among others; Kinsella's Emma and her colleague Artemis recapitulate this dynamic. The heroines of *The Nanny Diaries* and *The Devil Wears Prada* are variants of this rule: both gain our sympathy by being far more humane than their selfish employers and make mistakes only in interpreting their employers' bizarre demands. Whether a chick-lit heroine is actually incompetent or merely perceived to be so, she inevitably learns to appreciate herself for who she is, an endeavor generally aided by her eventual partner's approbation—although, commonly, he was earlier the occasion, or at least the witness, of some of her most embarrassing gaffes.

Bridget Jones's experience is archetypal. Whether making her misinformed appearance at the Tarts and Vicars party or sliding down a fireman's pole on camera, Bridget seems constantly to be stating that she has "never been so humiliated in [her] life" (*Bridget Jones's Diary* 222).[3] For Bridget, as for subsequent chick-lit heroines, any new sense of herself as truly competent is always vulnerable to disruption. The maturation of chick-lit heroines, like the conclusion of their love plots, often seems temporary or conditional; both circumstances, of course, leave the door open to sequels.

In its interest in heroines' emotional maturation and the role of humiliation in that process, chick lit owes a direct debt to Frances Burney and Jane Austen, by way of the Hollywood screwball comedies that were influenced by those writers. Burney's *Evelina* and Austen's novels tell variations of the same story: a young woman is repeatedly misconstrued by, and/or embarrassed in front of, the man who turns out to love her. In *Evelina* the heroine has early identified the hero as her desired mate and longs to correct his persistent misimpressions of her; in *Emma* the heroine is unaware of the hero's interest in her, while in *Pride and Prejudice* she heartily dislikes him. In each of these cases, the heroine's humiliation in the hero's presence—and often at his instigation—is crucial both to her education in proper behavior and to her recognition of his worth as a husband.

In Burney's and Austen's novels, the stakes of misunderstandings and embarrassments are much higher than in chick lit, thanks again to rigid cultural standards of feminine morality. For Evelina, being misapprehended by Lord Orville doesn't just imperil her chances of marrying him; it jeopardizes her entire reputation. When Austen's Mr. Knightley roundly reprimands Emma for overstepping propriety and speaking cruelly to a woman whose age and social position demand respect and forbearance, he does so to improve her character, which has a decided tendency toward conceit. Forced to confront the pain that her lack of consideration has caused others, Emma gains humility and consoles herself "in the resolution of her own better conduct" (384). Elizabeth Bennet's humbling in *Pride and Prejudice* is less severe, though still effective: she grows "absolutely ashamed of herself" when she realizes that she has placed her trust in the wrong man (156).

As writers of novels that supposedly afford their readers vicarious moral improvement as well as entertainment, Burney and Austen must correct any defects in their heroines' characters before rewarding them with marriage. Because chick lit has no such moral imperative, it can extract humor value from embarrassments and misunderstandings without belaboring them. At its most formulaic, chick lit adheres to the convention of humiliating the heroine in front of the hero without achieving notable humor at all: Plum Sykes's heroine, for instance, dutifully notes that "every time I saw Charlie I was somehow at a disadvantage" (278), but what wit the novel possesses is visible not in those encounters but instead in Sykes's skewering of ultrarich women's behavior.

The Heroine at Work

Not every chick-lit heroine has a career, but all of thei⸻ ⸻ jobs. Some heroines, such as Bridget Jones or Kinsella's Emma C⸻gan, languish unappreciated in low-level positions, anxious to show abilities that they worry they may not actually possess. Others, such as McLaughlin and Kraus's Nanny, have love–hate relationships with work that reward them in some ways and punish them in others. Still others, such as Kate Reddy in Allison Pearson's *I Don't Know How She Does It,* thrive in extremely high-powered professions, while regretting the effect of career pressure on their families. Heroines' professional identities and workday experiences are certainly important to the texture of chick-lit novels, and sometimes central to their plot: Weisberger's *The Devil Wears Prada,* for instance, is built around the young heroine's relationship with her fashion magazine boss, and the heroine of Buchan's *Revenge of the Middle-Aged Woman* must reinvent herself on professional and personal fronts when her young assistant annexes her husband and her job.

I Don't Know How She Does It, The Nanny Diaries, and *The Devil Wears Prada* are rare among chick-lit novels, however, in focusing as fully and vividly on the heroine's work life as on her love life. Of the three, only Pearson's novel examines the effects—ultimately corrosive in that case—of the heroine's own intense professional ambition. McLaughlin and Kraus's Nanny is deeply emotionally invested in her charges but hardly considers child care a lifelong career, and Weisberger distinguishes carefully between Andrea's aspiration to work at the *New Yorker* magazine and the all-consuming drive that transformed her boss from Miriam Princhek to Miranda Priestly. Most chick lit hews instead to the balance gigglingly revealed by Sykes's narrator, and for the same reasons: "finding a man … is *all* we think about 95 percent of the time. We just don't admit it in public. It's way more acceptable to say you worry about your career all the time. Although I generally find the more career a girl has, the more man she thinks about" (264).

Although few heroines expend as little energy on their ostensible careers as does Sykes's, it is certainly true that the love plot, much more than any professional plot, drives the great majority of chick lit. Many writers extract substantial amusement value from office scenes and make sure that their heroines end the novel better off professionally than they began, but it is requited love, not significant career advancement, that brings about the novels' conclusions. Even the end of Pearson's novel is a version of this trope: in a move that was highly controversial among readers, Kate almost completely renounces career ambition in favor of rededicating herself to the welfare of her children and husband, who have suffered as much or more from her work-related travel and long hours in the office as from her romantic dalliance.

The world of work in chick lit is thus essentially window dressing: a backdrop to the real business of finding love. In this respect, chick lit has a great deal in common with those novels of manners, from Burney's to Edith Wharton's, that chronicle a heroine's search for a suitable mate. In *The House of Mirth* (1905), Wharton depicts husband hunting as a quasi-professional endeavor: Lily Bart, the heroine, educates herself in the particular interests of prospective spouses, invests in the fashionable clothing necessary to make a fine impression at society gatherings, and devises—though she does not always implement—strategies designed to bring a romantic deal to a successful close. Many of the same tactics and stratagems are visible in other courtship fiction from the eighteenth and nineteenth centuries, although they are most often deployed by mothers and female guardians, not by the heroines. (That Lily, whose mother died before securing her a marriage, must direct her own search for a husband is one of the reasons, according to Wharton, that she ultimately fails: a hard-hearted, experienced mother is a much better negotiator than a young woman subject to whims and to love.) Mrs. Bennet in Austen's *Pride and Prejudice,* to take but one example, happily takes upon herself the task of marrying off her five daughters, though she is too silly and incompetent to complete it properly.

That chick lit capitalizes on the enduring popularity of courtship plots among women readers is hardly remarkable. What is noteworthy is that so much of chick lit, while otherwise taking great advantage of changes in social mores, essentially sidesteps the opportunity to treat the subject of women's careers. In Burney's and Austen's day, novels did not address remunerated work done by respectable women because such work was not supposed to exist, either in real life or in fiction. Although a gentlewoman might well teach or publish to support herself in the absence of family money, she would hardly call attention to this fact, and she would surely not broadcast any other less acceptable motives, such as a desire to exercise her talents or seek fame.

Austen's literary reputation is a case in point. For decades after her death, readers tended to think of her not as an ambitious, professionally minded author but instead as a spinster who happened to write amusing novels, an impression reinforced by her relatives' depictions of her as an unimpeachable lady who shunned publicity and stole time for writing when she was not engaged in family and household duties. For instance, her brother Henry Austen described her in 1818 as a deeply religious woman who shrank "so much ... from notoriety, that no accumulation of fame would have induced her, had she lived, to affix her name to any productions of her pen" (*Northanger Abbey* 6).[4] Our most enduring impression of Austen's writing practice comes from her nephew James Edward Austen-Leigh, who reported in his 1870 *Memoir of Jane Austen* that she wrote "in the general sitting-room," listening to a creaking door to alert her to interruptions, and preferred "small sheets of paper which could easily be put away, or covered with a piece of blotting paper" (102). Jan Fergus's recent biography of Austen counters this myth by emphasizing the evidence of her interest in and dedication to publication, from her youthful writings that imitated the look of the printed page to her concern with the sales and copyrights of her finished novels. Nevertheless, the distance between Austen and today's marketing-savvy writers of chick lit, who aim at best-sellerdom, is still substantial.

In their way chick-lit writers are as coy as Austen about any financial motives for their writing. Chick lit is a big business, and even readers not particularly attuned to what successful writers earn can deduce that a woman whose first novel is a hardcover *New York Times* best-seller for six months and has been published in twenty-seven countries—as the back cover of the paperback of *The Devil Wears Prada* informs us is true of Lauren Weisberger—has put a lot of money in the bank, even without the sale of movie rights. With the exception of Allison Pearson's Kate Reddy, however, when a chick-lit heroine makes an enormous amount of money, she does so through marrying a rich man, not by reaping the fruits of professional success. Not every chick-lit hero is extraordinarily wealthy, but none is just scraping by: Sykes's Charlie Dunlain turns out to be a landed nobleman, Kaplan and Schnurnberger's Josh Gordon is an über business-man, and even McLaughlin and Kraus's Harvard boy is, in the words of Nanny's employer, "quite a catch" for her (284).

With one notable exception, which I will discuss shortly, chick-lit novels also imitate their predecessors in avoiding the subject of the development of women's literary talents, an evasion that is particularly remarkable in light of the overwhelming popularity in the genre of first-person narration and the prevalence of heroines' careers that involve some kind of writing.[5] Every heroine who tells her own story to the reader is, in a sense, writing her own novel, yet in no case does she acknowledge this. (Kaplan and Schnurnberger's novel does end with a character successfully pitching a pilot for a television series called *The Botox Diaries*, a twist that highlights the novel's—and the genre's—debt to that medium.) Nor do any of the heroines who contribute to magazines, write marketing reports, or host television segments dream of trading in their day jobs to write a fantastically successful chick-lit novel, as many of the writers themselves must have done.

Several decades after the women's movement, chick-lit writers cannot defend themselves, as could their predecessors in women's literature, on the grounds that women's work and ambition are considered inappropriate subjects for fiction. Mary Gordon, Gail Godwin, A.S. Byatt, Margaret Atwood, and countless other prominent contemporary authors have conclusively disproved that notion. That the authors of chick lit take such an oddly conservative approach to these topics may bear out arguments made about backlash against feminism, ideology fatigue among the "post-feminist" age group, and the persistence of anxieties about women's ambition; the issue is worthy of further exploration. What is certain is that when a chick-lit writer claims kinship with prominent women novelists of previous centuries, she is trying to have it both ways: profiting from the literary associations of her predecessors without acknowledging her own financially driven compromises and evasions.

One of those evasions is evident in the way that individual examples of the chick-lit genre pretend not to be part of a trend. Chick-lit writers may refer to Austen or other women authors in the public domain, but they do not cite each other or show their heroines reading *Bridget Jones's Diary.* Although successful chick-lit writers are frequently called on to provide what publishers term "advance praise" for each other's new work, they studiously avoid comparing a new chick-lit novel to its predecessors, preferring to reach further into literary history: Jane Heller's back-cover blurb of *The Nanny Diaries,* for instance, characterizes it as "*The Bonfire of the Vanities* meets *Mary Poppins.*"[6] In the current publishing market, every writer of chick lit vies with every other, and none can spare a sisterly defense of a fellow author or of the genre as a whole.

This competitiveness stands in marked contrast to Austen's effort to promote women's contributions to fiction. Before Austen, women novelists tended to respond to the contemporary perception that novels endangered women's minds and characters by claiming that their own fiction was less deleterious than that written by others. Frances Burney, for instance, contended that *Evelina,* thanks to its reliance on "Reason," "Probability," and "Nature" rather than "Romance," "Imagination," and the "*Marvellous*" (55–56), was a comparatively wholesome alternative to other novels on the market. Far from endorsing novels in general, Burney mustered only a very qualified defense of the genre: "All attempts to contribute to the number of those [novels] which may be read, if not with advantage, at least without injury, ought rather to be encouraged than contemned," she declared (xii). Unlike Burney, Austen was not content to argue that her own novels were not as harmful as others' novels. At the end of chapter 5 of *Northanger Abbey,* she mounts a spirited campaign on behalf of all writers of fiction:

> I will not adopt that ungenerous and impolitic custom so common
> with novel writers, of degrading by their contemptuous censure the
> very performances, to the number of which they are themselves
> adding. ... Alas! if the heroine of one novel be not patronized by
> the heroine of another, from whom can she expect protection and
> regard? ... Let us not desert one another; we are an injured body.
> (33–34)

Catherine Morland, the heroine of *Northanger Abbey,* avidly reads some of
the most popular fiction of her day, Gothic tales of suspense, horror, and
sensation—many of which were written by women. If Austen were alive
today, it is quite likely that Catherine would be reading chick lit.

Although the heroine of Weisberger's *The Devil Wears Prada,* Andrea
Sachs, does not read chick lit, she is a significant exception in almost every
other way to the genre's convention of remaining silent on the subject of
women's literary talents and aspirations. Andrea announces her literary
ambitions almost immediately: "Although I knew it was highly unlikely I'd
get hired at *The New Yorker* directly out of school, I was determined to be
writing for them before my fifth reunion" (11). This intention sustains her
through her grueling year assisting the fashion magazine editor Miranda
Priestly, whose influence Andrea hopes and expects will decisively advance
her career. Although Andrea has no time to sleep, much less write, she
does brush against the world of New York literary fame, pursuing an inter-
mittent flirtation with a hot young novelist and even meeting his agent,
who tells her that he's "looking forward to reading [her] work" and hopes
she'll "keep [him] in mind" (236). When Andrea is finally fired for insub-
ordination and realizes that Miranda will be making no calls to the *New
Yorker,* she takes stock of her work experiences, "pull[s] an old notebook
from [her] bottom desk drawer and [begins] to write" (352). By the end of
the novel, she has had an autobiographical short story published in *Seventeen* and found an encouraging literary mentor in that magazine's editor.
Weisberger does stop just short of depicting Andrea writing a ragingly
successful roman à clef about her experience, but the connection is hardly
difficult for the reader to make.

While neither Weisberger nor her heroine ever alludes to the tradition
of women's writing, *The Devil Wears Prada* can be read as a present-day
answer to those nineteenth-century novels, most prominently *Jane Eyre,*
that hint at but shy away from actually depicting the development of a
woman writer.[7] By subtitling her novel *An Autobiography,* Brontë encourages us to read it as "written" by its heroine, yet she does not depict Jane
actually composing it. Brontë's readers are left to infer that Jane, like

Brontë, harbors literary ambitions and applies herself to their fulfillment. Weisberger connects the dots.

Beauty

With beauty, chick-lit writers must toe a fine line. If the heroine is too stunning, readers may resent her; if she is too ordinary looking (let alone unattractive), she gives readers nothing to admire. If she is utterly obsessed with her looks, she risks turning off readers, although the immense popularity of Bridget Jones demonstrates the comic and satiric potential of excessive preoccupation with weight gain and appearance. A heroine who is completely free of care about her looks and happily self-accepting is nowhere to be found in chick lit, an absence that suggests that such a character is too unrealistic to appeal to image-conscious women readers. (The absence of the self-accepting heroine marks but one of chick lit's many departures from second-wave feminist theory, which deconstructed the very myths of beauty that chick lit, for the most part, vigorously upholds.)

Many chick-lit writers handle the beauty issue by providing their essentially good-looking though anxious heroine with a more gorgeous foil who is also much more irritating on the subject of beauty maintenance and makes the heroine seem appealingly normal by contrast. In *The Botox Diaries,* for instance, the writers play the heroine Jess off her much more glamorous and expensively turned out best friend Lucy. Lucy indulges in the title concoction and views it as essential to fortysomething beauty, whereas Jess, though she never conclusively accepts the aging process, holds out against plastic surgery, relying instead on the glow that results from a handsome man's compliment, satisfying sex, or a pair of Tiffany diamond earrings.

In being beautiful but not too beautiful, chick lit's heroines are the direct descendants of Austen's. Nearly every Austen novel features a very attractive heroine whose wit and good temper more than elevate her above her more glamorous but less likeable romantic rivals. Elizabeth Bennet of *Pride and Prejudice,* for example, might have been outshone by the Bingley sisters' flashy looks and dress, if those women were less catty and grasping. Austen's oldest heroine, twenty-seven-year-old Anne Elliot in *Persuasion,* unites renewed loveliness with goodness and generosity, a combination that more than outmatches any younger, prettier contenders for Captain Wentworth's affections. An Austen heroine may be one of several equally beautiful women characters—as is Emma Woodhouse of *Emma,* whose looks are neither inferior nor superior to Harriet Smith's and Jane Fairfax's—but she is never the most beautiful.

In making her heroines not quite the most beautiful women in the room, Austen responded to a vogue in the fiction of her day for flawlessly gorgeous protagonists. Burney's *Evelina,* for instance, manifests what the author called "conspicuous beauty" (55), and she was hardly alone. Austen satirized this vogue most explicitly in *Northanger Abbey,* whose heroine, Catherine Morland, does not live up to the demanding standards of beauty evident in the fiction that she so avidly reads: "To look *almost* pretty, is an acquisition of higher delight to a girl who has been looking plain the first fifteen years of her life, than a beauty from her cradle can ever receive" (14).

Many of Austen's most prominent successors in the nineteenth-century novel were even more skeptical of beauty than she was. Brontë's Jane Eyre is famously small of stature and plain of face, characteristics that hardly prevent her from gaining the affections of Mr. Rochester, in spite of his previous attachments to Europe's most alluring courtesans. George Eliot, like Austen, created heroines who are lovely and radiant rather than stunning, including Dinah Morris of *Adam Bede,* Dorothea Brooke of *Middlemarch,* and Mirah Lapidoth of *Daniel Deronda.* Rather than relegating stunning characters to minor roles as Austen did, however, Eliot explored in depth the psychological costs of cultivating beauty rather than mind or soul, through such characters as Hetty Sorrel of *Adam Bede,* Rosamond Vincy of *Middlemarch,* and Gwendolen Harleth of *Daniel Deronda.* All three of these characters experience pain and disillusionment—and inflict the same sensations on others—thanks to the looks that they have been taught, and have taught themselves, to privilege over all other characteristics.

In the hands of Edith Wharton, whose fictional depictions of New York society are the recognizable forerunners of many a Manhattan chick-lit novel, beauty is an even more fatal burden than it is to Eliot's characters. When Lily Bart's father suddenly loses his wealth, her desperate mother puts all of her faith in what she views as "the last asset in their fortunes" (34): Lily's exquisite good looks. Lily, the narrator comments, has been bred for show and display much like a championship rose, "fashioned to adorn and delight" (301); she has no other means of support, no other social currency, to fall back on when she realizes first that looks alone can't guarantee her financial future, and then—ironically—that her very worry threatens to erode her beauty even faster. In the absence of plastic surgery, and in an era when wearing makeup was still not considered strictly respectable, Lily's options for enhancing her looks are few.

Although Wharton analyzed the effects on Lily of having been cultivated for her beauty, she did not, as would a chick-lit writer, examine in detail what we would call Lily's beauty regimen. Lily looks at herself in the mirror occasionally, usually to assess fearfully whether her anxieties are producing more lines on her face, but Wharton does not load us with particulars of Lily's maintenance of her skin, her hair, or her body. In part, this difference in emphasis can be attributed to changing standards of feminine beauty: before physical fitness became an inescapable element of beauty, no heroine, and no ordinary woman, would have exercised for the sake of making herself more attractive. The gap between Lily and one of Sykes's Bergdorf blondes, whose "dedication ... to be[ing] a gorgeous, flaxen-haired, dermatologically perfect New York girl" (1) the writer chronicles in enormous detail, is wider than mere chronology, however. Wharton did not consider the minutiae of beautification to be appropriate or adequate materials for fiction, even satirical fiction, whereas chick-lit writers do—an assumption that is certainly borne out by the novels' commercial popularity.

In its great interest in how beauty is created and maintained, chick lit allies itself to the genre not of the novel but of women's magazines.[8] The prominence of magazines over novels in chick lit underscores this link. Chick-lit heroines do occasionally mention, though rarely read, a classic novel. One of the shameful secrets of Kinsella's Emma Corrigan, for instance, is that she faked having read *Great Expectations* for her book club, while Sykes's heroine—although proud to tell us that she was, improbably, an "English lit major" at Princeton (5)—gains her cultural references from movies and television, not books, although she claims to have read "lots of important literature, like *Mrs. Dalloway* and *Valley of the Dolls*" (136). The attentive reading that is done by chick-lit heroines, from Bridget Jones onward, is instead of the articles and quizzes found in *Cosmopolitan* and its like. Women's magazines retain readers by capitalizing on their anxieties about their looks, anxieties for which the magazines promise but do not fully deliver relief.[9] Like women's magazines, chick lit immerses the reader in a world in which the pursuit of beauty is never ending; what distinguishes chick lit from magazines is that its heroines frankly admit to the drain of energy and resources demanded by this pursuit, even as they persist in it.

It is worth emphasizing that the subject of beauty is not inherently an unliterary one. In fact, Virginia Woolf's *A Room of One's Own* (1929)—a book-length meditation on women and authorship that is often considered to have inaugurated feminist literary criticism—specifically mentions attitudes toward beauty when encouraging women to write about what has long been considered unimportant. Arguing that masculine values have long prevailed in fiction as in real life, Woolf declares that "the worship of fashion, the buying of clothes" have been considered "trivial," that books that deal "with the feelings of women in a drawing-room" are thought "insignificant" (80). Although chick lit does not answer her call to record the "infinitely obscure lives" of "violet-sellers and match-sellers and old crones," it certainly does address her urging to women to "illumine your own soul with its profundities and its shallows, and its vanities and its generosities, and say what your beauty means to you or your plainness and what is your relation to the ever-changing and turning world of gloves and shoes and stuffs" (97–98).

Shopping and Consumption

Without shopping, could chick lit exist? Such is the primacy of the shopping scene in chick-lit novels that many of them could accurately be titled, as was Sophie Kinsella's first, *Confessions of a Shopaholic*. Countless heroines cheer themselves up by buying expensive lingerie, indulging in pricey spa treatments, and adding to their often already impressive collections of shoes, handbags, and outfits. Brand-name items are not always what they seem: Kinsella's Emma Corrigan in *Can You Keep a Secret?* acquires her wardrobe at charity shops, whereas Weisberger's Andrea amasses her ultrafashionable ensembles from the "Closet" of goods for the taking at the fashion magazine at which she works. Regardless of their source, however, consumer goods are essential to chick-lit heroines' self-conception and self-presentation, and writers commonly give as much attention to the obtaining and assembling of outfits as to the maintenance of faces and bodies.

As with beauty, writers of chick lit commonly garner sympathy for their heroines by making them slightly less fervent consumers than their best friends or foils. Kaplan and Schnurnberger's Jess, for example, marvels at the indulgent shopping habits of her friend Lucy, a television producer, whose wardrobe makes Jess's seem comparatively drab. Kinsella's Emma Corrigan likewise endears herself to us by passing off her secondhand clothing for new, in contrast to the predatory shoppers with whom she works and shares her flat. In no case, however, does a heroine's different style of consumption equal a contempt for shopping and fashion altogether. Even Weisberger's Andrea, who is initially almost indifferent to fashion, most unlike her obsessive coworkers at *Runway* magazine, gains a firm appreciation for the advantages conferred by truly up-to-the-minute accouterments.

Although the novel, unlike the more "elevated" genre of poetry, has always been concerned with the material world, chick lit is distinguished both by the centrality of what Woolf called "the ever-changing and turning world of gloves and shoes and stuffs" (98) and by the implicit message that, while indulgence may not always bring happiness, happiness cannot be found without a good dose of indulgence. In contrast, novelists from

Austen to Wharton cast a questioning, and often a critical, eye on women's relationships to consumer goods and consumption.

Austen's focus on the dailiness of women's lives has given her the reputation of being deeply absorbed in domestic and material detail, a reputation reinforced by the visual dominance of these elements in recent film adaptations of her novels. Scenes of shopping are relatively few in her works, however, and are largely confined to minimal purchases such as a ribbon or pair of gloves. She is economical, too, in her descriptions of her characters' dress: she usually singles out for mention clothes or jewelry only to satirize those characters, such as Lydia Bennet of *Pride and Prejudice,* who concern themselves more with adornment than with behavior. In Austen's moral universe, an extreme focus on externals—whether beauty or clothing—betrays superficiality of character, a damning characteristic indeed.

Although Brontë shares Austen's distrust of extravagance, she considers women who care for it to be not silly but oppressed. The fiercely independent Jane Eyre strongly resists Mr. Rochester's efforts to deck her with lavish clothes and jewels because she associates such luxuries with kept women: "The more he bought me," Jane declares, "the more my cheek burned with a sense of annoyance and degradation" (301). Referring to one of Mr. Rochester's French mistresses, Jane asks him if he remembers what he said "of Céline Varens?—of the diamonds, the cashmeres you gave her? I will not be your English Céline Varens" (302). For Jane, maintaining the plainness of her dress is a way to assert both her independence and her refusal to make herself into a man's image of a desirable woman.

Unlike Jane Eyre and Austen's characters, the heroines of Wharton's society novels, especially *The House of Mirth* and *The Custom of the Country* (1913), are strongly attracted to ultrafashionable dresses and magnificent jewels, as well as to spacious and elaborately furnished houses and extravagant travel, whose lure Wharton effectively conveyed. Although Wharton did not offer moral condemnation of her heroines' desire for these luxuries, she made plain the personal cost of placing consumption above all other goals. Undine Spragg of *The Custom of the Country* is driven by desires that always outpace what she can achieve, leaving her perpetually unsatisfied. Finally, she realizes to her angry dismay that "there was something she could never get, something that neither beauty nor influence nor millions could ever buy for her" (594), and she ends the novel as discontented as she began. Lily Bart's fate in *The House of Mirth* is far more tragic: unwilling or unable to shrug off the expensive tastes that she developed before her father lost his fortune, she dies ostracized by the society that once embraced her, her disgrace having been set in motion by her persistent debts, many of them to her dressmaker.

Although chick-lit writers certainly satirize the excesses they depict, they do not attack, as does Wharton, the very foundations of consumer culture, which in her view teaches women in particular to crave luxuries and to create themselves—and their friends and daughters—as veritable objects of consumption. Although many of chick lit's heroines, unlike Wharton's, earn the money they spend and are financially autonomous, the genre as a whole does not cast any lasting doubt on the notion that self-indulgence is key to a rewarding life.

"Lit" versus Literature

Many of the differences between chick lit and the tradition of women's writing discussed so far can be attributed, at least in part, to changes in social customs and expectations that have affected both writers and readers. No such explanation is possible for the wide gap in what we might call literary achievement between chick lit and women's novels. When we look in chick lit for such literary elements as imaginative use of language, inventive and thought-provoking metaphors, layers of meaning, complex characters, and innovative handling of conventional structure, we come up essentially empty-handed. Only in its deployment of humor can the best of chick lit stand up favorably to the tradition of women's writing, and humor—perhaps unfairly, as many have argued—has never been the most valued and respected of literary elements.[10]

It is important to note that chick-lit novels—in their content, packaging, and promotion—do not claim to be literary rather than popular fiction. Novels aiming at literary stature or prizes are rarely, as chick lit invariably is, unabashedly focused on the daily experiences of comparatively privileged English-speaking women to the exclusion of all other subject matter. Their covers are not adorned with sorbet colors, high heels, and curly fonts. They are not puffed purely in terms of their enjoyment value, with frequent comparisons of the reading experience to those of eating, shopping, or even successful plastic surgery.[11] Nevertheless, the persistent appearance of literary women authors' names—particularly, though not solely, Austen's—in discussions of, and judgments about, chick lit suggests that many readers and reviewers wish to case the genre as the descendant of literary, not popular, fiction.

In terms of language, chick lit's greatest achievement is its satiric employment, and sometimes invention, of contemporary slang and lingo. From *Bridget Jones's Diary*'s "fuckwittage" (manipulative behavior by a male significant other) to *Bergdorf Blondes*'s "fake bakes" (spray-on tans) and "PJs" (private jets), chick lit supplies its readers with amusing, evocative, and occasionally useful terms. Aside from these words and phrases, though, the language of chick-lit novels is unremarkable, in a literary sense. Richly descriptive or poetic passages, the very bread and butter of literary novels, both historical and contemporary, are virtually nonexistent in chick lit. Consider the contrast between the following sentences, both of which describe the appealing physical presence of the heroine's beloved:

> He looked gorgeous in his work suit with the top buttons of his shirt undone. (*Bridget Jones: The Edge of Reason* 18)

> My master's colourless, olive face, square, massive brow, broad and jetty eyebrows, deep eyes, strong features, firm, grim mouth—all energy, decision, will—were not beautiful, according to rule; but they were more than beautiful to me: they were full of an interest, an influence that quite mastered me—that took my feelings from my own power and fettered them in his. (*Jane Eyre* 198)

While Helen Fielding supplies us only with a succinct, declarative statement about Mark Darcy's looks, Charlotte Brontë captures in words the features of Mr. Rochester's face, relates them to the qualities of his personality, convincingly explains why Jane should be so drawn to a man who would not usually be considered handsome, and tantalizes our interpretive skills by insistently using language of mastery and enslavement. Fielding's sentence, immediately comprehensible, passes by almost without our noticing it; Brontë's sentence invites us to savor and ponder her choice of words.

In general, the narrators of chick lit devote as little time to metaphors and similes—elements common, if not overabundant, in contemporary fiction that aspires to be considered literary—as to descriptive language. Those similes and metaphors that do exist in chick lit tend toward the silly, even when a narrator is grappling for a means to describe serious emotion, and do not interact in thought-provoking ways with the book's overall themes, as they would in literary fiction. The following passage from Kinsella's *Can You Keep a Secret?* is representative:

> As I leave the office in the evening, I feel all agitated, like one of those snow globes you see resting peacefully on shop counters. I was perfectly happy being an ordinary, dull little Swiss village. But now Jack Harper's come and shaken me up, and there are snow-flakes all over the place, whirling around until I don't know what I think anymore. (120)

It could be argued, at a great stretch, that the heroine's later discovery that Jack is interested in her in part because she represents the target demographic for his company's new product relates to her description of herself here as "an ordinary, dull little Swiss village"—but the connection is tenuous at best and unlikely to be made by a reader concerned primarily in finding out whether Jack and Emma will end up together. Contrast Kinsella's snow globe to the following simple but suggestive simile employed by Wharton when characterizing Lily Bart's effort to make a rational decision when agitated: "She had to stop and consider that, in the stress of her other anxieties, as a breathless fugitive may have to pause at the cross-roads and try to decide coolly which turn to take" (*House of Mirth* 177). Likening beautiful, socially gifted Lily to a fugitive at first seems preposterous, yet the simile reminds us of her underlying desperation and hints that she may not ultimately succeed in fleeing her past and her limitations.

Both descriptive language and metaphor contribute crucially to the layers of meaning that make literature worth discussing, examining, and rereading. Karen Joy Fowler's 2004 novel *The Jane Austen Book Club* vividly presents contemporary readers' differing interpretations of Austen's novels as love stories, high comedy, irony, and social criticism. Although each of these elements is certainly present in some (if not all) chick lit, no chick-lit novel is multilayered enough to allow its readers to come to truly divergent conclusions about its nature. *The Devil Wears Prada*, for example, is full of criticism of its heroine's working conditions, yet—aside from very brief mentions of roommates who toil as investment bankers—it makes no broader claims about the grueling nature of apprenticeships in different fields, as would be characteristic of a more literary treatment of this theme.

Literary fiction's openness to interpretation depends in large part on the complexity of its characters, which results not merely from competing impulses but also from fundamentally opposed traits. It is fully possible, for instance, for one reader to approve of the maturation, by the novel's end, of Austen's Marianne Dashwood from a selfish and histrionic young woman into a responsible one, and another reader to regret that Marianne has lost the confidence and freedom of expression that once so distinguished her from her sister Elinor; *Sense and Sensibility* supports both these readings (and more). Although the heroines of *The Nanny Diaries* and *The Devil Wears Prada* are often torn between loyalties to their employers and to others (and to themselves), each young woman's gradual realization that she must walk away from her job to keep her self-respect lends itself to no alternative interpretation.

In terms of their narrative structure, chick-lit novels make more use of literary models than in the case of language and characterization, although the genre's goal of entertaining readers requires the careful adaptation of techniques that might interfere with comprehension and easy digestion. The immediate, informal style of chick-lit narration is reminiscent of the epistolary form popular among eighteenth-century novelists such as Frances Burney, as well as of the stream-of-consciousness technique pioneered by Virginia Woolf and other modernists, which gives the reader the sense of being inside the mind of each character and watching her or his perceptions unfold, rather than of reading a planned, crafted narrative. Yet no chick-lit novel demands of its readers the kind of attention and detective work required by the epistolary form or the stream of consciousness technique. Nor does chick lit dare deprive the reader of the satisfaction of a conclusion that ties up all plot strands and rewards the heroine with the object of her desires, whether mate, job, or both.

Conclusions

Does chick lit, then, belong in the company of Jane Austen and Edith Wharton, Charlotte Brontë and Frances Burney? Are these writers, who were both popular and critically admired in their own day, and who have come to be esteemed as major literary figures, the "mothers" of chick lit? As a final means of answering these questions, let's consider again the passage from *Northanger Abbey* in which Austen defends novelists and their work. It continues,

> Although our productions have afforded more extensive and unaffected pleasure than those of any other literary corporation in the world, no species of composition has been so much decried. ... While the abilities of the nine-hundredth abridger of the History of England, or of the man who collects and publishes in a volume some dozen lines of Milton, Pope, and Prior ... are eulogized by a thousand pens,—there seems almost a general wish of decrying the capacity and undervaluing the labour of the novelist, and of slighting the performances which have only genius, wit, and taste to recommend them. (34)

Chick-lit aficionados would certainly agree that their favored genre produces "extensive and unaffected pleasure" and that it is often "decried" at the expense of more sober works, whether treatises on current events or highbrow literature. While wit is undeniably abundant in chick lit, however, the genre can hardly be said to be overflowing in either taste or genius, even allowing for changes in the meaning of these terms since Austen's day. Chick lit amuses and engrosses, but it does not richly reimagine in literary form the worlds that inspire it.

Earlier in this essay, I declared that if Catherine Morland of *Northanger Abbey* were alive today, she'd be reading chick lit. This is a less ringing endorsement of the genre than it may sound. Austen certainly acknowledges the pleasure and diversion to be found in reading popular fiction: not just Catherine and her female friends but even the novel's estimable hero, Henry Tilney, enjoys gothic tales. Yet Austen makes plain the dangers, especially to a relatively uninformed young woman, of taking her reading too seriously. Catherine, saturated in the adventures of her favorite genre, expects to meet ghosts and ogres; she finds only morally flawed human beings, for whom she is less prepared.

If the readers' lists at Amazon.com are to be believed, Catherine Morland's real-life, present-day counterparts are indeed a major audience for chick lit.[12] This should come as no surprise: all of chick lit's signature elements, from the love plot to shopping, appeal strongly to teenagers' interests, and the genre poses none of literature's demands on attention and intellect. When grown women read chick lit, then, they are shrugging off the serious concerns of adult life to escape into fictional worlds in which pleasure and self-indulgence are paramount, and in which they don't have to think too hard. Chick lit's heroines may grapple with difficult questions about careers, mates, and relationships with family members and friends, but the novels themselves skirt truly challenging territory, whether social or literary.

What women prefer to read, and to write, has historically received less respect than what men create and consume. The *New Yorker* cartoon's mother in the window seat, reading "only" chick lit, is one of a long line of women readers reading "only" Frances Burney or Jane Austen. That women's reading and writing have for centuries been trivialized does not mean, however, that any genre currently favored by women writers and readers necessarily deserves *literary* regard. We can admire chick lit's appeal to contemporary women readers and the financial success it has brought to a number of women writers without claiming that a chick-lit novelist is the next Jane Austen or Edith Wharton. Rather than being the daughters of these authors, chick lit's writers are their younger sisters, inclined to take a more lighthearted and less complex approach to fiction, even as they benefit from changes in social mores and less conflicted attitudes toward women's professional success.

Notes

1. Plots featuring an unhappily married woman who survives the end of her marriage and begins a promising new liaison are hard, if not impossible, to find in chick lit, perhaps because the experience of divorce is just too wrenching for comic treatment.

2. Jacqueline Pearson thoroughly discusses these and other cultural anxieties surrounding women's reading in the eighteenth century, as Kate Flint does for the nineteenth.
3. Fielding, unlike most of her successors, supplies her hero with mortifying scenes as well, beginning with his appearance in an unfortunate sweater at the outset of *Bridget Jones's Diary* and continuing with Bridget's discovery of a "lithe oriental boy, stark naked … and a baby rabbit" in his bed in *Bridget Jones: The Edge of Reason* (63).
4. The title page of Austen's first published novel, *Sense and Sensibility*, identified her only as "A Lady," and the title pages of her subsequent novels identified her as "The Author of" her previous works. Henry Austen's "Biographical Notice" was the first public acknowledgment of Austen's identity as author; it appeared as a preface to the first edition of *Northanger Abbey* and *Persuasion*, which were published together in one volume after her death.
5. Carrie Karasyov and Jill Kargman's *The Right Address* is rare in employing third-person narration, which mitigates the reader's sympathy for the novel's heroine, the social upstart Melanie Sartomsky.
6. General references in blurbs to the popularity of chick lit do not seem to be forbidden: Jacqueline Mitchard, for example, is quoted on the back cover of *The Botox Diaries* describing it, bafflingly, as "the Ur-Post-Chick-Lit novel."
7. *The Devil Wears Prada* also responds to *Jane Eyre* by identifying a plausible source of financial independence for Andrea, one she gains through her resourcefulness at reselling the designer leftovers from her job. Brontë's decision to endow Jane with a substantial, unexpected inheritance has often been criticized as improbable and contrived.
8. While chick lit's narrators commonly drop brand names of fragrances and makeup, it's rare that these references read more like advertising or product placement than mere contemporary detail. An exception is Sykes's heroine, who not only tells us that she is using "Bobbi Brown Black Ink Gel" but also proceeds to remark that "it's the best for smoky eyes, I totally recommend it" (78–79).
9. The social world of *Runway* magazine in *The Devil Wears Prada* suggests that these anxieties are also fully present among the staff of these periodicals.
10. In this section, I cite and refer to the best of chick lit; nothing would be gained here by pointing out flaws in the worst, which—as in any genre—are very bad indeed. (Anyone who objects that comparing early-twenty-first-century fiction with works a hundred or more years old is unfair is welcome to try the same experiment with contemporary literary fiction by women; I will wager that the same gap in achievement will be noticeable.)
11. See, for instance, these two blurbs on the back jacket of *The Botox Diaries:* "Far, far more satisfying than a carb-free éclair will ever be" and "a potent injection of humor and insight" (attributed to Karen Moline and Jeanne Wolf, respectively).
12. At the time of this writing, a search on *The Devil Wears Prada* called up lists submitted by a self-described "junior in highschool [*sic*]" and titled "a must read list for any girl!" and "read great teen books."

Works Cited

Austen, Jane. *Emma*. 1816. Oxford: Oxford University Press, 1995.
———. *Northanger Abbey*. 1818. New York: Penguin, 1995.
———. *Pride and Prejudice*. 1813. Boston: Houghton Mifflin, 1956.
Austen-Leigh, James-Edward. *A Memoir of Jane Austen*. Ed. R.W. Chapman. 1870. 2nd ed. Oxford: Oxford University Press, 1926.
Bank, Melissa. *The Girls' Guide to Hunting and Fishing*. New York: Viking, 1999.
Brontë, Charlotte. *Jane Eyre*. 1847. New York: Penguin, 1996.
Buchan, Elizabeth. *Revenge of the Middle-Aged Woman*. New York: Penguin, 2002.
Burney, Frances. *Evelina, or the History of a Young Lady's Entrance into the World*. 1778. Boston: Bedford, 1997.
Eliot, George. *Adam Bede*. 1857. Oxford: Oxford University Press, 1996.
———. *Daniel Deronda*. 1876. Oxford: Oxford University Press, 1998.
———. *Middlemarch*. 1871–72. Oxford: Oxford University Press, 1996.
Fielding, Helen. *Bridget Jones's Diary*. London: Picador, 1996.
———. *Bridget Jones: The Edge of Reason*. London: Picador, 1999.

Fergus, Jan. *Jane Austen: A Literary Life*. London: Macmillan, 1991.

Flint, Kate. *The Woman Reader 1837–1914*. Oxford: Clarendon, 1993.

Fowler, Karen Joy. *The Jane Austen Book Club*. New York: Putnam, 2004.

Kaplan, Janice, and Lynn Schnurnberger. *The Botox Diaries*. New York: Ballantine, 2004.

Karasyov, Carrie, and Jill Kargman. *The Right Address*. New York: Broadway Books, 2004.

Keyes, Marian. *Angels*. New York: William Morrow, 2002.

Kinsella, Sophie. *Can You Keep a Secret?* New York: Dial Press, 2004.

———. *Confessions of a Shopaholic*. New York: Random House, 2001.

McLaughlin, Emma, and Nicola Kraus. *The Nanny Diaries*. New York: St. Martin's, 2002.

Pearson, Allison. *I Don't Know How She Does It: The Life of Kate Reddy, Working Mother*. New York: Knopf, 2002.

Pearson, Jacqueline. *Women's Reading in Britain, 1750–1835: A Dangerous Recreation*. Cambridge: Cambridge University Press, 1999.

Solomon, Deborah. "Hazards of New Fortunes." *New York Times Magazine* 30, May 2004: 13.

Sykes, Plum. *Bergdorf Blondes*. New York: Miramax/Hyperion, 2004.

Weisberger, Lauren. *The Devil Wears Prada*. New York: Broadway Books, 2003.

Wharton, Edith. *The Custom of the Country*. 1913. New York: Scribner, 1956.

———. *The House of Mirth*. 1905. New York: Penguin, 1985.

Woolf, Virginia. *A Room of One's Own*. 1929. New York: Harcourt Brace Jovanovich, 1957.

4

Narrative and Cinematic Doubleness: *Pride and Prejudice* and *Bridget Jones's Diary*

SUZANNE FERRISS

Without question, the phenomenal success of *Bridget Jones's Diary*—both novel and film—comes largely from pilfering plot and narrative strategies from a writer who knew nothing of film: Jane Austen. Helen Fielding has freely admitted her debt to Austen: "The plot of *Bridget Jones's Diary* was actually stolen from *Pride and Prejudice*. I thought that Jane Austen's plots were very good and had been very well market-researched over a number of centuries, so I thought I would actually steal it. I thought she wouldn't mind and anyway, she's dead."[1] While clearly Fielding was referring to Austen's novel, she was writing the newspaper columns that eventually became the book while the British nation was obsessed with the BBC miniseries starring Colin Firth as Mr. Darcy and Jennifer Ehle as Elizabeth Bennet. In fact, Fielding freely admits that she had Colin Firth in mind as she created the character of Mark Darcy. As such, the novel owes as much to Andrew Davies's screenplay as to Austen's novel.

Perhaps it is not surprising that Davies, who also wrote the screenplay for *Emma* (1996), collaborated with Fielding and Richard Curtis on the film version of *Bridget Jones's Diary*. Their screenplay earned them a nomination at the USC Scripter Awards for best film adaptation of a book.

Although they lost to the screenwriters of *A Beautiful Mind,* their Scripter nomination recognizes their success in transforming Fielding's novel into film. This was no small achievement given that the novel was written entirely in diary form, an interior mode seemingly incompatible with the external perspective offered by the cinematic lens. An even greater achievement is that the film actually allies itself more directly with Austen's text. As such it is a doubled adaptation: Austen's work is transformed in Fielding's popular fiction and again in the film. And, in each instance, the transformation exploits the distinctive and incommensurate qualities of literature and cinema to represent the psychological development of a female character searching for self-esteem and security. Unexpectedly, the film, more than Fielding's novel, replicates and extends the narrative techniques introduced by Austen to capture the comic perils facing single women.

Fielding's debt to Austen is not surprising given their shared focus on the rituals of courtship as the central drama in a young woman's life. As Kathryn Robinson argued, "Anyone familiar with Jane Austen's oeuvre will immediately recognize in chick lit a kindred wit, the same obsession with choosing a mate, and a shared attention to the dailiness of women's lives." Fielding's novel playfully and overtly reveals its roots in Austen's texts. To cite only the most obvious, Bridget's love interest is Mark Darcy, a transparent reference to Austen's Mr. Darcy, the love interest of Elizabeth Bennet. Like Elizabeth, Bridget is embarrassed by her mother's shameless attempts to marry her off to an aristocrat—who, in contemporary Britain, is a "top-notch" barrister with "masses of money" (9). And, like Elizabeth, Bridget is initially turned off by Darcy's smugness but gradually overcomes her prejudice against him, swallows her pride, and falls in love.

In the novel, Bridget and her singleton friends know Austen only through television. They obsess over the *Pride and Prejudice* miniseries playing on the BBC. As Bridget explains, "The basis of my own addiction, I know, is my simple human need for Darcy to get off with Elizabeth." Darcy and Elizabeth "are my chosen representatives in the field of shagging, or, rather, courtship" (215).

Without mentioning Austen or the miniseries, the film version of Fielding's novel exploits this association as an inside joke, casting Colin Firth as Mark Darcy.[2] As film critic James Berardinelli commented, Firth plays Mr. Darcy "exactly as he played the earlier role, making it evident that the two Darcys are essentially the same" (qtd. in Ebert). Firth spends much of the film standing off to the side, apparently glowering condescendingly at Bridget, when, in fact, he is looking on with admiration and concern as he sees her fall for her womanizing boss, Daniel Cleaver (Hugh Grant). In the film, the publishing house where Bridget works is named Pemberley Press, after the name of Mr. Darcy's ancestral home in *Pride and Prejudice.* One voice-over even begins with the first part of the opening line of Austen's novel: "It is a truth universally acknowledged."[3]

As several literate film critics have noted, the movie version strengthens the allusions to Austen's novel.[4] The initial meeting between Bridget and Mark Darcy at the New Year's Day Turkey Curry Buffet more clearly parallels Elizabeth and Darcy's first meeting in Austen's novel, which establishes the basis for their "prejudices" against one another. In Fielding's novel the animosity between them results from Bridget's distaste of his manner and clothing: she says, "It struck me as pretty ridiculous to be called Mr. Darcy and to stand on your own looking snooty at a party" (13). His V-neck diamond-patterned sweater in shades of yellow and blue, "favored by the more elderly of the nation's sports reporters" (13), makes him decidedly *not* dating material. His refusal to take her telephone number, as a meddling family friend suggests, is the final insult.

In the film this gentle snub—and Darcy's sweater—are enhanced for comic effect while strengthening the ties to Austen. As Una Alconbury and her mother guide her unwillingly toward Darcy, Bridget initially glimpses him from behind. "*Ding-dong!*" she comments, just as Bridget does in the novel about Austen's Mr. Darcy. "Maybe this was the mysterious Mr. Right." As he turns around to reveal a giant reindeer appliqué on the front of his sweater, she adds, "Maybe not." As in the novel, her initial distaste originates in her reaction to his clothing. The film, however, turns a subtle rebuff into a wounding blow. Bridget hears Mark refuse his mother's insistence that he ask for Bridget's phone number: "Mother, I do not need a blind date, particularly not with some verbally incontinent spinster who smokes like a chimney, drinks like a fish and dresses like her mother!"

This directly invokes the scene in Austen's novel that establishes Elizabeth's prejudice against Darcy, which is faithfully reproduced in the BBC version. The Turkey Curry Buffet substitutes for the ball at Netherfield where Darcy's friend Bingley insists that he dance, "Come, Darcy. ... I must see you dance" (11). Darcy responds heatedly,

> I certainly shall not. You know how I detest it, unless I am particularly acquainted with my partner. At such an assembly as this it would be insupportable. Your sisters are engaged, and there is not another woman in the room whom it would not be punishment to me to stand up with. ... You are dancing with the only handsome girl in the room. (11)

To Bingley's suggestion of Elizabeth, Darcy replies, "She is tolerable, but not handsome enough to tempt *me*" (11). In the film, Bridget's growing disdain of Darcy's proud manner is far more overt than it is in Fielding's novel, making her a clearer heir to Elizabeth, who boasts that she always believes in first impressions.

In the film version of *Bridget Jones's Diary*, as in Austen's novel, Bridget's prejudice against Darcy is confirmed by a lie told by a rival for her affections. In this instance the film paradoxically strengthens its allegiances with Austen's novel while making a significant departure from Fielding's. The major impediment between Elizabeth and Darcy is Wickham, who features in two significant subplots in *Pride and Prejudice*. He first confirms Elizabeth's ill opinion of Darcy, claiming that Darcy hurt him economically. Wickham says that Darcy cheated him out of the living promised to him by Darcy's father before his death. In *Bridget Jones's Diary*, Daniel Cleaver, Bridget's boss and love interest, plays Wickham's part, claiming that Mark Darcy slept with his wife. (In the novel, by contrast, Daniel merely thinks that Darcy, whom he knew at Cambridge, is a "stupid nerd," a "bloody old woman" [103].)

In Austen's novel, Darcy eventually tells Elizabeth that Wickham asked for and was given a lump sum instead of continued support for his studies to be a lawyer and squandered the money on idleness and drink. His roguish ways are confirmed by his sudden engagement to a rich heiress. In the film, Bridget's mother reveals that it was in fact Daniel who slept with Mark Darcy's wife. In both instances these revelations show that Elizabeth/Bridget's prejudices are without foundation and pave the way for romance with Darcy.

In *Pride and Prejudice*, Wickham introduces a second impediment. His rich heiress breaks their engagement and he sets out to seduce Elizabeth's sister Lydia, spiriting her off to London. He compromises her reputation and, by association, the reputations of the Bennet sisters, placing the economic, as well as romantic, future of the family in jeopardy, because they would be unable to attract husbands of means. In Fielding's novel this second complication is introduced not by Daniel but by Julio, the man who seduces Bridget's mother and embezzles money from their family friends. Bridget's mother takes on the role of the naive sister Lydia, duped by a handsome yet dissolute man.

In both novels, Mr. Darcy saves the day. In *Pride and Prejudice* he secretly pays off Wickham and forces him to marry Lydia. In *Bridget Jones's Diary* he tracks down Julio and Bridget's mother in Portugal, arranges for her safe return, and then follows Julio back to England, where he makes an unexpected appearance at the New Year's Day Turkey Curry Buffet, with the police in tow. In the film, by contrast, Julio is changed into a QVC product slinger, whose romantic charms eventually wear thin.

Fielding explained the change, commenting on the difference between writing novels and screenplays: "It's different because, in a script, every line has to work. In a book you can get away with murder. You can write around things. And a lot of the dialogue in the book is ridiculous if you actually get them to say it. Like the mother. It's so over the top. And the plot with mum and the Portuguese lover—it's fine in the book, but in the film we're wondering if it will work. If it will just seem like we've gone into sitcom land" (qtd. in Welch).

Fielding's remarks emphasize the difference between visual and print media. The filmmakers made significant changes to be faithful to the novel in ways other than slavishly following the plot. Plot parallels suggest but the most simplistic dimension of the film's and Fielding's debt to Austen. What is more significant, Fielding's Bridget Jones novels emulate Austen's in presenting the interior states of their female characters. Both writers present intelligent but misguided women who learn the error of their perceptions of men and discover true love in the process. The chief delights of the novels are those moments when we recognize the female character's lack of insight into herself and others.

Fielding's novels use the diary form to capture Bridget's thoughts, and one achievement of the film lies in its cinematic representation of the first-person intimacy of the diary. Bridget is shown writing in her diary—beginning it, in fact, right after being insulted by Mark Darcy at the Turkey Curry Buffet. The film promotes the confessional dimension of diary writing, with Bridget's claiming to tell "the truth about Bridget Jones—the whole truth."

The film retains the diary entry openings as Bridget's psychograph, noting her weight, alcohol, cigarette, and calorie consumption as indices of her psychological state. They appear in shots of the diary pages and written as overlays on the screen. In at least one instance, the film pumps up their emotional content, when her "shag-drunkenness" (60) after her first night with Daniel is broadcast on a billboard in Piccadilly Square. As she passes, the screen spells out in giant letters, "Date: Weds, Something the something. Weight: 131 lbs, Have replaced food with sex. Cigarettes: 22 … all post-coital."

The diary even becomes a part of the plot at the end of the film, when, just before they are to consummate their relationship, Mark Darcy accidentally reads some of Bridget's early entries: "Mum was really scraping the barrel with Mark Darcy. He acts like he's got a giant gherkin thrust up his backside. … Mark Darcy is rude, he's unpleasant, he's DULL—no wonder his clever wife left him."

But the director and screenwriters cannily exploit the medium of film to incorporate the diary form in still other ways. Owing to the intrinsically incommensurate nature of the media, film can in no way substitute for the literary device of the diary. Note that the diary gives us direct access to Bridget's thoughts, while the film necessarily focuses visually on Bridget from without. Screenwriter Richard Curtis says the secret to adapting the book was deciding "how to stand outside a character who you've got to know from the inside" (*Pride and Prejudice*). The writer and director had to devise analogous ways of representing interior states using cinematic, not literary, devices.

For instance, the film employs voice-over narration in places, which retains the first-person intimacy of the diary. However, this introduces a temporal disjunction. The reader consuming *Bridget Jones's Diary* in print experiences events contemporaneously with the narrator—we learn of events as she records them after they have occurred in time. In the film, by contrast, Bridget's comments on events that have already happened are heard as we see the events unfold on the screen. Thus the past tense of the voiced-over narrative does not coincide with the present tense of the visually represented events.

But the film actually augments the comic dimension of the novel, for it can visually register the contrast between Bridget's thoughts and actions, something readers can only infer from Bridget's reports of events and recounted dialogue. For instance, when Bridget is caught by her boss engaging in a personal phone call with a friend, she tries to cover it over by pretending to speak to F.R. Leavis. She says, "This book is a searing vision of the wounds our century has inflicted on traditional masculinity. It is positively Vonnegut-esque. Thank you for calling, Prof. Leavis." When Daniel asks, "Was that F.R. Leavis? … The F.R. Leavis who died in 1978?" the f-word scrawls with multiple u's across the bottom of the screen. The written word registers the inward distress concealed—however inexpertly—by Bridget's outward display of nonchalance.

In at least one instance, the film dramatizes Bridget's thoughts, paradoxically capitalizing on the film's point of view to show us her interior world. Before the book launch for *Kafka's Motorcycle*, Bridget's friends had advised her to "introduce people with thoughtful details." In the novel, Bridget is startled by Mark's appearance as she is speaking to Perpetua. "Trying not to panic" (100), she remembers her friend's advice and begins to introduce them—"Mark. Perpetua is …"—but then pauses, thinking, "What to say? Perpetua is very fat and spends her whole time bossing me around? Mark is very rich and has a cruel-raced ex-wife?" (101). Her reveries interrupted by Mark's "Yes?" she continues, "… is my boss and is buying a flat in Fulham, and Mark is … a top human rights lawyer" (100–101).

By contrast no distinction between her thoughts and actions appears to the viewer of the film. As Perpetua approaches Bridget and Mark, asking, "Anyone going to introduce me?" Bridget says in voice-over, "Ah, introduce people with thoughtful details." She then introduces them: "Perpetua. This is Mark Darcy. Mark's a prematurely middle-aged prick with a cruel-raced ex-wife. Perpetua's a fat-assed old bag who spends her time bossing me around." Over shots of their horrified reactions, we hear Bridget say, "Maybe not." The scene replays from Perpetua's entrance and Bridget gives more conventionally appropriate introductions. Instead of focusing on Perpetua's and Mark's reactions, the camera lingers on Bridget's face, as she reacts with surprise to the arrival of Mark's date Natasha. Our attention is diverted to Bridget's nascent jealousy, offering us an unexpected insight into her developing feelings for Mark, feelings that appear to be as surprising to her as to us.

The film thus manages to fuse the first-person and omniscient points of view, again strengthening its ties to Austen. As Cecilia Salber argued, "By maintaining Bridget's voice throughout, the diary format [of the novel] allows readers to judge the characters and their predicaments for themselves. The omniscient narrator of Austen's novels is replaced by an unreliable, solipsistic voice that creates its own sense of reality and coherence." The film version reintroduces the limited omniscient point of view. It combines the first-person perspective of Bridget's diary with the third-person perspective of the cinematic frame. Although one must acknowledge the fundamental differences between the two media, the film, more than Fielding's novel, replicates and extends the narrative techniques introduced by Austen.

In *Pride and Prejudice*, Austen's comic irony emerges out of the disjunction between Elizabeth's overconfidence (or pride) in her perceptions of Darcy and the narrator's indications that her views are in fact partial and prejudicial. As in *Emma,* the female protagonist is revealed to be as blind about herself and her feelings as she is about the hero. In *Pride and Prejudice* the revelation comes midway through the novel when Elizabeth reads a letter from Darcy after she rejects his first proposal of marriage. "Far from suspecting that she was … becoming an object of some interest" (20) to Darcy, she is completely blindsided by his proposal and the extremity of his feelings. He blurts, "In vain have I struggled. It will not do. My feelings will not be repressed. You must allow me to tell you how ardently I admire and love you" (147). We learn from the narrator that "Elizabeth's astonishment was beyond expression. She stared, coloured, doubted, and was silent. This he considered sufficient encouragement; and the avowal of all he felt, and had long felt for her, immediately followed" (147). Mistaking his relief at having finally expressed his feelings for "security" that his proposal would not be rejected, Elizabeth heatedly rebuffs him: "I have never desired your good opinion, and you have certainly bestowed it most unwillingly" (148). His honest expression of having overcome his scruples regarding her family's inferior status only augments her preexisting conviction that he had misused Wickham and prevented her sister's marriage to his friend Bingley. She concludes,

> From the very beginning—from the first moment, I may almost say—of my acquaintance with you, your manners, impressing me with the fullest belief of your arrogance, your conceit, and your selfish disdain of the feelings of others, were such as to form a groundwork of disapprobation on which succeeding events have built so immovable a dislike, and I had not known you a month before I felt that you were the last man in the world whom I could ever be prevailed on to marry. (150–51)

His astonishment, mingled with "incredulity and mortification," is matched by her own and, as Darcy leaves her, the "tumult of her mind was now painfully great" (151).

Elizabeth recognizes the source of her agitation only when reading Darcy's letter defending his behavior. At first, her misperceptions color her reading: "With strong prejudice against everything he might say, she began his account" (159). Underscoring the superficiality of her judgment, the narrator presents Elizabeth as more concerned with Darcy's prose than the letter's contents: "His style was not penitent, but haughty. It was all pride and insolence" (159). Eventually the rational basis of his arguments convinces her that "she had been blind, partial, prejudiced, absurd" (162). As she reviews events, she sees not only Darcy and Wickham differently but also herself. She admits, "Till this moment I never knew myself" (162). She rereads his letter and so "widely different was the effect" (162) that it results in a "change so sudden and so important" (163) that she can think only of the letter.

A scene so dependent on writing and internal reflection would seem the least likely to be successfully transformed on film. The BBC version, to the contrary, invests the scenes of writing and reading with such cinematic import that the home video version successfully uses them as the break between the first and second volumes. With remarkable use of voice-over, flashback, and editing, the filmmakers collapse Elizabeth's initial and secondary reviews of the letter into one compressed scene visually linking the two protagonists. As Elizabeth's rejection echoes in his head in voice-over, Darcy returns home to write his letter. As we see him compose the letter, his defense of his actions regarding Wickham is rendered partly in voice-over, using exact quotations from Austen's text. The emotional heat of his defense is represented by the physicality of writing. Darcy, stripped to his shirt, open at the chest and wrists, writes furiously, physically expressing his desire to transform not only Elizabeth's views but also her feelings for him.[5] Partway through Darcy's recitation of the letter's contents in voice-over, we witness him deliver the letter to Elizabeth and then the scene switches to her reading his reservations about her family. Initially, the voice-over is punctuated by her outraged reaction—"insufferable presumption," "hateful man!"—but then flashbacks reveal Elizabeth's changing perceptions of events, thus fusing the first and second readings of the novel into one scene. The flashbacks appear to show us Elizabeth's growing acknowledgment of her family's boorish behavior at social events.

The film version of *Bridget Jones's Diary* revises Fielding's novel to incorporate equivalents of this key moment in Austen's text, making two significant modifications: Bridget discovers Daniel's philandering ways on her own and breaks up with him, giving Mark the opportunity to declare his affections. While Fielding's Wickham has been exposed, Mark still nonetheless defends his view of Daniel and Bridget's family, as Darcy does in his letter to Elizabeth, in a dinner scene with the "Smug Marrieds" at Magda and Jeremy's. The dinner with the Smug Marrieds fuses two scenes from the novel: an earlier dinner where, to cover for her lack of a boyfriend, Bridget boasts that she has found a younger man, and Darcy's party for his parent's Ruby Wedding. In the film, the Ruby Wedding party becomes the scene of Bridget's declaration of her feelings for Darcy; in the novel it provides the occasion for Mark to ask her to dance and declare his feelings, as Fielding revises the proposal scene from Austen. The film's revisions present Bridget and Darcy's encounter as closer to the scene in Austen's text.

In both the film and the novel, Darcy's date Natasha belittles Bridget by referring to her disastrous appearance at the Tarts and Vicars' party: "Not in your bunny girl outfit today, then" (232). Cleverly, Bridget replies, "Actually, we bunnies wear these in the winter for warmth" (232). But the assault continues: in the novel as Natasha insults Jude's dress and in the film as the Smug Marrieds grill Bridget about why there are so many single women in their thirties. In both, Bridget escapes—outdoors in the novel and downstairs to catch a taxi in the film. Darcy follows. In the novel their exchange goes like this:

"I heard about Daniel. I'm sorry."

"I suppose you did try to warn me," I muttered sulkily. "What have you got against him, anyway?"

"He slept with my wife," he said. "Two weeks after our wedding."

I stared at him aghast ... (236)

Note that Elizabeth's astonishment at Darcy's proposal is transformed into Bridget's surprise at further evidence of Daniel's nefarious ways. Any hesitancy about revising her views evaporates. She accepts his declaration with little evidence of suspicion or shock. As Natasha can be heard summoning him, Mark hurriedly explains, "Last Christmas, ... I thought if my mother said the words 'Bridget Jones' just once more I would go to the *Sunday People* and accuse her of abusing me as a child with a bicycle pump. Then when I met you ... and I was wearing that ridiculous diamond-patterned jumper that Una had bought for Christmas. ... Bridget, all the other girls I know are so lacquered over. I don't know anyone else who would fasten a bunny tail to their pants or ..." (236–37). Assured of his esteem and his own apparently imminent break with Natasha, Bridget agrees to his invitation to dinner.

In the film, by contrast, Bridget shows some of Elizabeth's continuing prejudice while Mark retains Darcy's criticism as he reveals his attraction. As Bridget prepares to leave, Mark descends the stairs, complimenting her Lewisham fire report, the notorious "up the fireman's pole" shot broadcast by "Sit Up Britain." She misperceives his remark as mockery. On the defensive, she also reacts to his question "Didn't work out with Daniel Cleaver?" with evident distrust and disdain. Learning that she has in fact broken up with Daniel, Mark says, "I'm delighted to hear it." She reacts with anger, saying, "You seem to go out of your way to try to make me feel like a complete idiot every time I see you and you really needn't bother. I already feel like an idiot most of the time anyway with or without a fireman's pole." As the cabdriver rings the bell, Mark attempts to apologize:

I don't think you're an idiot at all. I mean there *are* elements of the ridiculous about you. Your mother's pretty interesting and you really are an appallingly bad public speaker and you tend to let whatever is in your head come out of your mouth without much consideration of the consequences. I realized that when I met you at the Turkey Curry Buffet I was incredibly rude and wearing a reindeer jumper that my mother had given me the day before. ... But what I'm trying to say, very inarticulately, is that, in fact, perhaps despite appearances, I like you very much.

His reference to "appearances" emphasizes the obstacles of pride and prejudice standing between them and linking them to Austen's couple.

Stung by his perceived criticism, Bridget disdainfully interjects, "Apart from the smoking, and the drinking, and the vulgar mother, and the verbal diarrhea." He counters, "No, I like you very much, just as you are." As Mark ascends the stairs in response to Natasha's summons, the camera lingers on Bridget's look of astonishment.

Like Elizabeth, the cinematic Bridget initially remains unaware of her own feelings. In a conversation that follows with her friends, they puzzle over Mark's phrase "just as you are." Asked, "But this is someone you hate, right?" Bridget agrees, "Yes, yes, I hate him," but with little conviction. Her distracted look reveals that she is not at all sure and is still reviewing her own reaction.

It is ironic, in fact, that Austen's heroine seems far more secure in her feelings than Fielding's. Once she does see herself and Darcy without prejudice, Elizabeth recognizes her desire for Darcy: "Never had she so honestly felt that she could have loved him, as now, when all love must be in vain" (212). Fearful that Lydia's indecent behavior has completely eradicated all hope for an alliance between herself and Darcy, Elizabeth was "humbled" and "grieved" (238):

> She became jealous of his esteem, when she could no longer hope to be benefited by it. She wanted to hear of him, when there seemed the least chance of gaining intelligence. She was convinced that she could have been happy with him; when it was no longer likely that they should meet. ... She now began to comprehend that he was exactly the man who, in disposition and talents, would most suit her. (238–39)

When she learns that Darcy has bribed Wickham to marry Lydia, she realizes his motives lie in his love for her: "Her heart did whisper that he had done it for her" (250).

Bridget, by contrast, has to be told. After Mark has assisted in Julio's arrest, she asks him, "Why did you bother doing all this?" (306). He replies, "Isn't it rather obvious?" (306). Her reaction—"Oh my God" (306)—shows her genuine surprise. "I didn't think you liked me much," Darcy adds (306). One might expect that Bridget, the more worldly contemporary woman with previous romantic experiences and an arsenal of self-help books at her disposal, would have greater insight into her own feelings. To the contrary. After he has engineered her exclusive interview with his client Elena Rossini, she is still uncertain. Contemplating writing him a thank-you note, she tells herself, "It's not because I fancy him or anything. Simple good manners demands it" (243). As in *Pride and Prejudice,* family scandal appears to quash any possibility of a relationship:

"Had thought only silver lining in cloud of mother's criminality was that it might bring me and Mark Darcy closer together but have not heard a peep from him" (276). Her musings focus not as Elizabeth's on her own feelings but on anxieties about her perception by Mark: "Was obviously completely put off by culinary disasters and criminal element in family, but too polite to show it at the time" (277). She thinks, "Maybe Mark Darcy is too perfect, clean and finished off at the edges for me, with his capability, intelligence, lack of smoking, freedom from alcoholism, and his chauffer-driven cars" (286). Like Elizabeth, she fears that class differences prevent their union. But Elizabeth still perceives that they are "equal" (274), as she tells his interfering aunt, and dismisses any consideration of how their union might appear in the "eyes of everybody" (275). She remains firm in her conviction that "it was a union that must have been to the advantage of both" (239).

The film version of *Bridget Jones's Diary* does significantly alter the conclusion of Fielding's novel. It does so only partially and imperfectly to introduce a modicum of Elizabeth's confidence. Learning that Daniel slept with Mark's wife, Bridget speeds to the Ruby Wedding as "Ain't No Mountain High Enough" plays on the soundtrack. Just as Elizabeth's revised opinion of Wickham coincides with the discovery of her own feelings, the evidence in support of Mark's vision of Daniel impels Bridget to pursue her Darcy. The racing car conveys the intensity of her desire. Taking him aside at the party, she tells him, "You once said that you like me just as I am and I just wanted to say 'likewise.' I mean there are the stupid things your mum buys you and tonight is another classic. You're haughty and you always say the wrong thing in every situation and I seriously believe that you should rethink the length of your sideburns. But you're a nice man and I like you." The filmmakers revise Darcy's proposal in *Pride and Prejudice*, recasting it from Bridget's perspective. They thus grant this contemporary Elizabeth the initiative and "pride" of her male counterpart. Bridget invites him to "pop by," whereas Elizabeth waits for Darcy to renew his proposal. Before Mark can answer, however, they are interrupted for the toast that announces his job in New York and presumed engagement to Natasha. As the crowd lifts their glasses to "Mark and his Natasha," Bridget cries, "No! No!" She covers her feelings quite unsuccessfully by claiming that it's a shame that England should lose one of its "top people—our top person really." Even when Mark returns, her confidence is undercut by her mistaken belief that she's lost him after he's read her diary. The filmmakers underscore her vulnerability by picturing her in her underwear covered only by a flimsy sweater. As "Ain't No Mountain High Enough" plays again, her race after him has none of the confidence of her earlier drive. Instead, she appears desperate. In the previous scene she had wrested control of the car from her father, who was driving too slowly, thus asserting her power over her feelings and the course of her relationship. In the final chase she is out of control. Their dialogue compounds her fragility. Apologizing, she dismisses her writing as "only a diary," undermining her perceptions and feelings. They are "crap." As he presents her with the new diary he had run out to purchase for her, he agrees: "Time to make a new start." When she protests after their kiss that "Nice boys don't kiss like that," he replies, "Oh yes they fucking do," playfully but powerfully asserting his vision.

At the end of Austen's novel, by contrast, the narrator emphasizes Elizabeth's "lively, sportive manner of talking" to Darcy (299). His sister Georgiana learns from Elizabeth that "a woman may take liberties with her husband" (299). Elizabeth clearly has, if not the upper hand over Darcy, at least a position of more equal footing, whereas Bridget stands on tiptoe.

In Fielding's novel and in the film, it appears that increased professional and personal choice has led merely to greater uncertainty and confusion. Austen's women were faced with a far narrower range of choices—essentially one: whom to marry? Within this limited scope, they achieved a measure of power. Their power may have been limited to "the power of refusal" (Looser 168), but even this power is denied Bridget. As Anne Mellor argued, Austen's novels offer "a revolutionary criticism of the authority of the father and husband, a demand for more egalitarian marriages, and an insistence on the domestic affections as the basis of all public and private virtues and happiness" (41). It is worth remembering, however, that Austen's novels created a courtship balance to critique the *absence* of such balance in early nineteenth-century relationships between men and women (Hudson). The filmmakers' attraction to Austen's text may signal their own view that such inequities remain nearly two centuries later. Given the preponderance of similarities to *Pride and Prejudice* in the film version of *Bridget Jones's Diary,* the divergences at the end appear in stark contrast to the imaginative hope for equality promised by Austen's text. Instead, they emphasize contemporary women's renewed desire to be rescued by men from the complications of life as an independent woman.

Notes

1. Fielding delivers this line on the "Behind-the-Scenes Featurette" on the DVD version of the film, but she was repeatedly quoted as offering some variation of the same line in the popular press. See the *Daily Telegraph,* November 20, 1999.
2. On the extent to which Colin Firth's previous roles affect the viewer's perception of the film, see Ritrosky -Winslow.
3. The complete line in Austen's novel reads, "It is a truth universally acknowledged, that a single man in possession of a good fortune must be in want of a wife."
4. See Haskell, Rathke, and Turan.

5. Nixon observes, "Darcy's physical activities create a cinematic form of self-expression, a dialogue between mind and body that runs throughout the entire film but is absent from the novel" (31).

Works Cited

Austen, Jane. *Pride and Prejudice*. 1813. London: Penguin Classics, 1994.

Bridget Jones's Diary. Screenplay by Helen Fielding, Andrew Davies, and Richard Curtis. Dir. Sharon Maguire. Miramax, 2001.

Ebert, Roger. "*Bridget* Rules: Zellweger Finds Her Stride as Lovable Brit." *Chicago Sun-Times* 13, Apr. 2001.

Fielding, Helen. *Bridget Jones's Diary*. London: Picador, 1996.

Haskell, Molly. "The Innocent Ways of Renee Zellweger." *New York Times* 13, Apr. 2001.

Hudson, Glenda A. "Consolidated Communities: Masculine and Feminine Values in Jane Austen's Fiction." *Jane Austen and the Discourses of Feminism*. Ed. Devoney Looser. New York: St. Martin's, 1995. 101–14.

Looser, Devoney. "Feminist Implications of the Silver Screen Austen." *Jane Austen in Hollywood*. Ed. Linda Troost and Sayre Greenfield. Lexington: University of Kentucky Press, 1998. 159–76.

Mellor, Anne K. *Romanticism and Gender*. New York and London: Routledge, 1993.

Nixon, Cheryl L. "Balancing the Courtship Hero: Masculine Emotional Display in Film Adaptations of Austen's Novels." *Jane Austen in Hollywood*. Ed. Linda Troost and Sayre Greenfield. Lexington: University of Kentucky Press, 1998. 22–43.

Pride and Prejudice. Screenplay by Andrew Davies. Dir. Simon Langton. BBC/A&E, 1995.

Rathke, Renee Scolaro. "*Bridget Jones's Diary*." *Pop Matters*. <www.popmatters.com/film/reviews/b/bridget-jones-diary.html>.

Ritrosky-Winslow, Madelyn. "Colin & Mark & Renée & Bridget: The Intertextual Crowd." *Quarterly Review of Film and Video* 23 (forthcoming).

———. "Lust Actually: *Bridget Jones's* Men." *Entertainment Magazine*. 2003. <http://entertainmentmagazine.net/>.

Robinson, Kathryn. "Why I Heart Chick Lit." *Seattle Weekly* 22–28, Oct. 2003. <http://www.seattleweekly.com/features/0343/031022_arts_books_chicklit.php>.

Salber, Cecilia. "Bridget Jones and Mark Darcy: Art Imitating Art … Imitating Art." *Persuasions: The Jane Austin Journal On-Line* 2...1(Winter 2001) <http://www.jasna.org/pol04/salber.html>.

Turan, Kenneth. "Keeping up with Ms. Jones." *Los Angeles Times* 13, Apr. 2001.

Welch, Dave. "Helen Fielding Is Not Bridget Jones." *Powells.com Interviews*. 3, June 1999. <www.powells.com/authors/fielding.html>.

PART II

Free Range: Varieties and Variations

5

"Sistahs Are Doin' It for Themselves": Chick Lit in Black and White

LISA A. GUERRERO

R.E.S.P.E.C.T.

Most fans of contemporary women's fiction can immediately answer the following question: how *did* Stella get her groove back? Most likely they can also tell you the difference between a "singleton" and a "smug married"; sing one of Whitney Houston's songs from the soundtrack of *Waiting to Exhale;* marvel at length at Renee Zellweger's spot-on portrayal of Bridget Jones, self-deprecating vulnerability, fluctuating weight, English accent, and all; and recall with relish when Angela Bassett's character in *Waiting to Exhale,* Bernadine, sporting a fiercely flattering silk negligee set, sets her cheating husband's BMW on fire after selling all of his belongings in a bargain-basement garage sale. Sistah lit and chick lit, along with their respective film versions, have unalterably changed the attitudes and imaginations of the large female consumer public at the end of the twentieth century. They have been responsible for creating pop culture reflections of modern women that are at once honest, empowering, and profitable. Chicks and sistahs aren't just heroines; they're big business. But because of both the association to pop entertainment culture and the seemingly unstoppable popularity of the larger recognizable genre of chick lit, under which various subgenres, including sistah lit, often are subsumed, it has been easy for readers to critically disengage from the significant differences found between chick lit and sistah lit, often resulting in sistah lit's being looked at as simply chick lit in blackface. In this essay I look beyond the superficiality of racial difference between chicks and sistahs and examine how race socially, politically, and historically informs the ways in which these two powerhouse genres and their heroines diverge, especially in their attitudes toward and relationships to men, marriage, and the struggle for worth, fulfillment, and respect.

The Chick Cometh

During the 1990s, women's literature experienced a very public spike in both popular readership and commercial viability. It was the dawning of the era of chick lit. The women who had fought for equality in the 1960s and 1970s now had daughters who were reaping the rewards of those struggles and claiming a stake in society, ostensibly on their own terms. This was their literature. They were at once feminine and powerful; they knew how to accessorize and negotiate; they didn't know how to cook or clean, but they were skilled at mixing a mean cocktail, could quote verbatim from *Glamour, In Style, Cosmopolitan,* and British *Vogue,* and knew the best places to get dim sum and Indian takeout. This was the definition of the new modern woman, aka the chick. The new genre embraced all of the pleasures and problems of this new model of womanhood with wry irony and humor, and little sentimentality.

A flood of pop novels elevated the tribulations of the single, careerist, twenty- and thirtysomething women of the world to entertaining and eloquent farce. The heroines of this new genre were white and generally middle class, and all of them were in search of love, though arguably most chick lit deals with the desire for romantic relationships as an ironic fantasy, at once coveted and mocked. The protagonists seek not the grand love portrayed in the classic romance novel but rather a modern love that is only extraordinary in the difficulty of finding a man who is single, heterosexual, committal, manly, sensitive, successful, and attractive all at the same time. In chick lit, happiness, though often involving sex, *always,* and quite problematically, involves an ideal of monogamous coupling, the promise of domesticity, and the comfortable routinization that domesticity seems to provide.

It should be noted that, as several scholars argue articulately, marriage is not the ultimate goal, and very often is not the ultimate result in much of chick lit. However, it docs occupy an idealized place in the minds of many chick protagonists. It is, in fact, a chick's problematic relationship to the codified and commodified institution of marriage that presents one of the central negotiations she is constantly making as she begins to make sense of her life. Part of the chick's appeal, both comically and tragically, is her paradoxical existence of being successful and independent in society while simultaneously being rendered "less than" by that same society through media images and popular ideologies because she doesn't weigh 105 pounds, isn't married, can't cook, isn't married, doesn't have kids, isn't married, can't afford to dress in high fashion and still eat, and isn't married.

The readership of chick lit identified closely with these social absurdities. Much of the wild popularity of these novels can be traced to the reality of their readers—young women who, after reaping the benefits of the opportunities secured for them by the fights waged during the preceding decades, found themselves in the virtually uncharted territory of being professionally powerful and relationally adrift. The thirtysomething women composing the large fan base of chick lit at once expected more than their mothers and grandmothers economically and professionally while also hoping for the same romance and family as the female generation that had come before. They wanted careers, economic stability, and self-determination because those were the things they were taught they had a right to claim. But they also wanted to have husbands and children, to be taken care of, and to be the caretaker, because those were the things they had been socialized to recognize as characterizing real womanhood.

The Sistah Also Rises

During this same period, African-American female thirtysomethings had been embracing their own sistah lit, a group of series and authors that spoke to the modern condition of being female, independent, single, and black. The protagonists of sistah lit were also mainly careerist and middle class, but the implications of both of those positions for black women were what separated them from the white chicks. Being a career-centered, self-sufficient, and unmarried woman flew in the face of decades of social assumptions regarding *white* women. Black women represented an unprecedented challenge to American social structures that had, over centuries, put black women on the absolute bottom of the social hierarchy, confined and vilified through race, gender, and class. The space of black women in America had been normalized as belonging within the limited boundaries of servant and/or sex object from the time of slavery.

The indelible connection between black women, the domestic sphere, manual service labor, and the underclass had existed for so long in the American popular imagination and social reality that the emergence of this new model of the "sistah" onto the popular stage posed a nearly herculean move toward naturalizing a distinctly different vision of black womanhood. While the heroines' odysseys involved the complications of relationships, sistah lit more often showed its heroines running *from* domesticity in an attempt to assert an identity that is unconnected to histories of forced compliance with the roles of caretaker, breeder, and sexualized object. As such, sistah lit represented not only a reflection *of* a new African-American womanhood but also a revolution *for* this new African-American womanhood.

Black women authors, including Pearl Cleage and April Sinclair, presented pop novels for modern black women that interwove African-American cultural specificities and current social challenges facing the African-American community with the basic stories of their heroines' everyday struggles with careers and relationships. Their themes included racism, the rub of affirmative action, the wildfire-like spread of AIDS/HIV, and the shadow of the prison industrial complex. Among these writers, perhaps the most important originator of sistah lit is Terry McMillan. A popular and successful founding force in the genre of African American women's popular fiction, McMillan has written numerous novels, beginning with *Mama* (1987) and *Disappearing Acts* (1989). But the 1992 publication of her third novel, *Waiting to Exhale*, heralded the arrival of an original model of the African-American woman and solidified the presence and marketability of sistah lit.

Waiting to Exhale and *Bridget Jones's Diary*, six years later, marked a major shift in the ways in which the lives of women were portrayed in popular culture. Women had become agents, albeit oftentimes fumbling and awkward ones, in their own lives. And they were no longer exceptions to the rule as earlier literary heroines of strength and struggle, including Scarlett O'Hara, Iola Leroy, Carrie Meeber, Elizabeth Bennet, Helga Crane, and Becky Sharp, had been; now they were the rule. Admittedly, as "strong, independent women" became the commonplace protagonists in women's popular fiction, their trials and struggles also became less epic than the situations of their literary forebears; but with the pursuit of their conventional aspirations they succeeded in infusing the figure of the modern woman with a relevance and humanity that reimagined assumptions about female identity. Although their positions had changed, so too had the society in which they ruled. The roles of sex, love, marriage, domesticity, motherhood, and success had been radically transformed to shrug off the confinement of traditional notions of womanhood. But they would never be able to *completely* shake off the hand of history and feminine inheritance. And as it had been before—in life and in literature—white chicks and black sistahs were traveling different paths toward fulfillment, characterized by racial and cultural specificities, histories, and expectations.

Although it is clearly not the case that the readers of chick lit and sistah lit are exclusively of one race or the other, it is clear that even as African-American women can enjoy and, on multiple levels, relate to Bridget Jones and other literary chicks, it is more difficult to *see* themselves in these white heroines. Similarly, white women are certainly able to root for and empathize with the heroines of *Waiting to Exhale* and other sistah lit, but a distance remains between their own realities and those of the black female protagonists. As we will see as we look more closely at the touchstone works of the genres, *Waiting to Exhale* and *Bridget Jones's Diary,* several main components of the narratives separate the two fictions: the images of manhood, the relationships to friends and family, attitudes toward love and sex, ideas of marriage and domesticity, and perceptions of self-worth.

Of Chicks and Sistahs

Waiting to Exhale and *Bridget Jones's Diary* both begin with a similar tenor and framework. McMillan and Fielding introduce us to their narrators and establish the mood of yearning and frustration that is identifiable in both novels, as well as in their respective genres. Both introductions also work to create a familiar relationship between the reader and the protagonists. The appeal, and the power, of these genres was, and is, the remarkable ability to make the reading experience nearly indistinguishable from a conversation with our best girlfriends. It isn't fiction as much as it is the comfort of community.

McMillan employs a shifting narration throughout the novel, creating a tangible sense of the constant negotiation between intimacy and distance, between those things we hide and those things that are hidden from us. The four women of the story are all smart, professional women. Two are mothers, one is married, and none of them are happy. They all desire different lives from the ones they currently live bound by social expectation and fraught with disappointment.

Similarly personable and personal, as our tour guide through the social follies of single life at the end of the twentieth century, Bridget Jones proves a touching—sometimes obliviously so—native informant. The first-person narrative voice establishes our intimacy with Bridget and her life. Before the story even begins, the reader is confronted with Bridget's list of New Year's resolutions. Immediately we are introduced to the varied struggles in which our heroine is engaged, many of which, we imagine, we share. The entries of the narrative begin on January 1, giving a certain cyclical symmetry to the tedium of lives measured by overcoming unrelenting obstacles. The diary form makes the personal life public, infusing the situations of the novel with the palpable feeling of exposure, emphasizing the ways in which modern single life has created a community of isolates. The similarities between McMillan's and Fielding's works are immediately apparent. The stylistic and thematic convergence of these two introductions, however, belies the larger differences that exist between these two books specifically, and the two genres generally.

First, though the quests of both the black and white heroines are often romantic in nature, the flavor of and motivation behind them are distinct. White chicks are usually looking for a relationship that will give them the opportunity to fulfill domestic impulses, even if those impulses have been artificially instilled through an incessant barrage of stereotypes regarding womanhood. The mythic spaces of "hearth and home" have come to characterize womanly identity and represent a fortification of womanhood for the heroines of chick lit. Sistahs, alternatively, are usually looking for a relationship that will give them the opportunity to define their womanhood beyond domesticity. The same mythic spaces of hearth and home that provide an expansion of chick identity represent a reduction of sistah identity. Though arguably the ideas surrounding hearth and home have been used at various times in history to limit the identities of both black and white women, ideologically and actually, only black women have experienced that connection through systematic processes of violence, exploitation, and degradation. White femininity has historically been idealized as something that needed to be protected and preserved. Black femininity represented the antithesis of that ideal and was denigrated as unwomanly. As such, these divergent histories of black and white women's relation to their femininity inform the searches of chicks and sistahs. Chicks are looking for love because, as white women, they have been taught to believe in their preciousness and the fact that they should be loved, even worshipped. Having grown comfortable with the privilege these "truths" provide, chicks seem to be seeking actualization of these promises. For them fairy tales do come true; at least, they've come to expect that they do. Sistahs are looking for worth because, as black women, they have been taught by society to believe in their disposability and the fact that they should be loathed, even demonized. Having grown suspicious of these truths, sistahs seem to be seeking validation of their suspicions.

As we see in the story of Bridget's life as a singleton, the chick quest becomes comically rendered as the monotony of constantly searching for that *one* thing that will let us know that our life is finally complete. For twenty- to thirtysomething single women in the 1990s, that one thing was a husband. Even with all of the progress of modern women, chicks are still inextricably bound to the shadow of the "Cult of True Womanhood," a nineteenth-century construction that positioned white women as the moral center of families who reigned exclusively in the domestic sphere as a near-sacred calling. Men were meant to provide salary; women were to provide sanctity. And despite the other successes that modern women had to their credit, especially white women, their singleness somehow still diminished their claim to true womanhood. Bridget addresses this reduced status when she says of her friend Tom, "Tom, who has taken, unflatteringly, to calling himself a hag-fag ... has a theory that homosexuals and single women in their thirties have natural bonding: both being accustomed to disappointing their parents and being treated as freaks by society" (24). Tom's theory, at once humorous and accurate, emphasizes that both gay men and single women appear deviant by rejecting traditional social assumptions.

The plot of Bridget's story is a standard chick-lit plot, adhering to certain predictable formulas, even as it breaks molds and sets standards: Bridget is miserably single. Bridget is attracted to the "wrong" man and appalled by the "right" man. Bridget endures rituals of surface self-transformation in an attempt to gain the affections of "wrong" man. Bridget has sex with "wrong" man. "Wrong" man engages in "fuckwittage," the game playing, contradictory, cowardly, shallow, hurtful, ridiculous "logic" of eligible men deployed unpredictably in their pursuit of women—or sex. Bridget obsesses, but finally gets over "wrong" man and gains a new sense of self in the process. "Right" man does something to demonstrate why he is "right" man. Bridget falls in love with "right" man and ends up as part of a couple, thus ending her quest, and, significantly, the story, since now that she has been "naturalized," her identity has become subsumed into couple identity and is no longer interesting to us.[1]

On the other hand, for McMillan's four heroines—Savannah, Bernadine, Robin, and Gloria—the quest is not the same and, understandably, neither is the result of that quest. Though they too are searching for the love and protection of a man, their struggles are marked by much more than just *how* to get a man in order to fit into socially constructed ideas of womanhood; because of their race, they are first forced to forge their own sense of womanhood. Much of *Waiting to Exhale* deals implicitly (and oftentimes, explicitly) with the socially created battle between black womanhood and white womanhood over the mantle of beauty and worthiness.

In this quest Savannah and Robin stand as two sides of the same coin. They are both single and childless. They are both successful and recognized in their professions. They are both the primary caretakers of their aging and ailing parents. They are both attractive and aware of how to use sex appeal as a tool (and a weapon). And they have both had a string of unsuccessful relationships with undeserving men. Both women realize the bankruptcy of the romantic ideal, but they differ in their responses to this realization. Savannah complains,

> The truth of the matter is, I've spent nine years of my adult life living with three different men that I'm glad I didn't marry because all three of them were mistakes. Back then, I felt like I had to live with them in order to find out that I *couldn't* live with them ... I'll take my chances the next time around ... I'm also willing to spend the rest of my life alone if I have to, until I find someone that makes me feel like I was born with a tiara on my head. (11–12)

Here we see that unlike chicks for whom fairy tales can be incorporated realistically into their pursuits, Savannah, and sistahs generally, may indulge in fairy-tale fantasies where they are the crown princess, but their own life experiences have shown the futile emptiness of such dreams. Demonstrating the frustrating chasm between fairy tales and real life for sistahs, McMillan draws Savannah as wary and closed off; expecting little, she finds that romance consistently lives up to those expectations. On the other hand, McMillan characterizes Robin as resigned to the state of romance and proceeding by being generous and forgiving to the useless men in her life, while carrying much of the responsibility for their relationships herself. She says,

> I have always fantasized about what life would be like when I got married and had kids. I imagined it would be beautiful. I imagined it would be just like it was in the movies. We would fall hopelessly in love, and our wedding picture would get in *Jet* magazine. We would have a houseful of kids, because I hated being an only child. I would be a model mother. We would have an occasional fight, but we would always make up. And instead of drying up, our love would grow. We would be one hundred percent faithful to each other. People would envy us, wish they had what we had, and they'd ask us forty years later how we managed to beat the odds and still be so happy.
>
> I was this stupid for a long time. (44–45)

Robin has inherited this submissive stoicism from her mother, who, in the face of Robin's father's deterioration due to Alzheimer's disease, modifies her behavior to fit the wild swings of the disease, believing that it is her responsibility to make things right. Ultimately, Savannah and Robin realize that their responses to men, romance, and relationships have led them, in part, to their current lives, and that galvanizes their desire to change themselves. By rejecting social expectations and creating their own sense of real womanhood, they are able to remain self-possessed, even if that self-possession means staying single, *especially* if it means staying single. They are also able to recognize what *really* defines family and values, even if it means, as it does in Robin's case, having a child alone rather than being treated poorly by the baby's father just to fit the traditional model of motherhood.

Savannah's and Robin's tribulations are somewhat different from those of Gloria, who is an overweight, single mother of a teenage boy, Tarik. She is a business owner, a home owner, and a community activist, but because of her treatment by Tarik's father (which we discover is motivated mainly out of his own confusion over his homosexuality), as well as ideals of beauty that are rarely ever black *or* fat, she lacks self-confidence and the belief that she deserves more in her life than just taking care of others. A sudden heart attack forces her out of her role as caretaker and prompts the realization that she should confront her weight problem not to conform to society's ideals of beauty but rather to actualize *her own* ideals of life, such as watching the success of her son and falling in love with a kind neighbor. Gloria's character is the least explored of the four women in the novel, which ironically reproduces precisely the same experience of the women like Gloria that McMillan is hoping to give voice to. Although the social construction of womanhood influences the pursuits of Fielding's and McMillan's women alike, the sharp distance between the quest of Bridget and those of Savannah, Robin, and Gloria is ultimately marked as that between the romance fantasy that chicks are allowed to believe in and the real-life experiences that sistahs are forced to live in.

The second departure between the two texts hinges on the men in the lives of chicks and sistahs and the portraits of manhood they embody. In both genres there are the "good" men and the "bad" men, and they are drawn with the recognizable traits readers expect from each group. Bad men generally lie, cheat, and don't communicate, and they are unappreciative, unsupportive, patronizing, or a combination of all of the above. Good men generally work hard to be deserving of the heroines' affections, which typically means possessing the opposite characteristics from those on the previous list. The difference comes in the ways in which they manifest their manhood. For example, Bridget chooses between Daniel and Mark. Daniel is clearly a pompous cad to Mark's dashing gentleman, but both of them are unquestioned models of masculinity—professionals with the ability to provide, and lovers with the ability to satisfy. Conversely, the four women in *Waiting* go through a list of men that can be accurately described only as "triflin'" or useless. As Savannah says,

> What I want to know is this. How do you tell a man—in a nice way—that he makes you sick? ... And what if a man's a drag in bed? This list is too long to name names, but of course all black men think they can fuck because they all have at least ten-inch dicks. I wish I could tell some of them that they should start by checking the dictionary under *F* for "foreplay," *G* for "gentle," and *T* for "tender" or "take your time." ... And I'm not interested in rehabilitating anybody either. I've tried it, and it doesn't work. (13–14)

The issue of racialized masculinity makes the black male characters of sistah lit take on a different tenor than the white male characters of chick lit. In a parallel process to the one that systematically deprived black women of their womanhood, black men were denied certain claims to manhood. As a result, the modern black men that sistahs are faced with are asserting a kind of hypermasculinity to protect their fragile claims to manhood, an assertion that has never been socially necessary for white men. And though Savannah's list characterizes the bad men, even the good men in sistah lit are not idealized models of manhood. The good men are *too* faithful, to the point of being cloying and needy, and, although the sistahs don't say so, womanly, like Robin's comical, yet pitiful, rebound man, Michael; or they're faithful to you but not faithful in general, like Savannah's handsome, accomplished, devoted, and *married* lover, Kenneth. Seemingly in sistah lit, the bad men are always bad and the good men are never good enough.

A third distinction between chicks and sistahs is the different ways in which friends and family operate. Family for chicks generally means a nuclear family that represents a certain measure of stability, even if it's a stability in formality only, provided by the unquestioned normative nature of its makeup. Their parents are usually shown to be relatively reasonable, though often unreasonably expectant, people who don't need to be provided for and remain largely separate from chicks' everyday lives. Even in their lunacy, like Bridget's mother's rash affair and comical brush with crime, they are still portrayed as self-contained and comfortably removed from the central chaos of a chick's life. For sistahs, family tends to be a part of everyday concerns because sistahs are often the ones responsible for providing the stability, economic and otherwise, for their parents. In *Waiting,* three of the four main characters find themselves as the major source of their parents' well-being, whereas the parents of the fourth woman, Gloria, are deceased. Savannah and Bernadine provide financial care for their mothers, who are on prohibitively fixed incomes, while Robin is forced to supplement her parents' inadequate health care benefits, as well as to provide psychological grounding as she and her mother witness the rapid deterioration of her father to Alzheimer's disease. Although families aren't portrayed as particularly nurturing in either chick lit or sistah lit and, in fact, are more often drawn as generally annoying, the dysfunction of family remains, largely, outside of the chick's concern, whereas for sistahs that same dysfunction of family becomes the sistah's responsibility. For chicks, family can be a mere embarrassing inconvenience; for sistahs, family is often an inescapable burden.

As for friends, while they serve as the primary support system for both groups of women, a self-centeredness comes through in the friendships of chick lit, whereas in sistah lit the friends form a communal unit. Bridget's best friends, two single women and a gay man, tend to rally around each one of the group's individual crises; and though the support shown in these crises is genuine, it is also generally self-serving. As Bridget says, "If you are single the last thing you want is your best friend forming a functional relationship with somebody else" (91). In sistah lit the friend unit is a constant presence, and crises take on a communal sense regardless of which individual woman is experiencing them. This is apparent in Bernadine's sentiment in the face of her divorce settlement: "Bernadine knew her girlfriends were just as elated about her settlement as she was. She could hear it in their voices. Hell, they'd been waiting as long as she had. Now it seemed as if they'd *all* won the lottery. And as far as Bernadine was concerned, they had" (398). The level of responsibility to both friends and family in sistah lit is informed by the prevalence and tradition of the extended family found within the African-American community.

Finally, both sistahs and chicks seek self-worth. However, whereas chicks are shown as measuring their self-worth against their perceived proximity to the social *institutions* of womanhood, specifically marriage and childbearing, sistahs find themselves measuring their self-worth against their perceived proximity to the social *standard* of womanhood, the figure of the white woman.

The sistahs' overarching search for self-worth is vividly illustrated as Bernadine and the other women in *Waiting* face the force of the "Ideal of White Womanhood" and its effects on their lives. As Robin says, "I hate the fact that they think white girls epitomize beauty and femininity" (177). After eleven years of marriage, two kids, and all of the trappings of middle-class success, Bernadine's husband John leaves her for a white woman:

> Now she looked over at her husband, thinking she had wanted to
> be rid of him, had been trying to conjure up the courage, the nerve,
> the guts, to tell *him* to leave, but she didn't have that much courage

> yet. All she wanted to do was repossess her life. To feel that sense of
> relief when the single most contributing factor to her uttermost
> source of misery was gone. But he beat her to the punch. Not only
> was he leaving *her*. Not only was he leaving her for another woman.
> He was leaving her for a *white* woman. Bernadine hadn't expected
> this kind of betrayal, this kind of insult. (26)

For Bernadine it is not the fact of divorce that stuns her, or the breaking of
the traditional family model—because that model is imprisoning
her—but rather the fact that her courage has failed her, even as her husband has failed her, and she's not even left with the satisfaction of controlling her own life *again*. This betrayal by her own sense of self-preservation
is compounded by John's betrayal of her by his complicity in the elevation
of white womanhood over black womanhood. But as the divorce drags on,
Bernadine uses John's underestimation of her and society's misrepresenta-
tion of black women to begin to regain her sense of self. We can see her
initial steps in the following conversation:

> "Look, Bernadine. Let's not let this thing get any uglier than it
> already has, okay? I've already given you the house. I'll pay what-
> ever the court tells me to make sure my kids are taken care of. But
> I'd be willing to give you three hundred thousand. Today. Cash.
> And we can be done with this whole thing."

> "You're the one who sounds delirious now. My pussy is worth more
> than three hundred thousand dollars. And, John, this is already as
> ugly as it can be." (131)

This brief exchange between John and Bernadine is not just about their
marriage. It represents larger assumptions regarding black womanhood
that historically have been used to deny black women their humanity and
a fair chance at self-determination. John tells her he has given the house to
her and will give any amount necessary to make sure *his* children are taken
care of, two moves that reestablish the long historical connection between
black women, domestic spaces, and children who are not their own, but to
whom their futures are ineluctably bound. The insult in this moment is
that these are *her* children, and this is *her* house, yet they still must be
bestowed on her by a misguided attempt at magnanimity. John further
attempts to rob Bernadine of power and self-worth by offering her money
to "be done with this whole thing," implying the insignificance with which
he regards the whole of their lives together. He disregards the weight
of Bernadine's own experience by "buying" her. But as she responds,

"My pussy is worth more than three hundred thousand dollars." Recognizing his reduction of her worth empowers her to lay bare the *true* thing he is trying to pay for—her body, as both childbearing vessel and sex object—and then to refuse him *finally*. She punctuates the moment by reminding him, as well as herself, that relinquishing her identity to the social constructions of motherhood, marriage, and black womanhood has already made their situation "as ugly as it can be."

In Bridget's very different search for self-worth, her sense of inferiority is determined by her distance from marriage. Her isolation is particularly reiterated in the presence of her married friends, who patronize her. She complains,

> On top of everything else, must go to Smug Married dinner party at Magda and Jeremy's tonight. Such occasions always reduce my ego to size of snail, which is not to say am not grateful to be asked. I love Magda and Jeremy. Sometimes I stay at their house, admiring the crisp sheets and many storage jars full of different kinds of pasta, imagining that they are my parents. But when they are together with their married friends I feel as if I have turned into Miss Havisham. (35)

With her married friends she feels at once childlike *and* spinsterly. Neither association brings her any closer to embracing marriage, except as the institution that will liberate her from her deviant and suspended social status. Meanwhile, the novel frequently suggests that marriage is *not* the way for a person to achieve completion: Bridget's mother has an affair of slapstick proportions; Mark Darcy is defined almost singularly by his divorce from a woman who cheated on him; and "smug married" Jeremy is having an affair. The ultimate irony is that Bridget gauges her self-worth by reference to marriage, while the behavior of the married people surrounding her is consistently less than admirable.

Ultimately, we can see the split between sistah lit and chick lit in the endings of *Waiting to Exhale* and *Bridget Jones's Diary*. In the face of all of these examples of flawed couplehood, Bridget's quest remains unchanged, and she is eventually "victorious" as she finds a boyfriend, the previously offensive Mark Darcy, and commends herself on "an excellent year's progress." One is left to wonder what her assessment of the year's progress would be without the achievement of a boyfriend. Ironically, it seems less like progression and more like regression, with Bridget's succumbing to traditional expectations for white womanhood: she is satisfied, fulfilled, and identified through the love and protection of a man.

On the other hand, *Waiting* ends with each woman finding a place to begin to stake her claim to self and happiness. Through their reliance on one another's strength, the four women of McMillan's story are able to discover themselves outside of the relationships to men, children, and physical beauty that they had let define them for so long. More than just a novel about modern black women finding empowerment and happiness, *Waiting to Exhale* is a narrative about the significance of the community of other black women that contributes to those processes of empowerment and searches for happiness. In McMillan's novels, as in much of sistah lit, the overarching theme is the power of the black female community and the importance of asserting and cherishing that power in a society that has often made it difficult to do just that. Unlike Fielding, whose final portrait of Bridget's becoming coupled with Mark Darcy marks a triumphant *end,* McMillan shows her four heroines' ultimate relationships to men (two of the women are basking in singleness and two of them are entering into new relationships) as *beginnings.*

When both novels were turned into blockbuster movies, their marketing campaigns revealed differences in both interpretation and audience. *Waiting to Exhale,* released in 1995, was marketed as a story about friends. The tagline made it clear what the audience should expect from the film: "Friends are the people who let you be yourself ... and never let you forget it." *Bridget Jones's Diary,* released in 2001, was marketed as a romantic comedy, as is evident in its tagline: "Uncensored. Uninhibited. Unmarried." Each movie was able to create worlds for its heroines that were at once universally recognizable and yet oddly racially specific. Bridget lived in a London where few blacks seemed to live, and, perhaps what is more remarkable, Savannah, Bernadine, Robin, and Gloria lived in an Arizona where few white people seemed to live. This creation of societies in racial vacuums delineated, quite starkly, the boundaries of gendered experience that are captured in the genres of chick lit and sistah lit.

Birds of a Feather?

The focus on the genres of chick lit and sistah lit in this essay does not hint at the myriad groups of women who are left unrepresented by the publishing powerhouse that is chick lit. Still, new types of popular fiction that speak to the modern gendered experiences of other groups, such as Chicana–Latinas (Alisa Valdes-Rodriguez) and lesbians (Cameron Abbott, Gerri Hill), are growing in popularity. Furthermore, sistah lit has spawned a new wave of African-American women writers who are confronting the *Sex & the City* syndrome, a version of popular ethnocentrism that assumes that women of color don't exist in urban worlds of glamour.[2] All of these new popular fictions for women are challenging the social naturalizing of chick identity—in popular, literary, and consumer culture.

But even as this newest wave of sistah lit opens up popular imagination to the idea of a population of black women who are upper class, couture wearing, trendsetting, and powerful, culturally and economically, the trajectories of chick lit and sistah lit remain divided. Though the women of both of these races have "come a long way, baby," black women have had to come farther. They have had to fight for the recognition of their womanhood after long histories of the United States denying their affiliation with the feminine gender through the systematic violence and exploitation of their bodies, and the ideological distortion of their image and worth in the national imagination. White women have never had to convince society of their womanhood, though they have had to convince it of their equality. It is these differences in social battles that have made the resulting perspectives of each of these groups of women on domestic institutions significantly separate, and so too, the literature that caters to them and their desires. Under the skin they are all women with many shared oppressions and aspirations, but *in* the skin is where society defines, and frequently, in the case of African-American women, *con*fines their place within it, necessitating that "sistahs do it for themselves."

Notes

1. Fielding's much less popular sequel, *The Edge of Reason*, does deal with Bridget as part of a couple, but specifically with the ways in which being in a couple is transformative, and not always in a good way.
2. For more on this new wave of black chick lit, see Ogunnaike.

Works Cited

Bridget Jones's Diary. Screenplay by Helen Fielding, Andrew Davies, and Richard Curtis. Dir. Sharon Maguire. Perf. Renee Zellweger, Hugh Grant, and Colin Firth. Miramax Films, 2001.
Fielding, Helen. *Bridget Jones's Diary*. New York: Penguin Books, 1999.
McMillan, Terry. *Waiting to Exhale*. New York: Pocket Books, 1993.
Ogunnaike, Lola. "Black Writers Seize the Glamorous Ground around Chick Lit." *New York Times*, May 31, 2004. <http://www.nytimes.com/2004/05/31/books/31CHIC.html>.
Waiting to Exhale. Dir. Forest Whitaker. Perf. Whitney Houston, Angela Bassett, Lela Rochon, and Loretta Devine. Twentieth Century Fox, 1995.

6

Long-Suffering Professional Females: The Case of Nanny Lit

ELIZABETH HALE

A relatively recent branch of chick lit, known as "underling lit" or "assistant lit," focuses on young women, usually recent college graduates from comfortable and cultured backgrounds, and their uneasy entrance into the culture of the professional workplace. In these works the iniquities of disagreeable employers are revealed and the lunacies of bureaucratic systems are exposed. The suffering and superior knowledge of the narrator heroine is ultimately rewarded by removal from the bad workplace and the discovery of a new, far more suitable career. Such literature belies its frothy packaging. On the cover, the heroine may be an elegantly stalky-legged, martini-clutching silhouette; in the pages of the novel, she mutates into a disheveled, wild-eyed, self-righteous narrator with a victim mentality who informs the reader of every slight she received during the course of working for the horrific boss whose antics supply much of the novel's material.

I do not find reading such novels to be relaxing; indeed, I finished two underling novels (*The Devil Wears Prada* and *The Nanny Diaries*) feeling as if I had spent several evenings counseling a distressed colleague whom there was no possibility of helping. I wondered where the empowering aspects of chick lit had gone, such as the ability to poke fun at the ironies of one's life and career, so entertainingly on offer in the novels of the late

1990s, such as those by Marian Keyes, Fiona Walker, or Helen Fielding. Underling lit, too, seemed to have undone the model of the 1980s, the empowering career-based bonk-busters of Barbara Taylor Bradford, Judith Krantz, or Jackie Collins, in which the underling swiftly overcomes her boss, replacing him or her with a new, superior style of management. Instead, the heroine of underling lit wins only by leaving her workplace for one where her talents are appreciated. I wondered why the best reward for enduring a terrible workplace was not to reform it but to leave it.

The answer may lie in the long-ago antecedents of underling lit. Where Jane Austen's sparkling wit and brilliant romance plotting may be the point of inspiration for much of chick lit (*Bridget Jones's Diary* being the most self-aware of this inspiration), the darker, more realistic model for underling lit comes from nineteenth-century realist *bildungsromanen* focusing on the travails of young professionals. *David Copperfield, Jane Eyre, The Professor, Nicholas Nickleby,* and *The Way of All Flesh* are some famous examples: their narratives outline their protagonists' progress from uncertain youth to assured adulthood and their transition in their professional lives, from newness to established authority. Many of them have autobiographical qualities, and most are marked by the underlying assumption that although work may be noble and satisfying, the competent professional is best rewarded by gaining financial independence: the best reward for working hard is not to have to work any more.

One nineteenth-century novel in particular exemplifies this trend, a trend that I believe resonates with turn-of-the-twenty-first-century chick lit. *Agnes Grey,* by Anne Brontë, a meticulously crafted, realist, and darkly humorous narrative of a young, gently bred woman's travails on entering the workforce as a governess, was overlooked by literary critics for many years, overshadowed by the more fantastic novels of Brontë's sisters.[1] In the past fifteen years, it has been rediscovered, reissued, and increasingly is the focus of literary study. It offers a model for thinking about work and the workplace that is compellingly similar to the underling-lit novels published in the past few years. To make this comparison, I will examine closely the recent underling-lit best-seller *The Nanny Diaries* (2002), by Nicola Kraus and Emma McLaughlin. Each of these novels has a governess–heroine; each exposes the exploitation that underpins the nannying situation; each analyses a female employer–employee relationship. And each exposes the complexities of the mother–nanny relationship, in which the nanny is hired to substitute for a mother, and in which the mother fails to live up to her parental role, as a mother to her child, and as a mother–employer to her nanny.

Agnes Grey and *The Nanny Diaries* are written by women who have undergone, in some measure at least, what their protagonists have suffered. Anne Brontë worked for a period of six years as a governess to a number of families before returning to live with her family at Haworth. Her first employers were the Ingham family of Blake Hall, with whom the Brontës had a connection through a mutual friend. She was with them for about nine months, before leaving by mutual agreement (their addiction to blood sports sat ill with her pacifism; in contrast, the family viewed her as "ungrateful"). Her second post was with the daughters of the Reverend Edmund Robinson, where she was somewhat happier (Harrison and Stanford 62 ff.). The authors of *The Nanny Diaries*, Emma McLaughlin and Nicola Kraus, became friends while studying at New York University and sharing their experiences working for more than thirty New York families (vii). Reviewers of *The Nanny Diaries* were quick to latch on to the roman-à-clef possibilities of each book, and although the authors deny that their novel corresponds exactly to specific real-life employers and incidents (presumably to avoid lawsuits), they nevertheless claim that it is true to life. I do not propose in this essay to analyze whether the novels I discuss are dishing real dirt. Instead, I am concerned with the way the novels convey their narrators' (and authors') sense of real disappointment in their workplaces and working lives, as well as offering them an outlet for their anger and even a measure of vengeance. If Nan and Agnes are exorcizing their work demons in their narratives, it is worth analyzing what exactly it is about their employers and the terms of their employment that makes them so angry. It cannot only be that their employers are callous and morally defective. Rather, the cause of much of the pain in these narratives may be the gap between the heroine's expectations (and fantasies) about her working life and the reality of work.

Self-Worth versus Job Status

A major source of anger in the novels is the gap between the protagonists' perception of their own value and their status in the workplace. Agnes and Nanny are low in the pecking order. Outside the workplace, their social pedigrees are at least equivalent to their employers': Agnes is the daughter of a lady and a clergyman, which gives her a higher rank than her nouveau-riche first employers; Nan's grandmother is a grande dame of New York society, whereas Mrs. X has merely married into wealth. As the novel progresses, we see that the nanny heroines claim to have superior moral values to their upper-class employers, a claim that is common in middle-class literature. At work, however, they are at the bottom of the pecking order, in unusual ways.

Agnes's position as a governess puts her in limbo: the fact that she has to work robs her of any claim to equal her employers, while her middle-class background puts her at one remove from the servants, a social irony that is well documented in novels of the period, and has been the subject of a number of recent studies.[2] Lady Elizabeth Eastlake, an early advocate for governesses, observed in 1848, "There is no other class which so cruelly requires its members to be, in birth, mind, and manners, above their station, in order to fit them for their station."[3] The irony of her situation results in what M. Jeanne Peterson calls "status incongruence": the governess is neither a servant nor a lady, and both her employers and her fellow employees shun her, compounding her lonely state, and rendering her job extremely difficult (5). At Horton Lodge it is clear that the servants despise Agnes and resent assisting her in any way. Some are better dressed than she is and condescend to her "with the air of ... conferring an unusual favour"; others are not "very respectful in their demeanour towards [her]" (57).[4] Meanwhile, the parents of the children whom Agnes is hired to instruct undermine her authority continually, spoiling her delightful fantasies about entering the workforce:

> How delightful it would be to be a governess! To go out into the world; to enter upon a new life; to act for myself; to exercise my unused faculties; to try my unknown powers; to earn my own maintenance. [...] I had but to turn from my little pupils to myself at their age, and I should know, at once, how to win their confidence and affections; how to waken the contrition of the erring; how to embolden the timid, and console the afflicted; how to make Virtue practicable, Instruction desirable, and Religion lovely and comprehensible. (9)

Not only do her charges have no intention of becoming virtuous or learned or of paying more than lip service to religion, they and their parents seem to poor Agnes to conspire actively against her doing her job properly. For example, Mrs. Bloomfield makes a point of referring to her children in Agnes's presence as "Master" and "Miss" Bloomfield, demonstrating to her children that Agnes is only a servant, effectively undermining Agnes's ability to control the children. Agnes complains,

> I had been very slow to take the hint, because the whole affair struck me as so very absurd; but now I determined to be wiser, and begin at once with as much form and ceremony as any member of the family would be likely to require: and, indeed, the children being so much older, there would be less difficulty; though the little words Miss and Master seemed to have a surprising effect in

repressing all familiar, open-hearted kindness, and extinguishing every gleam of cordiality that might arise between us. (58)

Agnes sees how the Bloomfields' snobbery prevents her from creating a bond of affection between herself and the children, and hence from being able to teach them well.

When she is working for the Murrays, however, she is surprised to find that Rosalie Murray, the eldest daughter, becomes very fond of her, at the same time as openly despising her for her lower social rank, with the effect that she fails to learn anything of significance:

> Towards me, when I first came, she was cold and haughty, then insolent and overbearing; but, on a further acquaintance, she gradually laid aside her airs, and in time became as deeply attached to me as it was possible for *her* to be to one of my character and position: for she seldom lost sight, for above half an hour at a time, of the fact of my being a hireling and a poor curate's daughter. (61)

Agnes does her best to impart a sense of virtue to the flighty Rosalie, but to little avail, owing to Rosalie's conviction of Agnes's inferiority. Such snobbery on Rosalie's part may be because Mrs. Murray has hitherto neglected the moral education of her children. Indeed, when she instructs Agnes in her duties, she seems set to continue:

> For the girls she seemed anxious only to render them as superficially attractive and showily accomplished as they could possibly be made, without present trouble or discomfort to themselves; and I was to act accordingly—to study and strive to amuse and oblige, instruct, refine, and polish, with the least possible exertion on their part, and no exercise of authority on mine. (60)

Mrs. Murray further compromises Agnes's authority by advising her that she is not to admonish the children herself, as it would violate the appropriate boundaries of her position: "Remember, on all occasions, when any of the young people do anything improper, if persuasion and gentle remonstrance will not do, let one of the others come and tell me; for I can speak to them more plainly than it would be proper for you to do" (61). Well might Agnes sound bitter when she observes that she is expected to educate the Murray children "with the least possible exertion on their part, and no exercise of authority on mine" (60). Thus the skills and knowledge that Agnes has been hired to impart, which she believes should give her sufficient authority over her charges, are rendered worthless because of her perceived social inferiority.

Across the Atlantic, 150 years later, Nanny Drew is fighting a similar battle with Mr. and Mrs. X, social-climbing Manhattanites who have hired her as a nanny to their four-year-old son, Grayer. Nan, whose social credentials include solidly middle-class parents, is a graduate of the prestigious Chapin School, supporting herself through her degree in arts in education and child psychology at New York University by taking a series of nannying jobs. She is aware that her background makes her more comfortably off than many other child care workers, often immigrants in difficult positions, such as Sima, an engineer from San Salvador, who sends money back each month to her husband and children, or Murnel, from the West Indies. These workers' lives are hostage to their employers' demands (47 ff and 173 ff). Although the main focus of *The Nanny Diaries* is Nan's narrative, the authors take pains to make it clear that Nanny's situation is rather easier than some and to make serious points about the exploitation of immigrant workers. As she dryly observes, at first her class and race make her more desirable to employers: "Nanny Fact: in every one of my interviews, references are never checked. I am white. I speak French. My parents are college educated. I have no visible piercings and have been to Lincoln Center in the last two months. I'm hired" (4).[5]

Nevertheless, Nan is sufficiently exploited herself, to create a narrative that painfully belies the claim made by the novel's blurb that "Funny, touching and true-to-life, *The Nanny Diaries* is a modern-day Mary Poppins story—with attitude."[6] Like Agnes Grey, Nanny Drew's expertise as a child caregiver is ignored and undermined by her employers, and she is often reminded of her lowly position in the servants' hierarchy. For instance, when it's time for the Christmas bonus, while the Xs' other employees get "money *and* a handbag," Nanny is insulted to receive earmuffs instead of the requisite "hefty Christmas bonus," recognition for putting in "so much extra time" (121). Nanny never receives this recognition; she is also poorly paid for a part-time job that stretches at short notice, and seemingly at random, to full-time.

Although Nan has a measure of authority over her charge, Grayer—after an initial rocky adjustment period, they have a warm relationship—Mrs. X undermines Nan's methods of dealing with the four-year-old, calling her knowledge and skills into question on a number of occasions. The most spectacular of these is the occasion when Grayer's application to "Collegiate," a prestigious private elementary school, is rejected. Although Grayer has not been consulted on whether he would like to attend, the application has gone in, and his mother has presented Grayer with a Collegiate sweatshirt, which he has insisted on wearing nearly every day.

To Nan's surprise, she is blamed for Grayer's potential "disappointment" at his rejection, because she has allowed him to wear the sweatshirt:

> "I'm concerned that your encouragement of his fixation on Collegiate may have set him up for a potentially deleterious self-esteem adjustment."
>
> "I—"
>
> "No, please don't feel bad. It's really my fault for allowing you to do it. I should have been more on top of you." (175)

To be more "on top" of Nanny, Mrs. X arranges for a "Long-Term Development Consultant" to interview herself and Mr. X, Grayer, and Nanny. Nanny's interview is a humiliating, jargon-filled put-down fest in which her performance is assessed and found wanting. As Nanny disentangles the jargon and gives hesitant answers, answers that demonstrate her real knowledge of the little boy, Jane, the Long-Term Development Consultant, sighs and "scribbles furiously on her pad" (178). And when Nanny reveals that she is not, in fact, using an Apparel Chart to help Grayer pick out his clothes or "documenting his choices with him on a Closet Diagram" or "having him translate his colors and sizes into the Latin" (179), Jane announces that she has to "question whether you're leveraging your assets to escalate Grayer's performance. ... I understand you are getting your degree in arts-in-education so, frankly, I'm surprised by the lack of depth surrounding your knowledge base here" (179).

Nanny's explanation that although she wants to help educate Grayer, he is, in fact, "really stressed out right now," and that "the best thing I can give him is some downtime so that his imagination can grow without being forced in one direction or another" receives a skeptical reaction (179–80). To the consultant, and to Mrs. X, understanding and reacting to Grayer on the level of his emotional needs is incomprehensible, and Nanny is sharply reminded to focus harder on bringing Grayer to his "optimal state" (180).

In contrast to Agnes Grey, who works with almost unlovable children and whose attempts to educate them are futile, here Nanny's ability to love and understand Grayer is undermined and undervalued, a point that I think can be given a class coding. The implication in Jane the Consultant's diatribe, and in Mrs. X's comments throughout the book, is that Nanny's emotional attachment to Grayer (and his to her) is somehow déclassé, inappropriate for the son of an X. Nan, who is helpless to stop the rampant and destructive social ambition of Mrs. X or the emotional absence of Mr. X, is also helpless to heal the emotional scarring of Grayer, who has been subjected to a string of nannies, replaced without notice or explanation, so low is their status and so insecure are their jobs. It is only a matter of time, too, until Nanny is replaced, continuing the damage. For both Agnes and Nanny, then, governessing or nannying is a losing battle for the young woman who tries to impart sound middle-class values (such as the value of manners, an education, and a loving family) to the aristocrats of their world, for whom social climbing is more important than their children.

"Are You My Mother?" Female Bosses without Maternal Streaks

The mothers of Agnes and Nan would be surprised to hear that their daughters are spoiled. After all, they brought them up carefully, provided them with moral fiber, self-respect, cultural capital, and ambition. And they have been rewarded with intelligent, driven daughters, who still seek their advice, no mean feat in the world of chick lit, where mothers tend to be monstrous or exasperatingly daffy. Mrs. Grey, Agnes's mother, is a gentlewoman from a wealthy family who has married beneath her: marrying a mere parson for love, and becoming an excellent wife and doyenne of the parish.[7] Mrs. Drew, who is rather less clearly depicted, is nevertheless strong-minded and resourceful, and an excellent mother, who provides sound advice and support when her troubled daughter needs it. These solid mothering forces, then, provide our heroines with strong role models and an idealized vision of what mothers should be like. Having had good mothers, they assume that all mothers are equally good, and they are inclined to judge other styles of mothering as defective.

Agnes and Nan, who are hired as substitute mothers, judge their employers harshly in these terms. When Agnes arrives at her first governessing post with the Bloomfields, she is very disappointed by the reception she receives from Mrs. Bloomfield. She had hoped that if her new employer were "warm" and "motherly," she would get on very well: instead, Mrs. Bloomfield is as "chilly" as the servants' quarters in her establishment, and her supercilious gaze infantilizes Agnes, though such infantilization is not accompanied by any maternal warmth. Such warmth is available only to her children, whom she dotingly spoils, shifting the responsibility of discipline unfairly onto Agnes. Matters come to a head when Agnes discovers Tom Bloomfield, the spoiled eldest son, preparing to torture a nest of baby sparrows. A passionate advocate of animal rights, like her author, Agnes feels forced to kill the nestlings with a large rock, rather than allow them to be tortured inhumanely by the boy. She confidently expects that Mrs. Bloomfield will uphold such moral instruction in this instance but is stunned to be blamed for spoiling the boy's pleasure.

"I think," said she, "a child's amusement is scarcely to be weighed against the welfare of a soulless brute."

"But, for the child's own sake, it ought not to be encouraged to have such amusements," answered I, as meekly as I could, to make up for such unusual pertinacity.

"Blessed are the merciful, for they shall obtain mercy."

"Oh, of course! But that refers to our conduct towards each other." *"The merciful man shews mercy to his beast,"* I ventured to add.

"I think *you* have not shewn much mercy," replied she, with a short, bitter laugh, "killing the poor birds by wholesale, in that shocking manner, and putting the dear boy to such misery, for a mere whim!"

I judged it prudent to say no more. (45–46)

Not long after this conversation, Agnes is dismissed by Mrs. Bloomfield, who informs her that "Though superior to most children of their years in abilities, [her children] were uncultivated and their tempers unruly. And this she attributed to a want of sufficient firmness and diligent, persevering care on my part" (47). Thus Agnes, who has prided herself specifically on her "unshaken firmness, devoted diligence, unwearied perseverance, [and] unceasing care," is dismissed for failing to correct the very faults in the Bloomfield children that their mother has refused to acknowledge and has hindered her from disciplining.

However, as Dara Rossman Regaignon points out, Mrs. Bloomfield is right to dismiss Agnes (86–108). Agnes's gentle ways are so unlikely to succeed with the children and her moral code is so at odds with the prevailing ethics of the household that clashes are inevitable; indeed, in the encounter above, Agnes refuses to subordinate her wishes to her employer's. Such clashes were inevitable in the governess's life, not merely because of the inconsistencies of her class position, and that of her charges, but also because of the complexities of her role as a substitute mother. In *Agnes Grey,* Mrs. Bloomfield and, later, Mrs. Murray (and Mrs. X in *The Nancy Diaries*) have proved themselves to be inadequate mothers, simply by having to hire an outsider to do work that they should do themselves, and yet they seem to view themselves in competition with Agnes to bring up their children.[8] The governess, or the nanny, is thus prevented from fulfilling her role by the woman who has hired her to do it. Such women are not merely bad mothers, they are also bad employers. For example, Mrs. Murray's maternal instincts extend only to the comfort of her children, at least theoretically, while she spells out to Agnes how she will maintain it, and not to the comfort of her newest employee, as Agnes notes sardonically:

> While Mrs. Murray was so extremely solicitous for the comfort and happiness of her children, and continually talking about it, she never once mentioned mine; though they were at home, surrounded by friends, and I an alien among strangers; and I did not yet know enough of the world, not to be considerably surprised at this anomaly. (61)

Mrs. Murray would be considerably surprised to learn that Agnes expects her to be "motherly." This lack of maternal instinct explains the Murrays' and the Bloomfields' failure to understand that as employers they are *in loco parentis* to their employees. They thus fail to live up to the aristocratic standards of *noblesse oblige* increasingly located, in Victorian times, in the values of the middle classes.[9]

It has now become commonplace for middle-class readers to turn with delight to stories that reveal the moral bankruptcy of the extremely rich. "I suspected as much!" we cry triumphantly to ourselves as we discover the emotional vacuum at the heart of what Kraus and McLaughlin call the "Midwest of Manhattan," the wealthy avenues where the population density shrinks in proportion to the swelling of the apartments' floor space. We are unsurprised to discover that the fragile, lilac-clad Mrs. X of the initial chapters is as steely in her resolve to parade her son as a trophy in front of her social circle as she is to avoid spending time with him. She pays lip service to the idea of bringing up a child, in her elaborate planning of the "right" kind of improving activities and after-school events for Grayer, down to her choice of bedtime reading ("one verse from your Shakespeare reader" [220]) and dinner ("he loves Coquilles Saint-Jacques" [56]), and her obsession with getting him into the prestigious elementary school, Collegiate. But she is absent at critical moments, such as when she spends a week at a spa resort while Grayer is severely ill. When his fever develops into croup, Nanny is unable to reach Mrs. X because, the receptionist at the spa informs her, she is "in a sensory-deprivation tank all day" (140). In desperation, Nanny calls her own mother, who calmly identifies the problem and solution (steam inhalation, to calm his wheezing). As they sit together in a steamy bathroom, Grayer cries into Nanny's shoulder: " 'I ... want ... my mommmmmmmm.' He shudders with the effort, seemingly unaware that I am here. My pajama pants soak in the warm water. I drop my head against his, rocking slowly. Tears of exhaustion and worry drip down my face and into his hair. 'Oh, Grove [Nanny's nickname for Grayer], I know. I want my mom, too' " (141).

The contrast between Mrs. X and Nan's own mother is made explicit on a number of occasions, both in terms of their maternalism and in terms of their professionalism. Mrs. Drew coaches Nan in employee–employer negotiations when the job demands start to spiral out of control, and she gives Nan a friendly kick in the pants when her obsession with her exploitation by the Xs threatens to ruin her and their Christmas (121). She provides a stable model for Nan, as a self-sufficient woman, and as part of a happily married liberal and artistic couple, and a successful mother herself. In contrast, Mrs. X, who stole Mr. X from his previous wife, is distraught at the signs that he is straying once more (Nanny wastes a great deal of time trying to hide the evidence of his infidelity from Mrs. X), and she uses Grayer as a weapon to keep the unit together (another clear indication of her moral defectiveness). While the family, with Nanny unwillingly in tow, is on holiday on Nantucket Island, she manipulates Mr. X into impregnating her, thus forcing the family unit to remain together, at least for a few more years.

Mrs. X's second pregnancy sounds the death knell for Nanny's job with the family; she's unceremoniously dumped at the ferry terminal within what seems like minutes of the announcement, sacked with the following words:

> Frankly, Nanny, I just don't feel that your heart's in it anymore and I think Grayer can sense that, too. We need someone who can give Grayer their full commitment, don't you agree? I mean, for the money we're paying you, with the new baby coming, we should really have someone more professional. (295)

Masterfully blaming Nanny for her own halfheartedness, Mrs. X is not merely replacing her with "someone more professional," she is also getting rid of someone who has simply witnessed too much—the cracks in the marriage, the moral bankruptcy, the exploitation of their child. And when Nanny, who is genuinely appalled that Mrs. X would want to stay with her philandering husband, clumsily tries to warn her about his mistress, she is dismissed: " 'You fucking child.' She comes back at me ... with all the force of years of suppressed rage and humiliation. '*You. Have no idea. What you're talking about. Is that clear?*' Each word feels like a punch. 'And I'd be very careful. If I were you. How you regard our family—' " (296). She is interrupted by Mr. X's honking the car horn, ready to whisk Nanny off to the ferry terminal.

The sexual politics of *The Nanny Diaries* are more explicit than those in *Agnes Grey*: clearly Mrs. X is fighting with the viciousness of the desperately unhappy to keep her worthless marriage.[10] The crux of the tragedy, however, is summed up by Grayer's urgent cries, which echo through the house as she leaves: " 'NAAAANNNNYYY! *I NEEEEEED YOU!* ' " (297). Nan observed in the prologue to the novel, "Looking back, it was a setup to begin with. They want you. You want the job. But to do it well is to lose it" (12). To "do it well" Nanny must love, and be loved by, the child whom she will have to leave when she inevitably loses the job; to do it well she must supplant her employer, the defective mother who has hired her, which will result in her firing. Tellingly, the novel's dedication underscores the connection between good nannying and good parenting: "To our parents, for always reading at least one bedtime story (with voices) no matter how tuckered out they were. And to all the fabulous kids who have danced, giggled, and hiccupped their way into our hearts. We root for you still" (v).

Sticky Endings and Damp Squibs

Perhaps the most disturbing aspect of *The Nanny Diaries* and *Agnes Grey* is the heroine's inability to stand up for herself. Despite Nanny's assertiveness training sessions with her mother, in which she practices stating her needs and limits to the Xs, Nanny is constantly interrupted and silenced, reduced to the inarticulacy of a timid child. And when, in the middle of the family holiday to Nantucket, the Xs fire her, leaving her virtually stranded, she is hustled out of the house before she can object in any meaningful way. Back in Manhattan, on discovering that she has been paid $500 instead of the $1,900 she is owed, she lets herself into their silent apartment. "I switch on the brass lamps, as if illuminating their home will shed some light on how I could have worked so hard and been hated so much" (300). Flicking through Mrs. X's calendar, she discovers that the Xs had been interviewing new nannies well before the Nantucket trip. Finally, after enduring three hundred pages of exploitation in silence, Nanny is sufficiently outraged to speak up for herself. She goes to Grayer's bedroom, and sets the Nanny-cam (that she has recently discovered the Xs have installed to spy on her) to record, running through all the abuse and neglect and warped priorities she has been witness to during the course of the novel. But her anger soon evaporates, she rewinds the tape, and, true to self-effacing form, leaves a short, caring message to the Xs, warning them that they are running out of time with Grayer, who "won't love you unconditionally that much longer. And soon he won't love you at all. So if there's one thing I could do for you tonight, it would be to give you the desire to know him. ... I really cherished him. And I want that for you. For both of you, because it's just, well, priceless" (305). Nanny characterizes her parting message as "leaving with grace" (305): she rises above the pettiness that has marked her employment with the Xs, demonstrating once again her moral superiority. Nevertheless, the lack of confrontation or resolution in this novel is hard to take, particularly given the demands of the fantasy chick-lit genre. Although it is clear that Nanny has a good job lined up, having graduated with distinction, and that she is well provided for emotionally, having found a boyfriend who shares her cultural capital and socialist leanings, it is nonetheless disappointing that her tenure at the Xs' dribbles to a halt in such a way.

In "leaving with grace," Nanny behaves like Agnes Grey, who, rather than challenging her employers, draws her virtue tightly around her like a protective shield and makes a virtue out of self-sufficiency in the face of isolation (Knapp 63–73). Thus, while she has retained her dignity, rigor, and standards, she fails to instill them in her charges or their parents. Agnes's employment at her mother's school is a happy period: the children are eager to learn, her mother presumably having winnowed them out from applicants, and, significantly, they are removed from the disruptive influence of their parents. *Agnes Grey* implies that children are far easier to teach when they are not surrounded by the distractions and contradictory advice of the family. The novel suggests, too, that unless the governess is employed by parents who share her values and educational standards, the governessing system is guaranteed to fail. In fact, the best educator is the good mother. Agnes is granted a happy ending by her author, in which, like Nanny, she finds a partner who shares her faith and views: the novel ends with Agnes's telling us that she has become the mother of two girls and a boy, whom she delights in educating.

Agnes Grey and Nanny Drew thus gain happy endings that reward them for their endurance in the workplace. But it is noticeable that each is removed from her dysfunctional job before she has to act on her desire to leave. Nanny is fired before she can hand in her notice; Agnes's mother effectively makes the decision for her. The implication is that the workplace can never be changed, at least as far as employers are concerned; instead of examining their own responsibilities, Mrs. X and Mrs. Bloomfield will continue to bemoan the difficulty of getting good staff, and Rosalie Murray will replicate her own vain, dilettantish mother's behavior, while ignoring Agnes's sensible advice. It is far better for the unhappy employee to absent herself from the scene of bad employment.

Thus the underling lit I have discussed here lacks the kind of satisfying revenge or comeuppance scenes that can be seen in such workplace films as *Working Girl* or in *Bridget Jones's Diary*. Even though novels such as *The Devil Wears Prada* and *The Nanny Diaries* are best-sellers, their damp-squib endings sit ill with readers, who wonder where the reward is in reading novels that, far from being escapist fantasies, become stressful and frustrating reading. Their desire for Nanny and even Agnes to stand up for themselves and to take revenge on their employers can be summed up by the review of *The Nanny Diaries* by "beatchik-books":

> The only reason I kept reading this book was to get to the point where Nanny told the Xes off. And when it never happened, I realized that I hated this book. Sure, some of it was funny, but mostly it was sad. Sad for the kid, sad for the puppy, but mostly sad that anyone would put up with all the crap and never say her piece. The whole bit about grace at the end was a crock.

It is indeed frustrating to wait for the underling narrator to "say her piece" to her employers. But perhaps this desire for escapist fantasy is unrealistic, first on the grounds of truth to life (how many young women, and men for that matter, slide away from unrewarding or exploitative first jobs into better workplaces, without voicing their complaints?), and second, because each novel does in fact allow its author to speak for herself. Despite the fact that Kraus and McLaughlin deny that there is one specific Mrs. X, readers have played guessing games, identifying various New Yorkers. If underling lit does not allow the protagonist to take revenge, it at least allows the former underling writer to make some sharp points, as Janet Maslin comments in her review of *The Nanny Diaries*: "Sorry, Madam, but your worst nightmare has arrived. It appears that the help has been taking notes, and good ones. The help is very sharp-eyed indeed." Indeed, such novels may cause a number of employers some uncomfortable moments, and may even go some way to encouraging the reform of an abusive industry. Anne Brontë's novels were surely uncomfortable for Victorian readers, because they realistically exposed the abuses of servants, animals, and governesses, and were part of a general movement toward improving conditions for a wide range of workers. The revenge that is possible in these novels is of the literary, rather than any other, kind. Anne Brontë refines her and her sister's governessing experiences into a novel that explicitly exposes the abuses that occur among families who hire governesses. Nicola Kraus and Emma McLaughlin boil down the more than thirty families they have nannied for, and the myriads more they have heard stories about, into the Xs (thus causing panic among the nanny hirers of the Upper West Side). Thus, although the narratives of Agnes Grey and Nanny Drew fail to deliver the kind of excitement generated by a confrontation, the fact that they are written at all offers a kind of revenge, and may result in reform that goes wider than the specific targets.

In his acerbic *The Way of All Flesh* (written 1870, published 1901), Samuel Butler suggested that Victorian public schoolmasters pay close attention to their behavior to pupils, lest they end up realistically depicted in memoirs:

> O schoolmasters—if any of you read this book—bear in mind when any particularly timid drivelling urchin is brought by his papa into your study, and you treat him with the contempt which he deserves, and afterwards make his life a burden to him for years—bear in mind that it is exactly in the disguise of such a boy as this that your future chronicler will appear. Never see a wretched little heavy-eyed mite sitting on the edge of a chair against your study wall without saying to yourselves, "perhaps this boy is he who, if I am not careful, will one day tell the world what manner of man I was." If even two or three schoolmasters learn this lesson and remember it, the preceding chapters will not have been written in vain. (148)

The grim details of *The Nanny Diaries* carry on the work of *Agnes Grey* in exposing and commenting on workplace abuse. Its failure to depict the *reform* of the workplace should not be taken as novelistic failure, or even as the failure of girl power. Rather, it offers a broader, darker, and even more realistic set of boundaries for chick lit to operate within; boundaries, perhaps, that those involved with the packaging, marketing, and even the reading of chick lit need to take account of. If they do, perhaps these novels will not have been written in vain.

Notes

1. For example, Kathryn Hughes, in her critical work *The Victorian Governess*, makes almost no mention of *Agnes Grey*, though she devotes some time to the much less realistic *Jane Eyre*.
2. See, for example, M. Jeanne Peterson's essay "The Victorian Governess: Status Incongruence in Family and Society" in *Suffer and Be Still: Women in the Victorian Age* (pp. 3–19); Kathryn Hughes's *The Victorian Governess;* James Simmons's essay "Class, Matriarchy, and Power: Contextualizing the Governess in *Agnes Grey*"; or Dara Rossman Regaignon's "Instructive Sufficiency: Re-reading the Governess through *Agnes Grey.*"
3. Elizabeth Eastlake, "*Vanity Fair, Jane Eyre,* and the Governesses' Benevolent Institution," *Quarterly Review* 84 (December 1848): 176 (qtd. in Peterson 11).
4. Eastlake observes, "The servants invariably detest [the governess], for she is a dependant like themselves, and yet, for all that, as much their superior in other respects as the family they both serve" (qtd. in Peterson 15).
5. The novel has been cited in the growing movement to unionize among U.S. household workers. See Chisun Lee's *Women Raise the City* series in the *Village Voice,* especially "Domestic Disturbance: The Help Set out to Help Themselves," April 3–9, 2002.

6. The marketing of this novel borders on false advertising: I and many readers (see, for instance, the bulk of reviews on Amazon.com) found this novel excruciatingly sad. Not to mention that Mary Poppins has far more "attitude" than the downtrodden Nanny.

7. Though she steps down a rung or two in the social ladder, in the economy of the novel, she steps up a rung or two in the moral ladder: by marrying for love, rather than money, she conforms to middle-class romantic goals. Her birth family responds by cutting her off, thus reinforcing Agnes's prejudices against aristocratic models of behavior.

8. See James Simmons, "Class, Matriarchy, and Power: Contextualizing the Governess in *Agnes Grey*."

9. Robin Gilmour's *The Idea of the Gentleman in the Victorian Novel* traces the adoption of aristocratic ideals of gentility by nineteenth-century middle classes.

10. Another area in which the middle classes vaunt their superiority over the aristocracy is the attitude to marriage. The happy and faithful marriages of Nanny's and Agnes's parents are contrasted with the infidelity and chilliness of aristocratic unions.

Works Cited

Beatchik-books. "A Sad Story, Really." Rev. of *The Nanny Diaries*. Amazon.com. 14, Nov. 2003.

Butler, Samuel. *The Way of All Flesh*. Harmondsworth: Penguin, 1966.

Gilmour, Robin. *The Idea of the Gentleman in the Victorian Novel*. London: Allen & Unwin, 1981.

Harrison, Ada, and Derek Stanford. *Anne Brontë: Her Life and Work*. London: Methuen, 1959.

Hughes, Kathryn. *The Victorian Governess*. London: Hambledon, 1993.

Knapp, Bettina L. "Anne Brontë's *Agnes Grey*: The Feminist 'I Must Stand Alone.' " *New Approaches to the Literary Art of Anne Brontë*. Ed. Julie Nash and Barbara A. Suess. Aldershot, England: Ashgate, 2001. 63–73.

Kraus, Nicola, and Emma McLaughlin. *The Nanny Diaries*. Harmondsworth: Penguin, 2002.

Lee, Chisun. "The Help Set out to Help Themselves." *Village Voice* 3–9, Apr. 2002.

Maslin, Janet. "Ex-Nannies Skewer Lives of the Rich." *Detroit Free Press* 31, Mar. 2001.

Peterson, M. Jeanne. "The Victorian Governess: Status Incongruence in Family and Society." *Suffer and Be Still: Women in the Victorian Age*. Ed. Martha Vicinus. Bloomington: Indiana University Press, 1973. 3–19.

Regaignon, Dara Rossman. "Instructive Sufficiency: Re-reading the Governess through *Agnes Grey*." *Victorian Literature and Culture* 29.1 (2001): 85–108.

Simmons, James. "Class, Matriarchy, and Power: Contextualizing the Governess in *Agnes Grey*." *New Approaches to the Literary Art of Anne Brontë*. Ed. Julie Nash and Barbara A. Suess. Aldershot, England: Ashgate, 2001. 25–43.

7

You Are Not Alone: The Personal, the Political, and the "New" Mommy Lit

HEATHER HEWETT

Six years after the initial publication of *Bridget Jones's Diary*, Allison Pearson's *I Don't Know How She Does It: The Life of Kate Reddy, Working Mother* appeared in the United States.[1] Pearson's novel, a darkly comic tale of one woman's frenzied attempt to have it all, was quickly heralded as the next step for chick lit, the story of Bridget Jones after she got married and had children. Like the essay collection *The Bitch in the House: 26 Women Tell the Truth about Sex, Solitude, Work, Motherhood, and Marriage*, which was also published in 2002, Pearson's book struck a chord among readers. Decades-long debates about motherhood and work were reignited, and both books spent time on best-seller lists, Pearson's for eleven weeks. Journalists and critics discussed Kate Reddy, at times as though she were a real person, in publications such as the *New York Times, USA Today, Business Week, Time, People*, and Salon.com.[2] Pearson sold the movie rights to Miramax. Mommy lit was born.

Not to be left behind, other publishing houses followed suit, with titles such as Jane Green's *Babyville*, Laura Wolf's *Diary of a Mad Mom-to-Be*, Fiona Gibson's *Babyface*, and Danielle Crittenden's *Amanda Bright@Home*. Like Pearson's novel, they featured fallible but likeable narrators (all middle class and white) who, although overwhelmed by diapers, lack of sleep, and incompetent husbands, managed to survive the self-transformation into motherhood without losing their sense of humor (at least, not permanently).[3] Like chick lit, the plot of these books centered on their heroine's quest.[4] But the mommy heroine, unlike her single counterpart, isn't on the prowl for Mr. Right. She is, instead, on a journey from womanhood to motherhood, and her challenge lies in integrating her new role into her former identity. And because she's accustomed to spending her days at the office—for the mommy-lit heroine used to be a working girl, like the heroines of chick lit—this struggle manifests itself in the task of reconciling work with motherhood.

If anyone was the target audience, it was me. I was a middle-class, thirtysomething white woman who was pregnant for the first time. I was, to put it mildly, apprehensive about all the changes to come. I'd spent much of my adult life worrying about what would happen to my career, my development as a writer, and my marriage when I became a mother. Although I knew it was a luxury to worry about these things, it did not always feel like a luxury; having witnessed my own mother engage in a terrible, self-destructive struggle to reconcile work, an artistic career, and parenthood, I wasn't at all certain it could be done with one's sanity (and family) left intact. At the same time, I was excited about becoming a mother, and my personal anticipation was at least a little heightened by the sense that "everyone" was having a baby—not only the other women in the streets of New York, where I lived, but also Miranda on *Sex and the City,* Rachel on *Friends,* and Brooke Shields on the cover of *Vogue.* Motherhood certainly seemed to be all the rage: it was featured in the cover stories of magazines such as *Time,* the *New York Times Magazine,* and *New York;* it was the topic of books such as Sylvia Ann Hewlett's *Creating a Life: Professional Women and the Quest for Children* and Julie Shields's *How to Avoid the Mommy Trap: A Roadmap for Sharing Parenting and Making It Work.*[5] But while these books and articles were supposed to be helpful, they served only to make me more anxious. They all seemed to confirm my worst fears: that balancing work and motherhood was at best a very, very difficult task, and at worst impossible.

I was not alone in my anxiety. In *The Mommy Myth: The Idealization of Motherhood and How It Has Undermined Women,* scholars Susan Douglas and Meredith Michaels argue that a wide array of cultural phenomena over the past thirty years—media stories about celebrity moms, welfare mothers, and abusive day care workers; an explosion of parenting books and magazines; the right-wing propaganda campaign to redomesticate women; the popularity of attachment parenting—has created an ideology of motherhood, the "new momism," which has increased the standard of what it takes to be a good mother to unattainable heights. The new momism is the "insistence that no woman is truly complete or fulfilled unless she has kids, that women remain the best primary caretakers of children, and that to be a remotely decent mother, a woman has to devote her entire physical, psychological, emotional, and intellectual being, 24/7, to her children" (Douglas and Michaels 4). It represents a backlash against many of the changes brought on by the feminist movement, and its power lies in its ability to make women experience a "thick, sedimented layer of guilt, fear, and anxiety" surrounding motherhood (14). I wasn't a mother yet, and already I was feeling like I had to dig myself out from under several strata of worry and concern.

As my due date quickly approached, I became more and more apprehensive. I found myself craving books on the subject of motherhood, but not books that made me feel worse (I'd already been made to feel guilty for eating—horrors—a bran muffin by What to Expect When You're Expecting). I wanted something else: the stories of other mothers, their collective wisdom, and the bigger picture of motherhood in America. Fortunately, there were plenty of books to choose from. I started with the moms in The Bitch in the House and searched the library and bookstores for more: Anne Lamott's memoir Operating Instructions: A Journal of My Son's First Year, Rachel Cusk's memoir A Life's Work: On Becoming a Mother, and Ann Crittenden's The Price of Motherhood: Why the Most Important Job in the World Is Still the Least Valued. I noticed, as I devoured these books and the discussions about them, that journalists and critics were increasingly using "mommy lit" to describe what I was reading.[6] Apparently mommy lit encompassed more than Pearson's novel and the genre fiction written by those who came after her. The only requirement seemed to be that it explored the "real" experience of motherhood honestly, without sentimentality or idealization or judgment, from the point of view of the mother.[7] And more often than not, it circled around the issues of work, identity, and motherhood.

Of course, much of the expansion of this category was driven by marketing: publishers wanted to garner press attention and sell copies, and mommy lit was hot. But at the same time, the outpouring of writing about motherhood, much of it predating Pearson's novel—mommy memoirs, mommy manifestos, mommy humor, mommy anthologies—suggests that something else was at work.[8] Two new publications—Hip Mama and Brain, Child: The Magazine for Thinking Mothers—were founded in a deliberate attempt to provide an alternative to the advice- and service-oriented mainstream parenting magazines.[9] In 1997 the Internet magazine Salon launched the department Mothers Who Think, providing a forum for writers to debate the issues surrounding motherhood. These were joined by playful zines such as memoirist

Ayun Halliday's *The East Village Inky*. Finally, increasing numbers of mothers began posting their stories on personal Web logs and creating communities on Internet sites such as Hip Mama, Literary Mama, and Mommy Too! Magazine.[10]

True, women had been writing about motherhood for more than a century, but the latest incarnation of mommy lit, which dates to the early 1990s and continues through the present moment, represents a veritable eruption of mothers' voices opining on diapers, breast-feeding, and maternity leave. On the one hand, then, mommy lit does not represent an entirely "new" genre, as the publishers would have us believe, but it does, in fact, differ from what came before in several respects. Although much of it continues to be written by white, middle-class women, this has begun to change, as the voices of working-class mothers and mothers of all ethnicities—plus single, queer, and teenage mothers—have claimed a space, found publishers, and stormed the Internet. As opposed to the poetry and fiction of previous generations, autobiographical writing and the "memoir" are increasingly popular genres. The stories told by these writers—about struggles with ambivalence and self-doubt, bouts with depression, searches for a new self-identity—often feel familiar, though today's writers have more latitude to take on taboo subjects. In their unmasking of the still-powerful myths of motherhood, this wave of writers frequently challenges the dictates of parenting manuals and the sentimental images in mainstream mothering magazines; and like their foremothers, they make use of anger and rage as well as humor, irony, and satire in their commentaries on contemporary child-rearing culture. Yet in spite of decades of feminism, many of them find themselves writing about similar issues as their predecessors: the pain of living in a world that pits mothering against work and self-fulfillment, and the joy of finding connections between mothering and the outside world.[11]

Mommy lit, then, is the latest incarnation of what Jane Smiley calls the "literature of real, live motherhood," which she contrasts with literature written from the point of view of the child (14). As such, it provides us with a powerful lens onto late-twentieth- and early-twenty-first-century motherhood in the United States. Given that we find ourselves in a period of heightened anxiety surrounding motherhood, as Douglas and Michaels assert, what does mommy lit reveal to us about our fixations, our needs, and our fears? What does the current surge of writing about motherhood tell us about our relationship to feminism, our families, and our careers? If much of mommy lit is personal, is it political? Is its use of humor? And what does it have to tell us about trying to have it all?

Having It All? The Juggling Act of Kate Reddy, Working Mother

I Don't Know How She Does It follows the life of Kate Reddy, a successful thirty-five-year-old hedge-fund manager at Edwin Morgan Forster, an investment bank in London's financial district, and harried mother of two young children. Kate's sharp, witty observations of her puerile office mates and her boss (who fortunately responds well to techniques borrowed from *Toddler Taming*) and clueless in-laws (who are scandalized to hear that Kate is the breadwinner of her family) feel very Bridget Jones–like. Like Fielding's satire, Pearson's is essentially an Austenesque comedy of manners, albeit one that begins after the happy ending, when the heroine has settled down with her Mark Darcy. Some of the same elements of Fielding's novel appear in Pearson's: both unfold in the office as well as at home, and both feature a narrator who, while prone to self-recrimination and self-doubt, manages to laugh at herself and others in the most painful of situations. Pearson does not dispense entirely with the romance plot. Like Bridget, Kate faces temptation in the figure of the wrong man, but instead of her boss, he's a client: the fun-loving American Jack Abelhammer, with whom Kate conducts an unconsummated love affair through e-mail. Of course, Pearson's novel isn't a romance; its heroine, after all, is a married mother, and Abelhammer primarily represents Kate's fantasy of escaping her own life. He poses too much of a threat to be taken seriously—both to her family, whom she loves too much, and to Pearson's story, which, as a comedy, must end happily—if not of the "ever after" variety, then at least happily enough.

Instead, the novel's central conflict emerges from the collision between Kate's high-powered career and her family. She loves her job and clearly excels at it. More than once—through a combination of street smarts, "balls," and luck—she manages to pull off something that looked impossible. Kate is a Superwoman in a job that requires her to put in grinding hours at the office and on the road. As she travels around the world to meet with clients and manage their multimillions, she suffers from guilt: too much time spent away from her children and her husband, too many household tasks left undone. (In most ways a model husband and devoted father, Richard still can't be counted on to dress the kids right or remember to change the roll of toilet paper.) Consequently, Kate's head is crammed full of frantic stream-of-consciousness lists:

Must Remember

Cut Ben's nails, Xmas thank-you letters? also letter bollocking council about failure to remove Christmas tree, humiliate ghastly Guy in front of Rod to show who's boss, learn to send txt messages,

Ben birthday—find Teletubbies cake, present—dancing Tinky Winky or improving wooden toy? Dancing Tinky Winky *and* improving wooden toy. Emily shoes/schools/teach her to read, call Mum, call Jill Cooper-Clark, *must* return sister's call—why Julie sounding so pissed off with me; only person in London not seen brill new film-Magic Tiger, Puffing Dragon? Half term when/what? Invite friends for Sunday lunch. Buy pine nuts and basil to make own pesto, cookery crash course (Leith's or similar). Summer holiday brochures. Get Jesus an exercise ball. Quote for stair carpet? Lightbulbs, tulips, lip salve, Botox? (86)

Like *Bridget Jones's Diary,* Pearson's novel is built out of narrative devices such as lists, computer messages, and diary entries. But whereas Fielding's style reflects the freewheeling nature of a singleton's life, in Kate's case, it reveals the frenzied breathlessness of her fragmented existence; there isn't even enough time to think or speak in complete sentences. At home and at work, Kate must constantly resort to shortcuts. The novel opens with one such scene, when Kate, having just returned from New York, is distressing store-bought mince pies in her kitchen at 1:37 a.m. on Monday morning. Her daughter has a Christmas party at school, and the narrator is trying to pass off her purchases as homemade—because, after all, a "proper" mother, one of the "self-sacrificing bakers of apple pies and well-scrubbed invigilators of the washtub," would have made one from scratch (4). But try as she might, she can never measure up to the "Mothers Superior," the "defiantly nonworking" women who, she fears, silently judge her for working (27).

Kate's inner conflict manifests itself in ways that many working mothers will recognize: her constant irritation toward her husband; her nagging feelings of inadequacy and guilt; and her dependence on their nanny, Paula, toward whom she feels both gratitude and envy. She loves her work and her children, but her constant juggling has precipitated an identity crisis. As a result, she feels like a fraud in both roles, a "double agent" who constantly "lie[s] for a living" (49): she claims that her daughter loves broccoli when she actually has no idea, and then she pretends that she's read the *Financial Times* when she was really spending time with her daughter. The author highlights this theme with the epigram that begins the novel, the dictionary definition of *juggle:*

v. & n. v. 1 *intr.* Perform feats of dexterity, esp. by tossing objects in the air and catching them, keeping several in the air at the same time. 2 *tr.* Continue to deal with (several activities) at once, esp, with ingenuity. 3 *intr. & tr.* (foll. by *with*) a deceive or cheat.

b misrepresent (facts). **c** rearrange adroitly. **n.** 1 a piece of juggling.
2 a fraud.

The definition, of course, begins with all the meanings the reader would expect, but it ends with the word *fraud,* which perfectly captures the narrator's fears about the end result of her juggling act.

Pearson sets up the conflict as irresolvable, an either–or dilemma that forces its heroine to make a choice: work or family? Kate, of course, chooses her family. But the author can't end the story on such a serious note, particularly one that's so depressing, and so in the epilogue, "What Kate Did Next," we find out that all is well. After moving to the country with her family, Kate spent more time with her children, got a little bored, and then started to look into buying her sister's former employer, a dollhouse factory, which just happened to be closing. It's an upbeat conclusion, and it ends, appropriately enough, late at night, with the narrator cleaning the kitchen and making lists of what she must do the next day: make Emily's lunch, take Ben to the doctor, and squeeze in a business trip to the factory. For the reader, it's a relief to know that our heroine hasn't changed; the smart, unstoppable Kate Reddy is going to take the world by storm once more, albeit on the slightly smaller scale and in the more feminine sphere of dollhouses. Pearson, in other words, requires her heroine to make a painful choice, thus resolving the novel's central conflict, but then she drops a factory out of the sky so that her character won't have to live with the consequences. Instead of cleaning houses, Kate will be producing them. And if Kate's life gets too frenetic once again—which it will, of course—it happens after the story ends, so the reader doesn't have to see it happen.[12] We're left feeling relieved (after all, if the unstoppable Kate Reddy can't balance motherhood with work, who can?), though also, perhaps, a bit confused. Does the ending mean that we can't have it all? Or does it mean that we can, but only after we redefine "all" to mean quitting our jobs and starting our own businesses?

The novel's ambiguity may actually reflect the cultural confusion surrounding motherhood and work. After all, the fictional life of Kate Reddy represents only a small fraction of women in the workforce: most working mothers are not managing hedge funds or bringing their nannies with them to Euro Disney, not to mention the fact that many women have little or no "choice" when it comes to work. Yet Pearson successfully turns an exceptional woman into an everywoman. The quick-witted Kate is exceedingly likeable; she blends "masculine" qualities such as aggressiveness, skill at math and investing, and fluency in locker-room humor with "feminine" ones. She's assertive at work but never challenges gender roles at home; she never talks about her ambition; and she rarely talks about the money she makes. Pearson gives her heroine a working-class background and a derelict father so that we'll more readily sympathize with her choice of career and her dilemma. Likewise, the author furthermore makes sure that the other woman—the nanny—is not an endearing Mary Poppins but rather a resentful and somewhat indifferent caretaker.[13] Perhaps because of Kate's appeal, journalists and pundits seized on the novel when it came out, reigniting a cultural conversation about work, motherhood, and social change. Pearson, herself a working mother, became a spokesperson for these issues. Her novel fueled the debate about what, if anything, can be done about the intransigence of the workplace to family life and the still mostly female work of raising children.

Of course, *I Don't Know How She Does It* isn't life but literature, and ultimately it draws from fantasy and humor to resolve the challenges facing its heroine. One of the best examples of this occurs in a scandal near the end of the novel. The men at the office are caught in the middle of their frat-boy antics, with a young female associate as the target of their sexually offensive behavior. Kate knows she cannot complain to her boss; the chief offender and instigator is too valuable to the firm. And she does not recommend that the young woman take legal action, a plot development that would take the story out of the comic realm. Instead our heroine masterminds a hilarious scheme in which a bad investment in biodegradable nappies takes the man in question down, to much applause and fanfare. Revenge is sweet, but the questions linger. What does the author want us to take away from her story—that we might as well laugh, extract our personal vengeance, and accept the way things are? Although I don't think Pearson intends this to be her message, one wonders whether some readers might come to this conclusion when they put the book down.

You Might as Well Laugh: The Harried Housewife and the Politics of Humor

Kate's brand of humor owes much to Bridget Jones, but it also owes a great deal to a central figure in twentieth-century American culture: the housewife humorist. In the years following World War II, writers such as Betty MacDonald, Shirley Jackson, Jean Kerr, Erma Bombeck, and Judith Viorst began publishing essays, columns, and poems in which the "autobiographical persona of a harried housewife describes her frantic and often unsuccessful efforts to cope with life in the slow (family- and home-centered) lane" (Dresner 93). They used and refined certain stereotypes—the beleaguered housewife, the inept and bumbling husband, the wild and uncivilized children—that continue to appear in much of today's writing about motherhood. As Sundae Horn observes, these writers represented the "first wave" of mommy lit. Their topics varied, but they usually addressed middle-class, white, and suburban concerns for an audience composed mainly of women like them. This differed by author, of course, and it changed over time. But generally, their writing used satire, caricature, and irony to entertain their readers.

The domestic humorists introduced certain templates for writing about motherhood that have endured until today. While this kind of writing appeared as early as 1945, with the publication of Betty MacDonald's *The Egg and I*, and became increasingly popular with the essays of Shirley Jackson and Jean Kerr (many of which appeared in magazines such as *Good Housekeeping, Ladies' Home Journal*, and the *Saturday Evening Post*), it was really Erma Bombeck who came to define housewife humor.[14] Her career was long and her output prodigious: between 1965 and her death in 1996, she wrote more than fifteen books and more than four thousand columns (Flanagan 149).[15] Her column "At Wit's End," which famously became syndicated within three weeks of its first appearance in the *Dayton Journal-Herald* in 1965, poked fun at her own ineptness at housework and at life in the suburbs (Colwell 50).[16] By the time she started appearing on *Good Morning America*, Bombeck was already a household name.[17] Through self-deprecating humor, she made her readers laugh and realize that they weren't the only miserable failures as housewives. Her jokes furthermore served to satirize (often quite darkly) the cultural expectations that created "impossibly high standards" for housewives and mothers (Walker, *A Very Serious Thing* 6). Her writing style—short, anecdotal, and full of one-liners—became the model for domestic humorists who followed her. But more than anything, it was her wisecracking, sarcastic, and wacky voice that defined her persona and made her the quintessential "rebellious" mother to whom Douglas and Michaels pay homage (and whom they emulate) in *The Mommy Myth* (13).[18] As a rebellious mother, she "talk[ed] back" to the dictates of "intensive mothering," resisted the dominant cultural scripts of motherhood, and defined mothering for herself (Douglas and Michaels 14).[19]

Today, writers such as Judy Gruen, Amy Krouse Rosenthal, Sandi Kahn Shelton, Ayun Halliday, and Debbie Farmer continue to plumb the daily experiences of motherhood in newspaper columns, magazines and books, and on the Internet. Their writing is remarkably similar to that of the early domestic humorists, and though they vary in style, their purpose can be summed up by the title of Sandi Kahn Shelton's first book: *You Might as Well Laugh ... Because Crying Will Only Smear Your Mascara*. A collection of *Working Mother* columns (aptly titled "Wit's End," an homage to Bombeck), *You Might as Well Laugh* draws from many of the conventions Bombeck perfected, and like many of her fellow humorists, Shelton is compared in blurbs to Bombeck.[20] As Horn observes, "Every publisher wants to grab the market share that Erma left behind," leading them to proclaim these writers as "bombeckian" ("Women").

But Bombeck's humor also survives in fictional characters such as Kate Reddy. Kate may be British, but her voice, with its combination of sarcasm and candor, hearkens back to Erma's willingness to talk back. Like Bombeck, Kate is all too well aware of her inferiority when compared to the "Mothers Superior" (the same mothers whom Bombeck dubbed the "Super Moms" in *The Grass Is Always Greener over the Septic Tank* [136]). In both cases, the speaker exposes her own shortcomings while simultaneously suggesting that it's actually more sensible (and quite possibly more fun) to be an inferior mother. After all, who wants to spend all her time aspiring to an impossible ideal? This use of self-deprecation is powerful; it links the narrator and the reader together in a kind of complicity. For example, when Kate castigates herself for all the things she "should" know how to do but doesn't (such as putting the rain cover over her one-year-old son's buggy), we laugh, and while some of us may sigh in relief (at least we haven't done *that*), others of us may recognize ourselves and laugh some more. Humor works as a coping device: when we suddenly realize that we aren't alone, we begin to view our own behavior as less shameful and possibly even normal. In recognizing the humor in these common experiences, we're able to forgive ourselves.

Some critics have charged that although this kind of humor may make us feel good, it preserves the status quo: because of its dependence on stereotypes and conventional gender roles, it actually reinforces them. By transforming anger into laughter, writers such as Bombeck prevent rage from being funneled into political involvement and social change.[21] This critique emerged in the 1960s during the second wave of the women's movement, when the politics of humor came under scrutiny.[22] Times had changed, and although the domestic humorists protested "the conditions of the homemaker's life through the covert means of humor rather than in a more direct, aggressive manner, allowing women to preserve their femininity," many feminists, by contrast, wanted to challenge the status quo directly (Walker, "Toward Solidarity" 62). Many of them began by questioning the idea that women should stay at home to raise children. In 1963, Betty Friedan led the charge in her landmark *The Feminine Mystique* by naming "The Problem That Has No Name," the quiet desperation and boredom plaguing housewives across the country. Women had been stymied by idealistic images of femininity, Friedan argued, and they needed social and personal change, not humor; the way out of the "housewife trap" lay not in laughter but in fulfilling one's intellectual and artistic potential, through finding and pursuing creative or professional work

(344). The author drives her point home when she observes that the housewife humorists, unlike many of their readers, had professional lives: "Shirley Jackson makes the beds, loves and laughs at her son—and writes another book. Jean Kerr's plays are produced on Broadway. The joke is not on *them*" (57).

Since then, scholars such as Nancy Walker and Zita Dresner have recuperated the housewife humorists, arguing that their humor did, in fact, act as a catalyst for social change. Although domestic humor may not have challenged the status quo directly, it did help women cope, in part through effectively "debunk[ing] the 'happy homemaker' myth" by exposing the unrealistic expectations placed on mothers (Dresner 109). It was an important first step in empowering women to examine their lives and realize that they weren't alone.

I Don't Know How She Does It revives the same debate over humor. On one hand, you could argue that its effect is ultimately depoliticizing: instead of connecting with other mothers, we sit at home, alone, and bond with a fictional character; instead of becoming angry, we laugh; and instead of changing the world, we buy more books. On the other hand, Pearson's book exposes the ways in which our culture still falls short, and combats the unrealistic expectations placed on working mothers through laughter. When you consider the potency of the new momism—the way that advertisements, television shows, toy companies, and publications sell an impossible-to-attain image of motherhood to so many of us—you realize how important, and how self-empowering, it is to laugh.

What's most revealing, however, is how little this particular debate has changed since it first appeared forty years ago. In fact, in many ways the current historical moment reveals distressing similarities with the period following World War II, a time of backlash against many of the social changes that had taken place during the war. By 1945, six million women had entered the workforce, only to be urged back home once the war ended (Dresner 93). At home they could aspire to the image of the "happy housewife heroine," extolled in books, magazines, and advertising (Friedan 44). More often than not, home was now in the suburbs, which grew tremendously during the 1950s and 1960s, but without the benefit of extended family, raising children became a more isolated undertaking (Dresner 94). In the midst of all these changes, many women found themselves confused about their role. Enter the domestic humor writers, whose writing represented one of the "by-product[s] of the 'bewilderment' that was generated by the post-war antifeminist sentiment, another response to the confusion that existed about woman's identity, purpose, and place" (Dresner 95).

The domestic humor so prevalent in today's mommy lit fulfills the same purposes it did fifty years ago: to alleviate anxiety, produce laughter, and expose cultural ideologies of parenting. It's not that our culture hasn't changed, because it has; but even though many families no longer fit traditional concepts of what constitutes a "family," these ideologies still hold sway.[23] Slowly, however, they are changing; for example, a few fathers have begun to write domestic humor, revising the persona of the harried housewife into the frenzied father.[24] But the ongoing popularity of the harried housewife suggests that while roles are shifting, the idealized roles of "mother" and "father" continue to produce anxiety for many people.

While mommy lit emerges from this cultural confusion, it varies in how successfully it clarifies the situation. Pearson's novel, for example, effectively mirrors the anxieties many middle-class women experience surrounding motherhood, but it does not provide any answers or get us closer to thinking about work and family in new ways. Pearson's novel presents the situation in terms we know well ("having it all," "juggling") and in a character who, though rebellious and assertive, ultimately remains trapped in a comedic plot. *I Don't Know How She Does It* doesn't suggest how Kate might change her world, or we ours. It seems impossible.

Granted, mommy lit shouldn't be required to provide solutions to dilemmas such as the conflict between work and family. Much of it aims to entertain, to make us laugh, and to hold real life at bay for just a little while. And that's okay. But it's also worth noting the many reasons why women read mommy lit. Besides entertainment, many mothers are looking for something more: for community and conversation, and as my own experience as a mommy-lit reader suggests, for models. The funniest writing about motherhood doesn't necessarily help with that. Even if it's combating dominant cultural narratives about motherhood, even if it's making us laugh our heads off, if it only reflects back to us our confusion, the relief is only temporary. And although it's certainly not part of the problem, it's not really helping, either.

Hip Mamas Speak Out: Autobiography, Community, and the Maternal Feminist Revolution

In *I Don't Know How She Does It*, Kate Reddy experiences herself as a fraud both at work and at home. Her identity crisis provides the inner conflict that propels the story forward. One way or another, she must find a way to stop feeling so divided, and if that means giving up work, which had been the source of her identity before her children, then work must go. This particular narrative of motherhood—that having a baby challenges and changes one's very sense of identity—recurs throughout the literature of motherhood of the past thirty years, particularly in autobiographical writing. In 1976, both Jane Lazarre and Adrienne Rich published books about motherhood that explored, in very different ways, the "psychic crisis" they experienced as young mothers (Rich 35). At the time it was revolutionary for women to admit that having children might entail psychological and emotional pain. Writers such as Jean Kerr and Shirley Jackson had kept their inner demons off the page, and even Erma Bombeck, who allowed some bitterness and ambivalence to creep in, didn't dwell on such dark feelings. Her purpose, as with the other humorists, was to make readers laugh. By contrast, Rich and Lazarre were not primarily interested in humor. They wanted to chart the true experience of motherhood and break the weighty silence surrounding it. As Rich writes in *Of Woman Born: Motherhood as Experience and Institution,* "The words are being spoken now, are being written down; the taboos are being broken, the masks of motherhood are cracking through" (24).

For Rich and Lazarre, motherhood did more than irrevocably change their sense of who they were. It also politicized them. Voicing their experiences in writing became an important step, perhaps even the crucial one, that enabled this to happen. By speaking out about formerly taboo subjects, they directly challenged and resisted cultural ideals of the good, patient mother. Their searching, passionate, and poetic voices added another dimension to the "talk back" tradition of mothering, and although humor wasn't their primary weapon, they were certainly engaged in rebellious mothering. For Rich, of course, this meant reclaiming the experience of mothering from the patriarchal construction of motherhood. For Lazarre this meant coming to understand racism when she mothered black sons, a story she began in *The Mother Knot* and continued in *Beyond the Whiteness of Whiteness: Memoir of a White Mother of Black Sons.* In both cases their personal experiences of motherhood birthed a new political vision. Out of the chaos of self-reconstruction emerged a new sense of purpose and a clarified voice.

Since the 1970s, many women have written memoirs about their experiences as mothers. Some, such as Rich and Lazarre, were writers before having children—Anne Lamott, Anne Roiphe, Marni Jackson, Rachel Cusk, Faulkner Fox—and motherhood provoked a crisis of identity that led them to the memoir form. Others—Ayun Halliday, Andrea Buchanan, Ariel Gore—have written about finding their voice as writers after becoming mothers. For many of these women, writing about motherhood echoed the experiences of Rich and Lazarre. It was an act of breaking the silence and finding the courage to write the truth about their lives. The mothers in *The Bitch in the House* "tell the truth" about their anger and their boredom; in her introduction to *Breeder: Real-Life Stories from the*

New Generation of Mothers, Ariel Gore writes, "We are sick of silences, so we are telling the truth" (xiv); Rachel Cusk observes, "It was my impression, when I became a mother, that nothing had been written about it at all" (4); the editors of the anthology *Mothers Who Think: Tales of Real-Life Parenthood* write that the "uncensored" essays in their book are "intended to be an antidote to the saccharine, oversimplified literature of motherhood" (Peri and Moses xviii).

Mothering is "the greatest story never written," declares Susan Maushart in *The Mask of Motherhood: How Becoming a Mother Changes Our Lives and Why We Never Talk about It* (246). Yet when we survey the outpouring of autobiographical writing over the past thirty years, it's clear that this isn't quite the case. Still, writers keep on coming to the subject of motherhood as if they are the first to chronicle their experience and the only ones to shatter the silence. Why? Is it because, as Maushart charges, we suffer from a culturewide "conspiracy of silence" (5) that causes women to withhold "what they feel and [be] suspicious of what they know" (2)? Or is the problem not so much silence as it is the deafening roar of culture—the images and ideologies of motherhood—that crowd out the individual voices of mothers? Or is it perhaps because, as Cusk writes, we're simply not interested until we have kids—and this "tone-deafness" of the nonparent, which "we acquire as children … leads us as adults to wonder in bemusement why we were never told—by our friends, *by our mothers!*—what parenthood was like" (4)?

Regardless, some measure of silence persists. And in an atmosphere where certain truths remain largely unspoken, the act of speaking out can be politicizing. As Bee Lavender, one of the editors of the Hip Mama Web site, writes, "I was radicalized by my experience of being a parent, yet never saw my story or any honest stories in the media."[25] Along with her coeditor Ariel Gore, the original founder of the print edition of *Hip Mama* in 1993, Lavender has helped to create a vibrant online community for mothers.[26] The zine began as a "forum for young mothers, single parents, and marginalized voices, but has grown to represent progressive families of all varieties"—working class and lower class; lesbian, bisexual, and queer; black, Chicano, Asian, and mixed race; young and old; bohemian, punk rocker, and slacker; single and divorced; on welfare—in other words, anyone who doesn't fit the traditional white, middle-class model of motherhood.[27] Both the zine and the Web site cover the "politics and culture of motherhood," and they actively deconstruct dominant cultural scripts about motherhood to acknowledge and celebrate the diverse ways of mothering (Gore, *The Mother Trip* 231).

Like many other third-wave (and fourth-wave) feminists, Gore and Lavender view the project of redefining motherhood, and particularly its language, as a political act. The name *hip mama* works like the third-wave terms *grrl* and *girlie* in its creation of an alternative vocabulary that replaces second-wave words such as *feminist*.[28] *Hip*, of course, is an adjective that originated with jazz-era hipsters, but on their Web site Gore and Lavender redefine it to describe someone who is "Aware; Informed" and who has claimed her (postpregnancy) body—after all, she has hips. *Mama* provides a third alternative to the more formal *mother* and the familiar terms *mommy* or *mom*, which arguably have become associated with middle-class motherhood; one thinks of "soccer mom, sneaker mom, stay-at-home mom, working mom, supermom" (Peri and Moses xviii).[29] By contrast, *mama* is used by infants and on the street. It has attitude; it's informal, yet—well, hip. Likewise, in their anthology *Breeder* the editors reclaim *breeder*, a word that has been used to denigrate (lower-class, trashy, slutty) women who procreate.[30] While they cherish their reproductive freedom and the right to have an abortion, they simultaneously claim and celebrate their right to reproduce. As Gore writes in the introduction, they are "willing breeders [who] refuse to be oppressed by the institution of motherhood" (xiii). A hip mama understands that the personal is political, but similar to the riot grrls in the early 1990s, she seeks to produce political change in the realm of culture. For Gore and Lavender this means revising the language and images of motherhood.

Gore is the ultimate rebellious mother—she's opinionated, defiant, funny, and smart—and she fuses humor with anger in her writing. In *The Mother Trip: Hip Mama's Guide to Staying Sane in the Chaos of Motherhood,* the author builds on the work of second-wave feminism in an easily accessible, irreverent voice, mixing autobiography with history and cultural analysis with advice. Like her feminist foremothers, she views mothering as a process of "personal transformation" that brings with it "chaos" (3), but embracing this chaos is made difficult by the "modern mama fantasy," which combines "the 1980s Super Mom, the 1950s happy housewife, the early twentieth-century domestic scientist and the Victorian fountain of moral purity" (4). Gore invites her readers to throw away their guilt and "sav[e] the rage to fuel social transformation": "Imagine if we took all of the energy we spend beating ourselves up for our failure to adjust to this insane world where mothers work double shifts and shoulder the blame for everything from individual children's bad behavior to global economic crises—imagine that we turned that energy outward and used it to make this world our home" (218).

Gore dispenses her wisdom with the self-effacing, self-mocking persona of the housewife humorists, and as she creates a humor that doesn't depend on stereotypes, she models another path to self-forgiveness. She redefines not only motherhood but also the anxieties that have come to dominate mainstream discussions about motherhood. In "My Headache" she addresses the question of whether moms "should" work or stay at home: "I have a limited amount of Advil at my disposal, so I'm only going to say this once: The kids are all right. Adaptable little creatures, they are" (83). On the related issue of juggling, she writes,

> To call our experiences "juggling" is laughable. It belittles the work we do. Perhaps we'll achieve the awkward grace of circus clowns at some point in our motherhood, yes. Perhaps we'll feel compartmentalized for a time, too. ... But ultimately each of us has to reinvent the art of living, integrating all the old and new aspects of ourselves into a whole. ... The task isn't to master the clown's art of juggling the broken pieces. The task is to remain whole. And it's in empty spaces that we catch glimpses of our whole selves, where we have time to fit the pieces together. (73)

Rather than trying to follow some "formula" to have it all—a relationship, children, a career—Gore suggests that we focus on the internal qualities and day-to-day moments that can bring true satisfaction and fulfillment (77).

Gore's political vision lies in what she calls the "maternal feminist" revolution (218).[31] She sees part of this revolution taking place in cyberspace communities; after all, for many women, sites such as Hip Mama provide a "support system [and] their room in the dark, their community and their consciousness-raising group" (220). Like *Mommy Too! Magazine*, the Mothers Movement Online, and Salon's now-defunct Mothers Who Think, Hip Mama provides a mix of news, autobiographical writing, and discussion boards. All anyone needs is a computer, or at least access to one at a local library. The pure volume of Internet mommy lit suggests that plenty of women are speaking out. At no other moment in history has the act of writing about motherhood been so democratic. It's a conversation carried on late at night, when the kids are in bed, and it provides a vibrant community to fill the "vacuum" experienced by many mothers.[32]

For many cybermoms, the act of coming together as mothers is inherently political, and along with other networks and organizations founded in recent years—Mothers Ought to Have Equal Rights (MOTHERS), Mothers & More, and the Motherhood Project—these online and grassroots communities are taking the cultural conversation about motherhood in new directions.[33] In the act of writing about themselves and connecting with one another, they're redefining and repoliticizing motherhood.

Notes toward a Conclusion; or, Where Do We Go from Here?

We find ourselves, at the current moment, in a time of great anxiety and hope surrounding motherhood. We see around us evidence of both despair and optimism, of both entrenched conservatism and radical change. It is a moment reminiscent of the early 1960s, when mothers could choose between Erma Bombeck or Betty Friedan, laughter or rage, acceptance or revolt. The vast amount of mommy lit presents us with similar choices today: we can decide between domestic humor or feminist rage, psychic crisis or self-transformation, hip mamas or harried housewives. Granted, the sheer number of choices reflects the workings of the marketplace, but we can also see, in the chaos of this postmodern pastiche, other trends: the unparalleled access of women's voices to publishing houses and the Internet, the demand of women for "real" writing about the diverse experiences of motherhood, and the call for new ways of thinking about, and structuring, our lives.

At a time of both national and global change, the category of mommy lit has come to signify, for many, all forms of writing that explore the private and public dimensions of motherhood. Both the prevalence and the popularity of mommy lit suggest the deep need among many mothers to speak out and listen to each other, to remember that no matter how difficult or challenging our lives are, we are not alone. As the conversation expands, it may finally leave the beleaguered question of whether mothers should "choose" to work or stay at home and instead begin to address the many problems that mothers *and* fathers face in the early twenty-first century: How do we create a culture in which parenting is valued and supported? How do we balance market work with the unpaid work of care for our families? Perhaps then we may destroy, for once and for all, the impossible, idealized images of motherhood that many of us still carry around in our heads.

At the beginning of this essay, I recounted my own experience of trying to grapple with the impending changes of motherhood. But interestingly, all of that reading did very little, in the end, to help me with my own transformation. Some of it gave me helpful tools for thinking about mothering. Some of it provided helpful contexts for understanding the invisible cultural ideologies, histories, and economic forces that were influencing my life. Some of it, in truth, just made me more anxious. But the most useful thing I came away with was not a piece of knowledge, an insight, or an argument. It came after I arrived home from the hospital with a new, fragile, mewling creature in my arms. It came when I stole away, for the first time, and picked up my pen. It was the sense that I was part of a tradition that extended back for generations, a tradition of mothers who laughed and cried, shouted and whispered, talked and sang—who mothered, and then wrote.

Notes

1. Like Fielding's novel, Pearson's was originally published in the United Kingdom.
2. See reviews by Donahue, Carlson, Neill and Wright, and Marlowe.
3. At the date of this writing, I am not aware of any mommy-lit titles written by writers of color or featuring women of color as the protagonists.
4. Jessica Jernigan provides a good definition of chick lit in "Slingbacks and Arrows: Chick Lit Comes of Age" (70).
5. See Belkin, Wallis, Gardner, Peterson, and Ingall.
6. Anthologies of short stories about motherhood, such as the collection *Mother Knows: 24 Tales of Motherhood,* were marketed as mommy lit, and the category was also used to describe Rachel Cusk's memoir *A Life's Work,* personal essay collections such as *Breeder: Real Tales from the New Generation of Mothers,* and nonacademic nonfiction such as Ann Crittenden's *The Price of Motherhood.* See articles by Janet Saidi, Peg Tyre, and Judith Stadtman Tucker.
7. I am indebted to an e-mail conversation with Sundae Horn in which she articulated this definition.
8. Since 1990, memoirists include Anne Lamott, Marni Jackson, Ayun Halliday, Faulkner Fox, Susan Cheever, Anne Roiphe, Andrea Buchanan, Louise Erdrich, and Rachel Cusk; nonfiction writers include Susan Maushart, Naomi Wolf, Susan Douglas and Meredith Michaels, Ann Crittenden, Janna Malamud Smith, and Judith Warner; humorists include Sandi Kahn Shelton, Judy Gruen, Amy Krouse Rosenthal, Debbie Farmer, and Muffy Mead-Ferro. Anthologies include *The Bitch in the House, Mother Knows, Mothers Who Think: Tales of Real-Life Parenthood, Close Company: Stories of Mothers and Daughters, Child of Mine: Writers Talk about the First Year of Motherhood, Mother Reader: Essential Writings on Motherhood, Rise Up Singing: Black Women Writers on Motherhood, Double Stitch: Black Women Write about Mothers and Daughters, The Essential Hip Mama: Writing from the Cutting Edge of Parenting,* and *Mamaphonic: Balancing Motherhood and Other Creative Acts.* This list, of course, is in no way exhaustive.
9. *Hip Mama* was founded in 1993 and *Brain, Child* in 2000.
10. It is impossible to provide an exhaustive list of the many Internet sites and Web logs, but see UrbanBaby, Girl-Mom, Mocha Moms Online, Mamaphonic, and AustinMama.com.
11. In her 1979 essay "Writing and Motherhood," Susan Rubin Suleiman argues that "opposition" and "integration" are the two major themes characterizing writing about motherhood (121).
12. This plot is quite similar to the 1987 movie *Baby Boom,* starring Diane Keaton.
13. It is interesting that Pearson does not provide any details of Paula's background. Such an omission steers her clear of any tricky racial and economic issues, particularly given the increasing globalization of caretaking. See the essays in Barbara Ehrenreich and Arlie Hochschild's *Global Woman.*
14. Jackson's writing was collected in books such as *Life among the Savages* (1953) and Kerr's in books such as *Please Don't Eat the Daisies* (1957). Recent writing on these humorists includes articles by Sundae Horn, Elizabeth Austin, and Susan Currie. Also see Flanagan on Erma Bombeck.
15. Bombeck's fifteen titles (plus a best-of anthology) were followed by three collections after her death in 1996.
16. Bombeck also wrote a column for *Good Housekeeping,* "Up the Wall," between 1969 and 1975 (Colwell 62).
17. *Good Morning America* launched in 1975 with Bombeck as its humorist; she was on the show for eleven years (Colwell 67).
18. The authors' list of other rebellious mothers includes both fictional and real mothers such as Roseanne, Marge Simpson, and the mothers in *The Bitch in the House.*
19. Also see Sharon Hays on the cultural ambivalences underlying the ideology of "intensive mothering."
20. Shelton has been described as the "true successor to Erma Bombeck's throne." See Horn, "The Women Who Would Be Erma (and Jean and Shirley)."

21. See Betty Friedan (57) and Patricia Meyer Spacks (221). In her 1975 book *The Female Imagination,* Spacks described the writing of the housewife humorists as "profoundly conservative in its social implications."
22. Nancy Walker observes that although humor did not play a large role in the feminist movement during the late 1960s, it did emerge as a potent force in subsequent decades. See "Toward Solidarity: Women's Humor and Group Identity" (73–76).
23. See Stephanie Coontz.
24. For example, see Ken Swarner.
25. See "About Us" on Hip Mama's Web site.
26. Lavender is also the founding editor of Girl-Mom and Mamaphonic and has authored her own zine.
27. See Hip Mama.
28. See Jennifer Baumgardner and Amy Richards's *Manifesta* (50–52). Also see Leslie Heywood and Jennifer Drake's *Third Wave Agenda* (4).
29. In *The Mommy Myth,* Douglas and Michaels argue that "mom" addresses mothers "from a child's-eye view. It assumes a familiarity, an approachability, to mothers that is, frankly, patronizing" (19).
30. This is similar to the reclamation of words such as *bitch, slut,* and *cunt* (Baumgardner and Richards 50–52).
31. A wide range of women has championed various forms of "maternal feminism." For example, the Motherhood Project made one of the first public proclamations on behalf of a mother-centered feminism at a maternal feminism symposium at the Barnard Center for Research on Women in 2002, when they issued a "momifesto" calling for a "fundamental reordering of the priorities of our society." See the "Call to a Motherhood Movement" on the Motherhood Project's Web site.
32. Sundae Horn, e-mail conversation.
33. Mothers Ought to Have Equal Rights, founded in 2002 by Ann Crittenden, Naomi Wolf, and the National Association of Mothers' Centers, is a "grassroots initiative seeking to improve caregivers' economic status" (see "About MOTHERS"). Mothers & More is a support network for mothers with local chapters founded in 1987 by Joanne Brundage. The mission of the Motherhood Project, founded in 1999 by Enola Aird and sponsored by the Institute for American Values, is to put "motherhood and mothering on the national agenda" (see "About Us").

Works Cited

Austin, Elizabeth. "Giving Mirth." *Washington Monthly* 35.2 (March 2003): 43–46.

Baumgardner, Jennifer, and Amy Richards. *Manifesta: Young Women, Feminism, and the Future.* New York: Farrar, Straus and Giroux, 2000.

Belkin, Lisa. "The Opt-Out Revolution." *New York Times Magazine* 26, Oct. 2003: 42+.

Bell-Scott, Patricia, and Beverly Guy-Sheftall, eds. *Double Stitch: Black Women Write about Mothers and Daughters.* Boston: Beacon Press, 1991.

Berry, Cecelie S., ed. *Rise Up Singing: Black Women Writers on Motherhood.* New York: Doubleday, 2004.

Bombeck, Erma. *The Grass Is Always Greener over the Septic Tank.* New York: McGraw-Hill, 1978.

Burmeister-Brown, Susan, and Linda B. Swanson-Davies, eds. *Mother Knows: 24 Tales of Motherhood.* New York: Washington Square Press, 2004.

Carlson, Margaret. "The Mummy Diaries." *Time* 7, Oct. 2002: 90.

Colwell, Lynn Hutner. *Erma Bombeck: Writer and Humorist.* Hillside, NJ: Enslow, 1992.

Coontz, Stephanie. *The Way We Really Are: Coming to Terms with America's Changing Families.* New York: Basic Books, 1997.

Crittenden, Ann. *The Price of Motherhood: Why the Most Important Job in the World Is Still the Least Valued.* New York: Henry Holt, 2001.

Crittenden, Danielle. *Amanda Bright@Home.* New York and Boston: Warner Books, 2003.

Currie, Susie. "Days of Wine and Daisies: The Happy Life and Work of Jean Kerr." *Weekly Standard* 14, Apr. 2003: 41–43.

Cusk, Rachel. *A Life's Work: On Becoming a Mother.* New York: Picador, 2001.

Davey, Moyra, ed. *Mother Reader: Essential Writings on Motherhood.* New York: Seven Stories Press, 2001.

Donahue, Deirdre. "Modern Women, Messy Lives." *USA Today* 1, Oct. 2002: 1D.

Douglas, Susan, and Meredith Michaels. *The Mommy Myth: The Idealization of Motherhood and How It Has Undermined Women.* New York: Free Press, 2004.

Dresner, Zita. "Domestic Comic Writers." *Women's Comic Visions.* Ed. June Sochen. Detroit: Wayne State University Press, 1991. 93–114.

Ehrenreich, Barbara, and Arlie Russell Hochschild, eds. *Global Woman: Nannies, Maids, and Sex Workers in the New Economy.* New York: Henry Holt, 2002.

Fielding, Helen. *Bridget Jones's Diary.* New York: Penguin, 1999.

Flanagan, Caitlin. "Housewife Confidential." *Atlantic Monthly* Sept. 2003: 141–50.

Friedan, Betty. *The Feminine Mystique.* New York: Norton, 2001.

Gardner, Ralph. "Mom vs. Mom." *New York* 21, Oct. 2002: 21–25.

Gibson, Fiona. *Babyface.* New York: Red Dress Ink, 2004.

Gore, Ariel. *The Essential Hip Mama: Writing from the Cutting Edge of Parenting.* Seattle, WA: Seal Press, 2004.

———, ed. *The Mother Trip: Hip Mama's Guide to Staying Sane in the Chaos of Motherhood.* Seattle, WA: Seal Press, 2000.

Gore, Ariel, and Bee Lavender, eds. *Breeder: Real-Life Stories from the New Generation of Mothers.* Emeryville, CA: Seal Press, 2001.

Green, Jane. *Babyville.* New York: Broadway Books/Random House, 2003.

Halliday, Ayun. *The Big Rumpus: A Mother's Tale from the Trenches.* New York: Seal Press, 2002.

Hanauer, Cathi, ed. *The Bitch in the House: 26 Women Tell the Truth about Sex, Solitude, Work, Motherhood, and Marriage.* New York: William Morrow, 2002.

Hays, Sharon. *The Cultural Contradictions of Motherhood.* New Haven and London: Yale University Press, 1996.

Hewlett, Sylvia Ann. *Creating a Life: Professional Women and the Quest for Children.* New York: Miramax Books, 2002.

Heywood, Leslie, and Jennifer Drake, eds. *Third Wave Agenda: Being Feminist, Doing Feminism.* Minneapolis and London: University of Minnesota Press, 1997.

Horn, Sundae. "The More Things Change … Revisiting the First Wave of Mother-Lit." *Brain, Child: The Magazine for Thinking Mothers* 4.3 (Summer 2003): 60–65.

———. Personal e-mail conversation. July 22, 2004.

———. "The Women Who Would Be Erma (and Jean and Shirley): Modern Adventures in Writing and Mothering." *Brain, Child: The Magazine for Thinking Mothers.* Summer 2003. <http://www.brainchildmag.com/essays/summer2003_horn2.htm>.

Ingall, Marjorie. "Having a Baby *and* a Life: How Will You Do It?" *Glamour* Mar. 2004: 200–205.

Jackson, Shirley. *Life among the Savages.* New York: Penguin Putnam, 1997.

Jernigan, Jessica. "Slingbacks and Arrows: Chick Lit Comes of Age." *Bitch* 25 (Summer 2004): 68–75.

Kerr, Jean. *Please Don't Eat the Daisies.* New York: Fawcett, 1965.

Kline, Christina Baker. *Child of Mine: Writers Talk about the First Year of Motherhood.* New York: Dell, 1997.

Lamott, Anne. *Operating Instructions: A Journal of My Son's First Year.* New York: Fawcett Columbine, 1993.

Lavender, Bee, and Maia Rossini, eds. *Mamaphonic: Balancing Motherhood and Other Creative Acts.* Brooklyn, NY: Soft Skull Press, 2004.

Lazarre, Jane. *Beyond the Whiteness of Whiteness: Memoir of a White Mother of Black Sons.* Durham and London: Duke University Press, 1996.

———. *The Mother Knot.* Durham and London: Duke University Press, 1997.

MacDonald, Betty. *The Egg and I.* New York: Harper and Row, 1987.

Marlowe, Ann. "The All-Too-Female Cluelessness of 'I Don't Know How She Does It.'" *Salon.* 23, Oct. 2002. <http://www.salon.com/books/feature/2002/10/23/pearson/index.html>.

Maushart, Susan. *The Mask of Motherhood: How Becoming a Mother Changes Our Lives and Why We Never Talk about It.* New York: Penguin Putnam, 2000.

Murkoff, Heidi, Sandee Hathaway, and Arlene Eisenberg. *What to Expect When You're Expecting.* New York: Workman Publishing, 2002.

Neill, Mike, and Lynda Wright. "Stressed for Success." *People* 21, Oct. 2002: 107–108.

Park, Christine, and Caroline Heaton. *Close Company: Stories of Mothers and Daughters.* New York: Houghton Mifflin, 1989.

Pearson, Allison. *I Don't Know How She Does It: The Life of Kate Reddy, Working Mother.* New York: Random House, 2002.

Peri, Camille, and Kate Moses, eds. *Mothers Who Think: Tales of Real-Life Parenthood.* New York: Washington Square Press, 1999.

Peterson, Karen S. "Gen X Moms Have It Their Way." *USA Today* 7, May 2003: 1D.

Rich, Adrienne. *Of Woman Born: Motherhood as Experience and Institution.* New York: Norton, 1986.

Saidi, Janet. "Baby Steps of Change for an Age-Old Genre: 'Mommy Lit.' " *Christian Science Monitor* 20, Mar. 2002: 20.

Shelton, Sandi Kahn. *You Might as Well Laugh ... Because Crying Will Only Smear Your Mascara.* New York: St. Martin's Press, 1999.

Shields, Julie. *How to Avoid the Mommy Trap: A Roadmap for Sharing and Parenting and Making It Work.* Herndon, VA: Capital Books, 2002.

Smiley, Jane. "Can Mothers Think?" *The True Subject: Writers on Life and Craft.* Ed. Kurt Brown. St. Paul, MN: Graywolf Press, 1993. 3–15.

Spacks, Patricia Meyer. *The Female Imagination.* New York: Knopf, 1975.

Suleiman, Susan Rubin. "Writing and Motherhood." *Mother Reader: Essential Writings on Motherhood.* Ed. Moyra Davey. New York: Seven Stories Press, 2001. 113–37.

Swarner, Ken. *Whose Kids Are These Anyway? True Confessions of a Family Man.* New York: Berkley Publishing Group, 2003.

Tucker, Judith Stadtman. "Wistful Thinking: A Flurry of New Articles Focus on an Earlier Generation of Mothers Writing about Motherhood." *Mothers Movement Online.* 27, Aug. 2003. <www.mothersmovement.org/books/reviews/wistful_thinking.htm>.

Tyre, Peg. "Bridget Jones Grows Up: 'Mommy Lit' Takes a Wry, Irreverent Look at Motherhood." *Newsweek* 11, Aug. 2003: 56.

Walker, Nancy. "Toward Solidarity: Women's Humor and Group Identity." *Women's Comic Visions.* Ed. June Sochen. Detroit: Wayne State University Press, 1991. 57–81.

———. *A Very Serious Thing: Women's Humor and American Culture.* Minneapolis: University of Minnesota Press, 1988.

Wallis, Claudia. "The Case for Staying Home." *Time* 22, Mar. 2004: 51–59.

Wolf, Laura. *Diary of a Mad-Mom-to-Be.* New York: Dell, 2003.

8

Chick Lit Jr.: More Than Glitz and Glamour for Teens and Tweens

JOANNA WEBB JOHNSON

Cut the word *literature* down to *lit* and suddenly you have implied lower quality work. "Chick lit," the latest incarnation of this diminutive term, has stirred up some literary excitement, sparking controversy over its value and limitations. The argument concerning literary merit is familiar to the dedicated scholars of children's and young adult (YA) literature. Few branches of literary scholarship have suffered the stigma of insignificance as much as "kiddie lit," which hangs precariously from the lowest rung of the literary ladder. Few research universities acknowledge children's and YA literature as a field worthy of rigorous study. Likewise, the immensely popular genre of chick lit receives the academic snub as well.

Arguably, then, a conflation of chick lit and YA literature seems to create a new genre that, although worthy of popular accolades, garners academic disdain. However, this genre, which I dub "chick lit jr.," builds on a feminist children's literary tradition, almost extinct during the first half of the twentieth century. These novels address classic issues of YA novels: coming of age, identity, sexuality, and material culture. Authors such as Louise Rennison, Ann Brashares, Carolyn Mackler, Megan McCafferty, Cecily von Ziegesar, Zoey Dean, Cathy Hopkins, and Meg Cabot dominate this growing chick-lit-jr. market with both teen and adult readers. Their novels work in much the same way as their adult counterparts, and thematically the two genres share much common ground. Both try to affirm flawed women, acknowledge insecurities involving physical attributes, and give lessons in negotiating relationships (usually by showing the wrong way first). With backdrops of fashion and shopping, these novels embrace, or at least acknowledge, the power of consumer culture. However, instead of addressing challenges faced by the singleton in women's novels, chick lit jr. stresses issues relevant to coming of age. The girl characters are typically in a borderland between childhood and adulthood, and the novels show how to move through this difficult transition. At the very least, they use humor to realistically portray emotionally difficult adolescent and preadolescent development and maturation, usually featuring a character whose search for identity is less than graceful, and thus, easily identifiable to the young reader. This "bumbling" quality is also present in the adult chick lit, where the characters often seem to be adolescent in at least one aspect of their lives. In addition, both versions of the genre usually feature stages of emotional and sexual maturity for their protagonists or, at their best, a grand moment of self-realization.

Chick-lit and chick-lit-jr. authors engage their audiences with perceptive interpretations of the ordinary. Critics of the adult genre assert that chick lit does not do any important cultural work. A superficial look at the genre would seem to indicate nothing but a glimpse into an unimportant person's life. This view fails to appreciate the purpose of the genre. Anjula Razdan asserts that adult chick lit "isn't big-canvas storytelling. It's kind of the mundane, everyday, obsessive and superficial details of women's lives," something she says she finds "comforting to read" ("Specialized Literary Subgenres"). But the very scrutiny of another's challenges and problems can be not only escapist but also affirming to the reader. Chick lit and its authors rarely stake a claim on Great American Novel territory. Instead, they serve an immediate need without pretense. Razdan points out that "most chick lit isn't out to change the world anyway, only to reflect a part of it" (21). The same could be said of its junior counterpart in its quest to entertain and guide through example (or, sometimes, antiexample).

Perhaps one of the major challenges facing chick lit and its defenders is the lack of a standard definition. Kelly James-Enger observes that "every editor and agent defines chick lit a little differently." Jennifer Weiner, the author of *In Her Shoes* and *Good in Bed,* has offered a generic description of the "traditional" chick-lit novel. She proposes that "chick lit is any novel where you have a smart, spunky, benighted female heroine who is anywhere between maybe 22 and 40ish, who will, in the course of the novel, have awful things happen to her but will persevere, usually with her cadre of eccentric friends, her semi-dysfunctional family and perhaps a pet"

("Specialized Literary Subgenres"). If we were to change the ages to between thirteen and seventeen, we would have a pretty solid description of chick lit jr. Although the central character might not always be "spunky," Weiner points out that at the very least she cannot be "mopey." "Quirky" is certainly allowed for both genres.

Successful chick lit echoes real life, if not in practice then at least in theory—most readers do not, after all, toddle around in Jimmy Choos carrying Prada bags. We could, however, be guilty of botching a friendship, choosing the wrong person for a relationship, screwing up at work, not getting along with family, and mishandling money. Adult readers find comfort or entertainment, or both, in reading about others making the same mistakes. Never is this sort of affirmation more appreciated than during young adulthood. If anything, the need to see others facing mundane obstacles is more important for the adolescent because one would hope that an adult has developed better tools to face daily challenges.

With few rules to govern it and the list of taboo subjects getting shorter every day, chick lit jr. covers a lot of territory. Like adult chick lit, the junior version also runs the gamut from the humorous slapstick in Louise Rennison's fiction to the privileged lifestyles in Cecily von Ziegesar's Gossip Girl novels to the serious contemplations in Ann Brashare's Traveling Pants books. Somewhere along the spectrum we have Meg Cabot's Princess Diaries series and *All-American Girl,* along with Megan McCafferty's *Sloppy Firsts* and *Second Helpings.* As representative novels of the genre, these works move beyond a traditional novel format, often incorporating e-mails, letters, cell phone calls, diary entries, text messages, instant messaging blurbs, and Web site postings in conjunction with first- and third-person narratives. They reflect current language (including slang) and methods of communication that were not present or popular as recently as five years ago. Because of their hip and trendy references, the genre is mistakenly seen as new.

Although the term is new, the genre is not. Chick lit can trace its roots back to works such as Samuel Richardson's *Pamela* (1740) and *Clarissa* (1747–48), Jane Austen's novels, and the plethora of sentimental U.S. women's novels in the nineteenth century. The book jackets and vernacular may have changed, but thematically the modern novels continue the historical focus on daily trials, fashion challenges (as there have always been the "haves" and "have nots"), relationship issues, and family problems. By definition, Louisa May Alcott's *Little Women* (1868–69), arguably a YA text, follows this literary tradition with its "laments" about not having the right dress, sibling squabbles, heartache, and run-ins with classmates. The unpolished but lovable Jo March set the stage for many young literary heroines for the next centuries, and she continues to gain fans today.

Although nineteenth-century popular novels probably do not immediately come to mind when one thinks of "chick lit jr.," the twentieth- and twenty-first-century phenomenon finds its roots in these nineteenth-century precursors with the realistically flawed young female protagonist featured in most present-day YA novels. Even Alcott's title, referring to "little" women, implies a particular transitional stage for the characters. As a classic coming-of-age story, the novel features characters on a constant quest to find themselves. In particular, Jo March struggles with her identity, as she is faced with essential self-versus-cultural expectations. Alcott addresses sexuality by following her characters from childhood to courtship to marriage. She ties the novel together at the end by creating comfortable male–female relationships that indicate the need for women to fulfill cultural expectations. In rejecting Laurie as a partner for Jo, however, Alcott rejects the idea of the nineteenth-century traditional marriage. Knowing that she was bound by publishing conventions, Alcott needed to marry off her free-spirited heroine. By pairing Jo and Professor Bhaer, Alcott points to a more egalitarian relationship instead of a patriarchal one.[1] Jo can be empowered while still outwardly subscribing to nineteenth-century American culture.

In addition to questions of gender roles, class issues surface in the March girls' continuous mourning for their loss of station and property. They must continue to go through the motions of dressing appropriately and keeping up appearances despite their lack of funds. One can almost envision a twenty-first-century *Little Women* with a hot pink cover decorated with a crumpled glove, scorched dress, birdhouse turned mailbox, and locks of hair bundled together. Perhaps this vision borders on travesty when one considers the darker and more serious tone of Book Two (Beth's death, Amy's maturity, Jo's engagement). However, are Jo's "scrapes" in Book One essentially so different from those of fourteen-year-old Georgia Nicolson, the quirky and confused protagonist of Rennison's "confessions" books? Georgia, like Jo, means well, but her youthful self-centeredness often clouds her view of the big picture. On the one hand she displays motherly qualities to her three-year-old sister, Libby. But she also cannot resist childish calls to prank playing and silliness with her friends. Nineteenth-century Jo and twenty-first-century Georgia are portrayed as loving and well-intentioned girls, but their immaturity and attachment to childhood hampers their decision making and often leads to poor choices.

Thematically, then, chick lit jr. shares much common ground with the best-selling novels of the nineteenth century. Representative novels include

Susan Warner's *The Wide, Wide World* (1850), Maria Cummins's *The Lamplighter* (1854), A.D.T. Whitney's *Faith Gartney's Girlhood* (1863), Elizabeth Stuart Phelps's *Gypsy* series (1865–66), and Helen Hunt Jackson's *Nelly's Silver Mine: A Story of Colorado Life* (1878). Their heroines all arguably evolve during the course of the stories, presenting lessons learned and reaching for higher moral ground. Novels since the nineteenth century have targeted young adults and even young adult women, but these novels featured more *acting* than *becoming*. Characters were not given the opportunities to change or develop. Although popular with readers, these characters remained static and predictable. Series such as Nancy Drew offered more entertainment than enlightenment. These novels showed a purposeful protagonist and a plot preoccupied with exterior action. Nancy Drew solves, finds, and pursues the mysterious. She is relieved of any other responsibility of introspection, hesitancy, or confusion about who she is and who she wants to be.

In the intervening years, the novels addressing important coming-of-age issues, similar to those faced by today's chick-lit-jr. heroines, focused on the male experience. Many YA novels in the latter half of the twentieth century showed a harsh, graceless, and often unsuccessful struggle to make the transition from childhood to adulthood portrayed as a singularly male experience, epitomized by J.D. Salinger's *A Catcher in the Rye* (1951). While filled with many humorous and clever moments, it lacks the sort of hope and optimism contemporary young readers are likely to find assuring. Likewise, John Knowles's *A Separate Peace* (1959), with its war looming ominously in the background, offers little in the way of comforting options. One must accept adulthood and sever all ties with childhood or suffer the consequences—insanity or death. Even Robert Cormier's *The Chocolate War* (1974), with its grim and violent ending, points to a Lord-of-the-Flies sort of ugliness that festers in adolescents who are put in adult power situations. Certainly I am oversimplifying three very complicated novels but, arguably, the very complexity and heavy-handedness of these works makes them no longer popular with contemporary young adult readers. Gene, in *A Separate Peace,* kills off his childhood (the childlike and innocent Phineas) so that he can move into adulthood. His transition is difficult and harsh, a reflection of the war that serves as a backdrop to the novel. Likewise, in *The Chocolate War,* both the child's world of Trinity and the adult world of his father and Brother Leon offer little hope to Jerry. Both worlds seem equally grim and unattractive. Unlike chick lit jr., these novels fail to offer positive choices and options for their characters. The transition to adulthood, then, becomes something to be feared. Any coming-of-age novel must deal with the rites of passage concerning emotional, physical, and sexual identity, but chick lit jr. attempts to reengage the adolescent by using many of the strategies employed by adult chick lit. And unlike so many novels in the American literary canon, both adult and junior chick lit center solely on the female experience.

A significant swing back to the more hopeful thematic formulas of nineteenth-century women's novels occurred in the 1970s, beginning with Judy Blume's work.[2] What has changed most tellingly over the past 150 years are the rules governing what is acceptable in YA literature. Permanent fixtures on challenged and banned book lists, Blume's novels explored new territory in children's literature by overtly addressing issues that were previously considered taboo—menstruation, masturbation, sex, divorce, and questioning religion. She presented these important thematic issues as current daily challenges using approachable vocabulary and references. With novels such as *Are You There God? It's Me, Margaret* (1970), *Deenie* (1973), and *Forever* (1975), Blume reopened the discussion on girls' cultural identity, sexuality, and the difficult passage to adulthood.

Chick lit jr. furthers the literary tradition started by Bloom, revising and updating it. While critics argue whether adult chick lit does significant feminist work ("lipstick" or otherwise), chick lit jr. stands largely removed from that conversation. YA literature tends to focus less on *changing* the world and instead looks to offer helpful solutions on how the individual protagonist *negotiates* the world in its present state. This is not to say that YA literature, even chick lit jr., is incapable of doing important work. One needs only to read a few pages of Mary Pipher's groundbreaking study of female adolescence, *Reviving Ophelia* (1994), to see the difficulties and repercussions during this stage of development. The effective writer of chick lit jr. is in the enviable position of actually reaching and communicating with a potentially resistant audience. During a time when young adults tend to tune out older adult voices, chick lit jr. is a chance to send positive and helpful messages concerning coming of age. Popular writers for young adults know that contemporary young readers have no use for preachy stories that point to parents always being right and suggest that all will end well regardless of circumstance. If we believe that today's youth are that gullible then we are certainly selling them short. Young women demand the same sort of entertainment and respect given to adult audiences. While writers such as Meg Cabot have been panned because of their use of slang and pop culture, it is Cabot's very use of teenage dialect and references to musicians such as Gwen Stefani that pull in her readership. It is important to remember that just because her novels are fun doesn't mean they are not effective. A novel can teach without being authoritarian, and this instructional aspect is an important function of the chick-lit-jr. genre.

In the mid- and late 1990s, the concern was that, because many adolescent readers were skipping YA fiction entirely, the literature was being read by a much younger audience than intended.[3] In the new millennium, YA authors are attempting to recapture the YA audience, at least through their early teen years, offering themes and plots that simultaneously echo those of their adult counterparts while still remaining true to a coming-of-age theme. By employing humor, this subgenre of YA literature offers an approachable path to understanding the challenges associated with leaving childhood and accepting adult responsibility.

Beginning with their titles, the novels entice young readers with humorous or seductive glimpses of the contents. Quite possibly the queen of chick lit jr., author Rennison attracts the reader with her intriguing titles: *Angus, Thongs, and Full-Frontal Snogging; On the Bright Side, I Am Now the Girlfriend of a Sex God; Knocked Out by My Nunga-Nungas; Dancing in My Nuddy-Pants;* and *Away Laughing on a Fast Camel.* Rennison, whose Georgia Nicolson novels are often compared to Fielding's Bridget Jones books, achieves success on both sides of the Atlantic with her creation of a real-time diary. Like Bridget's, Georgia's diary entries are hilarious with their minute-by-minute commentary (yet unrealistic since no one would keep a diary in real time). The timing of her entries highlights the missteps and misperceptions of the adolescent who, typically, is self-absorbed and overly concerned with appearance. The reader sees the young protagonist at her obsessive and comic best in the following passage where Georgia tries to rid herself of the "unibrow" look:

2:30 p.m.

I can't bear this. I've only taken about five hairs out and my eyes are swollen to twice their normal size.

4:00 p.m.

Cracked it. I'll use Dad's razor.

4:05 p.m.

Sharper than I thought. It's taken off a lot of hair just on one stroke. I'll have to even up the other one.

4:16 p.m.

Bugger it. It looks all right, I think, but I look very surprised in one eye. I'll have to even up the other one now.

6:00 p.m.

Mum nearly dropped Libby when she saw me. Her exact words were "What in the name of God have you done to yourself, you stupid girl?" (20)

Rennison presents a visual image of a mundane occurrence going very wrong. Readers, both young and "old," may cringe in their identification with Georgia's calamity, but the novel optimistically points toward seeing the humor of the situation as well. Quality YA literature, then, can be a sort of educational tool, not an alienating textbook but an engaging guidebook that uses entertaining scenarios to create an aware reader. While it may be the rare teen who can step back and laugh at herself when that embarrassing moment strikes, she seems to enjoy laughing at others. It takes only a quick look at the "Traumarama" section in *Seventeen* magazine to understand how devastating these incidents can be to the one experiencing them but how humorous the situations appear to readers. This section, featured monthly in this magazine targeting young women, lets readers share their most recent embarrassing moments and how they reacted. In some cases the victim faces her humiliation with a snappy line or a heroic moment, but more often her solution is to slink away in shame and confusion.

Chick lit jr. similarly gives the reader the chance to achieve distance to give her a clearer picture of herself. Ideally, if the reader can step back from a traumatic situation, perhaps she can cope with it more effectively. Adolescents, particularly female adolescents, are constantly bombarded with images in the media that seem bent on destroying their already fragile egos. Just as adult women are under constant physical scrutiny, girls also must struggle with inflexible guidelines typically not followed by their male counterparts. The adolescent females' need to control their world and their image sometimes comes with devastating results. North American teens fall victim to eating disorders, depression, and even suicide over matters many would consider unimportant. Chick lit jr. acknowledges that which may seem trivial (and yet is not) and validates a young woman's sense of insecurity and self-doubt. Kelly A. Marsh makes an insightful observation concerning the function of Fielding's Bridget Jones novels that I believe assimilates well into discussions of adolescent novels. She asserts, "Bridget's voice is authentic because it reveals what we all know but rarely face, and perhaps never face with such high spirits: control is a myth, and the experience of being out of control and of being forced into mutually dependent relationships is authentic" (53). Just as Bridget helps the adult reader to accept her own imperfection, the YA reader, by and large the more fragile of the two, can move toward accepting her own shortcomings as well. Characters such as Georgia in the confessions novels, Jessica from Megan McCafferty's books, or Mia from the Princess series are far from prom queen perfect and offer a more hopeful and affirming image of the typical teenager. They acknowledge a world that cannot be *controlled* but can be *negotiated*.

Not only is perfection frowned on in these books, it comes across as unnatural, uninteresting, and, what is more important, not fun. For instance, in Megan McCafferty's *Second Helpings,* Jessica feels alienated because she believes she does not have anything unique to offer in her gifted summer writing program. As a reflection of the disconnect between her private and public self, she keeps two journals—one for herself (arguably reflecting her *true* self) and one that she turns in to her writing teacher. In an attempt to continuously hide herself from the world, Jessica writes a "highly censored" class journal to turn in. Meanwhile, in her personal journal she obsesses about her former love interest, fawns over her writing teacher, and passes humorous judgment on her so-called friends and classmates. Conflict arises when she accidentally turns in the wrong journal and receives kudos for writing something exciting, funny, and worth reading. Her teacher affirms her "true" voice and indicates that her writing gifts stem from her ability to see and interpret the world around her.

Jessica's romantic life follows the same pattern often seen in adult chick lit. She spends much of *Second Helpings,* McCafferty's sequel to *Sloppy Firsts,* obsessing about her failed relationship with Marcus Flutie. She writes about how wrong she was to trust him and wonders how she could have ever believed that he cared for her or that they were compatible. In complete denial about her continuing attraction to him, she refers to him as "He Who Shall Remain Nameless." Of course, what the reader realizes early on is that Jessica still cares for Marcus and that they are right for each other. Even other characters in the novel plot to bring the two of them back together. However, the ending leaves the door open for a potential third installment and takes an unhappy but realistic turn as Marcus leaves for a school on the other side of the country. Marcus attempts to comfort a devastated Jessica by telling her that they have "all the time in the world," which, instead of a pat happily-ever-after ending, points to a more realistic one of recovery and opportunity (344). The open-endedness of the novel reflects Jessica's transition from childhood to adulthood. The novel concludes with her upbeat graduation address, indicating an excitement about what lies ahead. As with so many teen movies and YA novels, high school graduation marks the official end of childhood. Whether prepared or not, the young adult is now an adult (and, thus, the story must end).

Second Helpings intertwines romantic turmoil and issues of sexuality with its subtext of emotional maturity and speculations on the future. Like adult chick lit, chick lit jr. often includes at least a subplot focused on romantic interests. Although the women protagonists of the adult genre are not typically worldly or promiscuous, they are also not usually virgins. In contrast, most of the heroines in YA novels are new to their sexuality. Roberta Seelinger Trites observes, "Teenager characters in YA novels agonize about almost every aspect of human sexuality: decisions about whether to have sex, issues of sexual orientation, issues of birth control and responsibility, unwanted pregnancies, masturbation, orgasms, nocturnal emission, sexually transmitted diseases, pornography, and prostitution" (84). As a subgenre of YA literature, chick lit jr. is no exception. Protagonists may have a more experienced friend but they themselves lack physical and emotional experience with the opposite sex. In inner dialogues and conversations with their peers, they obsess about and speculate on potential interactions with boys. They question logistics, impose rules and rating systems, and offer advice to each other that stems from no real experience. For instance, in Rennison's novels, Georgia and her friends have developed a numbered list for evaluating and categorizing physical contact with the opposite sex. The list goes from "(1) hand holding" to "(10) the full monty," with a distinction between "upper body fondling—outdoors" (only a 7) and "upper body fondling—indoors (in bed)," which rates a more significant 8.

The list, while humorous, serves a practical purpose for both the characters and the YA reader. By classifying sexual behaviors, Rennison's novel demystifies the unfamiliar. The adult reader may have more of a sexual history based on experimentation and conversations with experienced peers, whereas the younger reader often relies on gossip, speculation, and third-hand knowledge. The novel takes on *almost* absurd proportions when Georgia, afraid of coming across as inexperienced when the moment comes with Mr. Right, takes kissing lessons from a seventeen-year-old local boy, Peter. The irony and humor are certainly not lost on the adolescent reader as Georgia endures the almost formal lesson to learn the logistics of kissing.

"Do you want to sit down?" he says, patting the bed.

I think, No thanks, I would rather put my head in a bag of eels, but I say, "OK," and sit down.

He puts his arm around me. I think of putting my arm around him but I don't because I remember the stuffed-olive incident. Then, with his other hand, Peter turns my face toward his. It's a good thing he didn't try that yesterday when I had rigor mortis of the head. Then he says, "Close your eyes and relax."

9:00 p.m.

Phew, I suppose I am a woman now … (75)

Clearly, Georgia finds herself willing to try anything to demystify and understand physical interactions between men and women. In another humorous scene, she lies on her arm until it goes numb and then lifts it onto her breasts "to see what it felt like to have a strange hand on them" (68). She decides that it feels "quite nice" but then worries that she is "too full of strange urges to think properly" (68), a predicament certainly faced by many an adolescent. Georgia's sexual questioning rings all too true to the adolescent ear. The humor of the situations serves to both entertain and bring understanding to the reader.

Not all chick lit jr. follows the same formula, however. These scenarios are opposed to Bridget's in Brashares's *Sisterhood of the Traveling Pants* (2001). Bridget, although close in age to Georgia, aggressively pursues her sexual target with disheartening consequences. Instead of taking the time to understand and interpret her sexuality, she blindly stumbles forward without contemplation and certainly without Georgia's good humor. If anything, Bridget comes to realize how much of a child she still is. Away at soccer camp in Mexico, she is separated from her friends and support system. Bridget uses her sexual energy and prowess to have sex with a male counselor at her camp. The experience, obvious after the fact to have been a huge mistake, diminishes her instead of affirming her sexuality. In the end, her friend Lena comes to comfort her and bring her home.

Brashares's novels, like so many adult chick lit novels, herald the importance of friendships, the clarity they bring, and the mistakes we sometimes make when we don't have our friends there to help us understand complicated situations. They acknowledge female solidarity and the idea of *socially* constructed families (versus biological ones) from which the single woman or girl can truly draw her strength. The dependence on friends or peers points to another theme across both chick-lit genres: the shortcomings of parents. When parents lack understanding or are too caught up in their own issues, one needs, then, to look elsewhere for comfort and support. From the quirky companions of *Bridget Jones's Diary* to the serious sisterhood of the Traveling Pants novels, friendship becomes a valuable replacement for the omniscient, dependable parents from young childhood books. Not only is this image of parenthood unrealistic, it is also unreasonable to expect parents to forsake their lives entirely in favor of their children's. In adult chick lit the protagonist is often hoping a parent will understand her. Much humor comes from the obvious generation gap and dysfunction of most families. The lack of, or rejection of, parenting in chick lit jr. becomes a more serious component because it requires that the protagonist make her own decisions and act on her own. This movement points to the character's maturing and severing ties that connected her to childhood. While she may turn to her friends for advice and guidance, the main character must ultimately face the reality that she is responsible for her own actions. This realization can be startling and unsettling.

To lighten this message, chick lit jr. often gives the joking impression that becoming an adult is fairly easy, more like a choice: one simply decides and then actions naturally follow. But the close reader will understand the irony of these situations. In Rennison's *Angus, Thongs, and Full-Frontal Snogging*, the main character, Georgia, falls for an older boy. Worried that he might consider her too young for him, she writes in her diary, "I must become more mature quickly. I'll start tomorrow" (50). As if it were that easy. Georgia has many moments where she believes she sees adulthood with great clarity (the irony being that she doesn't). After trying unsuccessfully to understand an article on men in a women's magazine she writes, "I am going to become a writer for *Cosmo*—you don't have to make any sense at all" (118). Her comments point to adulthood being confusing and sometimes unfathomable, and, in this, she would be right. Ideally, the reader will get the message that not everything about being an adult is "knowable" but that she will survive regardless.

What lies between the covers of a YA novel may be serving a higher purpose than that of adult chick lit. But to seduce the young buyer into actually reading the material, publishers must rely on a certain amount of marketing savvy. Cover art for chick lit jr. employs some of the same strategies used to spark interest in the adult versions. They feature the usual bright colors—pink, aqua, lime green—seen on chick-lit covers but tend to shy away from the unsophisticated cartoon drawings so frequently seen on the chick-lit trade paperbacks.[4] YA novels also tend to avoid the stereotypical feminine images that serve as icons of the chick-lit genre such as designer fashion (Lauren Weisberger's *The Devil Wears Prada*), designer fashion and a trendy purse (Carrie Karasyov and Jill Karman's *The Right Address,* Alisa Kwitney's *Does She or Doesn't She?*, and Clare Naylor's *Dog Handling*), high heels (Jennifer Weiner's *In Her Shoes: A Novel* and Candice Bushnell's *Trading Up*), cosmetics (Isabel Wolff's *The Trials of Tiffany Trott* and Sue Margolis's *Apocalipstick*), or generic drawings of shopping bags or a woman shopping (far too many to list). It is interesting that YA covers rarely feature these sorts of material trappings. Although the inner pages of chick lit jr. may be just as obsessed with makeup, shopping, and an interest in boys, the cover art implies a reluctance to acknowledge these tendencies, at least on the outside.[5]

Chick lit jr., instead, appears to aspire to a certain dignity for the younger reader, avoiding the trappings of feminine consumerism in favor of first affirming the teenage girl's insecurities and quest for identity. Cover art for the adult chick lit assumes a security with one's consumerism and need for male companionship. The adult chick-lit reader has, perhaps, moved beyond apologizing for enjoying shopping and wanting men. The adolescent reader, on the other hand, seems to be apologizing for and denying everything. With so many ways to potentially embarrass and alienate the teenage girl, the perfect cover for a YA novel would seem to be brown paper featuring only an intriguing title. And yet publishers have successfully moved beyond these limitations. Cover art often offers real-life photos of teens without revealing the person. The photo always chops off below the eyes and sometimes only features a body from the neck down. This method, employed on the covers of Megan McCafferty's and Cecily von Ziegesar's novels, allows the reader to impose herself into the story (see figure 8.1 and figure 8.2). She could, with a small stretch of the imagination, be that girl on the cover and in the story. The novels are not necessarily about visualizing a particular character. The writers, or at the very least the publishers, hope the reader will internalize the story. While an adult chick lit novel might get away with providing nothing beyond escapism, chick lit jr. might have to work much harder. With limited marketing opportunities and readership, YA chick-lit novels need to be edgy, clever, and approachable to their young women readers, who are less likely than an adult reader to continue with a novel if it does not completely engage them.

Chick lit jr. obviously attempts to address a multitude of issues but, because there is far more adult fiction than YA fiction, chick lit jr. must be less specific and more multi-purpose. It seems harsh to call chick lit jr. "generic," for it must, in fact, serve a broader purpose and target a larger audience. YA literature, inclusive of YA chick lit, often eludes hard and fast categorization. Patty Campbell says, "The complex nature of the dilemma begins with a paradox of two contradictory truths about adolescent literature. First, YA fiction by its very nature defies categorization. Like adolescence, its definition is constantly shifting." Historically, YA literature was the section of the library or bookstore where the adolescent briefly stopped before moving on to adult fiction. Borders Books' recent decision to move its YA section away from the children's department and into the middle of adult fiction hints at the young adult's pressing need to disassociate herself with her youthful ties. At an age when many believe that appearance is

Figure 8.1 Jacket cover from *Sloppy Firsts: A Novel* by Megan McCafferty, copyright ©2001 by Megan McCafferty. Used by permission of Crown Publishers, a division of Random House, Inc.

Figure 8.2 Jacket cover from *Gossip Girl #2: You Know You Love Me* by Cecily von Ziegesar. Used by permission of Little, Brown and Company.

everything, the stigma alone of even being seen in the children's section is enough to discourage a book purchase. A clever marketing strategy, this relocation implies that the teen reader is more of a "preadult" rather than still a child. With retailers acknowledging the buying power of teens, this change may be about more than just bookstore geography. The positive news is that interest in YA literature as a separate genre from children's literature continues to grow. The American Library Association has a Young Adult Library Services Association that, in 2000, introduced the Michael L. Printz award "that exemplifies literary excellence in young adult literature" (ala.org). With continued marketing success, the YA kiosk in the middle of adult mainstream fiction may even aspire to add a shelf or two.

As heated discussions regarding purpose and value continue, do scholars have a right to place expectations on chick lit and chick lit jr.? With its slick promotional Web sites, snappy cover art, glamour shots of authors, and aggressive marketing, chick lit has an obvious objective to sell books, and *lots* of them. Entertainment and enlightenment could certainly be part of this equation but, judging by the wide range of quality in the so-labeled chick-lit genre, these features may not be necessary. Chick lit jr., however, appears committed to educating and must do so carefully. Teenagers living in industrialized countries, particularly North American teens, have tremendous access to information and stimulation. In addition, technology has created a language all its own through instant messaging, e-mail, and text messaging. This overstimulated MTV generation wants its preferences and language affirmed. The most successful popular YA authors seem to understand this. To truly capture the hearts and minds of young readers, chick lit jr. must positively and respectfully acknowledge the world of the young adult instead of treating it condescendingly.

Chick lit jr., like young adulthood, maintains a precarious and often difficult position. The added function of the chick-lit-jr. novel is that it works to help the young female reader make the transition into adulthood or at least understand that she is not alone in her confusion. Some critics and scholars have argued that adult chick lit is on its way out, its fifteen minutes of fame over.[6] Chick lit jr., however, has deeper roots. Although linked to chick lit, chick lit jr. holds its own *separate* literary position because of its emphasis on coming of age. As history indicates, the genre will evolve and tomorrow may have a new label, cover art, and jargon. While the specific novels may date themselves with references to slang, fashion, technology, and music, their themes have functioned effectively over several centuries. They have offered guidance and direction to young women while providing insight into historical and popular culture. At its core chick lit jr. will continue to affirm and guide its young readers, we hope with good humor and dignity, as they make the transition into adulthood.

Notes

1. My discussion of Alcott's work is much simplified here. The novel has been appropriated as a feminist text because of its subversion of a traditional patriarchal culture and the prominence and strength of its female characters. Likeable male characters in this novel are feminized or absent altogether.
2. Obviously, other authors contributed to the progression and evolution of children's literature over the past century. I skip ahead one hundred years because Blume's work introduced the most significant change that directed popular YA novels to their present state.
3. A comprehensive discussion of this phenomenon can be read in Patty Campbell's "The Sand in the Oyster: Rescuing Young Adult Literature," *Horn Book*, May–June 1997: 363.
4. Louise Rennison's novels do tend to use cartoon drawings, but they vary from the adult versions in that they feature the adolescent female body from only the waist down. The adult counterparts usually show a stylized feminine (and complete) body, whereas the Rennison covers are clearly that of a uniformed school girl paired with other relevant, and usually humorous, images from the novels.
5. The exception to this rule seems to be Cecily von Ziegesar's Gossip Girl novels that often stray beyond the boundaries of traditional YA themes and topics. Her books tend to read like adult mass-market paperbacks with YA characters.
6. Although this debate is beyond the scope of my project, it appears that since adult chick lit is dynamic and eluding definition, it too will continue to evolve and exist in different incarnations. Saying there is only one kind of chick lit (and that its time is over) seems to imply a very narrow view of the genre and its objectives.
   I am indebted to my colleague Peggy Kulesz for her helpful criticism and suggestions on this chapter.

Works Cited

Campbell, Patty. "The Sand in the Oyster: Rescuing Young Adult Literature." *Horn Book* May–June 1997: 363.

James-Enger, Kelly. "The Scoop on Chick Lit." *The Writer* Nov. 2003: 42–46.

Marsh, Kelly A. "Contextualizing Bridget Jones." *College Literature* 31.1 (2004): 52–72.

McCafferty, Megan. *Second Helpings*. New York: Three Rivers Press, 2003.

Razdan, Anjula. "The Chick Lit Challenge." *Utne* Mar.–Apr. 2004: 20–21.

Rennison, Louise. *Angus, Thongs, and Full-Frontal Snogging: Confessions of Georgia Nicolson.* 1999. New York: HarperTempest, 2001.

"Specialized Literary Subgenres Known as Lits." Narr. Brooke Gladstone. *All Things Considered.* Natl. Public Radio. Apr. 23, 2004.

Trites, Roberta Seelinger. *Disturbing the Universe: Power and Repression in Adolescent Literature.* Iowa City: University of Iowa Press, 2000.

9

Ya Yas, Grits, and Sweet Potato Queens: Contemporary Southern Belles and the Prescriptions That Guide Them

ELIZABETH B. BOYD

Why is the twenty-first century all of a sudden the perfect time to attempt to become a southern lady or belle—gender icons rooted in nineteenth-century mythology? Why are so many conduct manuals on the subject of southern femininity suddenly enjoying ready publication and wide readership? Why would the flamboyant antics of the Sweet Potato Queens, a women's performance group dedicated to mocking traditional ideals of southern womanhood, be popular enough to attract thousands of women from across the country to a nondescript southern city every spring? It *is* curious.

Blame it on Rebecca Wells. Ever since the publication of *Divine Secrets of the Ya-Ya Sisterhood*, Wells's tale of a Louisiana sisterhood that bonds over the trials of patriarchy, prescriptive literature targeting southern belle wannabes—and their ironic sisters—has experienced a heyday. New titles have appeared and old ones have been reissued; the twenty-first century, strangely, seems a great time to attempt belledom—or to fly in its face. Both positions (apparently) require instruction. And who could go wrong, with so much advice close at hand? Following on the dyed-to-match heels of Maryln Schwartz's best-selling humor volume *A Southern Belle Primer*,

Or Why Princess Margaret Will Never Be a Kappa Kappa Gamma, and join-
ing newly available reissues of Florence King's classic satires on regional
gender roles, are a slew of books that either laud or lampoon time-
honored notions of southern womanhood. From Deborah Ford and Edie
Hand's *The Grits (Girls Raised in the South) Guide to Life* to Loraine
Despres's *The Southern Belle's Handbook: Sissy LeBlanc's Rules to Live By* to
Jill Conner Browne's Sweet Potato Queens series, the current retail book-
shelf is chock-full of titles that take an outdated gender ideal as their subject. Add to the mix volumes such as *Queen of the Turtle Derby and Other
Southern Phenomena, Vogue* writer Julia Reed's argument for southern difference, and Seale Ballenger's *Hell's Belles,* a pop history reader that aims to
redefine the belle in racially diverse terms (which pretty much negates the
whole idea of the belle, but I digress), and you have a veritable trend. Even
NASCAR's Ronda Rich (whose book about racetracks, *My Life in the Pits,*
is 180 degrees from belledom) couldn't resist cashing in on this market,
publishing *What Southern Women Know (That Every Woman Should):
Timeless Secrets to Get Everything You Want in Love, Life, and Work.* Riding
on their coattails is columnist Celia Rivenbark, whose *We're Just Like You,
Only Prettier: Confessions of a Tarnished Southern Belle* has absolutely
nothing to do with being *either* southern *or* a belle. But at least she can
spot a trend.

Characterized in turns by sincerity and irony, the books in this subgenre are simply too numerous to be dismissed as a mere collective joke
poking fun at an outmoded gender construction. Some are deadly serious,
aimed at convincing women that the old feminine ways of subordination-
as-strategy were actually highly pragmatic. Others are campy satire set on
skewering the very prescriptions that confined and defined generations of
southern women. Some are a bit of both, poking self-referential fun at the
classic habits and trappings of the southern belle, and yet in cataloging her
every amusing way also holding her up for adoration. Both the "wannabe a
belle" books and the "wannakill a belle" books stem from a common root:
the continued hold of gender prescriptions on contemporary women.
Although at first glance these books appear sharply divided, I would like to
suggest that they in fact constitute a continuum of femininity with as
many commonalities as differences. Despite their often opposing tactics,
they are successful because old feminine prescriptions continue to burden
American women. The Sweet Potato Queens followers who bond over
rejecting the dictums of traditional femininity found in the works of
Ronda Rich and Deborah Ford understand the radical message of Jill Conner Browne only because they know the old prescriptions all too well.

Moreover, the popularity of these books with nonsoutherners is clear
indication that feminine prescriptions are not the burden of southern

women alone. Sales across the genre are just as high in Washington, D.C. as in Atlanta—and both are eclipsed by those in New York. The prissy precepts of Ronda Rich are just as popular in the Bay Area as in Dallas. Sweet Potato Queens fans in Denver, Seattle, and Chicago rival those in New Orleans, Atlanta, and Jackson (Nielsen BookScan). Southern womanhood in all its mythological glory may represent, historically, the pinnacle of gender prescription, but women across the country seem to identify with its insidious influence.

The Grits (Girls Raised in the South) Guide to Life bills itself as "a bible of Southern style," and it certainly cites chapter and verse on everything from religion to manners to sports. Organized for browsing, not reading, this Fannie Farmer of femininity is a lighthearted mix of recipes, truisms, and prescriptions. Lists of every sort abound, as do pen-and-ink diagrams (how to make a mint julep, how to season your iron skillet, how to take care of your pearls). Lengthy sidebars address such burning issues as how to grow your own magnolia tree, how to flirt, and how to plan a southern wedding. Scattered throughout are "Pearls of Wisdom," such as "If you can be ready to go in less than thirty minutes, you probably shouldn't be leaving the house at all!" (43). Entries in the "Grits Glossary" are along these lines: "**Revival:** an all-day meeting where a large group of people get together to shout, shake, forget their cares, and get in touch with their roots; a.k.a. the religious equivalent of a football game" (173).

Interestingly readers needn't have been born or even reared in the South to become "girls raised in the South," although upon close inspection, Ford vacillates throughout the text between essentialist and constructivist definitions of southern womanhood. On the one hand Grits possess "absolutely irresistible charm, a relaxed southern drawl that leaves men hanging on every word, and the natural inclination to be cunning and caring" (xiii). On the other, like cultured pearls, "Grits aren't born, they're made" (23). Attention to detail, possession of the right attitude, and utter adherence to the Grits manual are far more important than birthplace, according to Ford, who writes, "Absolutely anyone can learn the secrets of southern charm, no matter where you're from or who your people are" (xvii).

Such a can-do attitude works for Birmingham author Ford, who was a high school volleyball coach before she discovered there was big money to be made helping southern women to claim their upbringing—and others to fake it. The slogan she emblazoned on team T-shirts one day on a whim met with quick demand for more Grits merchandise, so much so that today Grits, Inc. is a multimillion-dollar merchandising company specializing in women's apparel.

Scholars generally agree that in the absence of true regional distinctiveness, both southerners and nonsoutherners continue to contribute to this effort of maintaining a knowable South by trafficking in southern difference (Ayers 66). For those hankering for some past South of the imagination, one somehow more unified, more authentic, and more distinct, commodification is central to recreating this fiction (Ayers 66–68). Removed temporally from the things that made the South truly different—from poverty, slavery, one-crop agriculture, and one-party politics (Woodward 5, 17)—consumer products take on a heightened role in constructing regional identity. After all, it was only after the so-called Bulldozer Revolution, that massive wave of post-WWII southern migration directly from farm to suburb (Woodward 6), that *Southern Living* became so profitable (Roberts 86). A conduct manual on "how to be an upper-middle-class Southerner," *Southern Living* prescribed the silver patterns, garden plans, football weekends, and grits casseroles the southerner yearning for connection with the past could consume (Roberts 87).

Small wonder, then, that leafing through *The Grits Guide to Life* produces a certain nostalgia. Perusing it is a little like leafing through an old scrapbook or farmer's almanac from days gone by. There is the spark of recognition (That's how it was!) coupled with amusement and, for some, pride, over outdated ways. Above all there is identification. As much conduit for memory as yardstick for living, *Grits* and volumes like it are sites for constructing regional identity in a postmodern age. For the white southerner, at least, *Grits* and its ilk remind the reader of who she is and where she came from, and serve as a mechanism for identifying with an increasingly endangered sense of place. Despite gestures toward racial inclusiveness, the belle books are a *white* thing, just as southern identity long was, and the unmistakable subtext is that "lots of the old ways really were better." With remaining claims to regional distinctiveness tenuous at best, southerners wistful for lost race and class privilege look to the gender rituals around which such privileges were constructed in the first place. What is ostensibly a good laugh at her own expense is also the reader's education and fond reminder. Equal parts self-deprecating humor, instructional guide, and cultural memory mechanism, the current how-to-be-a-belle book sells so well because it speaks both to women's general ambivalence about current gender matters and to white southerners' sense of loss. In the likes of *Grits*, white southern women recognize what they both hope they have overcome and are a little sad to have lost. Small surprise that the ultimate figure of nostalgia for women wistful for the days of being "Daddy's girl" (namely, Daddy) occupies *Grits* pride of place. "The Right Men" are as follows: Daddy, Jimmy Carter, Martin Luther King, Jr.,

Andy Griffith, Daddy, Robert E. Lee, Samuel L. Jackson, Peyton Manning, and Daddy (66)!

Daddy also looms large in Ronda Rich's *What Southern Women Know (That Every Woman Should): Timeless Secrets to Get Everything You Want in Love, Life, and Work.* Rich, though, prefers Daddies of the sugar variety. "Every woman, at some time or other, has dreamed of marrying a successful man and having a comfortable, even luxurious life," notes Rich, who writes of "capturing" and "landing" men "with a high earning capacity" (39), as if she were bagging a ten-point buck on the first day of deer season or reeling in a trophy fish (and perhaps she is). A willingness to be flexible and patient, to "adapt to a man's lifestyle," are key to Rich's big-game strategy, lest you lose out to the dozens of "beautiful, sexy women waiting in line behind you should you choose to abort the mission" (40). "In the South we say 'If you can't run with the big dogs, stay on the porch with the puppies,' " writes Rich. "If your goal is to marry a corporate CEO or mega-millionaire businessman, learn right now to adjust. Or resign yourself to staying on the porch" (38).

Ronda Rich is one big dog. Like Deborah Ford, she goes back and forth over whether southern womanhood is something natural or achievable, although like Ford, she leans toward the latter. She too has a book to sell. In this guidebook to using old-school feminine wiles to get what you want, Rich is unabashed in both her ridicule of more feminist approaches and her contention that southern femininity is an art form worthy of emulation. Above all, she is adamant that southern women are best at "having it all" because they flaunt their femininity "from bedrooms to boardrooms" (20).

Like Ford, she opens her book with a lot of "steel magnolia" talk about southern women's remarkable composition. Southern women are not only "the magnolia-scented breath which sustains the life of the South" but also "an enchanting blend of silk and steel, ... whose carefully maintained exteriors beautifully camouflage[d] a fiery determination and indefatigable spirit" (1). But where Ford is sweet, Rich is strategic. Where Ford is whimsical, Rich is wily. Remember, Rich is at the hunt, and she means to have her way—with men, with coworkers, with salesmen, with her mother—all the while coming off like some sort of goddess of benevolence and sincerity. What you might call fakery and manipulation, Rich calls femininity and manners.

Positing herself as the keeper of the keys to southern womanhood's "titillating secrets" (10), Rich notes that, "We're specifically trained from the cradle to be feminine. ... But our charm is painstakingly developed. We spend years learning to wink, smile, flutter, flatter, and bedazzle" (15). Projecting yourself as "the perfect girlish woman—an irresistible blend of wide-eyed wonder, worldliness, and sexiness" is Rich's recommendation for success of every sort (189). At the office especially, Rich suggests women flaunt their femininity, right down to "color coordinating your lingerie to business suit to your toenail polish to your lip gloss. … We socially flirt at the office, wear feminine, soft clothing, and shamelessly use our feminine wiles to get what we want professionally—plum assignments, transfers, raises, and promotions" (20). You read it here first: southern women "powder and perfume not only ourselves *but* our bedsheets" (21).

Mostly, Rich is a master manipulator, although she is quick to claim that she is not. "Southern women are not manipulative," writes Rich. "We are merely persuasive. We use our charm to gently bring the other person around to our way of thinking" (30). Rich's fables of getting everything she wants (a luxury car, a home, a promotion, a divorce) with just the flutter of an eyelash have been successful enough that a sequel is in the works: *What Southern Women Know about Flirting.*

As a southerner, I learned so much about myself reading Rich. How was I to know the following?

> We don't wear curlers or yard clothes to the grocery store. We do wear lipstick and mascara. Always.

> We love bright colors and always find our most complementary shades. (You will never find a lot of solid black in a southern woman's closet.)

> Shoes always match or complement our outfits.

> Southern ladies rarely go braless.

> Hairstyles and makeup are regularly updated—at least every 12 to 18 months.

> Jeans are worn occasionally, not regularly.

> Maintenance is a must. (85–88)

This last item is crucial, because according to Rich, "We Southern women view ourselves as an overall marketing package that attracts people—particularly men—to us, personally and professionally" (85).

I'd like to put Ronda Rich and Jill Conner Browne in the same room and watch the fur fly. Browne is all for attracting men and for feminine maintenance (she calls plastic surgery her new hobby), but it's Rich's package she despises. In fact, the Sweet Potato Queens came about in response to just the sort of prescriptive gender definition Rich represents. Inspired in part by years of watching the Miss America pageant with a mixture of fascination and disgust, Browne noted that it was high time women quit waiting to be selected (typically by men) on the basis of dubious gender ideals; the self-actualized woman would simply *declare* herself Queen. As she tells it,

> What I'm saying here is that the Sweet Potato Queens are real live grown-up women—self-sufficient and self-actualized. But we were crownless, one and all. Who, I ask, would be more worthy and capable of wearing a crown—the women I've just described, or some eighteen-year old surgically altered twit whose sole accomplishment is finally learning all the words to "My Way"? (SPQBOL 8)

Declaring herself Boss Queen and all her accomplices "Tammy," Browne and some friends donned thrift-store gowns, red wigs, and cheap tiaras and tossed raw sweet potatoes from the back of a pickup truck in the 1982 St. Patrick's Day parade in her hometown of Jackson, Mississippi. The same year, Browne began writing columns for a local independent newspaper, which eventually led to *The Sweet Potato Queens' Book of Love* (1999), *God Save the Sweet Potato Queens* (2001), *The Sweet Potato Queens' Big-Ass Cookbook (and Financial Planner)* (2003), and *The Sweet Potato Queens' Field Guide to Men: Every Man I Love Is Either Married, Gay, or Dead* (2004). Collectively, the books have sold some 1.5 million copies.

What began as a lark quickly developed into a cult following for Browne as women across the country responded to her tales of dressing outrageously, shedding inhibitions, and having fun. Today, thousands of women make a pilgrimage to Jackson each March to do just that alongside the original Queens, whose green sequined parade outfits have morphed over the years to feature ever more enormous padded breasts and buttocks, paired with red wigs, cats-eye sunglasses, majorette boots, and hot pink feather boas.

Noting, "As far as we can tell, we are the only female drag queens in existence," Browne recognizes the masquerade central to all gender performance (SPQBOL 11). By dressing the Queens in costumes of outsized proportions ("For white males, it is impossible to have tits that are too big, and for black males, you cannot get the butt big enough" [SPQBOL 10]), she manages to simultaneously criticize traditional yardsticks of femininity and remove the Queens from such scrutiny. In this powerful, playful move, the Queens shift from object to subject, from recipients of the male gaze to gazers of men. I suspect it is this gender sleight of hand that women across the country find so appealing.

Browne's spud empire now includes more than two thousand Sweet Potato Queens chapters worldwide and a Web site that hosts an active message board and does a quarter-million-dollar business in merchandise. With a $1 million contract for four more books and a sitcom pilot in the can for WB, Browne is riding the zeitgeist of American gender anxieties.

Browne chronicles in the books the antics, camaraderie, social lives, and sex lives of her close-knit group of women friends in Jackson. The Queens act up, take road trips, wear trashy lingerie, have lots of sex and talk about it, criticize other people just because they can, and, in general, make their own fun. They shop for sex toys. They indulge in heart-clogging recipes for Pig Candy (bacon and brown sugar), Chocolate Stuff, and Love Lard (the Queens' four major food groups are sweet, salty, fried, and au gratin). They drink lots of Fat Mama's Knock You Naked Margaritas. Their favorite activity is Not Doing Jack Shit (also known as Lolling About). If the Queens have a modus operandi, it is "anti"—antipolitical correctness, anticonvention, and, above all, antibelle.

Many of the Queens' escapades and most of their nearly incessant discussions center on the pursuit of A Suitable Man. The Sweet Potato Queens *love* men—"they taste just like chicken" (GSTSPQ 165; SPQBOL 99)—and at first glance it seems that heterosexual romance is priority number one in the spud kingdom. Yet closer inspection reveals that men are merely the parlor-game means to a more significant end: the creation and nurturance of a community of women. First of all, as far as the Queens are concerned,

> There are five different men that you must endeavor to have in your life at all times in order to have the equivalent of one satisfactory man ... (1) a man who can fix things; (2) a man you can dance with; (3) a man who can pay for things; (4) a man you can talk to; and (5) a man to have great sex with. The great news is that four out of the five can be gay! As a matter of fact, it would be a plus if they were gay. (SPQBOL 105–106, 111)

As a central organizing principle, this stance frees the Queens to view men as amusing but dispensable, "like cat toys" (SPQBOL 95; GSTSPQ 77), a position subversive of traditional gender hierarchies. In fact, much of Browne's second book is devoted to backtracking to assure disaffected male readers that the Queens aren't ball-busting man-haters after all. But inherent in The Promise, the Queens' signature prank in which, in return for some favor, a targeted man is promised a group blow job just to see how foolishly he will react (*promise* being the operative word, because delivery never occurs), is the fact that the Queens' first loyalty and true interest is each other (SPQBOL 45). Men serve as viable props and passing fancies, but the care and feeding of the Queens represents the central desire.

Ann Patchett perhaps put it best. Writing in the *New York Times Magazine* on the appeal of *Sex and the City,* she noted, "I used to think that the core fantasy of [the show] was that you could have your ultimate core bond in your friendships with women, while getting everything else you might need from a man.... I think the deeper fantasy is having such close women friends and having the time to actually spend with them" (9–10). Realizing further that "it was this very maelstrom of talk, this bright and complicated intimacy, that first caught me up" in the program (9), Patchett hits on what is surely a key attraction to fans of the Sweet Potato Queens. In an age of disillusionment regarding gender matters, the colorful exploits and close talk of a tight-knit group of women who rebel against the gender rules is the stuff of fantasy.

It doesn't surprise me one bit that Jill Conner Browne and her Sweet Potato Queens arose out of Jackson, Mississippi, or that the same spot on Capitol Street where civil rights proponents once marched past segregationist governor Ross Barnett's mansion is now the site of the Bucket Head Judges viewing stand, the place where the Queens stop each year to gyrate, thrust, and, in general, behave badly to the tune of Don Ho's "Tiny Bubbles" and the Monotones' "Who Wrote the Book of Love?" After all, born and reared in Jackson, I well remember its strict gender codes, which in the 1970s were still governed by 1950s-era prescriptions. If elsewhere old gender arrangements were under revision, in Jackson, as in much of the post–civil rights movement South, whites tender over the steady erosion of white privilege celebrated traditional gender arrangements as an expression of continued resistance to a changing racial landscape.

Had it ever been otherwise? The original southern lady, after all, was the imaginative creation of white, slaveholding southern men, who looked to her to rationalize a race–gender system that placed the patriarchal father at the head of households of women, children, and slaves. Pious and passive, graceful and deferential, the southern lady—as essence of endangered purity—legitimated white supremacy; she was the linchpin without which the whole system crumbled (Scott 4, 16–17).

Then, as now, prescriptive literature (plantation novels, sermons, conduct books, public orations) told real, live women exactly what constituted the ideal (Scott 4). The message must have been hard to miss; the most articulate champions of the subordinate role of women were also the most outspoken proponents of slavery—and they had a lot riding on the bargain (17).

She was always, of course, more mythological than real. Yet the southern lady over time proved an image with remarkable staying power. Ditto her representational sidekick, the southern belle, whose bright surfaces, strategic flirtations, and noncommittal charms historically were tactics for maximizing position within a narrow marriage market but have since survived as the very essence of southern feminine performance (Farnham 180).

Next to her antebellum heyday, it was a full century later, during the height of modern segregation, that the lady experienced perhaps her finest hour. Jim Crow meant that the southern lady never really went away. In fact, she was back to stay. Upheld once more as the reason behind "our southern way of life," she became the silent but potent focal point for white southerners' massive resistance to racial equality. In ritual renditions of femininity that were public, popular, and highly specific—in beauty pageants, debutante displays, Old South tourist productions, sorority rituals, and the Junior League—women performed southern whiteness. Ensuring continuity of the performance was a steady stream of prescription.

As Anne Rivers Siddons writes in her novel *Heartbreak Hotel,* a tale of a young white woman coming of age amidst the civil rights drama of the 1950s and 1960s,

> In the cities of the South—in Atlanta and Birmingham and Charlotte and Mobile and Charleston—there were … girls planted, tended, and grown like prize roses, to be cut and massed and shown at debutante balls and cotillions in their eighteenth year. Unlike roses, they did not die after the sowing; instead, they moved gently into colleges and universities and Junior League chapters, and were then pressed between the leaves of substantial marriages to be dried and preserved. (4)

Behind this reproduction of femininity, writes Siddons, was "a process of rules, subtle, shaded, iron bylaws that were tacitly drafted in burned and torn households sometime during the Reconstruction" (5).

So if twenty years down the road, Browne and her gang of gutsy, fun, professional women still felt constrained by lagging gender codes magnified by regional mythology, the fact that the Sweet Potato Queens would emerge in Jackson, Mississippi seems from my point of view not only not surprising but also perfectly logical. Liberation may have come in the mid-1960s, but for white southern women, the pedestal still stood and, indeed, many clung to it—their race and class privilege depended on it. Remember, this was the era when white southern women helped defeat the Equal Rights Amendment by organizing a groundswell of support for what eventually became known as the religious right. Southern women provided key support for antifeminist Phyllis Schlafly's campaign called STOP ERA—for "Stop Taking Our Privileges" (Spruill and Wheeler). In a snapshot of southern gender relations during this era, Donna Tartt writes of disillusioned young Jackson women wistfully paging through the old sorority scrapbooks that documented their brightest moments of gender glory. The present—dominated by Junior League obligations, a steady round of barbecues with the same old friends from Ole Miss, and marriage to Bubba, who worked at the bank—paled in comparison. Was this all there was?

By 1982, though, the year the Equal Rights Amendment died and the Sweet Potato Queens made their parade debut, some women had had enough of the contradictions between the ever-present gender prescriptions that continued to nag and their otherwise self-actualized lives. Think about it: the contradictions were enough to send not one but two former officers in the Junior League of Jackson in search of sequins.

In the end, though, are the Sweet Potato Queens really that different from the Red Hat Society, that thriving association of purple-and-red-clad women begun in 1998 and dedicated to offbeat fun after fifty? Or the middle-aged rockers who will play sold-out shows in four major cities this year as part of Mamapalooza? From modest to loud to in-your-face with sequins, all represent reactions to the same confining rules of decorum that linger over American women's lives.

Although Browne exposes gender prescriptions as patriarchal, and offers an empowering set of rules in their place, she doesn't completely refute traditional sex and gender hierarchies. Amidst lingering prescriptions, the Sweet Potato Queens, like Rebecca Wells's Ya-Ya sisterhood, constitute a space of gender comfort, an idealized source of solace and support. Something of an imaginative halfway house for women, the group serves as a survival mechanism for navigating both feminist yearnings and southern patriarchy. The Queens stop short of espousing feminism, but they provide tips and tools for negotiating slow-to-change regional gender hierarchies through play. Like Janice Radway's romance readers in Smithton, Sweet Potato Queen readers find in Browne's books a space of female camaraderie and subversion absent from their day-to-day lives.

Like the Red Hat Society, the Queens both caricature southern womanhood's ways and replicate them, in form if not in content. Browne's books see the Queens celebrating all the usual rituals traditionally performed by southern women, but with a twist. Those rituals predicated on "getting together with the girls," naturally, occupy a place of honor. The Queens celebrate birthdays (but rent out a children's game palace, because youth is wasted on the young). They host bridal showers (but sex toys and raunchy lingerie, not sterling and crystal, are the favored gifts). They get together to watch the Miss America pageant (and everyone is issued a rubber dart gun at the door). Browne delivers a tirade about the damage done to generations of American women by the domestic prescriptions of "Betty-by-God-Crocker," and then fills her books with "white trash" recipes that both send up southern cooking at midcentury and nod nostalgically at the past (SPQBAC&FP 4–5, 14). Campy recipes—high in fat, salt, sugar, pork, and attitude—provide another mode for Browne to reject prescriptions about body image and idealized femininity, all the while paying tribute to southern foodways.

I would like to suggest that the production and consumption of all of these books represents an uneasy nostalgia for an earlier era of race and gender relations. Where Rich and Ford promote such backward glances, Browne attempts to destabilize them, but both camps respond to the lingering presence of old feminine codes. Caught between postmodern lives and regional gender prescriptions that (still) expect them to maintain "southern lady" and "belle" performances in their feminine repertoire, southern women find on the printed page a space for negotiating what in real life is all but irreconcilable.

Ronda Rich may write, "We have not chosen to participate in the career world by sacrificing our home lives. And though it can be exhausting, we have not given up on that old-fashioned notion that we can, indeed, have it all" (*What Southern Women Know* 128), but the truth is many southern women feel caught between economic demands, career aspirations, and feminist ideals on one hand and age-old regional gender prescriptions on the other. For them, Arlie Hochschild's second shift is joined by a third: the burden of maintaining appearances, rituals, and periodic performances associated with a specific, regional rendition of femininity even though their day-to-day lives are far removed from any semblance of gentility or leisure. Witness the emergency room surgeon who insists on receiving not just the *one* set of fine china upon her engagement but twelve place settings of her Christmas china, too. And the harried academic who burns the candle at both ends, writing cutting-edge criticism by night and making sure her daughters appear at Sunday School in properly smocked dresses by day. Such feminine enactments—essentially material displays of gendered leisure—belie the real time scarcity women everywhere actually experience. Reiterating as they do the very prescriptions that burden them, southern women turn to books like those discussed here for direction, validation, or a way to laugh about it all.

Although they have no intention of actually living their lives to the letter by the old prescriptions (or employing the new primer methods), southern women look to their bookshelves. Because just as the HGTV viewer relaxing in her slummy house likes knowing that she *could* accomplish the perfect remodel (should the time, money, and inclination suddenly appear), the twenty-first-century southern woman likes imagining, at least, that she possesses the feminine knowledge for enacting belledom or southern ladyhood should the penchant arise.

The Sweet Potato Queens act up (and how), but still they never directly challenge the gender status quo. Without men and heterosexual desire surrounding the periphery of the Queens' steadfast sisterhood, Browne's formula would be blown (pun intended). On the face of it, the Queens' wry commentary on southern rituals of femininity and status appears to subvert. But in the end they provide vast compendia of regional feminine knowledge alongside the laughter. Together with their more serious sisters, the ironic books comprise a feminine reference library for the white southern woman estranged in the contemporary field of manners. Such a widely varied prescriptive reading room at turns explains, lampoons, reveals, instructs, skewers, and blasts—and all in armchair comfort. Today's prescriptive belle literature keeps regional gender expectations both ready at hand and neatly contained—something not always possible in real life.

Works Cited

Ayers, Edward L. "What We Talk about When We Talk about the South." *All over the Map: Rethinking American Regions*. Ed. Edward L. Ayers et al. Baltimore: Johns Hopkins University Press, 1996. 62–82.

Ballenger, Seale. *Hell's Belles: A Tribute to the Spitfires, Bad Seeds and Steel Magnolias of the New and Old South*. Berkeley: Conari Press, 1997.

Browne, Jill Conner. *God Save the Sweet Potato Queens*. New York: Three Rivers Press, 2001.

———. *The Sweet Potato Queens' Big-Ass Cookbook (and Financial Planner)*. New York: Three Rivers Press, 2003.

———. *The Sweet Potato Queens' Book of Love*. New York: Three Rivers Press, 1999.

———. *The Sweet Potato Queens' Field Guide to Men: Every Man I Love Is Either Married, Gay, or Dead*. New York: Three Rivers Press, 2004.

Despres, Loraine. *The Southern Belle's Handbook: Sissy LeBlanc's Rules to Live By*. New York: William Morrow, 2003.

Farnham, Christie Anne. *The Education of the Southern Belle: Higher Education and Student Socialization in the Antebellum South*. New York: New York University Press, 1994.

Ford, Deborah, with Edie Hand. *The Grits (Girls Raised in the South) Guide to Life*. New York: Dutton, 2003.

Hochschild, Arlie. *The Second Shift: Working Parents and the Revolution at Home*. New York: Viking, 1989.

King, Florence. *Confessions of a Failed Southern Lady*. New York: St. Martin's Griffin, 1990.

———. *The Florence King Reader*. New York: St. Martin's Griffin, 1995.

———. *Southern Ladies and Gentlemen*. New York: Stein and Day, 1975.

Nielsen BookScan. Dedicated Market Analysis reports. February 2005.

Patchett, Ann. "Friendship Envy." *New York Times Magazine* 29, June 2003: 9–10.

Radway, Janice. *Reading the Romance: Women, Patriarchy, and Popular Literature*. Chapel Hill: University of North Carolina Press, 1984.

Reed, Julia. *Queen of the Turtle Derby and Other Southern Phenomena*. New York: Random House, 2004.

Rich, Ronda. *My Life in the Pits: Living and Learning in the NASCAR Winston Cup Circuit.* New York: Morrow/Avon, 2002.

———. *What Southern Women Know (That Every Woman Should): Timeless Secrets to Get Everything You Want in Love, Life, and Work.* New York: Perigee, 1999.

Rivenbark, Celia. *We're Just Like You, Only Prettier: Confessions of a Tarnished Southern Belle.* New York: St. Martin's, 2004.

Roberts, Diane. "Living Southern in Southern Living." *Dixie Debates: Perspectives on Southern Culture.* Ed. Richard King and Helen Taylor. New York: New York University Press, 1996. 85–98.

Schwartz, Maryln. *A Southern Belle Primer, Or Why Princess Margaret Will Never Be a Kappa Kappa Gamma.* New York: Doubleday, 1991.

Scott, Anne Firor. *The Southern Lady: From Pedestal to Politics, 1830–1930.* Charlottesville: University Press of Virginia, 1995.

Siddons, Anne Rivers. *Heartbreak Hotel.* New York: Simon and Schuster, 1976.

Spruill, Marjorie Julian, and Julian Spruill Wheeler. "The Equal Rights Amendment and Mississippi." *Mississippi History Now.* Mar. 2003. <http://mshistory.k12.ms.us/>.

Tartt, Donna. "The Belle and the Lady." *The Oxford American* 26 (March–May 1999): 94–105.

Wells, Rebecca. *Divine Secrets of the Ya-Ya Sisterhood.* New York: HarperTrade, 1997.

Woodward, C. Vann. *The Burden of Southern History.* Baton Rouge: Louisiana State University Press, 1960.

10
Bridget Jones and Hungarian Chick Lit

NÓRA SÉLLEI

Helen Fielding's *Bridget Jones's Diary* is, undoubtedly, one of Britain's major cultural export goods. In this essay I analyze what is called the "Bridget Jones effect" or "Bridget Jones phenomenon" in Hungary, particularly because it has had a direct impact on Hungarian chick lit, an impact that is radical in its cultural and ideological emphases and has brought about an unprecedented discourse. All the elements of the discourse surrounding the "Hungarian Bridget Jones" phenomenon are indicative of the complex sociocultural and historical moment in which they are implicated. Likewise, they are indicative of how chick lit both as a literary genre and as a social phenomenon has been received in postcommunist Hungary, which is coping with a social reality where certain values have disappeared or at the least are in need of readjustment and reconsideration, perhaps even a new interpretative framework. In spite of the undeniable influence of *Bridget Jones,* this cultural borrowing cannot be read fully in terms of cultural dominance and dependence—rather it has contributed to a new multi-national cultural creation.

Bridget Jones is clearly a major British cultural export, having, by 2002, sold eight million copies worldwide and been translated into at least thirty-three languages. Still, it did not travel quickly to Hungary. *Bridget Jones's Diary* was first published in 1996, with its sequel *The Edge of Reason* appearing in 1999, but both were translated into Hungarian only in 2001.

Yet the moment *Bridget Jones* reached the Hungarian market, it became a nationalized cultural product, turning into a kind of cultural import that young women, primarily university students and graduates, consumed eagerly. It does not come as much of a surprise, then, that in 2002 Zsuzsa Rácz, an English-major graduate and freelance journalist in her early thirties, published what came to be known as the Hungarian Bridget Jones, *Állítsátok meg Terézanyut! (Stop Mammatheresa!).*[1] The novelist gives explicit credit to Bridget Jones, and the novel explicitly acknowledges Bridget's influence.[2]

Mammatheresa, in turn, became a major national best-seller. Indeed, never before has a Hungarian first-novel writer achieved similar success: the book sold some 130,000 copies in a market where selling 3,000 copies is considered significant. It is estimated that at least 400,000 people have read it, four percent of Hungary's population.[3] The author became famous overnight. In an interview she says that whereas when she started to write the book she had nothing, now she has a publisher, a manager, a producer, a lawyer, and a psychologist who helps her to work through all the experiences she has encountered ("Terézanyu megpihenne"). The enormous success of the novel is also indicated by the fact that in hardly more than two years' time, as in the case of *Bridget Jones*, *Mammatheresa*'s film adaptation was released (December 16, 2004), and soon ranked as movie number three on the Budapest Top 10 list (*Cinematrix*).[4]

Bridget Jones in English and in England, *Bridget Jones* in Hungarian and in Hungary, and *Mammatheresa* in Hungarian and in Hungary; however, no matter how many common traits they share, are all different cultural products, with their own specific elements of cultural signification. A comparative analysis of how *Bridget Jones* and *Mammatheresa* became contextualized in Britain and in Hungary reveals much about the process of cultural production and social discourse in the two countries. I will focus on how the two works are interpreted at various levels ranging from more narrow literary terms to the broader social, political, and economic ones.

First, let us consider the obvious similarities between the British novel and its Hungarian successor. What the critic Imelda Whelehan claims of *Bridget Jones* is fully applicable to *Mammatheresa*:

> Whether Fielding actually generated a new market or simply helped to concretize the most successful factors of an existing one is open to some debate. But for many reasons a hugely diverse constituency of readers feel that there is a link between Bridget and their own realities, or at least that Bridget says something genuinely new about single life. (21)

This is the kind of recognition factor (that is, the effect on readers: "That's me, that's about my life") that has made identification with both protagonists possible, particularly among urban, middle-class, mostly university or college-educated (typically in the humanities) young women in their late twenties and early thirties. In this respect, both texts have a direct reference to reality, confirmed by the fact that in many cases writer and protagonist are blurred in the minds of the readers. Such blurring is partly due to the first-person diarylike format—and quite justifiably, as both authors admit the clear autobiographical relevance. Fielding, for example, has often pointed out that Bridget's friends are modeled on her own. Zsuzsa Rácz tells the story that she and her friends pondered (and were later to have a say in deciding) who would play their "own" characters in the film, and tells of her dates' fears that she would actually "write" about them sometime ("Terézanyu megpihenne").

The genre represented by these two novels is not only about the independent single woman creating both her career and a "functional relationship." It is also implicated in the most traditional romance plot: the Mills and Boon romance plot of Harlequin romances that, actually, traces its pedigree back to the more prestigious *Pride and Prejudice* by Jane Austen.

Apart from these common thematic concerns, the Hungarian singleton novel and British chick lit also share certain elements of textual organization, especially first-person narration—usually diary format, but at the least some confessional mode—resulting in the reader's "stolen pleasure and voyeuristic relationship" (Whelehan 22) to the text. In addition these texts are highly innovative in terms of language, not only incorporating contemporary slang but also creating it. In the case of *Bridget Jones,* we were introduced to such neologisms as "singleton," "functional relationship," "smug marrieds," and "emotional fuckwittage." In Hungarian the term "szingli," an appropriation of the term "singleton" that I will discuss below, is the most important such linguistic invention. But the title of the text is an innovation as well: "Mammatheresa" in one word refers ironically to the often altruistic, self-sacrificial character of the protagonist, which conflicts with her desired self-fashioning.

When we look more closely at the plot and protagonist of the Hungarian novel, however, we begin to notice some divergence from the British model. *Mammatheresa* proves, in fact, to be not merely a *cultural* translation of *Bridget Jones* but a transformation. The novel presents a complex central character who exposes several layers of her identity—or, put in another way, takes up a great number of subject positions that implicate her in contemporary social issues. As a result the text has a notable stylistic intricacy and complexity. Kata Kéki is a young woman from a major provincial city, but living in a part of Budapest famous for its Roma ghetto and illegal prostitution. She shares a small flat with her brother, who has just come off drugs, and with his girlfriend. Even this personal space is telling of Hungarian reality: they live in what is called a one-and-a-half-room flat, that is, a normal-sized room and a small one, the small one opening into the bigger one, and both used as bed-sitters: one that of Kata, the other that of the couple. This shared living space obviously results in tensions among the inhabitants of the flat. Yet there is no way out: no matter how absurd it sounds, renting a flat is disastrously expensive, and this place was bought, at the cost of great family sacrifice and renunciation, by the parents for their children to live in the capital.

This is the district of Budapest and this is the flat from where Kata Kéki launches off on her series of job interviews, which indicates in itself that the social reality of the Hungarian Bridget Jones is fundamentally different from her English (and other, nonpostcommunist) counterparts. When depressed, she cannot go on shopping sprees—she is happy enough to buy more than one kind of cheese when she is paid well, and on time, for a temporary job. This difference in economic terms is supported by the sociologist Ágnes Utasi's research on Hungarian singletons, which reveals that whereas in the United States, France, and England whole marketing industries consider the singleton as a target group, Hungarian incomes hardly make a consumer lifestyle possible, either in terms of daily shopping or in terms of living conditions (Farkas).

In this respect Kata Kéki exemplifies the Hungarian singleton as a social phenomenon. Kata's social and economic context also causes her to be more empathetic both toward social issues (she and her friends establish a program for the prevention of drug addiction for secondary school children) and toward her family. In her case, family is not just a "problem," as is, for example, Bridget Jones's mother, but also an intimate emotional link. This family connectedness is indicated by the moving and lyrical passages in which Kata's dead grandmother is recalled, and by Kata's attempts to integrate her grandmother's wisdom into her present and future life.

In general Kata Kéki is caught in a web of reality that is not only characterized by the modern, alienated, and urban singleton life model but also rooted in a more traditional, familial network of allegiances—which inspires her to be "Mammatheresa," that is, to help anyone and everyone who needs help, including her partners, the very reason she loses them. Hence the title of the text: *Stop Mammatheresa!* To become the modern, urban, fashionable, independent individual, Kata must change, yet she cannot reject her Mammatheresa attitude. As a punch line, the text concludes with Mother Theresa's "Hymn of Life," an unexpectedly ambiguous ending. Instead of unambiguously reconfirming the idea of service to others, the "Hymn" is a celebration of life in its totality, opening up a vast array of potential subject positions.

In generic terms both *Bridget Jones* and *Mammatheresa* have paved the way in their respective contexts: each created a new genre in its respective culture, one that cannot be literally translated into the other. Even the concepts suggested in the names for the two genres have different implications. Although the terms for the genre—"chick lit" (and its masculine counterpart, lad lit) in English, and "szingliregény" ("the singleton" novel) in Hungarian—share basic elements, their connotations place them in different signifying systems.

With respect to its history, the Hungarian "szingliregény" differs markedly from the term "chick lit." The word "szingli" did not exist in its current meaning until a few years ago. Anyone with a most basic knowledge of, or even an ear or eye for, Hungarian can guess that the word "szingli" is not based on ancient Finno-Ugric roots. Furthermore, any speaker of Hungarian is aware that the word in the sense of a young, educated, urban single person (primarily woman) has come about only recently. Obviously influenced by Fielding's word "singleton," it is a new expression in the Hungarian language that has eclipsed the word's previous semiotic fields.[5]

It is this word that has become the basis for the name of the literary genre as well. At the same time, the word has initiated a social and cultural discourse about the singleton: a (female) person living on her own, with a distinct sociocultural background. The Hungarian genre term "szingliregény" obviously puts emphasis on an aspect of *Bridget Jones* and *Mammatheresa* that may be less of a novelty in Britain: the lifestyle—and very existence—of the single woman. The English phrase appropriates an old and rather sexist cliché and metaphor that can be interpreted as a derogatory and pejorative gesture or as a feminist attempt at reappropriation, or, as a third solution, an oscillation between, and play with, both of these. The Hungarian phrase, by contrast, is based on linguistic and cultural innovation. In Hungarian, just a few years ago, there was no colloquial name for a single person—and no social reality corresponding to the lifestyle it suggests.

"Szingli," with its obvious status as loan word, with its playfulness, novelty, and literateness, very quickly created a plethora of connotations that also contributed to the amazingly quick creation and canonization of the genre "szingliregény." Both terms very easily found their way into popular discourse. A reviewer for Hungary's most prestigious literary weekly, *Élet és Irodalom* (Life and Literature), starts her review in the following way: "The genre does exist. The terminological certainty of the saleswoman in the bookstore dispelled all my doubts. When I asked her about books like *Bridget Jones's Diary*, she responded: a singleton novel?" (Menyhért 23;

translation mine). The offhand manner of the saleswoman indicates the extent to which the term has entered Hungarian culture and saturated the discourse.

It is likely, as critics have noted, that Helen Fielding consciously used the term "singleton" to replace the negative "spinster" (cf. Menyhért 23). The new term brings with it playful connotations but, at the same time, includes a negative association, echoing the word "simpleton." In this respect "szingli" is an equivalent surpassing its original—no connotation of the simpleton there. Also, it provided the basis for a far more positive expression to designate the genre—even if, as we shall see, the social discourse surrounding it includes elements of a desire to put singletons back in their place, framing them in conservative, and often misogynistic, terms.

Another particularly interesting area indicative of differences in how the two terms are located in the two signifying systems—the British, and in general English-speaking, and Hungarian cultures—is seen in the scholarly and critical discourse on the texts. Apparently no serious review of *Bridget Jones* in England or in English can avoid raising the question of whether it is a postfeminist novel and what that might mean. Does it mean leaving the feminism and feminist achievements of the 1970s and 1980s behind? Or does postfeminism incorporate emancipatory impulses and aims, at the same time airing problems and unresolved tensions created by those freedoms? The 1990s everywoman increasingly has to face and cope with the impact of glossy magazines, consumerism, and the almost unavoidable obsession with the body and body weight, which goes clearly against major feminist achievements of the 1970s.

These issues of female empowerment and consumerism are discussed within a cultural studies and postfeminist framework, focusing on chick lit as an element of popular culture and also as a phenomenon implicated in a whole range of signifying systems, including the economic, the political, the generational, and the social. The discursive framework of popular culture and that of cultural materialism, however, in the English-language context, is *not* derogatory or pejorative in any way, as it is becoming less and less politically correct to interpret texts that used to be labeled as lowbrow in an offhand critical manner.

When it comes to the academic, scholarly reception of the genre in Hungary, one encounters an utterly different cultural discourse. In the Hungarian literary discourse of "szingliregény," the questions of the text as a popular cultural product or what postfeminism might mean are not issues at all. Indeed feminism and feminist criticism, along with cultural studies and cultural criticism, are difficult if not impossible to locate. As a sample, let me rely on a review of *Bridget Jones* in the prestigious literary weekly mentioned previously, by a highly sophisticated critic. She does raise questions that pertain to feminist literary criticism from the 1970s on: for example, she claims that this new genre provides a literary space for those female characters who, beforehand, did not have a life story worth writing and telling. Still, in her analysis of *Bridget Jones,* she does not articulate the kind of double pull and the resulting tension in the book in which most of its humor and irony reside. In her interpretation the major liberating message of the text is that the happy ending is not the result of the coupling off but primarily due to the mental growth and the psychic development of the heroine. She adds that even this happy ending is just a momentary repose on the way to self-knowledge (Menyhért 23). What is lost in this discursive framework is the very contemporaneity of the novel. On the basis of this review, I admit that I would not be inclined to read the novel. Rather, I would be inclined to repeat Katherine Mansfield's rather nasty and dismissive comment on Virginia Woolf's most Victorian novel *Night and Day:* "Jane Austen up-to-date." In fact, judging by this review, *Bridget Jones* appears to be not even Jane Austen up-to-date, but Jane Austen repeated, which is not actually the case.

The relative lack of a *scholarly* discursive framework and terminology that could address the specificity of these texts does not, however, mean that *Bridget Jones* and *Mammatheresa* did not initiate a cultural dialogue of the singleton. The various responses are, to a great extent, symptomatic of how contemporary Hungarian culture handles a relatively new literary and social phenomenon. The literary response to the Hungarian embodiment of chick lit may be even more revealing than the critical discussion. Whereas *Bridget Jones* spawned dozens of English wannabes—similar novels with similar heroines—*Mammatheresa* triggered two unflattering parodies, both by men. These literary responses both appeared in print within a year of the original novel's publication. *Mammatheresa,* as suggested earlier, is a witty text spiced with substantial humor and self-irony, rooted in a complex but subtle way in Hungary's postcommunist present. The two works that followed it, however, bear little resemblance to this model.

One of the responses to the text, *Freak-Out for Daddytheresa, Or Stop the Blondies!* written by two men, Tamás Dián and Belinszki Zoltán, under a female pseudonym, Diána Zoltán, presents itself as a parody at the level of authorial intentions.[6] But because *Mammatheresa* has a strong self-parodying current, the effect of *Daddytheresa*—which alludes to yet another recent novel, *Freak-Out for Daddy* by Richárd Salinger (itself a *Catcher in the Rye* intertext, and a female version at that)—seems to have lost its parodistic intertextual focus. Consequently, it is difficult to state if *Daddytheresa* is a parody of, or a sequel to, any of these potential intertexts, or, actually, a failure as both a sequel to and a parody of all of them.

The cover, particularly compared to that of *Mammatheresa,* certainly suggests a grotesque parody. The original novel's cover portrays a young woman, shown only from the shoulders down, seated on a staircase. Her pose is languid, her arms crossed loosely in her lap and her toes pointed inward. Most prominent are her long legs and stylishly feminine high heels (see figure 10.1). In the case of the second cover, we again see what appear to be female legs and shoes. This time, however, the dangling legs look more like those of a dummy than a human being, with its shoes not clearly pointing in any direction. At the top of the image, a tuft of false-looking blond hair hangs, apparently from an unseen hand (see figure 10.2). The text of the book, however, does not succeed in creating this effect of either parody or grotesque. What is more, it falls back on the worst dumb-blond clichés, stereotypes, and jokes, clearly a major fault of the novel. In the middle of the text, the heroine decides to have her hair dyed blond and to defy all the cultural stereotypes of the dumb blond. Yet the moment her hair is dyed, she utterly loses her intelligence, skills, and capacities. She cannot even find her way out of the hairdresser's and falls flat on the pavement. The narrative continues in the same vein, presenting a series of platitudes in the most blatant sexist tradition.

The other literary response to *Mammatheresa,* Károly Sáringer's *Woman I Want—A Response to Mammatheresa* is problematic for other reasons.[7] The cover, in this case, too, evokes the cover of *Mammatheresa*—not only by picturing the lower part of the human body—this time a young man's—with the focus on legs and shoes but also by what the image suggests: uncertainty, disappointment, and a touch of self-irony. This suggestion appears in the slightly flagging tennis socks worn with "sensible" black shoes and trousers—a trace of bad taste—and in the hands grasping a withering flower, an obvious sign of rejection (see figure 10.3). One would, on the basis of the cover, foretell some lack of self-confidence, a slightly shattered sense of masculinity—in general, those ideas that tend to characterize lad lit, as represented by Nick Hornby's *Fever Pitch* and *High Fidelity* or Sue Townsend's *The Cappuccino Years.*

Woman I Want, however, does not live up to its cover's promise. The text proves to be an *autobiographia sexualis* of a self-confident man who presents his own sexual power as irresistible and almost omnipotent. In this narrative there is no doubt and almost no humor or self-irony. The first-person narrator and protagonist gets all the women he wants—and the women, in turn, are reduced, in an almost soft-porn way, to their body parts. Also, the unified, self-identical subject of the narrative is amply expressed and indicated by the coherent, relatively continuous mode of storytelling. In that sense *Woman I Want* is far from being the masculine counterpart to *Mammatheresa.* Yet, as a cultural phenomenon, it is

Figure 10.1 Cover of the Hungarian edition of *Stop Mammatheresa!* by Zsuzsa Rácz (created by El Greco Ltd.).

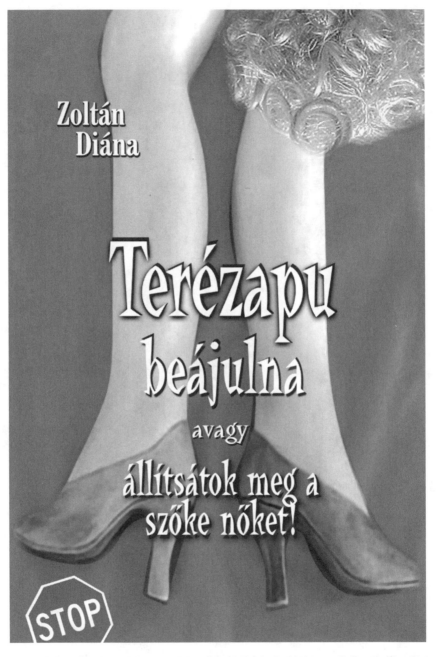

Figure 10.2 Cover of the Hungarian edition of *Freak-Out for Daddytheresa, Or Stop the Blondies!* by Diána Zoltán.

Figure 10.3 Cover of the Hungarian edition of *Woman I Want—A Response to Mammatheresa* by Károly Sáringer.

indicative of how both the singleton novel and the singleton phenomenon are understood and interpreted by many in contemporary Hungary.

Clearly, then, singleton culture has become a phenomenon, in terms of not only literary but also social discourse: the text seems to have touched a sensitive nerve in Hungary, perhaps a more sensitive one than *Bridget Jones* in Britain. The reason may lie in the very process of cultural exportation, and in the potential threat of a social-cultural "colonization" of an unstable culture. In this case the culture concerned is trying to find its way and whereabouts in a postcommunist atmosphere. Perhaps not surprisingly, then, one can observe almost paranoiac fears of being taken over—this time by the West and Western culture. One must not forget that the appearance of this new genre coincides with the stage in Hungary's postcommunist history when numerous social changes are no longer hidden or relegated into invisibility as supposed exceptions. University graduates' unemployment, young women working for an organization to save drug addicts, and the yuppie (singleton) lifestyle with its concomitant and conscious postponement of marriage were, not long ago, unheard of and inconceivable. Many Hungarians interpret all of these as the "evils" of postcommunist political change, and, as such, as the result of dangerous cultural importations.

This is why the following question is often posed: Is the singleton phenomenon artificially generated (and, in that sense, a simulacrum) or reality? I believe it is a social reality in that fifteen or twenty years ago the singleton—the single woman (or even man) in her thirties, living on her own, in a flat of her own (albeit a rented one) with all the freedom provided by this independent living—was simply inconceivable, or at least so rare that no one had to encounter it as a widespread social phenomenon that would have required a readjustment of thinking, terms, and concepts.

The reason is simple: in an economy of shortage and lack in which even married couples with children had to share a flat of one or two bedrooms with their own parents, in an economy in which you had to be married with at least two children to get access to an affordable mortgage, and in a culture where not getting married before graduation was considered a failure or at least weird, the singleton lifestyle was, quite simply, impossible. Its appearance obviously coincides with that economic, political, and cultural earthquake that erupted with the political changes of postcommunism. It should be expected then that responses to the new singleton lifestyle will be ambivalent. One major issue lies in the attitude toward feminism. Postcommunist cultures have tended to erase feminism and women's issues, considering them elements of communist thought, in particular, women's forced, imposed emancipation. Most people therefore assume that women's issues have been solved or at the least that women have no desire for emancipation. In this context, Barbara Einhorn argues, "The figure of the mother has eclipsed any expanded notions of alternative female role models such as woman-as-citizen.[...] Women's reproductive and 'feminine' nurturing roles are seen as crucial to the survival, not of a particular social system—as they were under state socialism—but of the national and ethnic community" (40), obviously a conservative turn concerning women, femininity, and feminism.

Given this conservative climate, it is not surprising that *Mammatheresa,* which upsets, and at the same time reinserts—but only after recontextualizing—several mainstream conservative ideas, caused an explosion of discourses that saturated Hungarian culture. Responses, not only from the critical and literary communities seen above but from the popular community as well, reinforce the point. The Web site of a women's magazine ("Szinglik"), for example, offered space for the discussion of the singleton phenomenon; the opinions given are indicative of popular conservative thought regarding young women's roles. Interestingly, but quite logically, the questions asked about single women are often close to Victorian articulations of similar conditions in the 1850s, when people realized the statistical abundance of women living on their own—but, much like present-day Hungarians, were not concerned about *men* living alone. The Victorians asked, "What shall we do with our old maids?"—and called them redundant, superfluous women (Nestor 4), an echo of ideas currently expressed in Hungary. Many contributors to the aforementioned Web site also suggest that these young women can blame only themselves and can only be blamed, in a discourse that can quite justifiably be read as a process of scapegoating women. According to this view, single women are egoists who just want freedom, money, and a career; they are incapable of adjustment, of a mutual give-and-take relationship. What is more, they are socially irresponsible—one contributor even claims that it is *her* children who will pay and work for the singletons' social security and retirement pensions.

Only a few comments open up the discussion in other directions, that is, away from the compulsory marriage plot or in the direction of a reconsideration or reconstruction of marriage or partnership. One exception is an article by Béla Buda, one of the most widely known and respected Hungarian psychologists, who sees not only the novelty of theme, tone, and style but also the novel's "educational" potential. He concludes his review by saying that "Mammatheresa should be encouraged to carry on with this search, this interpretation, to help us take a step forward in creating young people's relationship culture" (translation mine).

Parallel with the Internet discussion forum, the author of *Mammatheresa,* Zsuzsa Rácz, launched a phone-in radio program called "Mammatheresa

Club,"[8] which—before its launching—was explicitly advertised *not* to be feminist, again betraying a sign of the popular and widespread paranoia. The program undertook to offer strategies for the solution of partnership problems, an effort that clearly widened the popular discussion of the singleton phenomenon. Furthermore, in the spirit of consumerism, *Mammatheresa* has become an advertising catchword. Ads have appeared, for example, promoting luxury cruises on the Mediterranean for single women—and, by implication, for men interested in available young women—bringing to the surface an undercurrent of the singleton concept. Similarly, on New Year's Eve, a club in central Budapest (Gödör Klub) offered a program referencing singletons' supposed battle of the sexes: "Will Mammatheresa push down Daddytheresa—A literary armwrestling contest," featuring on the men's side, among others, Károly Sáringer, author of *Woman I Want* (www.holgyvilag.hu/index.php).

Still, most of these popular cultural resonances betray, at least implicitly, a fear of a general cultural—and within that, a gender—landslide, at the same time making an effort to put women back where they traditionally belong. The most *explicit* articulation of this fear was proposed by Vilmos Csányi, a member of the Hungarian Academy of Sciences and holder of the most prestigious award for scientists (Széchenyi Prize). In a popular TV broadcast lecture series ("University of Omniscience"—a kind of Open University), he presented the idea that from ancient communities on, human society has been in a state of disintegration, an ultimate—and rather pathetic—form of which is the singleton. He did not stop short at description, however; he also attached value judgments to this process. What he proposed about the cult of the singleton is symptomatic of a current mode of thinking. He apparently pours all the evils of modernity and postmodernity upon singletons: he blames them for the destruction of traditional communities, including the lack of shared value and belief systems; he claims that they are vulnerable to drugs, alcohol, and other destructive subcultures; he asserts that they have no lifestyle models to follow and are thus exposed to the manipulation of both the media and extreme political movements; and he concludes that they are therefore dependent on reality shows such as *Big Brother*. These claims and assumptions, no matter how bold they are, however, are not tested against reality and would surely be difficult if not impossible to support on the basis of sociological and anthropological research.

Yet we must not dismiss such responses to the emergence of the singleton or the singleton novel. Rather, the singleton phenomenon can be read as a perhaps extreme example of the social, cultural, and discursive repercussions of the Bridget Jones phenomenon. It exemplifies the idea that *Bridget Jones* is, undoubtedly, a major export good, one that behaves as proper export goods do: it has crossed the Channel and the social-political-economic divide that separates England and Hungary, but it has not remained untouched by this journey. Quite the contrary: while the English phenomenon has had a radical effect on the specific signifying system that is the Hungarian national language and culture, the meeting of the two cultures has also led to a new form of transnational cultural product, one that has become intrinsic to Hungarian discourse.

Notes

1. Although the Hungarian novels analyzed in this essay are not translated into English, I have provided tentative titles for all three. I subsequently refer to Zsuzsa Rácz's *Állítsátok meg Terézanyut!* as *Mammatheresa*.
2. The influence of Bridget Jones (among others, including "the Hungarian national water polo team, Frank Sinatra, Robbie Williams, Emir Kusturica") is credited in the acknowledgments (292; translation mine) but comes up in the form of explicit intertextual references several times in the text as well (e.g., 51, 75, 109).
3. Data from December 2004 based on oral information from András Novák, managing director of the publishing house.
4. Director Péter Bergendy; cameraman Gyula Pados; script Béla Rigó; starring Gabriella Hámori, Eszter Ónodi, Judit Schell, Melinda Major, Sándor Csányi, Ferenc Hujber, and Zsolt László. The film adaptation, however, was not an easy process. The novel's author had serious problems with the script, which turned the text into a Harlequin romance.
5. The word existed previously only in the areas of playing cards (in bridge when a player's hand includes only one card of a particular suit) and sports (as in a singles game, to play singles, etc.). Nowadays, however, if one asks a native speaker of Hungarian what "szingli" means, in my estimate eighty percent of those who are familiar with the word would give "singleton" as its first meaning.
6. Subsequently referred to as *Daddytheresa*.
7. Subsequently referred to as *Woman I Want*.
8. The program titled "Mammatheresa Club, or Kitchen Talks about the Essence" was run by Zsuzsa Rácz and Erika Barna, from 10 to 11 p.m. every Tuesday on Radio Petfi, a national channel.

Works Cited

Buda, Béla. "Jó nnek sem könny lenni: Kéki Kata világa." 10, Jan. 2005. <http://www.parkapcso-lat.ngo.hu/kekikata.htm>.
Cinematrix, 8, Jan. 2005. <http://cinematrix.index.hu>.
Csányi, Vilmos. "Az sközösségtl a szinglikig." 11, Jan. 2005. <www.magyarhirlap.hu/cikk.php?cikk=76482>.
Einhorn, Barbara. *Cinderella Goes to Market: Citizenship, Gender and Women's Movements in East Central Europe*. London: Verso, 1993.
Farkas, Tímea. "A magyar szingli férjhez akar menni." 11, Jan. 2005. <www.nol.hu./ cikk/149719>.
Menyhért, Anna. "A szingliregény: Helen Fielding, *Bridget Jones*, India Knight. *Szex, pasik, gyötrelmek* ..., Irena Obermanova, *Egy rült feleség naplója*, Jessica Adams, *Kalandorok email-jenek*." Ex libris. *Élet és Irodalom* 46 (May 10, 2002): 23.
Nestor, Pauline. *Female Friendships and Communities: Charlotte Brontë, George Eliot and Elizabeth Gaskell*. Oxford: Clarendon, 1985.
Rácz, Zsuzsa. *Állítsátok meg Terézanyut!* Budapest: Bestline, 2002.
Sáringer, Károly. *Nt akarok! Válasz Terézanyunak*. Gyöngyös: Pallas, 2002.
"Szinglik: gerjesztett divat vagy valóság?" 25, Nov. 2003. <www.holgyvilag.hu/index.php>.

"Terézanyu megpihenne: Interjú Rácz Zsuzsával." 25, Nov. 2003. <www.holgyvilag.hu/index.php>.

Whelehan, Imelda. *Helen Fielding's* Bridget Jones' Diary: *A Reader's Guide*. Continuum Contemporaries. New York: Continuum, 2002.

Zoltán Diána (Dián Tamás, Belinszki Zoltán). *Terézapu beájulna: Avagy állítsátok meg a szke nket!* Gyöngyös: Pallas, 2002.

Sex and the Single Chick: Feminism and Postfeminism, Sexuality and Self-Fashioning

11

About a Girl: Female Subjectivity and Sexuality in Contemporary 'Chick' Culture

A. ROCHELLE MABRY

Wednesday 15 March

Humph. Have woken up v. fed up. On top of everything, only two weeks to go until birthday, when will have to face up to the fact that another entire year has gone by, during which everyone else except me has mutated into Smug Married, having children plop, plop, left right and center and making hundreds of thousands of pounds and inroads into very hub of establishment, while I career rudderless and boyfriendless through dysfunctional relationships and professional stagnation. (67)

This quote from Helen Fielding's 1996 comic novel *Bridget Jones's Diary* highlights many of the issues addressed in the growing body of women's popular fiction commonly known as "chick lit." The story of a London "Singleton" attempting to make her way through a landscape fraught with feckless men, dead-end jobs, and the all-too-available temptations of shopping, cigarettes, and chardonnay, *Bridget Jones* is one example of the ways popular culture for women has changed in its portrayals of sexual relationships after the women's movement and the sexual revolution of the 1960s. Contemporary novels, films, and television shows aimed primarily at (younger) women do, like older forms such as the romance novel and the "woman's film," tend to present fairly conservative images of women and their place in society. Still, chick novels like *Bridget Jones's Diary,* as well as films such as *The Sweetest Thing* (2001) and television shows like *Sex and the City* (1998–2004)—collectively examples of "chick culture"—point to an important shift in women's popular texts, particularly in the ways they examine women's experiences and desires. Through various narrative and ideological shifts, chick novels and films give contemporary women voice and allow them to express desires that may lie outside of the "happily-ever-after" marriage to Prince Charming.

Although they represent a new direction in female-oriented popular texts, the works that began to emerge in the late 1990s do share a number of similarities with earlier films and novels produced for women. Like the woman's film and the romance novel, contemporary chick movies and chick lit are women's genres, not only in their focus on female voice and narrative point of view but also in their direct marketing and specific appeal to female consumers. According to Janice Radway, the growth of the paperback romance industry also "had much to do with the special characteristics of its audience, that is, with the unique situation of women in America." Radway notes that early romances, such as Harlequins, were sold largely at grocery stores and drugstores, two spaces American women had to visit regularly in their roles as housewives and mothers. The novels were marketed to an almost captive audience, ensuring that "the publishers could be sure of regularly reaching a large segment of the adult female audience" and at the same time "limit advertising expenditures because the potential or theoretical audience they hoped to attract already had been gathered for them" (Radway 32). Radway adds, however, that these tactics began to change in the 1960s and 1970s (perhaps because as the position of American women began to change, they couldn't be counted on to visit grocery stores and drugstores on a regular basis). She points to the 1972 publication of Kathleen Woodiwiss's *The Flame and the Flower,* which was "given all the publicity, advertising, and promotion usually reserved for proven bestsellers" as the first moment in which a romance novel was marketed and distributed, not as a "woman's" novel but as a mainstream work of fiction (34).

Although the changes in American women's circumstances over the past thirty years mean that the marketers of chick lit can't count on selling their product to the American housewife as she waits in line at the supermarket, the growth of the genre is also tied to market and demographic concerns. As the audience for traditional romance novels has begun to age (the average reader is estimated to be about forty-five years old), publishers have begun reaching out to the next generation of female readers (Wilson). A blueprint for the new genre came with the success of Helen Fielding's *Bridget Jones's Diary,* which Anna Weinberg calls the "Eve of the [chick lit] genre" (47). Published in 1996 in the United Kingdom and in 1998 in the United States, *Bridget* and the novels that followed it focused not on the romantic travails of an impossibly beautiful, undeniably wholesome heroine and her strong, hypermasculine hero but on the romantic escapades of contemporary young women similar to the novels' intended readers. With their fallible, funny heroines and breezy style, such books "navigated the perilous terrain of the modern woman's psyche with sassy aplomb" (Weinberg 47). Around the same time, television programs such as *Ally McBeal,* which premiered on FOX in September 1997, and *Sex and the City,* which bowed on HBO in June 1998 (and was based on Candace Bushnell's 1996 book of the same title) examined similar territory (imdb.com).

Nearly all of these works garnered significant commercial and critical success. *Bridget Jones's Diary* was an enormously popular best-seller in both Britain and in the United States. The 2001 film adaptation earned just over $71.5 million at the American box office (a very respectable showing for a romantic comedy) and earned a Golden Globe nomination for Best Comedy or Musical, as well as Golden Globe and Oscar nominations for star Renée Zellweger. *Sex and the City* resonated not only with its popular audience (a 1998 *Time* magazine cover featured all four of the show's leads) but also with the critical community. The show earned multiple Emmy and Golden Globe nominations (winning the Emmy in 2001, and Globes in 2001 and 2002), as did star and executive producer Sarah Jessica Parker, who won three Lead Actress Golden Globes (2000, 2001, 2002) and an Emmy (2004), and costar Kim Cattrall, who won a Supporting Actress Emmy in 2003 (imdb.com). Although sales figures and critical awards can't always tell us *how* readers and viewers read a book or a film, they do clearly indicate that these works have caught on with their intended audience(s).

The success of these early texts, especially *Bridget Jones's Diary,* revealed a market for stories about—and for—young, single women grappling with modern life and relationships. A whole host of *Bridget* imitators and successors emerged in the next years, including Sophie Kinsella's *Confessions of a Shopaholic* (2001), a particularly blatant—and arguably less charming and substantial—product of the *Bridget* formula. Chick lit soon became so popular that whole publishing lines were devoted to the genre. In 2001, Harlequin launched Red Dress Ink, an imprint focused mainly (at least in the beginning) on the adventures of single, urban twenty- and early thirtysomething women. A 2001 press release announcing the launch of Red Dress Ink established the tone and intended audience of the new line: "Red Dress Ink is a women's fiction program that depicts young, single, mostly city-dwelling women coping with the pressures that accompany a career, the dating scene and all the other aspects of modern life in America … these books are *Ally McBeal* meets *Sex and the City*" ("Harlequin Launches"). A blurb on the Harlequin Web site promotes its strategy, proclaiming that "these books say I'm single, I'm female and I'm having a really good time (despite what my mother may have told you)" ("About Red Dress Ink"). Despite recent complaints of a glut in the field, these new popular novels have had a significant impact on the industry. The emergence of chick lit, according to Anita Jain in *Crain's New York Business,* "is breathing life into a sagging book industry dominated by older readers" (3).

To reach their intended readers, chick novels and films, like the romance novels and women's films before them, must be marketed in a way that makes it easy for the potential reader to recognize them *as* chick lit. A brief overview in *Marketing for Women* notes that "most bookstores have created chick-lit display areas, such as prominent tables by the door, [although] none have created separate aisles for them the way they would shelve romance or mystery titles" ("Is 'Chick Lit'" 9). Marketing chick lit concentrates on the books' covers, which are often brightly colored and feature such images of modern "chick-ness" as lipstick, purses, cocktail glasses, and stiletto-heeled shoes. *Confessions of a Shopaholic,* for example, was released with a hot pink spine and a drawing of a high-heeled shoe on the bottom corner of the cover. Similarly, Anna Maxted's novels *Running in Heels* (2001) and *Behaving Like Adults* (2003) are almost fluorescently bright and feature cartoon drawings of overly feminine women wearing high heels or exaggerated makeup. Such packaging not only makes the books easy for the potential reader to identify but also visually represents the hip young protagonist within the covers with whom the reader is meant to identify.

Chick movies, similarly to chick novels, are also often marketed in a way that marks them specifically *as* chick movies. In the case of the films, it is the trailer that most clearly says to the viewer, "Look! It's a chick flick!" Many chick movie trailers have a number of components in common, including at least one shot of the heroine being clumsy or suffering some kind of embarrassment. The trailer for *The Sweetest Thing,* for example, shows star Cameron Diaz taking several pratfalls, including one where a garishly dressed Diaz falls and interrupts a wedding ceremony. Likewise, probably the most memorable moment in the trailer for *Bridget Jones's Diary* is the clip of Bridget answering her phone with a sexually suggestive remark, only to find her mother at the other end of the line. In addition to these moments of humiliation, the trailers also include at least one image of the heroine in a lighthearted or exuberant moment, such as the shot of Ashley Judd performing a cheerleading high jump in the *Someone Like You* (2001) preview or the image of Jennifer Lopez dancing with her friends in the *Maid in Manhattan* (2002) trailer. And nearly all the trailers use pop songs (either easily recognizable classics or up-to-the-minute songs by young female artists) to convey the emotional tone of the film, from the Isley Brothers' "This Old Heart of Mine" in the *Sweetest Thing* trailer to Vanessa Carlton's "1000 Miles" in the preview for *Maid in Manhattan*. (Further proof that these songs are meant solely as marketing tools is the fact that they are often not used in the films themselves.) The formula for putting together a chick movie trailer is now so well known that viewers can immediately identify a film being advertised as a chick flick, even before the film's titles or stars are announced.

Like other popular "female" texts, such as the woman's film of the 1930s and 1940s and the romance novel, many chick movies and novels employ techniques that make them "feminine," both in the stories they tell and in the way they address their readers or viewers. Annette Kuhn writes that one of the distinguishing characteristics of a "[women's genre] as a textual system is its construction of narratives motivated by female point-of-view" (437). Mary Ann Doane writes that the woman's film, for example, "appears to allow [the female protagonist] significant access to point of view structures and the enunciative level of the filmic discourse" (3). In other words, the woman's film uses devices such as the voice-over, the flashback, and the fantasy sequence to give the female protagonist a voice and to emphasize that this is *her* story. Both *Rebecca* (1939) and *Letter from an Unknown Woman* (1948), for instance, use the devices of the voice-over and the flashback to signal that these are *women's* stories, no matter how narrative and visual strategies may ultimately undercut the authority of the female voice. The story in *Letter*, in fact, is literally told by its female protagonist. The narrative is framed by a letter written by Lisa (Joan Fontaine) to a man with whom she has been in love for years, and the film unfolds as a series of flashbacks (understood as Lisa's memories) narrated by Lisa's voice-overs.

Like their forebears, chick lit and chick movies usually focus on a female main character and use a variety of strategies to make her desires and motivations the focus of the story. *Bridget Jones* and many of the chick novels produced by publishing imprints like Red Dress Ink are written in first person, in the heroine's voice, conveying the notion that these novels, although fictional, are authentic, in-depth accounts of women's experiences. This move toward first-person narration is an especially significant change from the third-person narration employed in most traditional romance novels. As Tania Modleski notes, one of the effects of this third-person perspective was to reinforce the heroine's position as the (often literal) object of a (primarily male) gaze (*Loving* 56). The move toward first-person voice in most contemporary chick novels not only strengthens the heroine's voice and increases the reader's opportunities to identify with her but also offers at least a temporary escape from the feeling of constantly being watched or controlled by a male-dominated society. Of course, this doesn't mean that a female author or main character, or even the use of first-person narrative voice, guarantees that a particular film or novel is a "real" representation of female experience. More significant here is how hard these texts work to present themselves as authentic stories of women's lives and feelings.

The novel version of *Bridget Jones* puts this first-person voice into diary form. The style and structure of the novel further reinforce the notion of intimate, personal women's writing. Although some passages read like any other traditional works of fiction (they are first-person, past-tense accounts of events that have already occurred), many sections are written in an immediate, abbreviated style that makes it seem as if Bridget writes about her experiences as they happen. This style runs throughout the "diary entries," including the one in which Bridget begins a relationship with her boss, Daniel Cleaver.

> 5:45 p.m. Could not be more joyous. Computer messaging re: presence or otherwise of skirt continued obsessively all afternoon. Cannot imagine respected boss did stroke of work. Weird scenario with Perpetua (penultimate boss), since knew I was messaging and v. angry, but fact that was messaging ultimate boss gave self conflicting feelings of loyalty—distinctly unlevel playing field where anyone with an ounce of sense would say ultimate boss holds sway. (23)

An even clearer example of such writing in the moment can be found in one of several entries Bridget has supposedly written while drunk. In one case Bridget has just returned home after drowning her sorrows over Daniel with her girlfriends Shazzer and Jude. She writes, "2 a.m. Argor sworeal brilleve with Shazzan Jude. Dun stupid care about Daniel stupid prat. Feel sicky though. Oops" (59). Rather than describing the evening after the fact, Fielding uses almost phonetic spelling and stream-of-consciousness sentence structure to convey the idea that Bridget is actually writing the entry while she's still drunk. These moments give the reader an even more vivid image of Bridget's state of mind and reinforce the idea that *she* is the one telling her own story.

The film adaptation of *Bridget Jones's Diary* also uses a variety of strategies to announce itself as the heroine's story, including those used in the traditional Hollywood woman's film. The movie uses voice-overs, fantasy sequences, and images of text from Bridget's diary to add psychological depth to the character and to allow the viewer to identify more fully with her. The film opens literally as Bridget's story. Over shots of Bridget (Renée Zellweger) walking through the snow to a family function, Bridget's voice-over begins the narrative. "It all began on New Year's Day, my thirty-second year of being single." The music that accompanies the opening lines, as well as Zellweger's delivery of them, evoke not only the "Once Upon a Time" beginnings of many traditional fairy tales but also the introductory voice-overs such as the one performed by Joan Fontaine in *Rebecca*. Yet although aspects of this voice-over—and much of the film—are similar to those found in earlier popular texts for women, *Bridget Jones's Diary* works on another level both to emphasize Bridget's voice and to reinforce the idea that this is a "true" woman's story—a story "written" by a woman about her experiences for other women to read or watch—and at the same time poke fun at the earlier forms.

The film's opening voice-over, for example, continues throughout the first scene, in which Bridget attends a New Year's Day brunch and suffers the multiple indignities of maternal nagging over her wardrobe, inappropriate groping by an old family friend, and a particularly embarrassing first meeting with Mark Darcy (Colin Firth), the story's intended hero. The scene ends on a freeze-frame of Bridget at the moment she has been unceremoniously rejected by Mark, while her voice-over (which continues through the opening credits) declares that "that was it. Right there. That was the moment … I decided to take control of my life and start writing a diary to tell the truth about Bridget Jones. The whole truth." On the surface this moment can be read as a warning to single women who fail to assume their rightful place as wives and mothers: "I was so pathetic in my failure to build a monogamous relationship that I became even more narcissistic and began scribbling meaningless stuff in a diary like a ten-year-old girl." Furthermore it evokes moments in earlier women's films such as *Now, Voyager* where the woman's story is examined for clues as to how she came to a particular point (i.e., how she became a lonely spinster).

Yet beneath these conservative ideas about what a woman should be is a sense that the attempt to tell "the whole truth" about Bridget Jones is—at least as much as is possible in a commercial film produced in a male-dominated industry—an attempt to tell a woman's story *for* women. The fact that Bridget chooses to record her experiences in the privacy of a diary, rather than the more public form of a newspaper column, as in the TV version of *Sex and the City*,[1] or on a television show (Ashley Judd's declaration of love for Hugh Jackman in *Someone Like You* occurs on a live talk show broadcast) is a clear indication of this attempt. Of course Bridget's diary is only private and "hers" in the fictional world of the film (and even that is undercut by the end, as I discuss later). The use of the diary trope, however, at least shows an understanding that it is a private form of expression that can be used by the woman to document her own experiences and express her own identity in her own voice.

The film further undercuts the conventions of the woman's film—and by extension the conservative messages those films ultimately present their viewers—by turning those conventions into jokes. In one early moment of the film, a flirtatious exchange with her crush Daniel Cleaver (Hugh Grant) leads Bridget into an immediate, single-shot fantasy of her wedding to Daniel. Much like the flashback sequences of the woman's film, this sequence is intended to provide insight into Bridget's character, particularly to her desire for marriage. However, the fantasy adds a comedic layer that sets it apart from similar sequences in the woman's film. It questions the assumption that—to paraphrase the title of an earlier romantic comedy about a single woman in search of a husband—Every Girl Wants to Be Married. The humorous intent of the fantasy becomes clear from the beginning, as the shot opens with an exaggerated close-up of Bridget's mother's smiling face, then moves to the "happy couple." The stylized performances of Grant (who has the only real dialogue in the fantasy) and Zellweger further indicate that the moment is to be understood as comic. The clearest signal that this fantasy is not to be taken seriously, however, arguably comes on the soundtrack. In a voice-over at the beginning of the sequence, Bridget hums a quick, almost silly version of the "Wedding March," mocking one of the most easily identifiable symbols of traditional marriage. In this moment, as in others throughout the movie, the elements of the woman's film (and, indeed, of earlier romance films in general) are turned in on themselves, raising questions about what women *really* want and how those desires can be expressed in a "feminine" text.

Like the *Bridget Jones* novel(s) and film, the HBO television series *Sex and the City* focuses on women's experiences and voices. And, like the *Bridget* texts, *Sex and the City* borrows the conventions and themes of earlier films and novels for women, only to turn them into something unmistakably contemporary and arguably feminist. Women's writing and storytelling literally act as a central point of the program. The show's main character, Carrie Bradshaw (Sarah Jessica Parker), is a New York columnist who writes about sexual relationships in contemporary Manhattan—Carrie is, as she puts it in the pilot episode, a "sexual anthropologist." More important, in nearly every episode, Carrie's voice-overs narrate her own and the other characters' sexual (mis)adventures (including those of several male characters). The pilot episode, in fact, begins with Carrie intoning the timeless fairy-tale opening, "Once Upon a Time." These words connect *Sex and the City* to traditional folktales, as well as to the female-narrated woman's film and the often fairy-tale-like romance novel. The story Carrie narrates, however, undercuts traditional ideas about gender roles found in many fairy tales. This tale is not one of a beautiful princess finding love with a handsome prince but one of a modern career woman being dumped by her commitment-phobic boyfriend. It has a cynical, rather than a happy ending—one that proclaims the "end of love in Manhattan."

This is not to say that the show completely writes off the search for Prince Charming, or that it does not occasionally consciously play on women's perceived desire for the fairy tale. The series finale, in which Big, Carrie's newly reformed Knight in Shining Armor, rescues Carrie from her unhappy life with a cold, selfish Prince in the "Tower" of the Paris Ritz, bears this out. As we see in the pilot, however, the show doesn't completely buy into the fairy-tale fantasy. Furthermore, unlike the fairy tale—or the woman's film, another text that is supposed to be a woman's story—the stories in this program are being told *by* women, both in the world of the show (Carrie's columns are the basis for most episodes) and through other devices such as voice-overs.

While the voice-over clearly emphasizes the feminine voice anchoring the show, a second device marks this voice even more clearly as a specifically contemporary one. Each episode focuses on a particular question—nearly always about sex and relationships—that Carrie is examining in that week's column. The question is nearly always foregrounded in the episode, both visually and on the soundtrack. A typical scene shows Carrie in her apartment, working at her laptop, as the voice-over takes us through her thoughts on that week's topic. Then, at some point near the end of the scene, we see Carrie's computer screen in close-up as she types the question. At the same moment, Carrie repeats the question in a voice-over. The glib, sometimes cheesy manner in which the questions are often phrased—"Are We Sluts?" Carrie asks in one third-season episode—often deflects attention from their real significance. Although the questions cover a wide range of relationship issues—"Do Women Just Want to Be Rescued?" "Can You Be Friends with an Ex?"—perhaps the main point of the questions over six seasons can best be summed up in the question famously attributed to Sigmund Freud: "What do women want?" In this case, however, the question is not asked by a man trying to solve eternal female mystery or diagnose some feminine weakness—at least, not within the fiction of the show. Rather, in pondering friendship with an ex or how many sexual partners is too many, the "question of the week" device *represents* the desires and attempts of many real-life contemporary women to investigate the mysteries of modern sexual relationships and gender roles on their own terms and to determine their place within these relationships for themselves.

Beyond similar marketing strategies and textual devices, perhaps the most important connection—as well as the most significant point of departure—between emerging chick culture and the women's genres that preceded it is that the primary focus of each of these texts is not simply on the woman but on the woman's place in the world in general and in sexual relationships in particular. In both the romance novel and contemporary chick novel, this question is examined within the story of the central romance. In chick texts, however, the romantic relationship is often given much less narrative and emotional weight than the heroine's own experiences and her relationships—both platonic and sexual—with other characters. A number of contemporary chick novels, in fact, break one of the cardinal rules of the "ideal romance" identified in Radway's study: they do not focus solely on their female protagonist's developing relationship with the "right" man but often portray the woman engaging in one or more sexual relationships (with varying degrees of success and pleasure) before she settles down with the right man. Thus, in these novels, sex becomes a way for the woman to explore her own identity and express her own desires, rather than merely part of a single romance narrative that emphasizes traditional gender roles.

Bridget Jones, for example, may write constantly about her desire for marriage and the right man, but the novel's emphasis on Bridget's growth as a person and her relationships with her friends outweigh the quest for romantic partnership. More important, much of the story's emotional and comic weight is given to Bridget's crush and subsequent relationship with the charming rogue Daniel Cleaver, rather than Mark Darcy, the story's hero. A flirtatious e-mail exchange early in the novel reveals Daniel to be irresistibly witty and sexy (to Bridget, at least), if not completely trustworthy. "You appear to have forgotten your skirt," he writes in his opening salvo. "As I think is made perfectly clear in your contract of employment, staff are expected to be fully dressed at all times" (20). He follows this message up with another, equally suggestive message:

> If walking past office was attempt to demonstrate presence of skirt can only say that it has failed miserably. Skirt is indisputably absent. Is skirt off sick? … If skirt is indeed sick, please look into how many days sick leave skirt has taken in previous twelvemonth. Spasmodic nature of recent skirt attendance suggests malingering. (21)

Far from being put off or considering herself sexually harassed, Bridget enjoys the "undeniably flirtatious" exchange and waits eagerly for his responses. The appeal of the charming bad boy (to Bridget and, we can assume, the reader) is further illustrated in Bridget's reaction to her first sexual encounter with Daniel. She spends the day after in a state of "shag-drunkenness, mooning about the flat, smiling, picking things up and putting them down again" (52). Although Daniel ultimately ends up betraying Bridget, the character and the relationship are presented in such a way that the reader can identify with Bridget's infatuation.

Mark Darcy, on the other hand, only makes a few brief appearances in the first half of the novel. True, his first appearance in the novel—a "meet cute" in which he and Bridget are constantly being shoved at each other by well-meaning mothers and family friends—makes it clear to anyone familiar with romantic-comedy conventions that he is the "right" partner for Bridget. Yet although Daniel's first exchange with Bridget is filled with flirtation and sexual innuendo, Mark barely manages to ask Bridget if she's "read any good books lately" when they are introduced to each other (13). Moreover, Mark is given much less narrative weight than Daniel—or, for that matter, Bridget's other friends and family—as he appears in only three scenes (though they are admittedly important moments) throughout the first three-fourths of the book. Even at the end of the novel, when the romance between the two is finally under way, Mark exists more in Bridget's thoughts than as a present character participating in the action. (He spends much of the last part of the story out of the country, attempting to save Bridget's mother from imprisonment due to her adulterous lover's fraudulent dealings.) Although it is clear from the beginning that Mark is the right man for Bridget (he's good-looking, brave, noble, and a wealthy barrister), other elements of the story are recounted in a way that threatens to overwhelm the romance for which we're supposed to be rooting.[2]

Why women go for the charming cad and the place pop culture has in reinforcing the attractiveness of the "bad boy" are certainly important questions that merit further investigation. The point here, however, is that contemporary chick lit often presents the heroine in sexual relationships with men other than the narrative's intended hero, but without "punishing" her or questioning her actions. In the romance novel such relationships would almost necessarily be presented as rape scenarios, because the sexually innocent heroine could not be allowed to enjoy a sexual encounter with any man other than her intended mate. Because the dual components of feminine development and heterosexual romance are such integral parts of the romance narrative, those novels Radway categorizes as the "ideal romance" will focus exclusively on the growing relationship between a heroine and a hero, without any narrative diversions. Any rival for the heroine's affections is often presented as a villain who poses a real threat of sexual violence (133). Radway notes that the "one woman–one man" formula is so important to the readers she surveyed that they will categorically reject the novels that do not follow it (123). By giving the female protagonist a number of sexual partners and experiences, chick lit lets the story of the heroine's growth and experiences stand on its own, rather than simply making it part of a larger romance narrative. In addition these more experienced heroines are also easier for their intended readers to relate to, as it is not only accepted but also expected in contemporary culture that young women will have had at least some sexual experience before settling into a serious long-term relationship or marriage.

The communities portrayed in many chick-culture texts are equally as important as the central romantic relationship—sometimes arguably more important. In the *Bridget Jones* novels, this community takes the form of what Bridget calls her "urban family"—her equally single friends Shazzer, Jude, and Tom.[3] Bridget's actual family offers little emotional support: her overbearing, self-absorbed mother leaves her father after forty years of marriage to experience relationships with other men, and her brother plays almost no role in the story. By contrast she and her "singleton" friends are always available to offer each other support and (sometimes comically misguided) advice. When Tom disappears for a few days (and after they determine he's not just "enjoying honeymoon-style shag hideaway for a few days"), Bridget, Shazzer, and Jude alert his other friends to his absence and spend the day searching for him (227). He'd been hiding out in his own apartment after getting dumped by his boyfriend and undergoing plastic surgery. When Tom finally turns up, he claims, "nobody loves me" (231). Bridget, however, points out the number of people who are concerned about him. "I told him to ring my answerphone, which held twenty-two frantic messages from his friends, all distraught because he had disappeared for twenty-four hours," she records, "which put paid to all our fears about dying alone and being eaten by an Alsatian" (231). In *Bridget Jones's Diary,* and in other novels such as Marian Keyes's *Last Chance Saloon* and movies such as *The Sweetest Thing,* the "urban family" often provides—or at least supplements—the emotional closeness and support expected from the traditional nuclear family. More important, the bonds of the urban family are often as strong, if not stronger, than those of the romantic relationship.

The conclusion of the *Bridget Jones* sequel, *Bridget Jones: The Edge of Reason,* shows that the urban family—and indeed the woman's life outside the romantic relationship—can be such an attractive alternative that it can, at least momentarily, place question marks around the happy romantic conclusion. When, at the end of the novel, Mark asks Bridget to move to Los Angeles with him, her initial response is atypical of the traditional romantic heroine:

> I thought hard. I thought about Jude and Shazzer, and Agnès B on Westbourne Grove, and cappuccinos in Coins, and Oxford Street.
>
> "Bridget?" he said gently. "It's very warm and sunny there and they have swimming pools."
>
> "Oh," I said, eyes darting interestedly from one side to the other.
>
> "I'll wash up," he promised. (337)

Of course, the *Bridget Jones* novels remain true to chick-lit conventions (and the conventions of romantic comedy in general), and Bridget does go with Mark (although to Thailand, not to Los Angeles). After all, the thought of shopping and hanging out with her friends could never seriously tempt Bridget to give up her (presumably) happy future with Mark. But this brief moment may speak to the anxieties of many modern women considering marriage or other long-term commitments after years of social, financial, and emotional independence.

Like the *Bridget* novels, *Sex and the City* presents a similar community—this time a group of four upper-middle-class Manhattan women. The show is, on the surface, all about the women's romantic and sexual misadventures. (Three of the characters have been either engaged or married over the run of the series.) Indeed, one of the most appealing parts of the series is following these women as they attempt to find love and romance in a large, impersonal, status- and consumer-oriented world. A long view of the series, however, reveals that the most significant relationships in these women's lives are those they have with each other. As Astrid Henry notes, "The women's relationships with each other—both as a group and individually—are continually depicted as these characters' primary community and family, their source of love and care" (67). The relationship among the four friends regularly overshadows their various romantic entanglements.

Although the point has been made directly throughout the series, it is illustrated even more clearly in the show's final season. Samantha, the outgoing, most sexually adventurous member of the group, is diagnosed with breast cancer in the same episode in which Miranda marries Steve, her on-again/off-again boyfriend and the father of her son. The rest of the women find out about Samantha's diagnosis over the course of the episode—Samantha tells Carrie in the cab on the way to the wedding, and Charlotte and Miranda both find out at Miranda's wedding reception. Although most television series would end a wedding episode with an image of the bride and groom (especially if the relationship had played out over several seasons, as Miranda and Steve's has), this particular show ends with an image that emphasizes the series' interest in women's relationships and community. The episode ends at Miranda's wedding reception, but not, as we might expect, with a shot of the bride and groom. Instead, we see the four women sitting at a table together, comforting and supporting each other during an uncertain time.

Yet even though shows like *Sex and the City* and movies and novels like *Bridget Jones's Diary* offer arguably more progressive alternatives to their female readers and viewers, they still ultimately emphasize that what a woman really wants is to find the right guy with whom to spend the rest of her life. *Sex and the City,* which has carefully developed its female community over six seasons, ends on a note that threatens to overturn any of its more overt feminist messages. By the show's final season, both Charlotte and Miranda (the show's most vocal feminist) have entered into marriage and (impending) motherhood, Carrie has a happy—although somewhat open-ended—reunion with Mr. Big (another powerful white male), and even Samantha has given up her promiscuous ways for a monogamous relationship (although this is a slightly less traditional relationship, as Samantha's boyfriend is both younger and less socially and financially powerful than she is). In and of themselves, these storylines are not necessarily problematic. After all, the women still have their careers and their relationships with each other. What *is* important is the fact that these pretty conservative endings happen in the series' finale. For six seasons this show has supposedly been about the lives and the relationships of these four strong, independent women, but the finale tells us that the *real* point of the show has been to place these sexually powerful, economically independent women in traditional heterosexual relationships.

Even more disturbing is the way that a number of contemporary chick novels, movies, or programs actually end up silencing the (arguably) prominent female voice that sets them apart from earlier women's texts. The most chilling example of the silenced chick heroine can be found in the final scene of the *Bridget Jones* film adaptation. Just as Mark and Bridget are about to come together as a couple, Mark discovers Bridget's diary and reads the less-than-flattering things Bridget has written about him over the course of their sometimes contentious relationship. He strides out of Bridget's apartment, leaving Bridget (clad only in a tank top, underwear, and a cardigan sweater) to chase after him in the snow, pleading and offering apologies. When Bridget finally catches up with him, her words disavow not only what she wrote about Mark (she didn't really mean it) but also the significance of woman's writing itself. "It's only a diary," she pleads, begging his forgiveness. "Everyone knows diaries are just full of crap." The scene does not, however, stop at having the woman reject her own voice. Mark replies that he knows she didn't mean what she wrote, and that he was just buying her a new diary for a "new start." All is forgiven, and Bridget is wrapped in Mark's strong arms and warm winter coat. It is a happy romantic ending, accompanied by snow, warm lighting, and the chick-flick staple "Someone Like You" on the soundtrack. But it can be achieved only when the woman submits her story and her voice to masculine control.

In the end, then, chick lit, movies, and television programs can be just as conservative as older works like the woman's film and the romance novel in their portrayals of women's concerns. Perhaps this should not be surprising. They are, after all, produced by and within the same male-dominated culture. Still, these contemporary works provide important new visions of women's voices, communities, and experiences as sexual beings. They are not perfect visions by any means, but they are a step beyond earlier "women's texts," which have been even more tightly bound by traditional ideas of what women should be and how women should behave. Chick novels, films, and television provide spaces for the expression of women's experiences and desires, suggesting possibilities for women outside the role of girlfriend, wife, or mother. In doing so, these "women's texts" truly are *for* women, presenting affirmative notions of female identity, sexuality, and community.

Notes

1. Ironically, both *Bridget Jones's Diary* and *Sex and the City* began as newspaper columns before being condensed into book form and eventually being adapted into a film and television show, respectively.
2. *Bridget Jones's Diary* and its sequel *Bridget Jones: The Edge of Reason* are, of course, both updated, comedic takes on two Jane Austen novels: *Diary* is a retelling of *Pride and Prejudice* and *Edge* incorporates elements of *Persuasion*. Although a discussion of the direct connections between Austen's novels and Fielding's updates are beyond the scope of this essay, the fact that the stories could be so easily translated to a contemporary setting perhaps says a lot about how little women's circumstances have changed in two hundred years.
3. One of the most disappointing aspects of the *Bridget Jones* film adaptation is the diminished presence and importance of Bridget's "urban family." The decreased role of Bridget's friends in the film could be attributed to the constraints of adapting a two-hundred-page novel into a ninety-minute motion picture. However, the fact that the friends' screen time is cut to allow more time for the central romance(s) speaks to mainstream films' continued reliance on—and reification of—heterosexual romance narratives.

Works Cited

"About Red Dress Ink." eHarlequin.com. <http://store.eharlequin.com/continuities/RDIOnlineConti-nuity.jhtml?PRODID=8454>.

"The Agony and the Ex-tasy." *Sex and the City*. HBO. 3, June 2001.

"Ally McBeal." Internet Movie Database. http://www.imdb.com.

"An American Girl in Paris (part une)." *Sex and the City*. HBO. 15, Feb. 2004.

"An American Girl in Paris (part deux)." *Sex and the City*. HBO. 22, Feb. 2004.

"Are We Sluts?" *Sex and the City*. HBO. 16, June 2000.

Bridget Jones's Diary. Dir. Sharon Maguire. Perf. Renée Zellweger, Colin Firth, Hugh Grant. Mira-max/Universal/Studio Canal. 2001. DVD Miramax. 2001.

"Bridget Jones's Diary." Internet Movie Database. http://www.imdb.com.

Doane, Mary Ann. *The Desire to Desire: The Woman's Film of the 1940s*. Bloomington: Indiana University Press, 1987.

"Ex and the City." *Sex and the City*. HBO. 3, Oct. 1999.

Fielding, Helen. *Bridget Jones's Diary*. 1996. New York: Penguin, 1999.

———. *Bridget Jones: The Edge of Reason*. 1999. New York: Viking Penguin, 2000.

"Harlequin Launches Red Dress Ink." *The Write News*. 30, Nov. 2001. <www.writenews.com>.

Henry, Astrid. "Orgasms and Empowerment: *Sex and the City* and the Third Wave Feminism." *Reading* Sex and the City. Ed. Kim Akass and Janet McCabe. London: I.B. Tauris, 2004. 65–82.

"The Ick Factor." *Sex and the City*. HBO. 11, Jan. 2004.

"Is 'Chick Lit' Here to Stay? " *Marketing to Women*. Dec. 2003: 9.

Jain, Anita. "Head over Heels for Sassy Chick Lit: Publishers Add Imprints for Plucky Novels as Genre Catches on with Young Women." *Crain's New York Business* 27, Oct. 2003: p1+.

Keyes, Marian. *Last Chance Saloon*. New York: Avon Books, 1999.

Kinsella, Sophie. *Confessions of a Shopaholic*. New York: Delta Fiction, 2001.

Kuhn, Annette. "Women's Genres. " *Feminism and Film*. Ed. E. Ann Kaplan. New York: Oxford University Press, 2000. 437–49.

Maxted, Anna. *Behaving Like Adults*. New York: ReaganBooks-HarperCollins, 2003.

———. *Running in Heels*. New York: ReaganBooks-HarperCollins, 2001.

Modleski, Tania. *Feminism without Women: Culture and Criticism in a "Postfeminist" Age*. New York: Routledge, 1991.

———. *Loving with a Vengeance: Mass-Produced Fantasies for Women*. 1982. New York: Routledge, 1990.

Radway, Janice. *Reading the Romance: Women, Patriarchy, and Popular Literature*. Rev. ed. Chapel Hill: University of North Carolina Press, 1991.

Rebecca. Dir. Alfred Hitchcock. Perf. Joan Fontaine, Laurence Olivier. Prod. David O. Selznick. 1939.

"Sex and the City." *Sex and the City*. HBO. 6, June 1998.

"Sex and the City." Internet Movie Database. http://www.imdb.com.

"Sex and the City (a titles and airdates guide by Murdok)." Epiguides.com. <http://epguides.com/SexandtheCity/>.

Someone Like You. Dir. Tony Goldwyn. Perf. Ashley Judd, Hugh Jackman. 20th Century Fox. 2001. DVD 20th Century Fox Home Entertainment. 2001.

"Theatrical Trailers." *The Sweetest Thing*. DVD Columbia Pictures. 2002.

"Trailers." *Maid in Manhattan*. DVD Columbia Pictures. 2003.

Weinberg, Anna. "She's Come Undone: Chick Lit Was Supposed to Be a Bright Light of Post-feminist Writing. What Happened?" *Book* July–Aug. 2003: 46–49.

"Where There's Smoke ..." *Sex and the City*. HBO. 4, June 2000.

Wilson, Amy. "Traditional Romance Formula Gets a Dose of 'Chick Lit.'" *Orange County Register* 5, Sept. 2001: K5484.

12

No Satisfaction: *Sex and the City, Run Catch Kiss,* and the Conflict of Desires in Chick Lit's New Heroines

ANNA KIERNAN

There is no disputing the thematic dominance of love and romance in chick-lit fictions. Given that chick lit can be said to fuse the literary and narrative conventions of Austen's novels with the mass-market, rose-tinted amorous projects of Mills and Boon or Harlequin romances, it is little wonder that so many of these novels are concerned with finding Mr. Right. And although Bridget Jones represents a version of the independent, upwardly mobile, postfeminist woman, she is also singularly obsessed with men and marriage. For her, the acquisition of a husband seems to represent success. Still, the genre's negotiations with desire, and, more specifically, sexual desire, are less secure.

Amy Sohn's *Run Catch Kiss*, like Candace Bushnell's *Sex and the City*, maps out new narratives of desire that can be read as signaling a shift away from the primacy of romantic closure in traditional romances. In these sex-column-turned-novels, the heroines often demonstrate a greater concern for getting sexual kicks than for getting hitched. But even within this shared central focus, the two novels reveal fundamental differences: *Run Catch Kiss* is about the pursuit of sexual liberation through pleasure whereas *Sex and the City* is about the pursuit of sexual liberation through power.

Rereading the Romance

Given the narrative traditions of chick lit, it is perhaps not surprising that the genre has been attributed such a lowly status by the literary establishment. For the most part, chick lit is viewed as being an insubstantial contribution to the canon by the more traditional stable of feminist novelists and cultural critics. Doris Lessing's and Beryl Bainbridge's respective views are that chick lit is "instantly forgettable" and "froth" (Ezard). That the traditional romantic formula has to some extent been reinvented to take account of new romantic heroines is seldom acknowledged.

The traditional romantic formula is dependent on a number of familiar factors. An attractive (but not beautiful) single woman meets an older man whom she is desperately drawn to. She encounters some difficulty in her pursuit of love, often based on some misunderstanding between the two romantic leads, but is finally rewarded with love or marriage, or both. *Bridget Jones's Diary* is perhaps the best known of such romances in recent years, and its explicit debt to Jane Austen's *Pride and Prejudice* underpins the narrative (as Suzanne Ferriss explains elsewhere in this anthology).

Sex in such romances is a rather alluring but elusive idea, because the heroine's progress is dependent on the ongoing suspense of seeking love. Once she finds love, "normal" relations commence, and the novel ends. Typically, as Anne Snitow suggests in "Mass Market Romance: Pornography for Women Is Different," romance readers' amorous investment is in the unknown: "Whatever [men] are, it is more exciting to wonder about them than to know them. In romanticized sexuality the pleasure lies in the distance itself. Waiting, anticipation, anxiety—these represent the high point of sexual experience" (263).

Not so in chick lit. The characteristic cynicism about "the ways of men" is key to understanding the motivations of newer metropolitan heroines and their conquests. Context is key to understanding this shift: whereas the Harlequin romances discussed by Snitow were specifically targeted at provincial secretaries and rural housewives (i.e., low or no-earners), chick lit is marketed more broadly, to both the typical "Harlequin lady" and the urban single woman with a disposable income.

The crossover in readerships is integral to my discussion, since the opening up of new markets is concurrent with the genre's partial departure from romantic conventions. Chick lit, as a relatively new form of romance, offers a more sophisticated insight into the lives, loves, and aspirations of the women it speaks for and to: "anticipating pleasure" has largely been superseded by actively seeking and experiencing pleasure. And sex, romance's new variable, has heralded a new phase of women's fiction—one that raises questions about how feminine desire is constructed, articulated, and received in and beyond fiction.

But such developments should be treated with caution. It is tempting to think that this new trajectory signals some kind of feminist triumph and that it implies the realization of the hopeful claim that women "can have it all." Of course it is far more complicated than that. *Sex and the City* and *Run Catch Kiss* may be about "sex and the single girl" but the heroines of both are sometimes wistful—they too want their knight in shining armor. In which case, what do Carrie Bradshaw and Amy Sohn tell us about the politics of love and sex that we don't already know?

Sexual Power in Sex and the City

> Welcome to the Age of Un-Innocence. The glittering lights of Manhattan that served as backdrops for Edith Wharton's bodice-heaving trysts are still glowing—but the stage is empty ... Truman Capote understood our nineties dilemma—the dilemma of Love vs. the deal—all too well. (Bushnell 2)

"The deal" in this passage from *Sex and the City* can be understood as being the opposite of the romantic ideal. Business concerns and career aspirations are attributed equal status to love, and the Capote comparison implies that love, too, is "a deal," as relations between the two leads and their benefactors in *Breakfast at Tiffany's* suggest.

Presented thus, romance and anticipation, deep sighs and uncertainties seem, for the most part, to be part of a different language to that of this hardheaded, business-oriented version of love, in which closure (of the deal) is paramount.

Bushnell's salute to literary romances, evoked in this passage as faded melodramas, demonstrates not only an affectionate appreciation of the cultural significance of Wharton's society novel *The Age of Innocence* but also a sense of resignation that such romances are largely irrelevant to affairs of the heart in New York in the 1990s: "There's still plenty of sex in Manhattan but the kind of sex that results in friendship and business deals, not romance" (3).

In the coolly confident world of Bushnell's Manhattan, to enjoy meaningless one night stands and to attain satisfaction from fleeting physical encounters, as men apparently do, is considered a triumph: "We were hard and proud of it, and it hadn't been easy getting to this singular position—this place of complete independence where we had the luxury of treating men like sex objects" (Bushnell qtd. in Zeisler).

Pulling off the patriarchal trick of sexual objectification is apparently a hard-earned skill for these women. This "singular position" implies an acceptance of individualistic imperatives, that is, a disavowal of womanhood as being contiguous with being supportive, loving, romantic, and in need of a partner to justify an otherwise incomplete existence.

Much of the novel's residual humor can be found in the inversion of sexual power and romantic ideals in the lead characters. Charlotte observes of one slighted lover, "He'd recently stopped calling: he wanted to read me his poetry and I wouldn't let him" (42). Carrie, in her brief involvement with twenty-five-year-old artist Barkley, similarly balks at the romantic clichés he expects her to crave. After a night out during which Barkley disappeared with another woman, he calls her, anticipating a scene of recriminations.

> "I didn't sleep with her. I didn't even kiss her," Barkley said. "I don't care. I'll never see her again if you don't want me to."
>
> "I really don't give a shit." And the scary thing was, she didn't. (8)

Such are the conventions of the mating game that both parties expect Carrie to be devastated by her new boyfriend's indiscretion. Even as she admits her disinterest, Carrie is aware that her lack of emotional attachment is more controversial than Barkley's infidelity. Her power lies in her sense of control, which is rooted in an inversion of gendered sexual codes. As such, it emasculates Barkley, whose unconvincing admission seems set up to provoke a standard lovers' tiff based on a misunderstanding (a standard trope of the traditional romance). His planned performance of "playboy of the Western world battles with needy woman for independence" is undercut by Carrie's pithy response.

In *Sex and the City*, each foray seems to debunk a different sexual myth, in a manner that is at odds with conventional wisdom about a woman's sexual and emotional needs and desires. When Carrie debriefs her friends regarding her trip to Le Trapeze, a couples-only sex club, she is typically nonchalant:

> "Didn't you love it?" asked Charlotte, the English journalist. "I'd love to go to a place like that. Didn't it turn you on, watching all those people having sex?"
>
> "Nope," I said, stuffing my mouth with a corn fritter topped with salmon eggs. (15)

That Carrie dips a toe into so-called sexually deviant practices and announces that for her, they are lukewarm, is further evidence of her comfortable detachment from sexual norms.

Positioned thus, Bushnell's heroines can be seen to act out Naomi Wolf's challenge in *The Beauty Myth* that, "Women could probably be trained quite easily to see men first as sexual" (154). But such an inversion of gendered sexual practice is problematic. After all, doesn't it simply reinstate the limitations of the value system that feminism purports to reject, namely, the objectification of women?

That Carrie et al. speak in the same Martini-cool tones as Bret Easton Ellis nihilists is telling, because *American Psycho* (1991) is a cautionary tale about exactly such reductive identifying practices. The dehumanizing impulse of objectifying women finds echoes in Bushnell's references to a certain type of male "sociopath", for whom a typical comment might be, "George says he doesn't care about getting laid. 'It's a sport' " (34). The attitudes of these unsympathetic characters are simultaneously repulsive and influential to Carrie and her friends' own philosophy of love.

The conflict of desires that this implies is played out on a day trip to a baby shower. Carrie and her single friends' primary response to the sanitized, moneyed world of the suburbs is to demand vodka and plan a hasty escape. At one point Miranda, a thirty-two-year-old cable exec says, "If I see gardening tools, I'm going to scream" (81). But despite the sense of horror they feel on observing a friend's acceptance of such domesticity, Carrie is momentarily mesmerized by the romantic myth she finds encapsulated in the photographs in the bathroom:

> Carrie stared at those photographs for a long time. What was it like to be Jolie? How did it happen? How did you find someone who fell in love with you and gave you all this? She was thirty-four and she'd never even come close, and there was a good chance she never would. (85)

The fairy-tale life she has stumbled into is as alien to Carrie as that of Snow White and the Seven Dwarves: she is intrigued but cannot really relate. Her philosophy—"to give up on love … and throttle up on power" (41)—to find contentment seems less certain in the light of these reflections. Carrie's dilemma here is the nexus of the novel. She must either "play hardball" with the boys or obey "The Rules," whereby the passive heroine is exalted.

Run Catch Kiss and the Pleasure Principle

As a novel, *Run Catch Kiss* lacks the authorial and narrative assurance of *Sex and the City*. And Sohn's debt to Bushnell's literary niche is evident in her rise to fame, the form she uses, and the issues she explores. Both authors even employ the same trick of retaining their own initials for their heroine's names. In fact, Ariel Steiner, the fledgling sex columnist in *Run Catch Kiss*, might be viewed as Carrie Bradshaw's naughty little sister. But rather than consciously protecting herself from destructive relationships, as Carrie does, Ariel seems set on seeking them out.

Having just arrived in New York, Ariel is intent on making her presence felt. Introducing herself to her readers by saying, "I was the Hester Prynne of Downtown," Ariel aligns herself with the protagonist in Nathaniel Hawthorne's *The Scarlet Letter* (1850), the tale of one woman's suffering after her sexual transgression. Ariel's identification with Prynne as an outcast in American society is partly self-parody (Ariel is marked with her own scarlet letter—her weekly sex column) but also an acknowledgment that both characters transgress society's prescribed sexual norms and suffer the consequences.

After a brief stint acting in dubious fringe theatre performances such as *Lolita: Rock On!*, Ariel stumbles into her new vocation as a sex columnist for a free weekly paper, *City Week*. Thrilled to be engaged in a more exciting venture than pushing paper in her temping job, or playing to empty theaters, Ariel seizes the opportunity, without a thought for the implications of her new identity.

Her editors' original brief for her column is that she should write about "the weekly struggles of a single girl in the city. A Perils of Pauline from a slacker slut perspective. We're seeing it as 'Reality Bites My Ass'" (Sohn 76). In this, Ariel's purpose is quite different from that of either Carrie Bradshaw, who is "some sort of journalist" (Bushnell 80), or Candace Bushnell herself, who writes about the Manhattan high life from the perspective of a set of women who are "smart, attractive, successful, and ... never married" (25). While *Run Catch Kiss* is a coming-of-age novel, *Sex and the City* is aspirational, because it is about women who have *arrived*.

This difference in intent is important: Carrie Bradshaw is "hard and proud"; when she feels vulnerable, she bolts. Ariel Steiner, on the other hand, is a two-bit graduate with something to prove—and when she feels vulnerable, she seems to cling to the source of pain. Her vulnerability, though, is also what allows her to experience sex as something more than a conquest, at least outside of the confines of her sex column.

For the purposes of her weekly column, Ariel soon learns that there is a correct form for titillation. Editor Jensen's brief, "You can write about whatever you want … as long as it's true" (77), might just as easily have read, "You can write about whatever you want … as long as you stay true to the winning formula." When Ariel reflects on an unsuccessful audition one week, instead of writing about her latest conquest, her editors reprimand her, because such honest accounts don't sell newspapers. Despite editor Turner's admission that any record of an event will contain "an element of distortion," it becomes clear that such distortion must be sexual or risk rejection.

As a cub columnist Ariel swallows her unpalatable brief and overlooks the ambiguities of her role. Even so, the disparity between intention (here understood as how the protagonist would *like* to behave and be understood sexually) and reception (the way that the men she sleeps with, her editor, and her readers *respond* to her sexuality) emerges as a central tension in this novel. What becomes apparent is that the doublespeak of editors Jensen and Turner regarding the necessary authenticity of Ariel's journalism is symptomatic of the confusing sexual landscape in which Ariel becomes an intrepid explorer.

For Ariel the production of fantasies for her column is largely an empty experience for public consumption, in which she soon discovers that the simplistic and ultimately pornographic readings of her writing do not correlate with any sense of eroticism. Stylistically each of her columns is in stark contrast to the body text of the novel. Both contain elements of the confessional, but whereas her column presents contrived sexual confessions, the main first-person narrative is self-deprecating, amusing, and characteristically (for the genre) concerned with the absurd minutiae of everyday life.

A typical preamble to writing her column, in which the pressure of finding a suitable subject seems insurmountable, occurs when her friend Sara makes off with the man Ariel wanted:

> The worst part of our breakup was the timing. She had left me with no one to go out with … I thought about going out alone, but it seemed too desperate. When two girls go out together, they look cool but when a girl goes out by herself, she looks pathetic. So every night that week, while Sara was probably lying spread-eagled on her bed, I was watching TV, chugging Carlo Rossi, rereading *Notes of a Dirty Old Man,* and praying some guy from my past would call me out of the blue so I could have an interaction worthy of a column. (83)

There is little here of the strident glamour of Bushnell's Manhattan; instead, it is more reminiscent of Bridget Jones's Chardonnay-fueled musings. Notwithstanding the opening reference to Hawthorne, Ariel's literary and literal muses are more often noted for trawling the underside of respectable society, the one that Ariel imagines she wants to explore but discovers holds little allure.

As a result it is Ariel's ongoing attempts to navigate her way between reality and fantasy, the respectable and the illicit, that drives the narrative in *Run Catch Kiss*. Of course the tensions between real sex and column porn, Ariel Steiner and her nymphomaniac persona, raise issues of identity that highlight the anxieties many women feel in trying to conform to impossible sexual ideals. As the novel progresses, the stress of trying to sustain a stereotypical version of herself as a liberated sex goddess begins to show as Ariel becomes increasingly alienated from her fleeting lovers.

When Ariel agrees to go with Charlton to a twenty-five-cent porn cinema downtown, her optimism can find a voice only in an abstracted third-person reference to herself, in which she contends that her adventurous alter ego would want to go: "Ariel Steiner sought out adventure at all costs" (144). When the extent of the venue's tawdriness becomes apparent, she says, "Ariel Steiner can fuck in a porno booth and come out feeling liberated, not gross" (146). But she can't; instead she "goes underground"—divorces herself from the grime of a porn booth by first disengaging from it, and subsequently reinscribing her experience as a standard pornographic fantasy in the form of her weekly column.[1] She writes, "I've always wanted to have sex in a porno movie booth, so last week I finally did" (151).

Of course there is nothing to say that Ariel shouldn't enjoy the experience of having sex in a porn booth. But her pleasure is denied because of her passivity in the proceedings. Charlton seems to treat Ariel like a sex doll, and in her passive state Ariel colludes with this eroticization of "only the woman's body and the man's desire" (Wolf 154). There is nothing erotic or even liberated about this scenario. Unlike Bradshaw's research trip to a sex club, Ariel has no real desire to view the inside of a porn booth, and her lack of agency combined with the self-serving performance of her porn-booth lover effect an annihilating experience.

Unlike *Sex and the City*, in which every episode seems to debunk a different sexual myth, *Run Catch Kiss* seems to play out elements of feminist debates, particularly with regard to the production of pornography. The scene above, for instance, seems to support Catherine MacKinnon's view:

> Sexual desire in women, at least in this culture, is socially constructed
> as that by which we come to want our own self-annihilation; that is,

> our subordination is eroticized ... we get off on it, to a degree. This
> is our stake in this system that is not in our interest, our stake in
> this system that is killing us. I'm saying that femininity as we know
> it is how we come to want male dominance, which most emphati-
> cally is not in our interest. (qtd. in Sommers 231)

Ariel's unconvincing statement of intent regarding visiting a porn booth
seems to ape the desire to be "hard and proud," which characterizes the
rather more worldly women in *Sex and the City*. Attempting to invert exis-
tent sexual norms in favor of the feminine here seems to risk annihilation.
But the possibility of adopting the stereotypically masculine approach to
sex, as I have suggested earlier, doesn't signify liberation; rather it seems to
suggest a resigned view toward revising feminist sexual politics.

Such a stalemate is symptomatic of the porn debate: To like porn is to
be complicit in the subjugation of women. To disallow porn is to be
complicit with neoconservatism that seems to seek to control sexuality as a
necessary means of reinforcing traditional power structures.[2]

Both positions are frustrating in that they disallow a free play of sexual
signifiers. A desire viewed thus must be experienced within an annihilating,
subordinating context. Within this framework, women are always victims.

Both novels under discussion would, in different ways, refute this assertion. Carrie's interest in porn is almost scientific in its detachment,
whereas Ariel's unsatisfactory experience of porn and her brief attempt to
produce porn are merely scenes that exemplify the need for an alternative
to the outdated and reductive discourses that dominate sexual behavior.

That Ariel is "more entranced by the idea of it than the act itself" is not
surprising given this context. It is also indicative of the disparity between
her real sex life (which is dull, sometimes painful, and in which she is
objectified) and her fantasy sex life (in which play is central, and satisfaction is a possible outcome). This, of course, is the great irony of the
novel—that the sex columnist here doesn't enjoy sex but is perceived to do
so by her lovers and her readers.

Ariel's sense of her own inadequacy is also partly due to her understanding that her column, at best, functions as a redress to her frustrations
(i.e., lovers). The package of herself that she presents to her readers is as
neat as that she offers up to her lovers. The narrative has altered but the
story remains the same—Ariel Steiner experiences and writes about a
version of sex that is geared toward masculine dominance, objectification,
and, apparently, pornography.

> When I got home from the diner I wrote a column about Evan, but
> I altered a few of the relevant details ... I said I'd broken up with

him because of his heroin problem, and said the one time he'd been hard enough to fuck, I came. It was the last fiction that was most important. There was no way I could let my readers know my saddest confession of all: ever since I was a teenager, my orgasms had been as elusive as the boys themselves. (113)

When Ariel is exposed by a disgruntled ex as making up the stories in her column—a position into which she was forced by her editors—she is sacked and her readers pour scorn on her. Ironically, Ariel was articulating a cheap fantasy of unconvincing sexual pleasure that her readers wanted to believe was true. Once she is exposed as a fraud, her fans might be forced to question their attachment to such unlikely fictions. But rethinking what are arguably fraudulent mythologies is, of course, an uncomfortable experience, as her editors' response to her fictions suggests:

"Didn't we make it clear when you started the column that you had to tell the truth?"

"Don't tell me you guys really thought everything I wrote was true! *Nobody's* that depraved!"

"We thought you were!" (222)

Of course her editors didn't make it clear that Ariel had to tell the truth. And their belief that she was that "depraved" is less to do with her "depravity" than their own need for her to be. In reality Ariel's column "normalizes" her experience of sex for a predominantly male readership. Her account of sex with Evan, for example, redresses her own sense of shame (at not having orgasmed and at having had sex with a heroin addict), which is complicit, up to a point, with an idealized conception of a woman with a high sex drive, who is easily pleased in bed.

This version of eroticism (and it is a singular version) is at odds with what Ariel is capable of experiencing and what she craves. What Ariel exposes is that the fantasies she is tasked with recounting do not tap into the wilder workings of her imagination but rather stunt their growth. During the course of the novel, Ariel's eroticism is replaced with irony, and her authentic fantasies find a voice only *outside* her sex columns:

That night, under the covers, I pretended my vagina was the trash compactor in *Star Wars* and James was this tiny Han Solo trapped inside me. The hotter I got, the faster my walls began to close and the harder he had to struggle to get out. After a few minutes he found this pole in there and desperately tried to pry me open with it, but it was to no avail … each move he made only intensified my arousal and crushed him further. (26)

This description of masturbation has more in common with Kathy Acker's work than Candace Bushnell's sex scenes, specifically "Girls Who Like to Fuck," a story about incest and promiscuity, and a masculine "need" to have ownership over women. Acker writes, "My hand was still there and there plus my hand had something to do with the ocean. It wasn't the ocean. It was a thick pole in the middle of the ocean. I could come around it he was inside" (162).

"Unusual" as her "trash compactor" analogy is, orgasm for Ariel has to do not with self-loathing but rather with power. Ariel knows that this fantasy is absurd, but its absurdity—its pointless playfulness—is part of what turns her on. This is not an image to massage a male ego but, rather, a fantasy of empowerment. The accepted interiority of intimacy is disrupted in the expansive images of orgasm transported to scenes characterized by their weightlessness—the ocean and outer space, respectively, in Acker's and Sohn's accounts. Such imaginary spaces are often used in sexually explicit accounts produced by women and highlight the disparity between sex as a functional discourse and sex as open-ended discourse. Here fantasy is not about obvious "transgressions" (such as visiting a porn booth) but rather about the transgression of rejecting the limitations of prescriptive sexual norms.

Both novels, like *Bridget Jones* before them, sign off with a typical romantic closure. The final line of *Sex and the City* reads, "Carrie and Mr. Big are still together" (Bushnell 228), whereas Ariel Steiner's final update is that, "Although I'd finally found someone to share my life with, it wasn't much of a life to share" (Sohn 255). It would be easy, then, to contend that nothing has changed, that the romantic formula is entirely intact.

Despite these similarities, the stories and ideologies of these novels are quite different. Sohn takes issue with reductiveness, with the notion that a person can be confined to one identity, through the various personas she ascribes Ariel Steiner in *Run Catch Kiss*. Sohn also positions her protagonist within the framework of feminist identity politics in which singular notions of the self are roundly rejected.[3] One of the strengths of *Run Catch Kiss* is, conversely, its inconsistency—its conflict of desires, because, of course, the consistency of the linear romantic myth is what must be put into question for more complex heroines to take form in commercial women's fiction.

Notes

1. In *Bitch*, Elizabeth Wurtzel discusses the notion of "going underground" with reference to the work of psychologists Carol Gilligan and Lyn Mikel Brown. In particular, *Meeting at the Crossroads: Women's Psychology and Girls' Development* concentrates on "losing voice"—teenage girls' dissociation during sexual development, often resulting in "separating themselves or their psyches from their bodies so as not to know what they were feeling, dissociating their voice from their feelings and thoughts so that others would not know what they were experiencing, taking themselves out of relationship [with themselves] so that they could better approximate what others want and desire" (110).
2. Hybrids of these views have found a greater readership in the works of Naomi Wolf, Susan Faludi, and Elizabeth Wurtzel. Wolf and Faludi, in particular, in their respective works *The Beauty Myth* (1991) and *Backlash* (1993), write of the constrictive conservatism that has encroached on developments in feminism since the second wave in the 1960s and 1970s. Viewed by neoconservative "feminists" such as Christina Hoff Summers as promoting conspiracy theories regarding, for example, the number of deaths suffered in the United States as a result of anorexia, *The Beauty Myth*'s journalistic style and questionable research are cause for concern.
3. Kathy Acker's commitment to multiplicity is, once more, an influence here. Consider this excerpt from an interview with R.U. Sirius:

   RUS: If he succeeds in dragging you into a singular "I," that's the death of Kathy Acker the writer.

   KA: Yeah, it sure is. But I don't think he'll succeed. He doesn't have a fuckin' chance. I'm just trying to fuck him. If he won't fuck, we're not going anywhere. He can't make me into this singular "I" I told him, "You gotta consider the pleasure principle—namely my pleasure. 'He didn't like that.'"

Works Cited

Acker, Kathy. "Girls Who Like to Fuck." *Memorium to Identity.* London: Pandora Press, 1990. 156–75.

Bushnell, Candace. *Sex and the City.* London: Picador, 1997.

Ellis, Bret Easton. *American Psycho.* London: Picador, 1991.

Ezard, John. "Bainbridge Tilts at 'Chick Lit' Cult: Novelist Says Bridget Jones Genre Is Just a Lot of Froth." *The Guardian* 24, Aug. 2001. <http://books.guardian.co.uk/departments/generalfiction/story/0,6000,541954,00.html>.

Faludi, Susan. *Backlash: The Undeclared War against Women.* London: Vintage, 1993.

Fielding, Helen. *Bridget Jones's Diary.* London: Picador, 1996.

Sirius, R.U. "Kathy Acker: Where Does She Get Off?" <http://www.altx.com/io/acker.html>.

Snitow, Ann. "Mass Market Romance: Pornography for Women Is Different." *Desire: The Politics of Sexuality.* Ed. Ann Snitow, Christine Stansell, and Sharon Thompson. London: Virago, 1984. 258–75.

Sohn, Amy. *Run Catch Kiss.* London: Scribner, 1999.

Sommers, Christina Hoff. *Who Stole Feminism?* New York: Simon and Schuster, 1994.

Wolf, Naomi. *The Beauty Myth.* London: Vintage, 1991.

Wurtzel, Elizabeth. *Bitch.* London: Quartet, 1998.

Zeisler, Andi. "Marketing Miss Right." "Our Bridgets, Ourselves: Why We Can't Stop Reading—and Reading into—*Bridget Jones's Diary*." Bitch. August 2001. <http://www.bitchmagazine.com/archives/08_01bridget/bridget.shtml>.

13

Fashionably Indebted: Conspicuous Consumption, Fashion, and Romance in Sophie Kinsella's Shopaholic Trilogy

JESSICA LYN VAN SLOOTEN

Prada. Vera Wang. Kate Spade. Tiffany. To a fashionista like Becky Bloom-wood, heroine of Sophie Kinsella's Shopaholic novels, these names evoke luxury, possibility, and romance. In the fashionable, hip, single societies of London and Manhattan that Becky inhabits, these labels are de rigueur. Like many of her chick-lit sisters, Becky fully engages in a culture of con-spicuous consumption, fashioning and refashioning her identity by means of her label-driven purchases. Insecure about both personal and profes-sional fulfillment, Becky engages in serious retail therapy and consump-tion binges to assuage her anxieties. Such behavior only feeds her insecurities, and Becky's world threatens to spin out of control as she sinks deeper in debt. Throughout the series, however, Becky never *really* suffers privation because of her spending habits. Instead, her problems almost miraculously disappear, suggesting to readers that there are no real conse-quences to Becky's behavior and providing readers a "safe" consumerist fantasy world.

All three novels, *Confessions of a Shopaholic, Shopaholic Takes Manhat-tan,* and *Shopaholic Ties the Knot,* share the same informal, chatty first-person voice of Becky, who begins each book trying to calm herself from a state of alarm: "OK. Don't panic." Becky immediately panics, often ignoring or running away from both personal and professional conflicts. Kinsella includes letters and memos from Becky's financial institutions throughout the novels to remind us (and Becky, lest she forget) of the authority of the bank and the supposed consequences of her endless spending. Yet the letters create mixed messages about financial responsibility, at once admonishing and encouraging Becky's compulsive, credit-driven spending sprees: the letters inquire about overdue payments—"You will also be aware that you have substantially exceeded the agreed limit of £2,000"—and offer credit extensions—"We are therefore offering you, Ms. Bloomwood—as a graduate—a free extended overdraft facility of £2,000 during the first two years of your career"—with the same polite tone (*Confessions* 1–2). The well-mannered and at times ridiculous doublespeak of these letters keeps readers from worrying too much about Becky's financial scrapes, while simultaneously reminding us that in the real world, Becky must eventually pay for her excesses. She *does* pay, but she always orchestrates a financially advantageous solution just before her predicament becomes dire.

Becky's exaggerated irresponsibility, delivered by means of a confessional first-person narrator, prevents readers from taking her or her problems too seriously; a common reader's response is "at least *I'm* not that bad." The fact that Becky's problems are easily solved ultimately suggests that the novels are not particularly critical of such spending. Though Becky's financial irresponsibility temporarily threatens her personal and professional lives, both actually benefit from her folly. In turn the novels become objects of conspicuous consumption, allowing readers a "safe" outlet for their own consumerist fantasies, reinforcing the luxury lifestyle as a means of creating identity and achieving success in both personal and professional spheres. The novels zero in on many modern professional women's concerns and suggest that conspicuous consumption at least provides the temporary illusion of decadently and stylishly "having it all."

How to Spend: Confessions of a Shopaholic

Becky Bloomwood represents what psychologists Annette Lieberman and Vicki Lindner label the "transitional woman." Women in this category embrace more modern, feminist ideas and identities than their predecessors, though they also seem to be conscious of vestiges of prefeminist ideas about women and money. Although feminism supports women's right to careers and access to their own money, some women may still feel insecure about making their own salary, competing with men in the marketplace, and often exceeding their male partners' earnings. For transitional women, "money can symbolize conflicted desires" (11). Many women want their own money, yet still want to marry well and do not want to appear to be more money motivated than the men in their lives. Because of the lingering conflicts between feminist and prefeminist ideologies, "Modern women are afraid of money" (3). The emotional premise underscores much contemporary writing on women and money. Lieberman and Lindner, as well as C. Diane Ealy and Kay Lesh, urge women to uncover their personal, hidden money myths and break free from the money myths and patterns that keep them from reaching their full financial potential.

Becky represents what Lieberman and Lindner label "Moneyfolly." The spender subject to this disorder "does not make rational or informed decisions about how she wants to use her money, but spends in order to achieve emotional goals. Because she buys to resolve emotional problems instead of to obtain goods and services, her concept of money is subjective" (144). Becky's view of money changes as emotional needs and anxieties change. This pattern of spending begins in *Confessions of a Shopaholic* and is most pronounced in situations where Becky's personal and professional insecurities are conflated. One of many examples occurs when Becky loses a retail sales job on her very first day (she tries to hide a pair of zebra print jeans from a customer because she wants them herself). After leaving the store, Becky runs into her childhood neighbor Tom Webster and his girlfriend, who are en route to Tiffany. Tom thinks Becky has feelings for him (she doesn't) and confronts her, letting her down gently. The cumulative effect of these incidents leaves Becky feeling "a bit low" on both the personal and the professional fronts: "I give a gusty sigh, stand up, and start walking along the street again. All in all, it hasn't been a great day. I've lost a job and been patronized by Tom Webster. And now I haven't got anything to do tonight" (134). Suddenly, Becky's life seems empty and unfulfilled, and she has no plans to help assuage her feelings of loss and humiliation.

Becky's plummeting spirits lift when she realizes "at least I've got twenty quid" (134). In typical Becky mode, she begins to fantasize about what she will buy:

> Twenty quid. I'll buy myself a nice cappuccino and a chocolate brownie. And a couple of magazines. And maybe something from Accessorize. Or some boots. In fact I really *need* some new boots. [...] God, I deserve a treat, after today. And I need some new tights for work, and a nail file. And maybe a book to read on the tube. (134–35)

Even Becky's fantasy purchases reflect her personal and professional identities. The luxury food items, magazines, and books comfort her personal woes by providing "nourishment" and escapism; these items are consumed quickly and temporarily replace the emotional need for a boyfriend. The goods from Accessorize—boots, tights, and nail file—are more "fashionable" purchases that she presumably needs to project her desired image at work: that of a well-groomed, stylish professional.

What begins as a tasty afternoon treat turns into a full-blown shopping trip for items that Becky feels are necessary. As Lieberman and Lindner note, "[The Moneyfolly woman] buys goods and services she unquestionably regards as 'necessities,' and loathes the idea of keeping track of expenses" (145). To Becky all of these items are justified and necessary. Even before she buys any of these "necessary" items, her mood improves because in her mind the shopping has already begun: "By the time I join the queue at Starbucks, I feel happier already" (135). The mere thought of shopping alleviates her worries and promises diversion. As Lieberman and Lindner note, "As they shop, the anxieties give way to pleasurable fantasies, which offer a real, if brief sensation of relief" (162). Becky's shopping compulsion seemingly offers her an escape from her dejection and promises to "outfit" her with a sense of success.

Becky's emotional needs are temporarily fulfilled by the idea of shopping and the act of shopping because both are pleasurable activities. Becky's behavior nicely fits Colin Campbell's model of "modern autonomous imaginative hedonism." According to Campbell,

> The central insight required is the realization that individuals do not so much seek satisfaction from products, as pleasure from the self-illusory experiences which they construct from their associated meanings. The essential activity of consumption is thus not the actual selection, purchase or use of products, but the imaginative pleasure-seeking to which the product image lends itself. (89)

The actual products are not as important as the fantasies that revolve around the products, which explains Becky's continually expanding list of necessities. The particular items are not significant beyond their role in her rationalizations of her *need* for some products more than others. Any of these products will theoretically assist Becky in escaping the reality of her bad day and transport her into her fantasy world where she achieves fulfillment.

The happiness and fulfillment Becky receives from her impromptu shopping trip quickly fade:

> On Monday morning I wake early, feeling rather hollow inside. My gaze flits to the pile of unopened carrier bags in the corner of my room and then quickly flits away again. I know I spent too much money on Saturday. [...] In all, I spent ... Actually, I don't want to think about how much I spent. Think about something else, quick, I instruct myself. (137)

At this point Becky has forgotten the reason for her purchases. Becky once again suffers anxiety, though not because of personal and professional insecurities. Instead, her anxiety revolves around her spending, further distancing her from the original problems that drove her to shop in the first place. Moneyfolly may also be a way of displacing the real emotional problem and creating instead a money problem, which is theoretically more distanced from the self.

The pleasure of her shopping binge passes and she feels "the twin horrors of Guilt and Panic" (137). The aftermath of her binge elicits a sense of shame and fear.

Becky's oh-so-necessary purchases remain in the bag, and Becky no longer feels happy. Instead, she feels worse because the reality of her financial situation is staring her in the face. No *thing* can fulfill Becky's needs beyond instant gratification, because her needs are emotional and not material.

Yet the culture of conspicuous consumption creates an endless cycle to replicate those brief moments of shopping-induced euphoria. Campbell theorizes the relationship between the idealized daydream and the disillusioned reality:

> [Modern consumers'] basic motivation is the desire to experience in reality the pleasurable dramas which they have already enjoyed in imagination, and each "new" product is seen as offering a possibility of realizing this ambition. However, since reality can never provide the perfected pleasures encountered in day-dreams (or, if at all, only in part, and very occasionally), each purchase leads to literal disillusionment, something which explains how wanting is extinguished so quickly, and why people disacquire goods as rapidly as they acquire them. What is not extinguished, however, is the fundamental longing which day-dreaming itself generates, and hence there is as much determination as ever to find new products to serve as replacement objects of desire. (89–90)

These ecstatic moments of shopping represent the promise of attaining the idealized self Becky fashions in her mind. After Becky's euphoria passes, she feels increased longing, despair, and disillusionment. She now must begin the cycle anew by centering herself through fashion.

Becky deals with her postshopping guilt by trying to consciously block out worrisome thoughts. To aid in this process, she checks her appearance, meticulously detailing her outfit: "Top: River Island, Skirt: French Connection, Tights: Pretty Polly Velvets, Shoes: Ravel ... Coat: House of Fraser sale" (138). These particular fashionable items, described not through physical details but through brands, help Becky create herself as fashionable and trendy. This act of listing, which occurs throughout the novels, becomes a way for Becky to reinforce her own sense of identity, which is intrinsically linked to what she wears. As Douglas Kellner notes, "Fashion and modernity go hand in hand to produce modern personalities who seek their identities in constantly new and trendy clothes, looks, attitudes, and behavior, and who are fearful of being out of date or unfashionable" (161). Because Becky defines herself through the fickle fashion industry, she must keep up with the trends so she does not become "last year's look." The act of listing "centers" her identity around a particular set of items.

Keeping up with the ever-changing fashion system costs Becky her financial security. Her peaceful listing reverie is rudely broken by the delivery of the mail, and the "two ominous-looking window envelopes. One from VISA, one from Endwich Bank" (138). With classic childlike avoidance, Becky wonders why these lenders cannot "just leave me alone?" (138). Becky "cleverly" drops the letters into a tempting dumpster on the way to work, and feels relieved, "purged of guilt ... as though neither of those letters ever existed" (139). Becky cannot face these letters because she knows the reality they contain: she simply cannot afford to live out her fashionable fantasy. Yet because her identity is so contingent on the fantasy self created through fashion, she cannot bear to live without indulging her dreams.

When denial is no longer an option, Becky resolves to either CB (cut back) or MMM (make more money), following the advice of her father and a financial self-help book. Becky takes the disastrous route of CB. Lieberman and Lindner warn that "the Moneyfolly victim in search of a cure must prepare herself to experience what will at first seem like deprivation as she trades in her habitual overspending pattern for a higher goal—getting a grip on her financial life" (167–68). Becky prepares to eat cheap watercress sandwiches and bring her coffee to work in a flask. Her plan goes awry when she realizes she must invest in necessary supplies to practice cutting back. For how can she make a chicken and mushroom Balti without the proper curry spices, a cute apron, and a special Balti pan? Because Becky's needs are not material, cutting off consumption only further exacerbates the situation of longing and drives Becky back to her practice of conspicuous consumption to reestablish herself. Once again Becky is entrenched in old spending patterns, deeming everything a necessity. When she attempts MMM, she likewise fails; Becky sends away for frame-making kits, hoping to raise her income through a cottage industry. Becky spends three hours stretching and gluing fabric to produce "one dodgy-looking frame" (*Confessions* 121).

Becky's financial windfall and personal turning point occur when she writes an exposé of Flagstaff Bank, who tricked her childhood neighbors out of a large sum of money. She draws on her professional knowledge of the financial world, her interest in interpersonal relationships, and her journalistic connections to help out her friends. In the process she comes face to face with romantic interest Luke Brandon in a television debate. Becky's spirited candor and ability to dispense financial advice as a "financial guru meets girl next door" win her a regular gig on television and a salary that allows her to immediately erase her debt and win Luke's heart. Although not the fantasy of a stranger paying off her debt as she formerly daydreamed, this turn of events is, for readers, a stroke of luck that is pure fantasy. Becky learns that money problems are solved in a flash, and one's compassionate concern for others will pay off financially and romantically. At this moment other characters and readers finally recognize Becky as capable and loveable, and she begins to believe it herself. Her fantasies of celebrity culture and wealth are achieved in her *real* life through her new television career on *Morning Coffee* and romance with the affluent, handsome A-list bachelor Luke Brandon.

However, because Becky's spending habits are motivated by deeper emotional concerns and issues, this windfall only benefits her in the short term. *Confessions of a Shopaholic* concludes with a blissful Becky waking up in a posh room at the Ritz-Carlton with Luke. Turning on the television, Becky becomes mesmerized by an unbelievable offer for NK Malone sunglasses; she succumbs to the allure of this fashion accessory and places an order. Clearly, Becky's need to shop persists despite her relative personal and professional stability. She still feels the need to adorn herself with the latest luxury trends to face the blessings and challenges of her personal and professional lives.

Becky reverts to her old Moneyfolly ways in the remaining two novels, which suggests that true reformation has not occurred. This also suggests that Kinsella is not wholly indicting this culture of conspicuous consumption that encourages and even demands the kind of Moneyfolly that Becky exhibits. In fact, one message that emerges from the novels is that "shopping habits [...] are not always ultimately destructive. Sometimes shopping can put women in touch with buried skills, as well as problems" (Lieberman and Lindner 164). Indeed, Becky's knowledge of the financial world and her personal experience as someone with a financial "past" enable her to better relate with the folks who call in to her TV spot. And even more significant, her love for shopping and knowledge of fashion leads her to a career as a personal shopper at Barneys. Becky finally taps into her full potential by helping others do what she loves best: shop. And through her blossoming relationship with Luke Brandon, she is transported to Manhattan, one of the great shopping meccas of the modern world.

What to Wear: Shopaholic Takes Manhattan

Life in Manhattan affords Becky an array of luxury shopping experiences that leave her exhilarated, transformed, and, ultimately, both financially and emotionally bereft. From her first outing in Manhattan, when she mistakes Saks for St. Peter's as a place of worship, the city's glitzy shopping districts enthrall Becky. She plunges into frenzied spending, grabbing a Kate Spade purse in Saks and wandering off to the unparalleled world of sample sales, where designer fashions, fresh from the runways, are sold for a fraction of the cost. Once again Becky displays the primary behaviors of a compulsive shopper and Moneyfolly victim. She thinks of American money as play money, a trend that Lieberman and Lindner note is all too common with troubled spenders while abroad (144). Becky feels she is "made to live in America," because "Everything is so grand, and luxurious, and kind of ... *more*" (158). Manhattan, even more so than London, exudes an air of affluent, fashionable luxury. Becky finds herself admired for her British accent, and she enjoys being the toast of the television studios. Because of Manhattan's association with affluence and celebrity culture, Becky's shopping takes on a new level of intensity.

The majority of Becky's purchases are status-laden items of clothing, accessories, and cosmetics that purportedly "enhance female sexuality" and "furnish costumes for a woman's fantasy life and also deck out her fantasy-persona—the different self she might like to be" (Lieberman and Lindner 148, 153). And for Becky this different self has endless variations. Through fashion each self becomes a "work of art," as Elizabeth Wilson notes (123). In London, and more intensely in Manhattan, Becky uses fashion to create both costumes and imitations of celebrity culture. Becky's creation of both suggests dissatisfaction with the actual self. For Becky such imitations of celebrity culture allow her to launch herself into realized fantasies of her imagined worlds of wealth and recognition.

Shopaholic Takes Manhattan opens with Becky's surveying her closet in London, attempting to pack for a weekend getaway. Her eyes light on a recent purchase: a fencing mask and sword. The fencing mask and sword—symbols of strength, agility, and privilege—are Becky's entrée to her fantasies of celebrity culture. She muses on her purchases: "It was a real coincidence, because I've been meaning to take up fencing forever, ever since I read this article about it in *The Daily World*" (6). Her secret fantasy is to become a gold-star fencing pro and serve as Catherine Zeta-Jones's body double, which will lead to a close friendship. Here, as elsewhere throughout the books, Becky defines herself through her purchases, many of which serve the person (or, more aptly, people) she would like to be rather than the Becky she is.

Although perhaps less overtly than the fencing suit, fashion becomes Becky's vehicle for creating a self. James Twitchell explains the role of consumption in self-presentation: "When this consumption of brands inside constellations is elaborated, it becomes a 'look,' a fashion. And creating fashion is what defines the modern self" (85). As Michael R. Solomon and Susan P. Douglas further explain,

> Traditionally, important uses of clothing for many women have been to project a role image and to communicate location or status in society. The clothing a woman wore thus revealed her self-identity and demonstrated her aesthetic taste [...] a clothing item was assessed on the basis of its "look," the fit with lifestyle and social position, and the self-image a woman wished to convey. (387)

Becky continuously creates looks for herself, describing herself by what she wears, such as "the Girl in the Denny and George scarf" (*Confessions* 14). Such high-end, luxury goods allow Becky to change herself by changing her clothes. By wearing recognizable, distinctive, coveted high-end brands like Prada and Jimmy Choo, what Twitchell labels "opuluxe," Becky projects an image of luxury and status to others and creates a feeling of inner satisfaction and self-worth. The Denny and George scarf gives her an established identity, one she can recall simply by winding the scarf around her neck. The scarf also functions as a memento that binds Becky and Luke's relationship; in *Confessions of a Shopaholic*, Becky borrows twenty quid from Luke to buy the scarf. This particular luxury scarf, then, conveys to the public wealth and taste, while simultaneously reminding Becky of her status as Luke's girlfriend.

Through dress, Becky purportedly conveys her financial standing and hence communicates her status. As Thorstein Veblen notes in his indictment of conspicuous consumption,

> Expenditure on dress has this advantage over most other methods, that our apparel is always in evidence and affords an indication of

> our pecuniary standing to all observers at the first glance. It is also
> true that admitted expenditure for display is more obviously
> present, and is, perhaps, more universally practiced in the matter of
> dress than in any other line of consumption. (167)

Veblen's insight remains relevant today only on the level of *appearance* of
pecuniary standing. With the advent of mass credit, anyone with an
extended line of credit can "afford" to appear wealthy. Becky is the perfect
example of someone who dresses above her means, for her dreams.

And yet Becky's encounters with Elinor Brandon, Luke's distant Manhattan
socialite mother, reveal the limits of fashion in creating an identity of
wealth and class. Becky dresses carefully and attentively for her first
meeting with Elinor, but in the taxi she notices, alongside a chipped nail
and a smeared shoe, a stray thread hanging from her skirt. Beside the
immaculate Elinor, Becky is veritably disheveled. Elinor wordlessly
hands Becky a small pair of scissors to repair this breach of grooming,
then coldly remarks, "The English are incapable of good grooming, [...]
unless it's a horse," reminding Becky that despite her posh new clothes,
she is an imposter in Manhattan (223). Elinor, a stylishly clad, well-pol-
ished woman—everything Becky *tries* to be—is ultimately without
warmth and compassion. While celebrating the opuluxe culture of Manhattan, Kinsella is also quietly reminding readers that such conspicuous
consumption has its limits and its dangers. Elinor also reflects Fred
Davis's point that a flawless appearance quickly loses value as a status
marker:

> Were everyone constantly trying to claim superior status via opu-
> lence of dress, immaculateness of grooming, and glitter of jewelry,
> the symbolic worth of such status markers would soon
> undergo—as indeed often happens—marked devaluation, thereby
> defeating the invidious ends they meant to serve. (60–61)

Elinor's case is a variation of Davis's warning; readers do not question
Elinor's financial status but question her emotional status. What are the
nonmaterial costs of such a flawless appearance? As Kinsella further develops Elinor's character, we learn that such immaculateness exacts a tremendous interpersonal cost, primarily in her relationship to her son, Luke.

Whereas Veblen indicted those members of the leisure class whose conspicuous consumption ruled the day, Twitchell responds more compassion-
ately to this culture of opuluxe. In his estimation the material world is not
meaningless, as its detractors (following Veblen's lead) posit. Rather, it is
"*too* meaningful" (Twitchell 54). In contemporary society "you are not what

you make. You are what you consume" (1). When you consume opuluxe clothing, "You are not *what* you wear but *who* you wear" (60). Thus Becky becomes "the Girl in the Vera Wang gown," her identity defined by a designer whose name holds certain cachet to those in the know.

Opuluxe items such as the Vera Wang gown garner their power from their link with the fantasy world: "The reaction to the material world can often be profound and transformative because it draws so much from dreamland. Salvation that used to be promised in the world beyond is now sited in the world of the here and now" (Twitchell 194). Opuluxe items have the potential to fulfill our dreams and fantasies, offering us an alternate "reality" to what we are currently living. And shopping for these high-end items can be "an almost transcendental experience" (Twitchell xv). Becky likens her discovery of luggage, a previous neglected consumption category, to "an incredible revelation in the middle of Harrods a bit like Saint Paul on the road to Mandalay" (*Shopaholic Takes* 7). Kinsella agrees with Twitchell's observation, though she makes her point in jest through Becky's erroneous simile. Shopping can be epiphanic, but, Kinsella suggests, it is not seriously *that* spiritual.

The Vera Wang gown figures prominently in the pivotal scene in *Shopaholic Takes Manhattan,* where Becky's New York fantasy of personal and professional fulfillment comes crashing down around her. The day begins when Becky takes advantage of complimentary personal shopping services at Barneys, the quintessential Manhattan department store for the wealthy and famous. Her major purchase is a cocktail dress, "inky purple, with a low back and glittering straps." When Becky tries on the gown, she muses,

> [I was] entranced by what I could look like, by the person I could be. There was no question. I had to have it. I *had* to. As I signed the credit card slip … I wasn't me anymore. I was Grace Kelly. I was Gwyneth Paltrow. I was a glittering somebody else, who can casually sign a credit card slip for thousands of dollars while smiling and laughing at the assistant, as though this were a nothing purchase. (251)

The dress transforms Becky into a princess, a movie star. This fabulously expensive gown allows Becky to look like the woman of her fantasies, and, more significant, to *be* the stylish, classy celebrities she emulates. Celebrity culture blends wealth, power, renown, and the fantasy of a glamorous, romantic life. Becky believes that buying the dress will allow her to experience the magic of the celebrity world. She is spellbound by her appearance in the couture gown, and her celebrity fantasy overtakes any rational thought of how much money the dream costs, or the immense distance between the fantasy and Becky's present reality.

Of course, as in *Confessions of a Shopaholic,* Becky cannot completely escape her feelings of buyer's remorse; in fact, she feels "slightly sick" after the purchase and once again begins her elaborate process of justification. When Becky arrives back "home"—the posh Four Seasons hotel—she suggests that she and Luke spend a glamorous night on the town so both of them can escape their woes. Becky dons her gown and the couple heads to a fabulous New York restaurant. Becky once again experiences that exhilaration of the opuluxe world:

> Maybe it's the Bellini, going to my head—but suddenly I feel again exactly as I did in Barneys. I'm not the old Becky—I'm someone new and sparkling. Surreptitiously I glance at myself in a nearby mirror, and feel a twinge of delight. I mean, just look at me! All poised and groomed, in a New York restaurant, wearing a thousands-of-dollars dress, with my wonderful, successful boyfriend—and a screen test tomorrow for American television! I feel completely intoxicated with happiness. This expensive, glossy world is where I've been heading all along. [...] My old life seems a million, zillion miles away, like a tiny dot on the horizon. [...] I mean, let's face it. That was never really me, was it? (255–56)

The designer dress, fancy restaurant, upscale cocktails, fabulous career prospects, and handsome, wealthy boyfriend all conspire to make Becky feel like a fairy-tale princess, who feels a rare sense of absolute personal and professional success. The couture dress makes her fantasy a reality, and the other trappings of the evening, also a nod to celebrity culture and affluence, amplify the transformation from fantasy to reality. For one perfect night Becky feels no disjunction between her imagined fantasy and her lived reality. In comparison her old life seems false. This night, spent cradled in the lap of luxury, is an absolute fantasy come true, and her identity is solidified by her opuluxe trappings.

The Vera Wang gown and its association with the wealthy, famous individuals who are able to afford such clothing create Becky's transformation. It is Becky's link to this magical luxury world, where she and Luke can dance the night away and forget their respective financial and business concerns. Becky is the wealthy, stylish, and glamorous woman she so longs to be—a self she knows lurks within her more prosaic life. Wilson explains the centrality of fashion to reclaiming a "lost" self:

> Fashion becomes an important—indeed a vital—medium in the recreation of the lost self or "decentered subject." If post-modernism articulates an experience of the world as fragmented, atomized

beyond recognition, then the plurality of styles in present day fashion [...] reflects this. At the same time, for the individual to lay claim to a particular style may be more than ever a lifeline, a proof that one does at least exist. (122)

For Becky, fashion proves not merely her existence but rather a particular type of existence, albeit a false existence built on ever-expanding debt.

The gown, though supplying one night of realized fantasy, does not contain the substance needed to truly alter reality, and like any moment that seems too good to be true, so is this night. Becky and Luke awake to face their troubles compounded—news of Becky's personal financial irresponsibility has hit the London tabloids. The magic disappears, Luke and Becky break up, and Becky heads back to England to regain control of her life. Her personal and professional lives are in shambles. Back in London, Becky resorts to an auction to sell her many luxury goods, repay her creditors with the profit, and reestablish her credibility. Selling possessions both prized (the Denny and George scarf, the Vera Wang gown) and indifferent (dozens of handmade picture frames) strips Becky of her multiple fantasies and identities, leaving her with a plainer version of herself. Becky does not have to survive with less for long, however, as she quickly reunites with Luke and finds her professional calling as a personal shopper at Barneys in Manhattan.

Once again the novel concludes with Becky and Luke's (re)establishing their relationship. In a mock proposal that foreshadows the third novel, Luke asks Becky to be his personal shopper. Material, opuluxe culture continuously frames their relationship, from Becky's designer clothing to their extended stays at luxury hotels such as the Ritz-Carlton and the Four Seasons. When all is well between them, they appear to be the modern fantasy couple, possessing money, good looks, and stylish clothing. This relationship brings Becky ever closer to the posh, affluent world of London and Manhattan. Here too, as in *Confessions of a Shopaholic*, turmoil and strife in personal and professional lives emerge through Becky's Moneyfolly. Yet Becky does not suffer any real, long-term effects. In each novel she briefly reforms her spending before reentering the cycle, buoyed up by promising new personal and professional beginnings.

Where to Wed: Shopaholic Ties the Knot

In the third novel in the series, Kinsella showcases the pinnacle of conspicuous consumption and the symbol of personal romantic and professional financial success for many modern women: the lavish wedding. *Shopaholic Ties the Knot* features three significant weddings: the wedding of Suze, Becky's best friend; the consummate fantasy wedding of Luke and Becky at the Plaza; and the heartfelt nuptials at Becky's childhood home in Oxshott, England. All three weddings present different interpretations of the modern lavish wedding. In *Cinderella Dreams,* Cele C. Otnes and Elizabeth H. Pleck detail the global domination of the lavish wedding. Much of its appeal emanates from its links to consumer culture, as Otnes and Pleck explain:

> The lavish wedding—more than any other event—has the ability to (1) "marry" the tenets of both consumer culture and romantic love; (2) offer magical transformation; (3) provide memories of a sacred and singular event; and (4) legitimate lavish consumption through the "ethic of perfection"—or the standard that includes the desire for both flawless beauty and a perfect performance—as well as an appreciation and recognition of the occasion by both participants and guests. (8–9)

The lavish wedding provides a sacred and public celebration of love and consumption. On this supposedly most important day of the bride's life, the lucky woman has one chance to enact a fairy-tale fantasy. And the emphasis on a perfect fairy-tale wedding is a vestige from earlier times when "marriage became the defining act of social place" for women (Twitchell 270). Still today the lavish wedding suggests a level of social standing—one has the money to create a lavish affair, proving to others not only the bond of marriage but also the appearance of affluent financial and elevated social status.

Over the course of the three novels, Kinsella sets readers up to expect nothing but a lavish wedding for Becky by showcasing her never-ending effort to make herself into the It Girl with the It Boyfriend. And yet the three vastly different weddings included in *Shopaholic Ties the Knot* suggest that Becky may not be the material girl we thought she was. Through the ensuing wedding fiasco, readers see the "real" Becky's ambivalence between pure fantasy and reality. Kinsella offers multiple weddings to suggest divergent identities but ultimately allows Becky to have *both* the fantasy and reality. Becky's relationship with admittedly wealthy Luke Brandon certainly aids in achieving her fantasy life. Yet Kinsella is careful to prove that Becky's marriage to Luke is not merely a calculated move to "marry up," as one might suspect. Once again Kinsella hints at both possibilities—true love and a financially advantageous match. Becky proves her genuine love and her economic disinterestedness when she signs the prenuptial agreement produced by Luke's mother, Elinor. However, much of Becky and Luke's relationship revolves around shopping and visiting posh hotels and restaurants on both sides of the Atlantic, benefits of Luke's financial and social status.

Before tackling Becky and Luke's wedding, Kinsella warms up with the understated and elegant nuptial celebration of two equal partners, Suze and Tarquin, distant cousins who do not need to showcase their wealth. Their family exudes a quiet, understated wealth mainly concerned with horses and country estates. According to Davis such understatement signals superior social and financial status:

> In the never-ending dialectic of status claims and demurrals, modesty and understatement in attire often come to be viewed as truer signs of superior social status than lavish displays of finery and bejeweled wealth. These latter, as we know, are usually taken as indicative of status posturing or, at best, a nouveau riche station. (62–63)

Suze and Tarquin's wedding lacks glamour and glitz because they have no need to prove their status—it is simply understood. Becky and Luke, however, need to prove their nouveau riche status, primarily for Elinor's benefit and her money-obsessed Manhattan social milieu. This need for lavish display speaks to anxiety about one's status and a need to receive external recognition and validation. Suze and Tarquin's calm, romantic wedding serves as the springboard to Becky's own nuptials, as Becky catches Suze's bouquet, in which Luke has hidden an engagement ring. From this moment on, Kinsella transitions into lavish wedding mode.

Kinsella heightens the excess witnessed in the two previous novels by bestowing Becky with *two* weddings, both of which are lavish, albeit on a different scale. Becky's Plaza wedding enacts a superficial fairy tale, created by a team of dedicated and overzealous wedding professionals and the calculating, frigid, and immaculate Elinor. The Plaza wedding, although planned with Becky's input, reflects the impersonality and lavish show that characterizes Elinor. This wedding is all glittering surface without an emotional substance. The Oxshott wedding, on the other hand, planned by Becky's mum and other women in the village, contains homey touches that are emotionally substantive *and* showy, although with a provincial and outdated appeal when compared to the cutting-edge trendiness of the Plaza wedding. For example, Becky's mum thinks that Thai filo parcels are the height of sophistication, whereas Robyn, the New York wedding planner, says that "filo parcels are a little passé" (249). By New York standards Becky's Oxshott wedding is not at all lavish, but looked at on its own, the wedding is indeed a sumptuous occasion into which the community women pour much of their creativity and energy to make it a grand celebration and show of luxury. Becky's family vows, "We're not going to spare any expense. We want you to have the wedding of your dreams" (47).

Compared to the Plaza wedding, a direct nod to celebrity culture as our standard of the fairy-tale wedding, any other wedding may seem devoid of luxury. Yet both are lavish affairs. As Twitchell notes, "What counts as luxury depends on who's doing the counting" (54).

Becky and Luke's Plaza wedding is the ultimate display of conspicuous consumption. Becky capriciously commits herself to a Sleeping Beauty theme, and every detail of the wedding is orchestrated to evoke the magic of the Disney-fied fairy tale of a beautiful princess awoken by the magical kiss of the handsome prince. Disney culture creates a desire to *be* the storybook princess rescued by the dashing prince, feeding into Becky's fantasy world of rescue and celebrity culture. For is not the quintessential Disney princess the "It Girl" of the fantasy kingdom? As Catherine Orenstein notes, "The modern romantic understanding of the fairy tale, and especially the romantic ideal of a 'fairy tale wedding,' owes most to the 20th century, when Americans began to glorify marriage and domesticity" (A23). This American fantasy is particularly appealing to British girls like Becky; Kinsella admits in an interview that "there's something magical about New York for British girls," and that Becky's Plaza wedding is "sort of the fulfillment of a dream" (Barker 7D). This dream merges romantic love and commerce into the fairy-tale wish of happily ever after. Otnes and Pleck explain this connection:

> The fairy tale, originally an oral tradition unconnected to commerce, became central imagery for a consumer culture and for the romantic version of that culture. [...] Two central ideas—romantic love as the basis for marrying and magic as the means of reversing fortune and realizing one's dreams—became embedded in products and services in a culture dependent on magazines, stores, visual imagery, advertising, radio, and finally, wedding services. (28)

Elinor, who has the cold demeanor and controlling nature that one might attribute to evil stepmothers rather than benevolent fairy godmothers, orchestrates and, more significant, pays for this magical wedding. Because of Elinor's strings-attached generosity, the wedding belongs not only to Becky and Luke's fantasies but also to Elinor's fantasies. Kinsella consistently presents Elinor as the negative embodiment of fashionable fantasies; her overt focus on status and wealth makes her emotionally distant and hollow. The Plaza wedding thus functions as a cautionary tale against pursuing one's lavish fantasies, because the cost of transforming reality can be too high.

The Oxshott wedding Becky's mum and her friends plan stands in sharp contrast to the Plaza wedding. The women invest their time learning new skills such as makeup application to make the wedding perfect for Becky. What their skills and plans lack in style, they make up for in true sentiment. From the "sausage roll" inducing wedding dress (her mum's) to her bright "Radiant Spring Bride" makeup (compliments of neighbor Janice), Becky could not be farther from her Plaza wedding. The only fashionable touch is her Christian Louboutin shoes, and yet Becky could not be happier. Ultimately Becky distinguishes the "real" from the fairy tale, and Kinsella posits that only when we move away from the lavish, opuluxe culture will we find what is authentic.

These three weddings suggest the multiplicity of Becky's dreams, and the role that conspicuous consumption and fashion play in their creation and enactment. Becky's never-ending search for the perfect wedding dress clearly illustrates her varied identities and dreams. Becky cannot choose just one dress because she cannot decide how she wants to be perceived and who she "really" is. She finally admits to a saleswoman that one dress is "the dress of *some* of my dreams ... I have a lot of dreams" (115). The wedding dress, which typically signifies the shift in role and status for the woman, holds even more value for Becky. This is yet another instance where "fashion persists in offering the allure of another life" (Finkelstein 103). By wearing a haute couture dress designed by her aspiring designer friend Danny and later her mother's dress, Becky fulfills some of her dreams, notably playing into the celebrity culture of haute couture and the passé yet emotionally fulfilling world of belonging to a particular family. In the end she rejects *most* of the glitz of Manhattan for the substance of Oxshott. Becky combines the best of both worlds, as she wears her fabulous Christian Louboutin shoes and her mother's wedding gown to marry her affluent boyfriend in a backyard wedding. Kinsella allows Becky to have it all—the glamour and the substance, all without footing the bill. No longer must Becky worry alone about money problems; now she and Luke work together to preserve their union of fantasy and reality, in a relationship bound by love and posh shopping trips.

Who to Read: Shopaholic and the Chick-Lit Phenomenon

With stylized type, bright covers, and colorful front-end pages that all glorify shopping, the Shopaholic novels, as well as the chick-lit genre in its entirety, become commodities akin to the very luxury items Kinsella presents throughout Becky's story. The fun artwork illustrates a shopaholic fashionista's fantasy of endless packages and abundant cutting-edge clothing. In a review of *Confessions of a Shopaholic*, as an example of "pink-covered-girl-centric fiction," *Publishers Weekly* notes, "This is a well-designed book, with a catchy magenta spine, and a colorful and kinetic double cover—which will attract many browsers" (53). The "pinkness" of the book and the colorful images grab attention and immediately signify chick lit. A consumer need only head toward such brightly colored books to find the latest tales of the thrilling and humorous lives of single women pursuing love. The Shopaholic novels are especially alluring because of their ingenious double covers.

In the mass-market edition of *Shopaholic Takes Manhattan,* these bright pages are followed by "Praise for Sophie Kinsella and the Shopaholic Trilogy" from a variety of popular press book reviews. Numerous reviews note the appeal to the primary chick-lit demographic. *Entertainment Weekly* notes that the Shopaholic novels give readers "a reason to stay home from the mall." Potential readers are urged by *US Weekly* not to "wait for a sale to buy this hilarious book." And finally, *New Woman,* a British publication, declares that "this book is an indulgence that's definitely worth every penny." These short blurbs, chosen to entice potential readers to buy the book, suggest that the book can be a commodity worth whatever the cost. Furthermore, reading tales of shopping will supplant the need for readers to make their daily trip to the mall.

However, because of their relatively low cost, the books provide us with "a have-your-cake-and-eat-it romp, done with brio and not a syllable of moralizing," as the blurb from *Kirkus Reviews* states. We need not suffer any pangs of buyer's regret or feel that the books are judging Becky or ourselves for engaging in this culture of conspicuous consumption. This ease of buying, together with Becky's example of always extricating herself from trouble with luck, ingenuity, and intuition, reassures us that our money troubles are nothing we cannot handle. And yet Becky's recurring patterns of Moneyfolly and compulsive shopping speak to a larger problem; despite her ability to emerge from immense debt, Becky inevitably falls into the abyss again and again. Once again Kinsella remains nonjudgmental and inconclusive in assessing Becky's fortunes. This could be partly because of our general cultural ambivalence toward shopping. Laura Paquet states, "We're conflicted about shopping—both fascinated and repelled—because shopping isn't a black-and-white endeavor. It doesn't have a fixed moral value. We all do it. To at least a basic degree, we all need to do it" (254). Of course Becky's shopping extends beyond a need for survival into the territory of emotional need. She needs to shop to fulfill her fantasies, or at least attempt to. Becky's shopping illustrates the endlessly replicating cycle of desire and longing that Campbell sets forth. Becky shops to fulfill her needs, to ostensibly close the gap between her imagined life and her real life, and to outfit herself for personal and professional success. This process, dependent on the whims of the fashion system, is ever replicating, and hence Becky returns to the shops again with a new possibility in mind. Despite her increasing personal and professional success, Becky remains ever anxious and unfulfilled, needing to prove through her fashionable attire that she can and does have it all.

The novels hover between fantasy and reality, much like Becky's life. The Shopaholic trilogy presents a consumerist fantasy world in which reality never fully intrudes. Becky repeatedly staves off her creditors until a brilliant plan comes to mind, and she never suffers bankruptcy, deprivation, or poverty. This allows readers to identify with Becky's struggles and dreams, make comparisons to their own lives, and live vicariously through Becky's shopping trips, without being troubled by the intrusion of reality, in the form of the expected real consequences. The novels are the perfect purchase for readers hoping to engage in carefree conspicuous consumption and to dream of fashion and romance! Despite receiving mixed reviews in publications as diverse as *Money* (positive) and *People* (lukewarm), Kinsella's Shopaholic novels are wildly popular. According to *USA Today*, close to three million copies of the three novels are in print in the United States (Memmott 4). Clearly the novels appeal to a large readership.

Combining consumption with romance makes for a powerful genre that plays into its readers' fantasies and desires, providing a safe substitute and continuing the cycle of conspicuous consumption. By purchasing and reading the novels, readers participate in a safer and cheaper alternative to the compulsive shopping in which Becky engages. We, too, experience the fantasy of self-creation through fashion and the allure of celebrity culture but without the high price tag that Becky encounters. In this way we, too, can have it all—the fantasy of a luxurious, romantic life—and the reality of our individual personal and professional struggles and successes. On a deeper level we can have both the spoils of material culture from the late twentieth century and the advantages advanced by the feminist movement. We, like Becky, may expect to have it all yet remain anxious about the disconnect between fantasy and reality. A niggling doubt crosses our minds as it does Becky's—what if we cannot have it all? Kinsella's Shopaholic novels reassure readers that such fantasies are attainable through conspicuous consumption and conscious self-fashioning through opuluxe items. The novels allow readers a safe haven to explore their own anxieties and assuage their fears with decadent fantasies. For a mere $10.95, readers can vicariously experience Becky's exploits and create their own fantasies with these alluring, fashionable books.

Works Cited

Barker, Olivia. "She Loves That 'Magical' New York." *USA Today* 20, Mar. 2003: 7D.

Campbell, Colin. *The Romantic Ethic and the Spirit of Modern Consumerism*. Oxford: Basil Blackwell, 1987.

Davis, Fred. *Fashion, Culture, and Identity*. Chicago: University of Chicago Press, 1992.

Ealy, C. Diane, and Kay Lesh. *Our Money, Ourselves: Redesigning Your Relationship with Money*. New York: AMACOM, 1999.

Finkelstein, Joanne. *After a Fashion*. Melbourne: Melbourne University Press, 1996.

Kellner, Douglas. "Madonna, Fashion, and Identity." *On Fashion*. Eds. Shari Benstock and Suzanne Ferriss. New Brunswick, NJ: Rutgers, 1994. 159–82.

Kinsella, Sophie. *Confessions of a Shopaholic*. New York: Delta, 2001.

———. *Shopaholic Takes Manhattan*. New York: Dell, 2002.

———. *Shopaholic Ties the Knot*. New York: Delta, 2003.

Lieberman, Annette, and Vicki Lindner. *Unbalanced Accounts: Why Women Are Still Afraid of Money*. New York: Atlantic Monthly Press, 1987.

Memmott, Carol. "For Mistress of Chick Lit, a 'Grown-Up' Success." *USA Today* 15, Apr. 2004: 4D.

Orenstein, Catherine. "Fairy Tales and a Dose of Reality." *New York Times* 3, Mar. 2003, late edition: A23.

Otnes, Cele C., and Elizabeth H. Pleck. *Cinderella Dreams: The Allure of the Lavish Wedding*. Berkeley: University of California Press, 2003.

Paquet, Laura Byrne. *The Urge to Splurge: A Social History of Shopping*. Toronto: ECW Press, 2003.

Publishers Weekly. Rev. of *Confessions of a Shopaholic*. 18, Dec. 2000: 53+.

Solomon, Michael R., and Susan P. Douglas. "The Female Clotheshorse: From Aesthetics to Tactics." *The Psychology of Fashion*. Ed. Michael R. Solomon. Lexington, MA: Lexington, 1985. 387–401.

Twitchell, James. *Living It Up: Our Love Affair with Luxury*. New York: Columbia University Press, 2002.

Veblen, Thorstein. *The Theory of the Leisure Class*. New York: Macmillan, 1912.

Wilson, Elizabeth. *Adorned in Dreams: Fashion and Modernity*. London: Virago, 1985.

14

Supersizing Bridget Jones: What's Really Eating the Women in Chick Lit

ALISON UMMINGER

In 1991, a scant five years before Helen Fielding's *Bridget Jones's Diary* came to dominate the pop-cultural landscape, Naomi Wolf published her scathing analysis of women's postfeminist disempowerment: *The Beauty Myth*. In this book Wolf claims that in the late twentieth century, "a private reality colonized female consciousness. By using ideas about 'beauty' it reconstructed an alternative female world with its own laws, economy, religion, sexuality, education, and culture, each element as repressive as any that had gone before" (16). Women who now had the right to vote, to build careers and identities of their own, were frittering away these advances in pursuit of eternal youth and thin bodies. Wolf warns that "there is a secret 'underlife' poisoning our freedom; infused with notions of beauty, it is a dark vein of self-hatred, physical obsessions, terror of aging, and dread of lost control" (10). Enter Bridget Jones, who cheerfully announces to her readers her weight of 129 pounds, along with a list of food she's consumed that day, before delving into a single detail of her actual life. Bridget's resonance with modern women was astounding: she humorously exposed Wolf's laundry list of obsessions as they lurked in the dark corners of the single, working woman's mind. The chapter titles—"An Exceptionally Bad Start," "Severe Birthday-Related Thirties

Panic," "Disintegration"—coupled with Bridget's self-policing of her (always wrong) behavior, and particularly her eating, show that even in a culture where many of chick lit's readers are loathe to self-identify as feminists, they are living with feminism's now-internalized backlash.

To those unfamiliar with the genre, chick lit might seem at first to be a category of novels primarily concerned with finding a mate—the search for a decent man in a sea of indecent "perverts and fuckwits," to quote Ms. Jones. And although this *is* a controlling feature of the genre, I maintain that in many of the books this quest for a partner is entirely secondary to the ongoing battle chick lit's heroines are engaging with themselves—particularly with regard to weight. Although Bridget Jones is arguably (and quite deliberately) a normal-sized woman obsessing over a perfectly healthy and culturally mainstream body type,[1] many of the protagonists who populate the novels she inspired are of a different build. Fat. Not 129 pounds, "fat-with-quotes-around-it" but genuinely obese—describing themselves with breasts that sink into their armpits when they lie on their backs, wardrobes from the upper sizes of Lane Bryant, and a related hyperconsciousness that the real relationship that must be mastered is one with their bodies and self-image.

Just as Edith Wharton's and Jane Austen's characters once negotiated their own social and financial disadvantages in a patriarchal world, Fielding and a host of other chick-lit authors have created a new breed of woman character similarly concerned with her ability to negotiate an equally hostile landscape. Although the Bridget Joneses and Jemima Js of the new millennium are free agents relative to their sister characters of past centuries, their freedom is mitigated by the "private reality" of which Wolf speaks—the self-imposed and culturally sanctioned tyranny of hating their own bodies. Jane Green's heroine Jemima J is perhaps the most extreme incarnation of this deal-with-the-weight versus find-a-man phenomenon. The novel opens with the line "God, I wish I were thin" (1) and closes with a chapter (after the heroine has paired off) that begins "Jemima Jones is no longer skinny, no longer hardbodied, no longer obsessed with what she eats. Jemima Jones is now a voluptuous, feminine, curvy size 10 who is completely happy with how she looks" (373). That she has found a man is almost an afterthought.

Yet these novels point to something greater than a narcissistic obsession with one's physique or sexual desirability; in virtually every novel, being thin has not only romantic but also financial rewards and repercussions. Looks are a form of currency that aid not only one's search for a mate but also one's ability to secure that promotion, get that next job, and become a fully realized human being. Jennifer Weiner's work stands relatively alone in allowing her heroines worldly success from the upper double digits of the dress-size range.

In this essay I investigate the extent to which the women of chick lit are looking for a way out of or around the "beauty myth," even as they unconsciously reinforce a number of its more destructive conclusions. Novels featuring plus-sized heroines—*Jemima J* by Jane Green, *Waking Beauty* by Elyse Friedman, and *Good in Bed* by Jennifer Weiner—play with some version of the following narrative: girl starts out fat, girl loses weight, girl finds true love or career fulfillment, girl makes peace with body (in relatively that order). While they vary in the extent to which they subscribe to the belief that a thin body and pretty face are indeed the glass slipper of the new millennium, all of these novels (and many others like them) address three larger categorical concerns. First, in addition to the more obvious issue of men and body image, all three books are preoccupied with the question of women and work—both the search for meaningful work and the ability to access certain jobs (and consequently resources) according to how beautiful one looks. Second, each of these novels depicts the often catty, rarely supportive, and deeply competitive world in which women view other women more often than not as the enemy. Even women who "succeed" in reaching that golden bar of "beauty" are trapped by their need to keep other women down, to hoard any scarce (and always fading) resources for themselves. Third, there is the problem of women and men. Aside from the obvious erotic dimension, I include in this category a profound mistrust of fathers, and of males, to accept or love a woman who is anything other than beautiful. By this token, men are as trapped as women by cultural standards, and this "trap" manifests itself most cruelly in the abandonment of ugly daughters by their attractive fathers. Fat women, by this token, are undeserving not only of romantic love but also of familial love.

Fat Chicks in the World: The Career–Calorie Connection

> Just as richness and thinness are linked, so are poverty and obesity. … The highest rates of obesity occur among people with the highest poverty rates. … Rather than speaking of obesity as a disease of the already poor, cultural commentator Laura Kipnis calls fat a predictor of downward mobility. A fat person has a lesser chance of being hired or, if employed, of being promoted. (Gross 70)

Jane Green's best-selling novel *Jemima J* updates the Cinderella story with modern-day ugly duckling Jemima Jones, who begins the novel as a low-on-the-totem-pole writer at a newspaper, overlooked in favor of her less-talented but perfectly coiffed, size-eight blonde coworker Geraldine. Geraldine has all the access in the world to men, sex, and power. Jemima describes Geraldine's "gleaming blond hair in a chic bob, her tiny size 8 figure squeezed into the latest fashions, [she] may not have one ounce of talent, but the men love her, and the editor thinks she's the biggest asset to the paper since, well, since himself. ... Geraldine is the woman I wish I was" (7). Unlike Geraldine, Jemima J has some real talent for writing, albeit overlooked, yet she would gladly trade her smarts and skills for the pretty packaging that far surpasses talent or personality in securing both men and work. Wolf warns, "When women breached the power structure in the 1980s, the two economies finally merged. Beauty was no longer just a symbolic form of currency; it literally *became* money" (21). In Jemima J's world, this means that she must accept the relative privileging of women like Geraldine, the all-style-no-talent packages who naturally secure the promotions at work, deserved or not.

Yet undeserved advancement at work is not Geraldine's only asset, so to speak. As a beautiful woman, ironically, even as she has easier access to jobs and money, she has less need for them in that she can easily attract a well-off mate. Thus the beautiful Geraldine has access not only to better jobs but also to richer men. When Jemima finally loses weight, Geraldine takes her out for the canonical makeover moment, when she will finally own clothes that fit her 121-pound body and 5-foot-7-inch frame; when her mousy brown hair will be transformed by an überswank hairdresser into golden blonde locks. This makeover, however, entails "reclassing" Jemima as much as it does redressing her. Although Jemima holds the same job and presumably makes the same paltry salary, Geraldine encourages her to break out the credit cards for designer clothes and the chi-chi hairdo. Once made over, Jemima and Geraldine walk down the high street as "two slim (slim!) blondes, laden down with fabulous goodies" (174). Not two paragraphs later, a rich man in his sportscar convertible stops to scope out the newly minted Jemima J.

This reclassing extends to Jemima's eventual trip overseas to meet her L.A. Internet love, Brad. Geraldine makes sure to give Jemima a Louis Vuitton bag and Cutler and Gross sunglasses "to look the part" (186). And in the cyclical economy where beauty begets money, which buys beauty, which begets more money, Jemima is immediately upgraded from economy class to first class. Jemima tells her reader that "the check-in girl seems to think I might be a made-it as well, and although she tells me it's not airline policy to upgrade those who simply look the part ... Virgin would like to upgrade me to first class" (189). And as a beautiful blonde, Jemima J exits the aircraft to be greeted by another beautiful man with a Porsche, ferried off to her new life as trophy girlfriend and L.A. accessory.

Perhaps the greatest irony of Jemima J's transformation involves what I call a "consumptive misreading of the obese body." In Joan Gross's article

"Phat," she notes, "Fat activists work hard at getting the message out that people should not automatically think of gluttony and overconsumption when they see an obese person" (72). In Western culture, fat people are equated visually with conspicuous consumption, scapegoats for the "ambivalence provoked by living in a society that deeply wishes us to over-consume, yet savagely punishes all bodily evidence of overconsumption" (70). Ironically, in her fat incarnation Jemima J hardly spends a cent on herself, yet as a thin person she all but hemorrhages money on gym memberships, expensive haircuts, and designer duds. While her obese body belies an extra dollar or two spent on bacon sandwiches, as a thin woman she is encouraged by Geraldine to treat herself, to indulge, to subscribe to that consumerist mentality that you only live once, and that all beautiful women are, to paraphrase the famous L'Oréal commercials, worth it. The latent message becomes clear: whereas fat women are punished for visible overconsumption, thin women are rewarded; the equally visible markers of high-end shopping—Louis Vuitton bags and Prada shoes—are met with appreciative nods, not disapproving glances.

By contrast, Jennifer Weiner's *Good in Bed* appears to get away from this equation of thin with rich. Her heroine Cannie is an accomplished reporter, and her career Cinderella-turn from journalist to successful screenwriter is accomplished at her heavy weight, not the thin one. Yet even as Weiner attempts to give Cannie a "protected" career (and stronger self-esteem than Jemima J), Cannie knows that she will be "read" publicly not only for her work but also for her appearance. When asked by a weight-loss expert whether she feels that her weight affects her performance at her job, Cannie responds,

> Not really. I mean, sometimes, some of the people I interview … you know, they're thin, I'm not, I get a little jealous, maybe, or wonder if they think I'm lazy or whatever, and then I have to be careful when I write the articles, not to let the way I'm feeling affect what I say about them. But I'm good at my job. People respect me. (41)

And even as Cannie carefully negotiates the way fat alters her perception of those around her, carefully monitors her own reactions, and carefully keeps her defenses in place, she remains uniquely vulnerable to size-ist attacks. After writing a defense of Monica Lewinsky in one of her columns, she receives hate mail that reads, "I can tell by what you wrote that you are overweight and that nobody loves you" (15), a comment that leaves Cannie temporarily reeling. Weiner shows that even an active, intelligent, self-aware, accomplished overweight woman has unique soft spots in her daily armor, sites of vulnerability that her thin sisters do not share.

On the surface, *Waking Beauty* is more like *Jemima J* in that it traces the transformation of its heroine Allison Penny from fat to thin, from social outcast to social savant. Unlike *Jemima J,* which seems tragically unaware of the ways in which the narrative undermines women's empowerment, or *Good in Bed,* which attempts to provide a way around or alternate solution to the fat unhappy–thin happy dilemma, *Waking Beauty* wears its allegorical and satirical affinities on its sleeve. The book's author, Elyse Friedman, unlike Jennifer Weiner or Jane Green, takes wicked pleasure in taking current cultural trends—which value surface over substance, the chic over the content driven—to their most cynical conclusions. Allison Penny—who unlike Jemima J is not so much a diamond in the rough as a coal lump in the discard bin of a diamond mine—goes to bed ugly, overweight, underemployed, and unloved, only to wake up (magically and inexplicably) beautiful.

Friedman is careful to differentiate Penny from her swan-turn sisters; her self-introduction to the reader announces,

> If I'd lost sixty pounds, I would have been a hideously ugly thin person. My dead-mouse hair would still have laid limp, my golf ball skin would have continued to ooze boils, my pellet eyes and potato nose would have remained, as would my broad back, hunched shoulders and flat ass. My teeth would still have sat snaggled and mossy in my thin-lipped mouth. (12)

The description continues, categorizing her various faults in a neo-Quasimodo vision of self-loathing and cold-hearted "reality." Allison shows far more self-awareness than Cannie or Jemima J as to what being fat means: no roommate wants to share space with such a woman, and certainly no man wants to share her bed.

Her experience fulfills the expectation of Gross's quote at the start of this section—ugly and unhireable, she appears destined to a life of blue-collar work, scraping by as a cleaning lady, invisible to those around her because of not only her fat but also her employment status. The single good quality she possesses, a lovely singing voice, serves only to remind her of the futility of real talent in a superficial culture. Allison laments the lost days when talent mattered more than packaging, a time when she might have envisioned a future for herself as a singer:

> There used to be room for Geddy Lee's schnoz. And Joey Ramone's teeth. No one cared if the "velvet Fog" was short and pudgy or if Janis Joplin had bags under her squinty eyes. The ratio was more sane. For every Jim Morrison, there was a Van Morrison. For every shimmying Tom Jones there was a simian Tom Waits. (42)

This catalog continues, with Allison's reaching the societally sanctioned conclusion that even in the world of music looks matter more than sound. She counts it an act of kindness that her romantic interest, Nathan, never patronizes her by saying, "oooh with a voice like that, you should be filling stadiums, not emptying trash cans," because at the end of the day, "it wasn't talent being managed, but genetic fortuity" (41–42).

As an ugly and overweight woman, Allison seems destined for a life lurking in the shadows, cleaning the trash from the bins of modeling agencies after-hours, and sharply critiquing a world that she feels powerless to change. Nothing short of a miracle could alter her position in the world, yet, relatively speaking, a miracle is visited upon her. She awakens the next morning in the body of a goddess, likening herself to "Grace Kelly's better looking cousin" (2). The moment she first sees herself in the mirror she waxes rhapsodic: "It was the truest, most essential moment of my life. All panic had flown, replaced by a feeling of profound relief. An exquisite joy, a supernatural happiness flooded through my perfect body" (61). Yet not only has Allison Penny's physique metamorphosed but her way of surveying the world also has literally changed. She closes the first chapter of the "After" section with this epiphanic observation:

> Not only did I look different, but I saw differently. The extra six inches or so of height had skewed my perspective and made everything appear slightly unusual and fresh. Also, I used to catch a bit of my potato nose in my peripheral vision. No more. My line of sight was suddenly unobstructed. For the first time ever, I could see clearly. (69)

Her newly "clear" vision reveals to her that she is not only now beautiful but also finally in possession of power categorically denied her in her prior body. While eating lunch at a McDonald's, Penny is approached by Fiona Ferguson, a B-rate talent agent who wants to have Allison's pictures taken for a potential modeling career. Until then, Allison had been working as a cleaning lady, making next to nothing, invisible to the world she served.

The ease with which the new Allison Penny enters the working world (of high-end modeling, no less) illustrates the commodified value of a pretty face and thin body. Allison recounts her experiences looking for a job in her old body as rife with discrimination based on appearance: "Offices didn't want me greeting their visitors or filing their files. The food service industry didn't want me mixing their drinks or serving their grub. Retailers, in particular, didn't want me anywhere near prospective customers" (91). In the contemporary consumer marketplace, Allison reports that there are whole categories of service work reserved for the attractive only.

This inability to advance because of one's appearance is not merely some hysterical fear of the unbeautiful but a true glass ceiling: an unseen but very real barricade to career success. As an attractive woman, Allison's life changes appreciably; not only have those long-closed doors suddenly opened but also people now go out of their way to open them for her.

And much like the makeover moment in *Jemima J,* many of those doors opening before Allison Penny appear to belong to retail establishments. Whereas the old Allison had once "stayed away from the mall, and prided [her]self on being an anti-consumer," the new Allison finds herself a born-again product whore. Whereas once her paycheck went to necessities (food) and "justifiable cultural items" like books and CDs, the new Allison comes to a disturbing conclusion about herself:

> My anticonsumerism might have less to do with my principles/ character, and more to do with the way I looked. Because suddenly all the products that Old Allison had deemed superfluous seemed not only desirable, but sometimes also necessary to New Allison. My flawless skin suddenly deserved, nay demanded, a comprehensive four-step system. (107)

Allison's cataloging continues, listing the new necessities of her thin, blonde, beautiful life. And once properly outfitted, she transforms from a cultural outsider to a commercial insider, a self-described product capable of soliciting rich men: "the ultimate option for a baby-blue Aston Martin convertible" (109).

This equation of self-as-product leads to a related problem in chick lit: competition among women. When women are reduced to the embodied equivalent of objects competing for shelf space in some consumer-based economy where men choose the newest, shiniest, thinnest, blondest models, a profound mistrust of "lesser brands" or envy of "designer models" develops. Green takes care to let us know that when Jemima receives some of the sexual attention normally reserved for Geraldine, Geraldine "if she hadn't been going out with Nick Maxwell ... would be green with jealousy" (175). In *Good in Bed,* Cannie's unlikely friendship with movie star Maxi Ryder is predicated on Maxi's once having been an ugly duckling herself, unable fully to shake her earlier "image" and singled out by the media for her inability to keep a man. Allison Penny puts this "fairy tale of female bonding and support" to rest with her crass assessment that this is a myth "perpetrated by yeast infection medication commercials and movies ... what a crock. *Dangerous Liaisons* is more like it. *All about Eve* got it just about right" (100). In fact, once Allison undergoes her magical transformation, she finds her one female friend unwilling to talk to her, her roommate becomes competition, and the only uncritical attention she receives is from members of the opposite sex.

Beyond Prince Charming: The Father–Lover Connection

> Simone de Beauvoir said that no man is truly free to love a fat woman. If that is true, how free are men? (Wolf 174)

Anyone with even a passing knowledge of the genre recognizes that chick-lit novels are most stereotypically about women and their problems with men. However, this man trouble masks a deeply sinister and cynical view of human relations, one in which obesity and a dearth of dating in the present mask unresolved issues with fathers, the "original abandoners," to paraphrase Cannie's description of her own. Not only does fat drive lovers away, its repulsive power is enough to sever the sacred parental bond.

Jemima J briefly glosses this subject. At the opening of the novel, Jemima's affection for food seems to have supplanted her affection for men. She secretly purchases forbidden foods on the way to work; the illicit pleasure of bacon and eggs gives her an almost sexual thrill:

> "Jemima" [the bacon sandwiches] whisper from the depths of your bag. "We're lovely and greasy, Jemima. Feel us. Taste us. Now." And you plunge your hand in, the craving fast overtaking any anxiety about eating in public, and in one, two, three, four bites the sandwiches have gone.
>
> And then to the office, wiping your mouth with your sleeve and stopping at the newsstand to buy some sugar-free mints to hide the smell of bacon. (16–17)

Jemima's relationship with her bacon sandwich brings to mind the sort of sordid and hidden meeting normally reserved for affairs. The eroticized "Feel us. Taste us. Now," followed by the "plunging in" and then the inevitable mints to cover up this momentary indiscretion all suggest that food has supplanted sex as an erotic, sensory experience. Jemima later explains that her love of food is a surrogate for the love she once experienced from her long-gone parent: "I discovered that the only thing to ease the pain of being abandoned by an uncaring father was food" (129). Not coincidentally, as Jemima undergoes her transformation to sex object, she substitutes orgasms for bacon sandwiches. In her 120-pound universe, it's either food or "love," not both.

One must then ask what this says about love. Throughout *Jemima J,* Jane Green presents love as a superficial pairing of equally attractive bodies, neglecting emotional connection and valorizing physical fetishism. Wolf warns of the danger of this sort of "fetishism" corroding male–female relations:

> When men are more aroused by symbols of sexuality than by the sexuality of women themselves, they are fetishists. Fetishism treats a part as if it were the whole; men who choose a lover on the basis of her "beauty" alone are treating the woman as a fetish—that is, treating a part of her, her visual image, not even her skin, as if it were her sexual self. Freud suggests that the fetish is a talisman against the failure to perform. (175)

Freud, of course, probably is using "performance" here in the sexual sense, yet *Jemima J* suggests that this performance is more social than personal. Late in the novel Jemima J finds out that her lover Brad in fact feels a far greater attraction for his overweight assistant Jenny than he does for Jemima. However, Brad cannot love Jenny in the world of the novel because he will no longer be performing his role as "successful man." In this way the myth of beauty and beauty-as-thin traps men and women equally and leaves all parties starving for authenticity (if not literally starving!).

Similarly, Allison Penny's problems go deeper than her modern model-versus-hag dilemma. An adopted child, she starts the story with a tense, almost servile, relationship with her adopted mother and no relationship with her adopted father. The father works as a designer, moving in hip, chic circles that Allison knows better than to attempt entering. Yet in her incarnation as "new" Allison she returns to her adoptive mother, who inadvertently gives her the horrific truth about her missing father. Not only does the mother blame Allison for their divorce, insisting that an ugly child didn't fit into her then-husband's image of the perfect family, she tells the incognito new Allison that her father used to call her "Thing" and that "he'd make all these bad taste jokes like: 'Maybe Thing would like to go play in traffic. Maybe Thing would like to go to the basement and play with matches' " (186). Allison soon after burns down her father's night-club, ironically thinking to herself that yes, the "thing" would indeed like to play with matches.

Although initially it appears that Allison's life has changed radically from the days of being Thing to her current supermodel incarnation, in a sense, her situation has remained remarkably similar. She's just gone from being one kind of thing to another—an undesirable past-the-date, dented generic knockoff of a human being to top-of-the-line, this-season's Prada. The problem then becomes that for all of Allison's duckling-to-swan epiphanies, she remains as trapped by notions of beauty and success as she was at the novel's start. Although she has found so-called happiness by the novel's end—a modeling contract, a happy relationship with Nathan, a burgeoning bond with her birth mother—all of these are possible only because of her newfound looks, and consequently all would presumably disappear were she to change back into the proverbial pumpkin at midnight.

In her final conversation with Nathan, Allison emphasizes the extent to which she believes in this surface-level fairy tale. She gives Nathan the bare-bones outline of her actual transformation, and he insists that the heroine of such a story would have to learn that beauty doesn't make her happy, and it's what's on the inside that counts. Allison counters with an impassioned monologue defending the opposite:

> No. That's the point. She learns the opposite. It's not what's inside that counts. It's what's outside. When she was ugly she had nothing. Nothing. Then she turns beautiful and gets everything. What she learns is that beauty is a tremendous power, and that its power is pervasive, more pervasive than even she realized. She learns that it's much much better to be beautiful, no matter how many clichés about skin deep and eye of the beholder. Being beautiful enables her to get whatever she wants. (243)

Although this so-called moral drips with cynicism guised as reality, one can't but think that the "new" Allison Penny has a point. The fairy tale is possible; still, Wolf warns of the dangers of treating the surface without finding a cure for the poison that remains. This placid panacea of beauty remains problematic because "the beautiful woman is excluded forever from the rewards and responsibilities of a particular human love, for she cannot trust that any man will love her 'for herself alone' " (172). Allison and Jemima may feel good about themselves, may sleep secure in their lovers' arms, yet both rest with the knowledge that they are loved *because* of how they look, not *regardless* of how they look.

These endings belie a deep cynicism not only about appearances but also about men. Men, it appears, are far too superficial and shallow ever to love a woman for her imperfect self. In these fictional worlds no man is strong or deep enough to love an overweight woman, not publicly at any rate. Thus all the characters remain trapped (or willingly ensnared) by a culture that values surface first, substance second. Friedman paints a portrait of a sadistic adoptive father who leaves his wife and daughter because the daughter does not "look" right, and although Jennifer Weiner handles the subject far more subtly and critically, she too hints that fathers cannot love fat daughters, and the trials of adulthood stem from familial abandonment and cruelty.

Unlike Jemima or Allison, even at her heaviest Cannie has a degree of romantic agency in *Good in Bed*. The novel begins with Cannie's decision to take a "break" from her boyfriend Bruce, who retaliates by publishing a first-person confessional in a national magazine *Moxie* titled "Loving a Larger Woman." The article details Bruce's ongoing struggle with Cannie's (or "C," as he refers to her in the piece) weight and Cannie's own struggle with self-love. Bruce describes her actual body both objectively and lovingly: "Her shoulders were as broad as mine, her hands were almost as big, and from her breasts to her belly, from her hips down the slope of her thighs, she was all sweet curves and warm welcome." However, not a paragraph later, Bruce reveals that his own appreciation of her form isn't enough:

> Being out with her didn't feel nearly as comfortable. Maybe it was the way I'd absorbed society's expectations, its dictates of what men are supposed to want and how women are supposed to appear. ... Loving a larger woman is an act of courage in this world, and maybe it's even an act of futility. Because, in loving C., I knew I was loving someone who didn't believe that she herself was worthy of anyone's love. (14–15)

Bruce's article hits painfully close to home. Cannie then embarks on a two-fold quest: to win back Bruce and to lose weight—thereby making peace with her body.

Along the way, though, she must also confront her plastic-surgeon father, the man she describes as "the author of all of my insecurities and fears" (305). Cannie virtually never mentions her problems with Bruce without an immediate reference back to her troubled childhood. Because of her father's chosen profession as an architect of physical perfection, Cannie had always felt "like a walking affront, like a collection of things my father spent his days waging war against." Cannie continues to say, "There was nothing beautiful about me at thirteen, nothing at all, and I could feel that fact confirmed in the hard, hateful way he looked at me, and in all the things he said" (105). Although Cannie can rationally recognize that her father failed and was a miserable disappointment in his role as parent and provider of unconditional love, the emotional toll of a solid decade of psychological abuse still wears on her.

Cannie's showdown with her father proves remarkably anticlimactic. He barely acknowledges her, and she fails to elicit any kind of response or apology. Cannie's lowest point comes soon after, when she nearly loses the child she conceived with Bruce during their brief reconciliation. In despair she equates her physical shortcomings with moral failure, lamenting, "I'd failed to be good enough, pretty enough, thin enough, lovable enough, to keep my father in my life. Or to keep Bruce. And now, I'd failed at keeping my baby safe" (323). Unlike Jemima J or Allison Penny, Cannie works past this superficial, destructive view of a fat self as an unworthy self. She finally loses the weight in an extreme postpartum depression, but this proves a bitter irony, not a triumphant swan-turn. Her new "hot" body comes courtesy of the "Placenta Abruptio Emergency Hysterectomy Premature and Possibly Brain-Damaged Baby Diet" (341). Although weight has been figured as the problem throughout the novel, weight loss cannot be the solution for finding a way to allow oneself to live and be happy in the world. Cannie's child recovers, and Cannie even finds romantic love along the way, but the happy woman at the end of the novel is happy at a size sixteen.

Even so, Cannie knows that her happiness is predicated on rejecting the cultural model that she has found so difficult to follow. She knows that certain fairy tales are no longer available to her, and that "if Prince Charming never shows up—or, worse yet, if he drives by, casts a cool and appraising glance at me, and tells me that I've got a beautiful face and have I ever considered Optifast?—I will make my peace with that" (365). What she's needed all along is not a new body but a new narrative: one without hard-bodied prince charmings, Aston Martins, modeling careers, and cheap happy endings.

Conclusion

Although this investigation has centered only on fictional scenarios and characters, the battles women have with their bodies are hardly limited to sojourns in the escapist Cinderella fantasies of chick-lit novels. One need only turn on a recent episode of the talk show *Dr. Phil* to see an episode on overweight brides who lament not only their weight but also their social undesirability, worrying to the doctor that their future husbands will be judged for having fat wives, that their perceived laziness or sloppiness or inability to conform to cultural standards of beauty will reflect badly on their mates. Or visit the rather grotesque Web site awfulplasticsurgery.com and take a look at media-whore Paris Hilton's before and after. Not so different from an Allison Penny or Jemima J, Hilton in the early shots is a mousy, brown-eyed girl who by sheer force of will and considerable chemical enhancement has transformed herself into a blond icon of processed beauty for processed beauty's sake. And now she has a television show, a modeling contract, even a failed singing career. Friedman's not-so-fantastic brave new world, readers know, already has *many* such Allison Penny's in it—transformed not by bizarre twists of fate but by botox and boob jobs.

The mental calculations Penny has made appear to hold: beauty means power, beauty means happiness, and beauty means success in family, work, and love. The problem, of course, is that beauty (even the most carefully manufactured) has a shelf life, and Friedman and Green present no real solution for what will happen to their Cinderellas when the clock inevitably chimes twelve.

Note

1. Naomi Wolf refers to Bridget's particular pathology as the "one stone solution"—the idea that life will become viable only once said woman loses those last ten to fifteen pounds.

Works Cited

Fielding, Helen. *Bridget Jones's Diary.* New York: Penguin, 1999.
Friedman, Elyse. *Waking Beauty.* New York: Three Rivers Press, 2004.
Green, Jane. *Jemima J.* New York: Broadway Books, 1999.
Gross, Joan. "Phat." *Fat: The Anthropology of an Obsession.* Ed. Don Kulick and Anne Meneley. New York: Tarcher, 2005: 63–76.
Weiner, Jennifer. *Good in Bed.* New York: Washington Square Press, 2001.
Wolf, Naomi. *The Beauty Myth.* New York: Perennial, 2001.

Afterword: The New Woman's Fiction

SHARI BENSTOCK

Having considered this volume, what conclusions can we now draw about the importance and direction of chick lit and chick-lit scholarship? This collection demonstrates that chick lit engages with complex and significant issues regarding women's fiction and lives—past, present, and future. Its undeniable popularity within the past decade suggests ongoing concerns with sexuality and femininity, genre and gender. As such, it is indeed a new "woman's fiction" as well as fiction about the "new woman."

Chick Lit and the "New Woman"

Scholarly attention to chick lit allows for an ideal confluence of gender, genre, and generation. It opens a space for second-wave and postfeminist scholars to "meet" together and assess where we are now. It gives younger scholars, in particular, a chance to consider issues that relate directly to their lives: particularly the postfeminist issue of whether a woman can be sexy and taken seriously at the same time—without taking herself too seriously.

In many ways women are no longer battling to come from the margins into the mainstream. The phenomenal success of chick lit, featuring independent, professional protagonists, testifies to the extent that women have left such battles behind. But that is not to say that women no longer face inequities. Despite their entry into the workplace, the new generation of women still receives less pay than their male counterparts and bears an inordinate burden in terms of household chores and child care. As chick lit

253

routinely reminds us, women now struggle to balance professional and personal satisfaction. Traditional expectations about women's roles as wives and mothers have proven remarkably persistent and even the most confident and self-assured women must negotiate conventional expectations.

As a result, the genre raises issues of major concern to contemporary cultural and feminist studies: the issues of commodification and consumerism, of race and class, of appearance and success. The essays in this volume make clear that chick lit crystallizes some of the most important cultural issues women are currently engaged in addressing. The contributors have subjected much of chick lit to cultural criticism that not only recognizes the genre's contributions to popular culture but also exposes many of the ways it replicates divisions and inequities characteristic of the early twenty-first century. Generational conflicts—between mothers and daughters, second- and third-wave feminists—loom large, as do divisions between women in terms of age, class, race, and ethnicity. Some chick-lit writers have tackled the competition between female bosses and their employees; others have tackled the competition between women over men. Chick lit featuring African American or Hispanic protagonists has challenged the genre's original overemphasis on white, middle-class characters.

We can expect subsequent scholarly studies to probe the extent to which chick lit engages with still other elements of women's lives. The genre's invasion of Europe, Indonesia, and beyond will test its malleability and engagement with the lives of women outside of Britain and America. Larger differences between women of the first and third worlds currently remain outside its pages. Few chick-lit texts have yet to fully or convincingly explore alternative sexualities. As more nuanced attention to the differences among women in contemporary culture has enhanced feminist criticism and gender theory, so can it advance scholarship of chick lit.

Chick Lit and the New "Woman's Fiction"

This collection clearly establishes then that chick lit has special resonance for the fields of cultural and women's studies. But what about literary studies? Not surprisingly, the essays collected here reflect the disagreements of our culture on that issue. Just as writers of "serious" literary fiction have entered the fray on opposite sides, so these scholars take a variety of perspectives. Of course any new genre or trend or individual work will ultimately be judged, not only by its contemporaries but also by the future. When time has made its inevitable judgment, will chick lit prove to have been a popular diversion, no more (or less) important than Harlequin romance? Is it just literary junk food for (semi-)professional turn-of-the-millennium women? Will its ability to speak to women be limited to its own time and place? Or will it prove to have literary significance beyond the here and now? These are questions that we will, naturally, have to leave to the next generations of readers and scholars. In the meantime, we can note the significant role chick lit already plays in the history of women's writing.

Without question, chick lit calls attention to questions of authorship, audience, and subject matter. But in an era when anxieties about women's right to write have largely disappeared, authors ask new questions, taking different approaches to the dilemmas facing women in contemporary culture.

Chick-lit authors approach such dilemmas with humor. Their heroines bear little resemblance, for instance, to the "new woman" of a century before. The self-sufficient, independent women in Ellen Glasgow's "vein of iron" novels share little in common with the fallible, sometimes bumbling protagonists of chick lit. In *Barren Ground* (1925), for instance, a woman struggles to become a successful farmer. In Willa Cather's *The Song of the Lark* (1915), the heroine bravely forgoes marriage, opting for a career instead. The high seriousness and simmering anger characteristic of earlier feminist fiction has given way to comedy. Part of the undeniable appeal of chick-lit fiction lies in its suggestion to readers that we can be ourselves even when we're beside ourselves.

Chick lit's use of the diary form, journals, letters, and e-mail links it to the epistolary tradition and to the novel that emerged out of private modes of writing commonly associated with women. It also links contemporary chick lit to the novel of psychological development that emerged in the early twentieth century. Women such as Virginia Woolf and Dorothy Richardson moved away from the social considerations of the novel of manners to explore the internal mental and emotional life of a central female protagonist. Richardson's *Pilgrimage* (1918) presented a woman's development between the ages of seventeen and forty—the same period that is the focus of much chick lit—employing stream of consciousness to replicate her character's thoughts and feelings with uncommon detail and nuance. In *Mrs. Dalloway* (1925) and *To the Lighthouse* (1927), Woolf did the same to capture the doubts, hopes, and reminiscences of women after World War I. Jean Rhys's *Good Morning Midnight* (1939) and Djuna Barnes's *Nightwood* (1936) powerfully represented the psychological torment of depression and psychosis. Well before them, in the closing pages of *The House of Mirth* (1907), Edith Wharton had used impressionistic interior monologue to capture Lily Bart's final moments. Although the somber tone of these novels divorces them from the lighter touch of chick lit, they share an interest in experimenting with modern means of communication. Just as the then cutting-edge technologies of the telephone, radio, telegraph, and cinema shaped modernist style, e-mail and instant messaging function in chick lit to capture the rapid, clipped pace of contemporary life and conversation.

The first-person, confessional mode of chick lit further enhances readers' identification. It also allies the genre with the equally popular contemporary genres of memoir and autobiography. The connection is not to the women of the 1950s and 1960s, such as Sylvia Plath and Anne Sexton, who railed against the restrictions of domestic life and the psychological damage it caused—loneliness, depression, and domestic violence—but to contemporary writers who look back not in anger or with self-pity but with humor stripped of sentimentality. Mary Karr, in *The Liar's Club* (1995), for example, treats traumatic events in her volatile childhood, such as fire, sexual assault, and her mother's mental illness, with an engaging mixture of horror and ironic distance. Her mother's depression is described as her "Empress Days," her parents' hangovers as "the Smirnoff flu." With wit, not sentimentality, chick-lit heroines recount their bafflement at their parents' behavior and expose their own flaws and failures.

Contrary to claims that chick lit has run its course, the genre still has room to grow, to enhance its cultural relevance and acknowledge the complexities of women's changing lives and experiences. Just as the "new woman's fiction" that preceded it was supplanted in its turn by more complex forms, covering a larger scope of women's experiences, so chick lit is expanding beyond its original definition. Our definition of the new "woman's fiction" will change as surely as our conception of the "new woman" does.

Selected Bibliography

Primary Sources

Baer, Judy. *The Whitney Chronicles.* Harlequin, 2004.
Bank, Melissa. *The Girls' Guide to Hunting and Fishing.* Viking, 1999.
Brown, Amanda. *Family Trust.* Dutton, 2003.
———. *Legally Blonde.* Plume, 2002.
Browne, Jill Conner. *God Save the Sweet Potato Queens.* Three Rivers Press, 2001.
———. *The Sweet Potato Queens' Big-Ass Cookbook (and Financial Planner).* Three Rivers Press, 2003.
———. *The Sweet Potato Queens' Book of Love.* Three Rivers Press, 1999.
———. *The Sweet Potato Queens' Field Guide to Men: Every Man I Love Is Either Married, Gay, or Dead.* Three Rivers Press, 2004.
Buchan, Elizabeth. *Revenge of the Middle-Aged Woman.* Viking, 2003.
Burkes, Cris. *SilkyDreamGirl.* Harlem Moon, 2002.
Burley, Charlotte, and Lyah Beth LeFlore. *Cosmopolitan Girls.* Harlem Moon/Doubleday, 2004.
Bushnell, Candace. *4 Blondes.* Atlantic Monthly, 2000.
———. *Sex and the City.* Atlantic Monthly, 1996.
———. *Trading Up.* Hyperion, 2003.
Cabot, Meg. *Boy Meets Girl.* Avon, 2004.
Cline, Rachel. *What to Keep.* Random House, 2004.
Colgan, Jenny. *Amanda's Wedding.* HarperCollins, 1998.
Culliford, Penny. *Theodora's Wedding.* Zondervan, 2004.
De Vries, Hilary. *So Five Minutes Ago.* Villard, 2004.
Dickey, Eric Jerome. *Cheaters.* Dutton, 1999.
———. *Drive Me Crazy.* Dutton, 2004.
———. *Sister, Sister.* Dutton, 1996.
Dyer, Chris. *Wanderlust.* Plume, 2003.
Fielding, Helen. *Bridget Jones's Diary.* Viking, 1996.
———. *Bridget Jones: The Edge of Reason.* Viking, 2000.
———. *Cause Celeb.* Viking, 2001.
———. *Olivia Joules and the Overactive Imagination.* Viking, 2004.
Finnamore, Suzanne. *Otherwise Engaged.* Vintage, 2000.
Grazer, Gigi Levangie. *Maneater.* Simon, 2003.
Harris, E. Lynn. *A Love of My Own.* Doubleday, 2002.
Holden, Wendy. *Gossip Hound.* Plume, 2003.
Juska, Elise. *Getting Over Jack Wagner.* Downtown, 2003.
Juska, Jane. *A Round-Heeled Woman: My Late-Life Adventures in Love and Sex.* Villard, 2003.

Kaplan, Janice, and Lynn Schnurnberger. *The Botox Diaries*. Ballantine, 2004.

Karasyov, Carrie, and Jill Kargman. *The Right Address*. Broadway, 2004.

Keltner, Kim Wong. *The Dim Sum of All Things*. Avon Trade, 2004.

Kennedy, Erica. *Bling*. Miramax Books, 2004

Kinsella, Sophie. *Confessions of a Shopaholic*. Delta, 2001.

———. *Shopaholic and Sister*. Dial, 2004.

———. *Shopaholic Takes Manhattan*. Delta, 2002.

———. *Shopaholic Ties the Knot*. Delta, 2003.

Lee, Tonya Lewis, and Crystal McCrary Anthony. *Gotham Diaries*. Hyperion, 2004.

Lissner, Caren. *Carrie Pilby*. Red Dress Ink, 2003.

———. *Starting from Square Two*. Red Dress Ink, 2004.

Maxted, Anna. *Behaving Like Adults*. ReganBooks, 2003.

———. *Running in Heels: A Novel*. ReganBooks, 2002.

McLaughlin, Emma, and Nicola Kraus. *The Nanny Diaries*. Griffin, 2002.

McMillan, Terry. *Waiting to Exhale*. Viking, 1992.

Mebus, Scott. *Booty Nomad*. Miramax Books, 2004.

Naylor, Clare, and Mimi Hare. *The Second Assistant: A Tale from the Bottom of the Hollywood Ladder*. Viking, 2004.

Pearson, Allison. *I Don't Know How She Does It*. Knopf, 2002.

Senate, Melissa. *See Jane Date*. Red Dress Ink, 2001.

———. *The Solomon Sisters Wise Up*. Red Dress Ink, 2003.

———. *Whose Wedding Is It Anyway?* Red Dress Ink, 2004.

Singh, Sonia. *Goddess for Hire*. Avon, 2003.

Smith, Kyle. *Love Monkey*. William Morrow, 2004.

Sohn, Amy. *Run Catch Kiss*. Scribner, 1999.

Sykes, Plum. *Bergdorf Blondes*. Miramax Books, 2004.

Valdes-Rodriguez, Alisa. *The Dirty Girls Social Club*. St. Martin's, 2003.

———. *Playing with Boys*. St. Martin's, 2004.

Weiner, Jennifer. *Good in Bed*. Pocket Books, 2001.

———. *In Her Shoes*. Pocket Books, 2002.

Weisberger, Lauren. *The Devil Wears Prada*. Doubleday, 2003.

Wells, Rebecca. *Divine Secrets of the Ya-Ya Sisterhood*. HarperTrade, 1997.

Williams, Tia. *The Accidental Diva*. Putnam, 2004.

Wolfe, Laura. *Diary of a Mad Bride*. Delta, 2002.

Secondary Sources

Akass, Kim, and Janet McCabe, eds. *Reading Sex and the City*. New York: I.B. Tauris, 2004.

Armstrong, Jennifer, and Clarissa Cruz. "Chick Lit 101: Feeding Your Heroine Addiction." *Entertainment Weekly* 16, Jan. 2004: 74.

"Bainbridge Denounces Chick-Lit as 'Froth.'" *Guardian Unlimited*. 23, Aug. 2001. <http://books.guardian.co.uk/bookerprize2001/story/0,1090,541335,00.html>.

Barrientos, Tanya. "Sassy, Kicky 'Chick Lit' Is the Hottest Trend in Publishing." *Philadelphia Inquirer*. 28, May 2003. <http://www.ledgerenquirer.com/mld/ledgerenquirer/entertainment/5960564.htm>.

Blase, Cazz. "Searching for Sense and Reason." *The F-Word: Contemporary UK Feminism*. 16, Oct. 2003. <http://www.thefword.ork.uk/reviews/books/chicklit.live>.

Cabot, Heather. "Chick Lit: Genre Aimed at Young Women Is Fueling Publishing Industry." abcnews.com. 30, Aug. 2003. <http://abcnews.go.com/sections/wnt/Entertainment/chicklit030830.html>.

Danford, Natalie. "The Chick Lit Question." *Publishers Weekly*. 20, Oct. 2003. <http://publishersweekly.reviewsnews.com/index.asp?layout=articlePrint&articleID=CA330294&publication=publishersweekly>.

De Vries, Hilary. "Bridget Jones? No, It's Jane Bond." *New York Times* 6, June 2004: 6.

Ezard, John. "Bainbridge Tilts at 'Chick Lit' Cult: Novelist Says Bridget Jones Genre Is Just a Lot of Froth." *The Guardian*. 24, Aug. 2001. <http://books.guardian.co.uk/departments/generalfiction/story/0,6000,541954,00.html>.

Felski, Rita. "Judith Krantz, Author of 'The Cultural Logics of Late Capitalism.'" *Women: A Cultural Review* 8 (1997): 129–42.

Finian, Kristin. "'Chick lit' for Teen Readers Comes of Age." *Houston Chronicle* 9, Feb. 2005. <http://www.chron.com/cs/CDA/ssistory.mpl/ae/books/news/3030242>.

Gelsomino, Tara. "Growing Pains." www.RomanticTimes.com. Aug. 2004: 28–29, 31–32, 104.

Gibbons, Fiachra. "Stop Rubbishing Chick Lit, Demands Novelist." *Guardian Unlimited.* 21, Aug. 2003. <www.guardian.co.uk>.

Gladstone, Brooke. "A Book for Every Girl and Boy." *On the Media.* WNYC Radio. 23, Apr. 2004.

Harzewski, Stephanie. " 'Chick Lit' and the Urban Code Heroine: Interview Symposium with Caren Lissner, Melissa Senate, Alisa Valdes-Rodriguez, and Jennifer Weiner." *New Voices of the Americas: Interviews with Contemporary Writers.* Ed. Laura Alonso Gallo. Cádiz, Spain: Aduana Vieja, 2004.

James-Enger, Kelly. "The Scoop on Chick Lit." *The Writer* Nov. 2003: 43–45.

Jernigan, Jessica. "Slingbacks and Arrows: Chick Lit Comes of Age." *Bitch* Summer 2004: 68–75.

Jones, Rebecca. "Female Fiction 'Dumbs Down.'" *BBC News* 23, Aug. 2001. <http://news.bbc.co.uk/1/hi/entertainment/arts/1504733.stm>.

Kuczynski, Alex. "Too Good Not to Be True: 'Gossip Lit' Dishes Up the Skinny without Quite Naming Names." *New York Times* 25, Apr. 2004.

Lee, Felicia R. "Chick-Lit King Imagines His Way into Women's Heads." *New York Times* 29, July 2004: B1, B5.

Leonard, Suzanne. "All Too Familiar." Review of *Playing with Boys,* by Alisa Valdes-Rodriguez. *Fort Worth Star-Telegram* 19, Sept. 2004: D6.

Lovell, Terry. *Consuming Fiction.* London and New York: Verso, 1987.

Ogunnaike, Lola. "Black Writers Seize Glamorous Ground around 'Chick-Lit.' " *New York Times.* 31, May 2004. <http:www.nytimes.com/2004/05/31/books/31CHIC.html>.

Rabine, Leslie. "Romance in the Age of Electronics: Harlequin Enterprises." *Feminist Studies* 11 (Spring 1985): 39–60.

Radford, Jean, ed. *The Progress of Romance: The Politics of Popular Fiction.* London: Routledge, 1986.

Radway, Janice. *Reading the Romance: Women, Patriarchy, and Popular Literature.* 1984. Chapel Hill: University of North Carolina Press, 1991.

Razdan, Anjula. "The Chick Lit Challenge: Do Trendy Novels for Young Women Smother Female Expression—Or Just Put a Little Fun in Feminism?" *Utne* Mar.–Apr. 2004: 20–21.

Robinson, Kathryn. "Why I Heart Chick Lit." *Seattle Weekly.* 22–28, Oct. 2003. <http://www.seattleweekly.com/features/o343/031022_arts_books_chicklit.php>.

"Selected Fiction List: Chick Lit." Chicago Public Library. Aug. 2003. <http://www.chipublib.org/001hwlc/litlists/chicklit.html>.

Skurnick, Lizzie. "Chick Lit 101: A Sex-Soaked, Candy-Colored, Indiscreet Romp through the Hottest Gal Tales of the Season." *Baltimore City Paper.* 10, Sept. 2003. <http://www.citypaper.com/2003-09-10/bigbooks.html>.

Ward, Alyson. "Black Authors Getting in on the 'Chick Lit' Circuit." *Fort Worth Star-Telegram* 2, Sept. 2003.

Weinberg, Anna. "She's Come Undone." *Book Magazine* July–Aug. 2003: 47–49.

Whitehead, Barbara Dafoe. "The Plaint by the Book." *Why There Are No Good Men Left: The Romantic Plight of the New Single Woman.* New York: Broadway, 2003. 44–54.

Wolcott, James. "Hear Me Purr: Maureen Dowd and the Rise of Postfeminist Chick Lit." *The New Yorker* 20, May 1996: 54–59.

Wolf, Naomi. *The Beauty Myth: How Images of Beauty Are Used against Women.* New York: William and Morrow, 1991.

Zernike, Kate. "Oh, to Write a 'Bridget Jones' for Men: A Guy Can Dream." *New York Times* 22, Feb. 2004: 9.1–2.

Contributors

Shari Benstock is professor of English at the University of Miami. She is the author of *Women of the Left Bank* (1986), *Textualizing the Feminine* (1991), and *"No Gifts from Chance": A Biography of Edith Wharton* (1994) and coauthor of *Who's He When He's at Home: A James Joyce Directory* and *A Handbook of Literary Feminisms* (2002). She has edited five volumes of work in feminist theory and gender studies, autobiography, and modernism, and was coeditor of the "Reading Women Writing" series at Cornell University Press.

Elizabeth B. Boyd is a senior lecturer in the American and Southern Studies Program at Vanderbilt University. She is currently working on the book *Southern Beauty: Performing Region on the Feminine Body*.

Suzanne Ferriss is professor of English at Nova Southeastern University. She has coedited two volumes on the cultural study of fashion: *On Fashion* (1994) and *Footnotes: On Shoes* (2001). She is also coauthor of *A Handbook of Literary Feminisms* (2002). Currently, she is editing *Chick Flicks: Contemporary Women at the Movies* with Mallory Young.

Lisa A. Guerrero is an assistant professor of African-American literature and culture in the Department of Comparative Ethnic Studies at Washington State University. She has recently published an essay on African-American popular culture and is currently at work on the book *Resistant Masculinity: Modes of Black Manhood as Racial Protest in the Cultural Work of African American Men*.

Elizabeth Hale is a lecturer in the School of English, Communication, and Theatre at the University of New England in New South Wales, Australia. She is coeditor with Sarah Winters of *Marvellous Codes: Critical Essays on the Fiction of Margaret Mahy,* forthcoming from Victoria University Press.

Stephanie Harzewski is completing her dissertation "The New Novel of Manners: 'Chick Lit' and the Urban Code Heroine" at the University of Pennsylvania. Her publications include an interview with chick-lit authors and essays on the cultural history of the wedding, *Sex and the City,* Eliza Haywood, Virginia Woolf, and Adrienne Rich.

Heather Hewett is an assistant professor of English and the coordinator of Women's Studies at SUNY-New Paltz. She has written for publications including the *Washington Post,* the *Women's Review of Books,* the *Scholar and Feminist Online,* and *Brain, Child: The Magazine for Thinking Mothers.*

Joanna Webb Johnson is a senior lecturer in English at the University of Texas at Arlington.

Anna Kiernan is a senior lecturer in journalism at Kingston University in London. She was previously fiction editor at Simon and Schuster UK.

A. Rochelle Mabry recently completed her PhD in film and media studies at the University of Florida. She is currently an assistant visiting professor of film studies at Florida Atlantic University.

Cris Mazza is winner of the 1984 PEN/Nelson Algren award and author of more than ten books of fiction. The anthologies *Chick-Lit: Postfeminist Fiction* (FC2, 1995) and *Chick-Lit: No Chick Vics* (FC2, 1996), which she coedited with Jeffrey DeShell, were the first to use the term *chick lit* in print.

Nóra Séllei is an associate professor in the Department of British Studies of the Institute of English and American Studies, University of Debrecen, Hungary. Her publications include *Katherine Mansfield and Virginia Woolf: A Personal and Professional Bond* (1996), a monograph on nineteenth-century British women writers' novels in Hungarian (1999), and a book on early-twentieth-century autobiographies by women writers (2001). She has published translations of Virginia Woolf's *Moments of Being,* Jean Rhys's *Smile Please,* and Virginia Woolf's *Three Guineas* (forthcoming). She is also the editor of two books and a journal issue.

Alison Umminger is an assistant professor of English at the University of West Georgia. She also writes chick lit under the pen name Grace Grant, and her coauthored novels *Flyover States* and *Coasting* are forthcoming from Red Dress Ink.

Jessica Lyn Van Slooten is a visiting assistant professor at Michigan State University.

Juliette Wells is an assistant professor of English at Manhattanville College. Her article on Jane Austen and the creative woman appears in the 2004 issue of *Persuasions: The Jane Austen Journal.*

Mallory Young is professor of English and French at Tarleton State University. She has published on a variety of topics, from the *Odyssey* to Texas women's literature. She is currently coediting *Chick Flicks: Contemporary Women at the Movies* with Suzanne Ferriss.

Index

A

Accidental Diva, The, 33
Acker, Kathy, 217
Adam Bede, 60
adolescent chick lit (chick lit jr.), 5, 156
    cover art, 152–55
    feminist children's literary tradition and,
        141
    genre discussed, 141–52
    readers of, 146–49
    subjects of, 141–42, 146
Age of Innocence, The, 209
Agnes Grey, 104, 109, 111, 114–15
Alcott, Louisa May, 143–44
All About Eve, 246
All-American Girl, 143
Ally McBeal, 193, 194
Amanda Bright@ Home, 119
Amanada's Wedding, 26
American Idle, 33
American Psycho, 211
Angels, 49
Angus, Thongs, and Full-Frontal Snogging, 147,
    152
Apocalipstick, 152
Are You There God? It's Me, Margaret, 146
Atwood, Margaret, 57
Austen, Jane, 5, 48, 53, 57–58, 59, 66, 104, 175,
    179, 207
    depiction of heroines, 39, 51, 53, 60, 63,
        81
    literary reputation, 55–56
    subjects, 41, 57, 68, 123, 143, 240

Austen-Leigh, James Edward, 56
Away Laughing on a Fast Camel,
    147

B

Babyface, 119
Babyville, 119
Bachelorette #1, 33
Bainbridge, Beryl, Dame, 1, 30, 208
Ballenger, Seale, 160
Baltimore City Paper, 1
Bank, Melissa, 50
Barnett, Ross, 167
Barth, John, 17
Barthelme, Donald, 17
Bassett, Angela, 87
BBC (British Broadcasting Corporation), 71,
    72, 78
Beautiful Mind, A, 72
Beauty Myth, The, 11, 211, 239
Behaving Like Adults, 194
Bergdorf Blondes, 49, 64
*Beyond the Whiteness of Whiteness: Memoir of
    a White Mother of Black Sons*, 131
Big Brother, 186
Bilungromanen, 104
Bitch, 7
*Bitch in the House: 26 Women Tell the Truth
    About Sex, Solitude, Motherhood, and
    Marriage, The*, 119, 121, 131
black fiction
    characteristics of, 8

Blume, Judy, 146
Bombeck, Irma, 126, 127, 128, 131, 135
Bonfire of the Vanities, 57
Booker Prize, 30
Book Magazine, 23
Boston Globe, The, 27
Botox Diaries, 50, 56, 59
Bradford, Barbara Taylor, 104
Bradshares, Ann, 141, 143, 151
Brain, Child: The Magazine for Thinking Mothers, 121
Breakfast at Tiffany's, 209
Breeder: Real-Life Stories from the New Generation of Mothers, 131–32
Brides, 36
Bridget Jones' Diary, 2, 23–24, 57, 64, 116, 119, 124, 151, 198
 appeal of, 38, 52–53, 91, 192–93, 239–40
 descendant of Austen's *Pride and Prejudice*, 4–5, 41, 49, 208
 narrative style, 4, 73, 92, 147, 148–49, 196–98
 screenplay for, 71–73, 75–83, 193–95
 urtext, 4–5, 33, 126, 173–75
Bridgit Jones: Edge of Reason, The, 65, 173
Brontë, Anne, 104–05, 116
Brontë, Charlotte, 39, 47, 51, 58–59, 60, 63, 65, 67
Brown, Amanda, 2
Browne, Jill Conner, 160, 164, 165, 167, 168–70
Buchan, Elizabeth, 49, 54
Buchanan, Andrea, 131
Buffy the Vampire Slayers, 2
Burney, Frances, 51, 52, 53, 55, 60, 67
Bushnell, Candace, 6, 10, 33, 38, 41, 152, 193, 207, 209, 214, 217
 Wharton principal influence on, 41
Business Week, 119
Butler, Samuel, 117
Byatt, A. S., 57

C

Cabot, Meg, 141, 143, 146
Can You Keep a Secret? 50, 62, 65
Capote, Truman, 209
Cappuccino Years, The, 180
Carrie Philby, 33

Carter, Charisma (Ward), 2
Carter, Jimmy, 162
Castillo, Mary, 8
Catcher in the Rye, A, 145, 179
Cattral, Kim, 193
Certain Age, A, 41
chica lit, 6, 8
chick lit. *See also subgenres*, adolescent chick lit (chick lit jr.); chica lit; Christian chick lit; mommy lit; sistah lit; southern chick lit; underling lit; working women's lit
 adoration of fans, 1, 237, 253–54
 autobiography and, 4
 beauty, 11–12, 39, 59–62, 239–42
 Bridget Jones Diary and, 4–5, 23–24, 33, 41, 48–49, 52–54, 93, 99, 175–78, 184, 191–92, 200–05
 centrality of irony, 3, 18, 28, 88
 commercial success of, 2, 4, 24, 35–36, 56, 57, 173–74, 254
 confessional narrative (instant messaging) style, 3, 4, 25, 38, 195–98, 255–56
 cultural phenomenon, 2, 173–74, 178, 254
 commodification of love, 10, 40, 186, 231–34
 consumerism, 2–4, 23, 35–36, 40; pleasures and dangers of, 10–11, 43, 48, 62–63, 178, 229, 255
 cover art, 1–2, 9–11, 30, 33–34, 35, 144, 194–95, 235–36
 disdain of critics, 1–2, 9–10, 22, 36; sexist bias of, 9 30–31, 35, 47, 208
 engagement with contemporary culture, 2–3
 family relationships, 142–43, 249, 254
 female friendship and, 6, 10, 50, 97, 151, 202–03
 first-wave of, 21
 genesis of, 3, 37
 genre's formula, discussion of, 1, 2–3, 4–5, 8, 9–10; 34, 37–40, 43, 50, 56, 59, 62, 64–68, 142–43, 195–98, 240, 254
 heroines, 3–4, 11, 37–39, 51–52, 60–61, 64, 208, 240, 243–46, 248–51, 256
 heterosexual hero and, 38, 40
 lucrative potential of, 2, 192–93
 media and, 33, 61
 novel of manners and, 41, 57
 opportunity for debut writers, 12

place in literary history, 3, 33, 255
primacy of shopping, 62, 219–37
quest for self-definition, 2, 37–38, 39, 66, 178, 200, 230–31
questionable literary merit, 5, 33, 48, 64–68,
realism of, 3, 39, 95, 117
romance tropes and, 37–39, 49–52, 55, 88, 99–100, 207, 208, 237, 247–48
scholarly reception, 19, 21, 178, 253
second-wave of, 21, 22, 53; primacy of male-female couple and, 3
sex in, 39, 50–52, 191–202, 207
singleness (singletons) in, 3, 24, 39, 87–89, 176–77, 184–85, 191–94; 208–09
target audience, 3–4, 12, 47, 48, 176, 193–94, 255
urban setting, 39
Web sites, proliferation of, 2, 23, 24
work world and, 7, 37, 39–40, 54–55, 103–17, 241, 254
Chick-Lit: No Chick Vics, 2
reviews of, 21
Chick-Lit: Post-Feminism, 2, 18
codification of literary term and, 3
Chocolate War, The, 145
Christian chick lit (church lit), 6, 50
Clarissa, 32, 143
Cleage, Pearl, 90
Colgan, Jenny, 2
Collins, Jackie, 4
Confessions of a Shopaholic, 62, 193, 219–25, 227, 230–31, 235
Connecticut Fashionista in King Arthur's Court, A, 33
Cormier, Robert, 145
Cosmopolitan, 41, 61, 88
Cosmopolitan Girls, 8
Coventry, Francis, 35
Crane, Stephen, 27
Creating a Life: Professional Women and the Quest for Children, 120
Crittenden, Ann, 121
Crittenden, Danielle, 119
Crucible, The, 27
Cumberland, Richard, 31
Cummins, Maria, 145
Cunnah, Michelle, 36, 41
Curnyn, Lynda, and Wendy Markham, 36
Cusk, Rachel, 121, 131, 132
Custom of the Country, The, 41, 48, 63

D

Dairy of A Mad Mom-to-Be, 119
Dancing in My Nuddy-Pants, 147
Dangerous Liasons, 246
Daniel Deronda, 51, 60
Dariaux, Genevieve Antoine, 41
David Copperfield, 104
Davies, Andrew, 71
Davies, Andrew, and Richard Curtis, 71–72
Dayton Journal-Herald, 127
Dean, Zoey, 141
de Beauvoir, Simone, 247
Deenie, 146
Depres, Loraine, 160
Details, 22
Detroit Free Press, 36
Devil Wears Prada, The, 7, 49, 52, 54, 56, 58, 66, 103, 116
Dewey Decimal System of Love, The, 24
Dián, Tamás, and Belinski Zoltán (Diána Zoltan), 179
Diary of a Mad Bride, 41
Diaz, Cameron, 194
Dickey, Eric Jerome, 7
Dirty Girls Social Club, The, 8
Disappearing Acts, 90
Divine Secrets of the Ya-Ya Sisterhood, 159
Does She or Doesn't She?, 152
Dog Handling, 152
Dunciad, The, 30
Dyer, Chris, 41

E

East Village Inky, The, 122
Egg and I, The, 127
Ehle, Jennifer, 71
Elegance, 38, 41
Élet és Irodalom, 177
Eliot, George, 29, 51, 60
Ellis, Bret Easton, 211
Emma, 51, 52 59, 68, 77
Emmy, 193
English novel, 47
Entertainment Weekly, 2
Evelina, 51, 57, 60

F

Faith Gartney's Girlhood, 145
Farmer, Debbie, 127

Fear of Flying, 25
Female Eunuch, The, 36
Feminine Mystique, The, 128
feminism, 9, 19
feminist scholarship, second-wave, 9–11, 30
Fever Pitch, 180
Fielding, Helen, 65, 104, 191, 193, 173, 239, 252; acknowledgment of source material, 4, 9, 25, 48, 71–72, 178
Fielding, Henry, 32
Financial Times, 124
Firth, Colin, 68, 72
Fitzgerald, F. Scott, 27
Flame and the Flower, The, 192
Ford, Deborah and Edie Hand, 160, 161, 163–64, 170
Forever, 146
Four Blondes, 38, 40
Fowler, Karen Joy, 66
Fox, Faulkner, 131
Freak-Out for Daddy, 179
Freak-Out for Daddytheresa, Or Stop the Blondies!, 179
Fresh Air, 33
Freud, Sigmund, 198, 248
Friday Night Chicas, 8
Friedan, Betty, 128, 135
Friedman, Elye, 241, 244
Friends, 119
Frye, Northrop, 30

G

General Hospital, 42
Getting over Jack Wagner, 42
Gibson, Fiona, 119
Girl's Best Friend, A, 38
Girl's Guide to Hunting and Fishing, The, 50
Glamour, 88
God Save the Sweet Potato Queens, 165
Godwin, Gail, 56
Golden Globe, 193
Goldsmith, Oliver, 31
Good House-keeping, 127
Good in Bed, 4, 11, 142, 241, 243, 246–47, 250–51
Good Morning America, 127
Gordon, Mar, 57
Gore, Ariel, 131–34
Grant, Hugh, 72
Grass Is Always Greener over the Septic Tank, The, 128

Grazer, Gigi Levangie, 2, 40
Great Expectations, 61
Green, Jane, 119, 240, 241, 244, 246, 247–48
Greer, Germaine, 36
Gregory, Dick, 28
Grescoe, Paul, 36
Griffith, Andy, 163
Grits (Girls Raised in the South), Guide to Life, The, 160, 161–62
Gruen, Judy, 127
Guardian Unlimited, 26

H

Halliday, Ayun, 122, 127, 131
Handbag Book of Girly Emergencies, The, 25
Harlequin (romance). *See also chick lit*
    characteristics of, 31, 37–40, 207, 208, 254–55
    criticism of, 36–37
    marketing, 2, 6, 36–37, 192
Harris, E. Lynn, 7
Hawthorne, Nathaniel, 30, 212
Haywood, Eliza, 30, 32
Heartbreak Hotel, 168
Hells Belles, 160
Helms, Jesse, 21
Hemingway, Ernest, 27
hen lit (post-fifty reader), 31
Hewitt, Sylvia Ann, 120
HGTV, 170
High Fidelity, 180
Hilton, Paris, 251
Hip Mama, 121, 132
History of Pompey the Little, The, 35
Holliday, Alesia, 9, 33
Hopkins, Cathy, 141
Hornby, Nick, 7, 180
House of Mirth, 41, 55, 63, 255
House Subcommittee on Oversight and Investigations, 21
Howells, William Dean, 30
How to Avoid the Money Trap: A Roadmap for Sharing Parenting and Making it Work, 120
How to Meet Cute Boys, 41

I

I Am Now the Girlfriend of a Sex God, 147
I Don't Know How She Does It, 5, 53, 119, 123, 126, 129, 130

In Her Shoes: A Novel, 142, 152
In Style, 88

J

Jackman, Hugh, 198
Jackson, Helen Hunt, 145
Jackson, Marni, 131
Jackson, Samuel L., 163
Jackson, Shirley, 126, 127, 131
Jane Austen Book Club, The, 66
Jane Eyre(An Autobiography), 39, 47, 49, 51, 58, 60, 104
Janowitz, Tama, 41
Jemima J, 241–43, 244–51
Jong, Erica, 25
Joseph Andrews, 32
Judd, Ashley, 195, 197
Juska, Elise, 42

K

Kaplan, Janice, and Lynn Schnurnberger, 50, 56, 62
Karasyov, Carrie, and Jill Karman, 152
Kerr, Jean, 126, 127, 131
Keyes, Marian, 49, 104, 202
King, Florence, 160
King, Martin Luther, Jr., 162
Kinsella, Sophie, 36, 50, 52, 62, 65–66, 219, 229
    Shopaholic series and, 11, 36, 62, 219–37
Kirkus, 23
Kizis, Deanna, 41
Knocked Out by My Nunga-Nungas, 147
Knowles, John, 145
Krantz, Judith, 4
Kwitney, Alisa, 152

L

Ladies Home Journal, 127
lad lit (dick lit), 6–7, 177
Lamott, Anne, 121, 131
Lamplighter, The, 145
Last Chance Saloon, 202
Lazarre, Jane, 131
Leavis, F. R., 76
Lee, Robert E., 163
Leflore, Lyah Beth, 8
Legally Blonde, 2

Lessing, Doris, 1, 208
Letter from an Unknown Woman, 195
Life á la Mode, 24
Life's Work: On Becoming a Mother, A, 121
Lissner, Caren, 33
Little Women, 143–44
Lopez, Jennifer, 195
Love in Excess, 32
Lucky (Magazine), 33

M

MacDonald, Betty, 126, 127
Mackler, Carolyn, 141
Maid in Manhattan, 195
Mama, 90
Mancusi, Marianne, 33
Maneater, 2, 40
Manley, Delarivière, 32
Manning, Peyton, 163
Mansfield, Katherine, 179
Mapplethorpe, Robert, 21
Margolis, Sue, 152
Mary Poppins, 57
Mask of Motherhood: How Becoming a Mother Changes Our Lives and Why We Never Talk about It, The, 132
Matthews, Carole, 35
Maushart, Susan, 132
Maxted, Anna, 194
Mazza, Cris, 3
McCafferty, Megan, 141, 143, 149, 153
McFedries, Paul, 27
McLaughlin, Emma, and Nicola Kraus, 7, 48–49, 54, 56, 104–05, 116
McMillan, Terry, 6, 8, 90, 100
Mebus, Scott, 7
Memoir of Jane Austen, 56
Merchants of Venus, 36
Me Times Three, 30
Michael L. Printz award (young adult literature), 156
Middlemarch, 51, 60
Miller, Karen E. Quinones, 33
Milton, John, 67
Modern Brides, 36
mommy lit, 5, 31, 119
    first-wave, 126–27
    genre defined, 119–20, 122–31
    house-wife humorist and, 126–27
    second-wave, 127–35
    subjects of, 120–21

third-wave, 133
work and motherhood in, 120
Web logs and, 122
Mommy Myth: The Idealization of Motherhood and How It Has Undermined Women, 120, 127
Mommy Too! Magazine, 134
Mother Knot, The, 131
Mother Trip, The: Hip Mama's Guide to Staying Sane in the Chaos of Motherhood, 132–34
Motley, Willard, 27
Mrs. Dalloway, 61
My Fair Lady, 50
My Life in the Pits, 160

N

Nanny Diaries, The, 4, 49, 52, 54, 57, 66, 103, 104, 111, 114–15
Naylor, Clare, 152
NEA (National Endowment for the Arts), 21
Nelly's Silver Mine: A Story of Colorado Life, 145
New York, 120
New Yorker, 22, 27, 54, 58
New York (Manhattan), 198
setting in chick lit, film, and television series, 8, 35, 60, 112, 209, 212, 214, 226–28
New York Times, The, 56, 119
New York Times Book Review, 23
New York Times Magazine, 120, 167
Nicholas Nickleby, 104
Nigger, 28
Night and Day, 179
Northanger Abbey, 57, 60, 67, 68
novels of manners, 55
NPR (National Public Radio), 33

O

O'Connell, Jennifer, 33
On the Bright Side, 147
Operating Instructions: The Journal of My Son's First Year, 121
Oscar, 193

P

Pamela, 32, 51, 143
Papa, Ariella, 33
Parker, Sarah Jessica, 193, 198

patriarchy, 9
romance novels and, 31–32
Pearson, Allison, 5, 53, 54, 56, 119, 130
People, 119, 237
Persuasion, 25, 59
Phelps, Elizabeth Stuart, 145
Philadelphia Enquirer, 33
Pipher, Mary, 146
Platas, Berta, 8
Playing with Boys, 8
Pope, Alexander, 30, 67
postfeminism, 9, 18–19, 22, 253
Post-Feminist Playground, 23
Price of Motherhood: Why the Most Important Job in the World is Still the Least Valued, The, 121
Pride and Prejudice, re-visioning of, 25, 48, 53, 63, 68, 72–75, 77–83, 175, 208
Prior, Matthew, 67
Professor, The, 104
Progress of Coquetry, The, 32
Progress of Dullness, The, 32
Progress of Romance, The, 32
Publishers Weekly, 2, 23, 26, 235

Q

Queen of the Turtle Derby and Other Southern Phenomena, 160
Quinterro, Sofia, 8

R

Rácz, Zsuzsa, 6, 174, 185
Radway, Janice, 3, 169, 192
Rebecca, 195, 197
Red Hat Society, 169
Reed, Julia, 160
Reeve, Clara, 32
Rennison, Louise, 141, 143, 147, 150, 152
Revenge of the Middle-Aged Woman, 49, 54
Reviving Ophelia, 146
Rich, Adrienne, 131
Rich, Ronda, 160–61, 163, 164, 170
Richardson, Samuel, 51, 143
Right Address, The, 152
Rivenbark, Celia, 160
Roife, Anne, 131
Room of One's Own, A, 61
romance novels. *See also Harlequin*
fixation with fashion, 35
genre stereotypes, 29–32, 37–39

history of, 31–32
instruments of debauchery and
corruption, 31–32, 35
modern, 24–25, 27, 32, 36, 43
patriarchy and, 9
reader of, 32
Rosenthal, Amy Krouse, 127
Royle, Nicholas, 22
Run Catch Kiss, 30, 207, 209, 212
Sex and the City and, 212–17
Running in Heels, 194

S

Salinger, J. D., 27, 145
Salinger, Richárd, 179
Salon, 121
Sáringer, Károly, 180, 186
sastra wangi (fragrant literature), 6
Saturday Evening Post, 127
Scarlet Letter, The, 27, 212
Schlafly, Phyllis, 169
Schwartz, Maryln, 159–60
Scordato, Caridad, 8
Second Helpings, 143, 149–50
second-wave feminism, 9
See Jane Date, 2, 30, 36
Senate, Melissa, 2
Sense and Sensibility, 66
Separate Peace, A, 145,
Seventeen, 58, 148
Sex and the City, 8, 10, 24, 33, 119, 167, 192,
193, 194, 197, 198, 203, 204, 212
chick lit and, 6, 207, 209, 210
Shelton, Sandi Kahn, 127
Shields, Brooke, 120
Shields, Julie, 120
Shopaholic and Sister, 11
Shopaholic Takes Manhattan, 219–23, 226–30
Shopaholic Ties the Knot, 219–23, 231–35
Siddons, Anne Rivers, 168
Sinclair, April, 90
sistah lit, 87- 90
African-American womanhood, 89,
100
chick lit and, 89–93
cultural specificities of, 8, 90, 97
debt to *Sex and the City*, 8
depiction of family, 96–97
Sisterhood of the Traveling Pants, 151
Sloppy Firsts, 143, 149
Smith, Kyle, 7
Sohn, Amy, 207, 209, 211

Someone Like You, 195, 197
southern belle (belledom) lit, 159–71
appeal of, 161–62, 165–67
rejection of belledom, 159, 163
subjects of, 160–63, 167–71
wannabees and, 159, 162
*Southern Belle Primer, Or Why Margaret Will
Never Be a Kappa Kappa Gamma, A*,
159–60
*Southern Belle's Handbook: Sissy LeBlanc's
Rules to Live By, The*, 160
Southern Living, 162
Steele, Danielle, 30
Stop Mammatheresa!, 6, 174–80,
185–86
Bridget Jones's Diary and, 174–79
cover art, 180–83
Swank, Hilary
purchase of rights to *Family Trust*, 2
Sweetest Taboo, The, 35
Sweetest Thing, The, 192, 194, 195, 202
Sweet Potato Queens, 159, 160–61, 164, 167,
168–69, 171
*Sweet Potato Queens' Big-Ass Cookbook (and
Financial Planner), The*, 165
Sweet Potato Queens' Book of Love, The,
165
*Sweet Potato Queens' Field Guide to Men: Every
Man I Love Is Either Married, Gay, or Dead,
The*, 165
Swendson, Shanna, 36
Sykes, Plum, 4, 26, 47–48, 53, 54, 56, 61

T

Tessaro, Kathleen, 38, 41
32 AA, 41
Time, 119, 120, 193
Time Out: London, 22
Tom Jones, 32
Townsend, Sue, 180
Trading Up, 41, 152
Trials of Tiffany Trott, The, 152
Trumball, John, 32
Twain, Mark, 27
Twitchell, James, 228–29
two girls review, 18

U

underling-lit (assistant-lit), 103
antecedents of, 104, 108, 109
chick-lit and, 103–04

genre characteristics, 103–06, 108,
111–12, 114–117
illustrative examples of, 103
mothers and mothering in, 110–13
Up and Out, 33
USA Today, 119, 237
USC Scripter Award, 71–72

V

Valdes-Rodriguez, Alisa, 8
Valley of the Dolls, 61
Veblen, Thorstein, 227–28
Villette, 52
Viorst, Judith, 126
Vogue, 120
Vogue (British), 88
von Ziegesar, Cecily, 141, 153

W

Waiting to Exhale, 6, 87, 90
Bridget Jones and, 90–96, 99–100
Waking Beauty, 241, 244–51
Walker, Fiona, 104
Wanderlust, 41
Warner, Susan, 145
Way of All Flesh, The, 104, 117
Weiner, Jennifer, 4, 142, 240, 241, 243, 244
Weisberger, Lauren, 4, 7, 49, 54, 56, 58–59, 62
Wells, Rebecca, 7, 159
We're Just Like You, Only Prettier: Confessions of a Tarnished Southern Belle, 160
Wharton, Edith, 41, 48, 55, 60–61, 63, 67, 209, 240, 255
What Southern Women Know about Flirting, 164

What Southern Women Know (That Everyone Should): Timeless Secrets to Get Everything You Want in Love, Life and Work, 160, 163
What to Expect When You're Expecting, 121
Whitney, A. D. T., 145
Wide, Wide World, The, 145
Williams, Jacqueline, 35
Williams, Tia, 8, 33
Winterson, Jeanette, 2
Wolf, Laura, 41, 119
Wolf, Naomi, 11, 211, 239
Wolff, Isabel, 152
Woolf, Virginia, 61, 67, 179
Woman Born: Motherhood as Experience and Institution, Of, 131
Woman I Want—A Response to Mammatheresa, 180, 186
Women's National Book Association, 2
women's writing, 30, 48–49, 50–51; 57, 61–63, 67, 68; *see also chick lit*
Woodiwiss, Kathleen, 192
Word Spy: The Word Lovers Guide to Modern Culture, The, 27
Working Girl, 116

Y

You Might as Well Laugh … Because Crying Will Only Smear Your Mascara, 127
Young Adult Library Services Association, 156
Young, Elizabeth, 38

Z

Zellweger, Renee, 87, 193, 197
Zeta-Jones, Catherine, 227